ABC Mathseeds

MATHS

Skills for Year 3

Megan Smith

Welcome to the ABC Mathseeds Workbook for Year 3!

This workbook covers core maths and problem-solving skills. Its carefully structured sequence of fun, interactive and rewarding lessons ensures everyone succeeds.

This workbook includes 50 lessons, 10 quizzes and regular reviews and rewards. Each lesson teaches a concept with four worksheets and lots of engaging activities to build skills.

Research shows that targeting a single skill in each lesson greatly improves long-term retention, builds a deeper understanding, and establishes a strong foundation for lifelong success in maths.

We know you'll enjoy learning maths with us because

Maths + Fun = Mathseeds

ABC Mathseeds Year 3 Workbook

www.mathseeds.com.au

ISBN: 978-1-923253-14-8

Distributed by:
Pascal Press
PO Box 250
Glebe NSW 2037

Written by Megan Smith
Publisher: Katy Pike
Editors: Laurence Trinh and Mark Stafford
Design and layout by Modern Art Production Group
Printed in China by 1010 Printing International Ltd

HOW TO USE THIS BOOK

ABC Mathseeds is a carefully sequenced program of 200 lessons. For Year 3 there are 50 lessons that comprehensively cover number, operations, fractions, geometry, measurement and statistics. The Year Planner on pages vi–x gives an overview of the teaching focus, skills and assessment tools, in a lesson-by-lesson format. You can see at a glance how this academically rigorous program covers the content for an entire school year.

Lessons

- Each lesson has 4 pages of activities to reinforce learning.

Lesson Review

- At the end of each lesson, the yellow review panel helps track achievement.

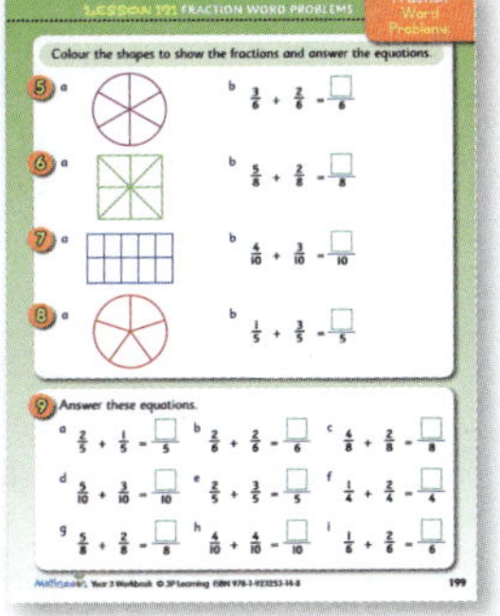

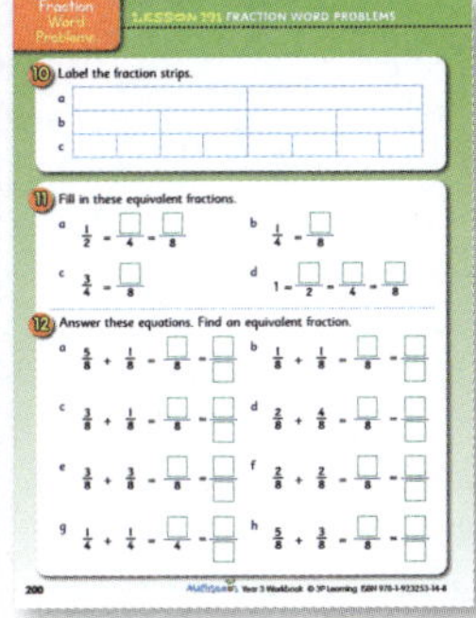

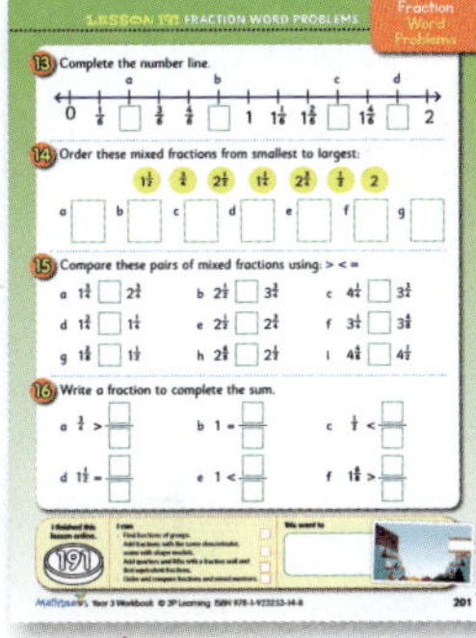

Colour when online lesson is complete.

I finished this lesson online.

I can

- Determine if a vessel holds >, < or = to 1 L.
- Use increments on measuring vessels in mL and L.
- Convert between litres and millilitres and solve capacity word problems.

We went to

Tick off each new skill to celebrate success.

Complete the name of the destination at the end of each online lesson.

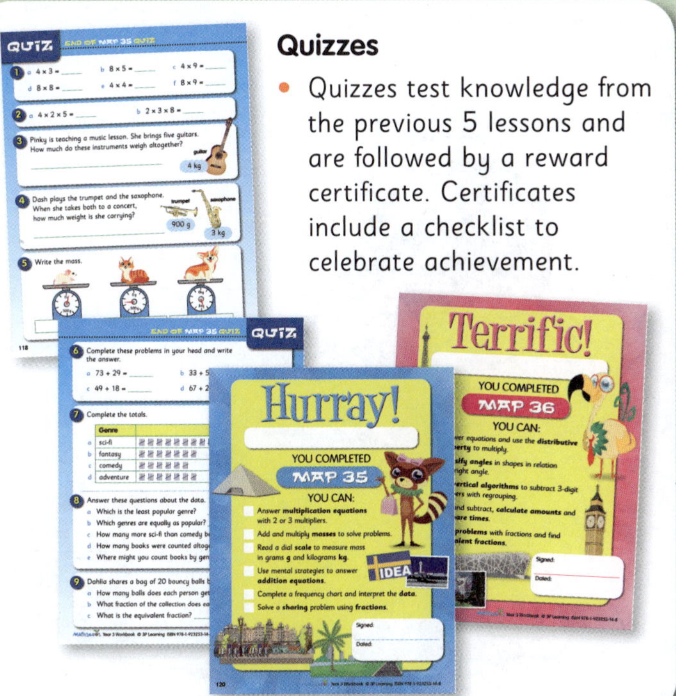

Quizzes

- Quizzes test knowledge from the previous 5 lessons and are followed by a reward certificate. Certificates include a checklist to celebrate achievement.

Online Lessons

These workbook lessons can be completed as a standalone maths program, but when combined with the online lessons, they act as a powerful boost for numeracy success. Best of all, each online lesson is aligned with the workbook, making an integrated approach easy to achieve.

Each online **ABC Mathseeds** lesson begins with a video of a new maths concept, followed by guided practice with activities, games and songs. By following each online lesson with the workbook lesson pages, learners are putting into practice their new skills and strategies.

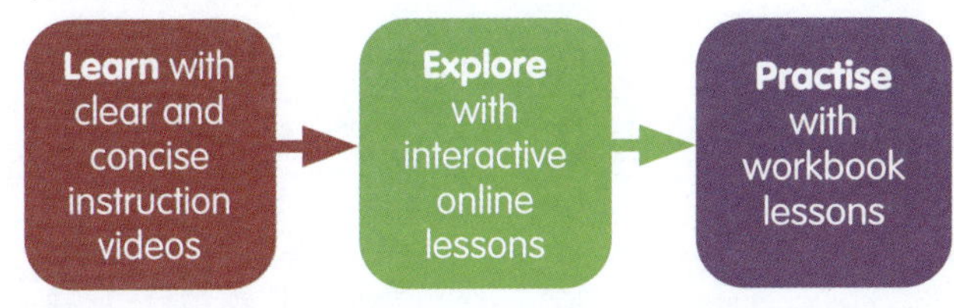

CONTENTS

Mathseeds Year 3 Workbook © 3P Learning ISBN 978-1-923253-14-8

CONTENTS

YEAR PLANNER

Map 31

Lesson	Teaching Focus	Book Pages	Skills
151	Numbers: Counting 1000–5000	2–5	✓ Order numbers to 5000 from smallest to largest and on a number line. ✓ Count to 5000 by hundreds and compare numbers to 5000. ✓ Write numbers to 5000 in words and vice versa. ✓ Make all 4-digit numbers given 4 digits.
152	Geometry: Symmetry	6–9	✓ Identify images that are symmetrical. ✓ Draw vertical and horizontal lines of symmetry. ✓ Draw symmetrical patterns and images.
153	Algebra: Number Patterns 2	10–13	✓ Explore the Fibonacci sequence. ✓ Identify and follow a rule to continue a number pattern. ✓ Correct mistakes in a given number pattern.
154	Measurement: Litres & Millilitres	14–17	✓ Determine if a vessel holds $>$, $<$ or $=$ to 1 L. ✓ Use increments on measuring vessels in mL and L. ✓ Convert between litres and millilitres and solve capacity word problems.
155	Operations: Multiplication Revision	18–21	✓ Use repeated addition, skip counting and the number line to multiply. ✓ Write equations for arrays and find missing numbers in equations. ✓ Solve multiplication word problems.
End of Map 31 Quiz	Revision	22–23	✓ Order numbers to 5000 and write numbers in words. ✓ Choose the line of symmetry on a shape. ✓ Identify and follow a rule to continue a number pattern. ✓ Read increments on measuring vessels in mL and L. ✓ Solve a multiplication word problem and answer multiplication equations.

Map 32

Lesson	Teaching Focus	Book Pages	Skills
156	Numbers: Counting 5000–10 000	26–29	✓ Model 4-digit numbers in base ten blocks, words and expanded form. ✓ Order 4-digit numbers forwards and backwards, and on a number line. ✓ Add 1, 10, 100, 1000 to a 4-digit number.
157	Measurement: Area 3	30–33	✓ Count squares and multiply length × width to measure area. ✓ Measure area in m^2 and solve area word problems.
158	Operations: Times Tables ×2, ×4	34–37	✓ Write multiplication equations based on groups and arrays. ✓ Fill in a multiplication table for ×2 and ×4. ✓ Use the commutative property of multiplication to write equations. ✓ Explore ×2 and ×4 using doubling.
159	Measurement: Money Equivalent Amounts 2	38–41	✓ Identify amounts of currency and make equivalent amounts. ✓ Find change from \$5 and \$20 using dollars and cents. ✓ Use an algorithm to add amounts of money in dollars and cents.
160	Fractions: Comparing & Ordering Fractions	42–45	✓ Work with fractions and mixed numbers with the same denominators. ✓ Work with the equivalencies between halves, quarters and eighths. ✓ Compare the sizes of fractions with and without models. ✓ Order fractions and fill in fraction number lines.
End of Map 32 Quiz	Revision	46–47	✓ Add 1, 10, 100 to a 4-digit number and write numbers in expanded form. ✓ Multiply length × width to find area and answer multiplication equations. ✓ Identify 2 ways to make an equivalent amount of money. ✓ Use an algorithm to add money and then calculate change from \$20. ✓ Order and compare fractions.

Mathseeds Year 3 Workbook © 3P Learning ISBN 978-1-923253-14-8

Map 33

Lesson	Teaching Focus	Book Pages	Skills
161	Numbers: Partitioning Numbers	50–53	✓ Recognise digit place values in 4-digit numbers. ✓ Write 4-digit numbers in expanded form then add 1, 10, 100, 1000. ✓ Order and compare 4-digit numbers. ✓ Make all 4-digit numbers given 4 digits and explain placement of 0.
162	Measurement: Time to the Minute	54–57	✓ Read and show time to the nearest minute on analog clocks. ✓ Read and write time in words and in digital format. ✓ Calculate the amount of time passed between two times.
163	Algebra: Equivalent Number Sentences (+ –)	58–61	✓ Complete number fact families. ✓ Calculate equivalent addition and subtraction equations. ✓ Use equivalent equations to solve word problems. ✓ Compare options in equivalent addition and subtraction equations.
164	Geometry: Maps	62–65	✓ Label the directions on a compass and use it to answer questions. ✓ Use grid coordinates to identify places and features on a map. ✓ Use grid coordinates and compass directions to map a route. ✓ Calculate distance on a map.
165	Operations: Division	66–69	✓ Answer division equations, with and without groups of shapes. ✓ Find missing divisors, with and without groups of shapes. ✓ Write related division equations, with and without arrays. ✓ Find multiple arrays and equations for division into 30.
End of Map 33 Quiz	Revision	70–71	✓ Write 4-digit numbers in expanded form. ✓ Make the largest odd and smallest even numbers given 4 digits. ✓ Make matching times on analog and digital clocks and in words. ✓ Complete equivalent equations and number fact families. ✓ Use grid coordinates to map a route. ✓ Answer division equations.

Map 34

Lesson	Teaching Focus	Book Pages	Skills
166	Numbers: Odd & Even Numbers 2	74–77	✓ Identify and make odd and even numbers. ✓ Find rules in odd and even number patterns with addition and use them to predict if answers to additions will be odd or even. ✓ Explore odd and even numbers given 4 digits – 3 odd and 1 even.
167	Probability: Chance 3	78–81	✓ Revise 'certain', 'impossible' and 'equal chance'. ✓ Write probability as a ratio, eg 1 in 6. ✓ Identify outcomes for chance experiments and predict frequency. ✓ Record results for chance experiments and compare to predictions.
168	Operations: Multiplication Word Problems 2	82–85	✓ Write commutative multiplication equations with arrays. ✓ Solve multiplication problems using arrays and equations. ✓ Solve multiplication problems with 3 multipliers.
169	Geometry: Prisms and Pyramids	86–89	✓ Identify prisms and pyramids and describe their key features. ✓ Name prisms for their end faces and identify all their faces. ✓ Name pyramids for their base, identify the apex and draw all faces. ✓ Match prisms and pyramids to their nets.
170	Operations: Addition 3	90–93	✓ Explore regrouping or trading with base ten blocks and algorithms. ✓ Use vertical algorithms to add 2 and 3-digit numbers. ✓ Solve problems using vertical addition algorithms.
End of Map 34 Quiz	Revision	94–95	✓ Use rules to predict if answers to additions will be odd or even. ✓ Write probability as a ratio, eg 1 in 6. ✓ Solve multiplication problems with 3 multipliers. ✓ Label the features of a prism and a pyramid and draw a net for each. ✓ Use vertical algorithms to add 3-digit numbers with regrouping.

Map 35

Lesson	Teaching Focus	Book Pages	Skills
171	Operations: Times Tables 2 ×8	98–101	✓ Write multiplication equations based on groups. ✓ Fill in a multiplication table for ×4 and ×8. ✓ Use the commutative property of multiplication to write equations. ✓ Find missing factors in multiplication equations. ✓ Solve multiplication problems with 3 multipliers.
172	Measurement: Kilograms & Grams	102–105	✓ Use balance scales to measure mass in kilograms kg. ✓ Order items from heaviest to lightest. ✓ Read a dial scale to measure mass in grams g and kilograms kg. ✓ Add and subtract masses to solve problems.
173	Operations: Mental + – Strategies	106–109	✓ Use the compensation strategy (round, adjust) to add and subtract. ✓ Use the jump strategy (split by place value) to add and subtract. ✓ Use mental strategies to solve problems or find the missing number. ✓ Compare the compensation and jump strategies.
174	Statistics: Data 3	110–113	✓ Explore how a frequency chart works and interpret its data. ✓ Draw a scaled picture graph. ✓ Interpret a scaled picture graph and apply the data to real life. ✓ Conduct a survey: write a question, collect data, make a graph.
175	Fractions: Comparing Fractions of a Collection	114–117	✓ Link fractions to sharing groups (division). ✓ Find equivalent fractions of groups. ✓ Compare fractions using groups.
End of Map 35 Quiz	Revision	118–119	✓ Answer multiplication equations with 2 or 3 multipliers. ✓ Add and multiply masses to solve problems. ✓ Read a dial scale to measure mass in grams g and kilograms kg. ✓ Use mental strategies to answer addition equations. ✓ Complete a frequency chart and interpret the data. ✓ Solve a sharing problem using fractions.

Map 36

Lesson	Teaching Focus	Book Pages	Skills
176	Operations: Times Tables 3 Mental Facts (×3, ×6)	126–129	✓ Write multiplication equations based on groups. ✓ Fill in a multiplication table for ×3 and ×6. ✓ Use the commutative property of multiplication to write equations. ✓ Use the distributive property to multiply larger numbers.
177	Measurement: Angles	130–133	✓ Name the parts of an angle and identify a right angle. ✓ Compare angles visually. ✓ Classify angles in relation to a right angle.
178	Operations: Subtraction with Regrouping	134–137	✓ Explore regrouping or trading in subtraction algorithms. ✓ Use vertical algorithms to subtract 2- and 3-digit numbers. ✓ Solve problems using vertical subtraction algorithms.
179	Measurement: Comparing Times	138–141	✓ Read and write amounts of time in words and digital format. ✓ Compare and order amounts of time in hours and minutes. ✓ Add time with and without a number line. ✓ Solve a complex word problem involving time.
180	Fractions: Equivalent Fractions	142–145	✓ Make fractions in shapes and write equivalent fractions. ✓ Use fraction walls or strips to identify equivalent fractions. ✓ Fill in number lines and use them to identify equivalent fractions.
End of Map 36 Quiz	Revision	146–147	✓ Answer equations and use the distributive property to multiply. ✓ Classify angles in shapes in relation to a right angle. ✓ Use vertical algorithms to subtract 3-digit numbers with regrouping. ✓ Add and subtract, calculate amounts and compare times. ✓ Solve problems with fractions and find equivalent fractions.

Mathseeds Year 3 Workbook © 3P Learning ISBN 978-1-923253-14-8

Map 37

Lesson	Teaching Focus	Book Pages	Skills
181	Operations: Number Fact Families 2	150–153	✓ Complete commutative number sentences for multiplying. ✓ Complete related number sentences for dividing. ✓ Complete number fact families for multiplying and dividing.
182	Measurement: Metres, Centimetres & Millimetres	154–157	✓ Use a ruler to measure lengths in centimetres and millimetres. ✓ Convert between metres m, centimetres cm and millimetres mm. ✓ Compare lengths and find the difference. ✓ Recognise the most appropriate unit of measure for an object.
183	Operations: Solving Word Problems	158–161	✓ Use bar diagrams to add and subtract up to 3-digit numbers. ✓ Use rounding, place value and number lines to add and subtract. ✓ Solve complex word problems using tables to organise information.
184	Geometry: Properties of 2D Shapes	162–165	✓ Identify polygons and their features. ✓ Identify and compare quadrilaterals and their features. ✓ Draw shapes to match descriptions. ✓ Classify angles in shapes in relation to a right angle.
185	Measurement: Minutes to the Hour	166–169	✓ Read and write time in words in minutes to and past the hour. ✓ Tell and draw times in minutes on analog clocks. ✓ Read and write digital times in minutes to and past the hour. ✓ Add and subtract times to solve word problems.
End of Map 37 Quiz	Revision	170–171	✓ Complete number fact families for multiplying and dividing. ✓ Interpret lengths and convert between units. ✓ Solve add and subtract problems with written and mental strategies. ✓ Draw quadrilaterals. ✓ Add time to solve a word problem.

Map 38

Lesson	Teaching Focus	Book Pages	Skills
186	Operations: Multiplication	174–177	✓ Use vertical algorithms to multiply 1 digit by 1 digit, and 2 digits by 1 digit. ✓ Match multiplication equations and arrays. ✓ Write vertical multiplication algorithms for arrays. ✓ Answer vertical multiplication algorithms using times tables. ✓ Match vertical multiplication algorithms and number lines. ✓ Write vertical multiplication algorithms to solve problems.
187	Statistics: Creating Graphs	178–181	✓ Complete the tally graph and interpret the data. ✓ Draw a scaled column graph. ✓ Interpret a scaled column graph. ✓ Conduct a survey: write a question, collect data, make a column graph.
188	Operations: Problem Solving	182–185	✓ Solve 1-, 2- and multi-step problems using all operations. ✓ Determine the appropriate operation/s and write equations.
189	Measurement: Time Word Problems	186–189	✓ Add and subtract, calculate amounts and compare times. ✓ Use these skills to solve word problems.
190	Operations: Division 2	190–193	✓ Complete number fact families for multiplying and dividing. ✓ Use number mountains to write number fact families. ✓ Use number mountains to find missing numbers in division equations.
End of Map 38 Quiz	Revision	194–195	✓ Write vertical algorithms to solve multiplication problems. ✓ Interpret a scaled bar graph. ✓ Write equations to solve problems using all operations. ✓ Add and subtract and calculate amounts of time to solve problems. ✓ Find the missing number in number mountains.

Map 39

Lesson	Teaching Focus	Book Pages	Skills
191	Fractions: Fraction Word Problems	198–201	✓ Find fractions of groups. ✓ Add fractions with the same denominator, some with shape models. ✓ Add quarters and 8ths with a fraction wall and find equivalent fractions. ✓ Order and compare fractions and mixed numbers.
192	Measurement: Perimeter	202–205	✓ Measure and add to find the perimeters of rectangles. ✓ Measure and multiply to find the perimeters of regular polygons. ✓ Add to find the perimeter of irregular shapes.
193	Operations: Multiplication 2	206–209	✓ Use vertical algorithms and equations to multiply by 10. ✓ Use the associative property to multiply multiples of ten. ✓ Solve 1- and 2-step problems involving multiplying multiples of ten.
194	Numbers: Rounding to the Nearest 100	210–213	✓ Use a number line to identify the 'midpoint' and round up or down. ✓ Round 3-digit numbers to the nearest ten or hundred. ✓ Use rounding and other clues to identify a number.
195	Algebra: Addition and Subtraction Patterns	214–217	✓ Complete place value patterns of addition and subtraction equations. ✓ Use place value patterns and vertical algorithms to solve problems.
End of Map 39 Quiz	Revision	218–219	✓ Find fractions of a group. ✓ Calculate the perimeter of a rectangle, a regular hexagon and an irregular shape. ✓ Use the associative property to solve a multiplication problem. ✓ Round 3-digit numbers to the nearest ten or hundred. ✓ Correct mistakes in addition and subtraction place value patterns.

Map 40

Lesson	Teaching Focus	Book Pages	Skills
196	Operations: Division Word Problems	222–225	✓ Solve division word problems by using equations and division facts. ✓ Write equations to solve problems using all operations. ✓ Solve multi-step word problems involving division.
197	Fractions: Whole Number Fractions	226–229	✓ Understand the terms numerator and denominator. ✓ Write, draw and match whole number fractions and shape models. ✓ Use division to find a whole number equivalent for a whole number fraction.
198	Statistics: Measurement Data	230–233	✓ Measure distance in centimetres and half centimetres. ✓ Record distance data in a table and make it into a column graph. ✓ Interpret the data in the column graph. ✓ Collect data, make a column graph and write statements on the data.
199	Operations: Fluent ×÷ within 100	234–237	✓ Complete timed quizzes on multiplication and division facts. ✓ Write inverse operations and number fact families. ✓ Solve multiplication and division word problems.
200	Measurement: Area Problem-Solving	238–241	✓ Solve irregular area problems involving adding and subtracting. ✓ Compare areas. ✓ Solve multi-step problems with area and money.
End of Map 40 Quiz	Revision	242–243	✓ Solve a 2-step word problem involving division. ✓ Complete sentences using the terms numerator and denominator. ✓ Find whole number equivalents for whole number fractions. ✓ Complete number fact families for multiplication and division. ✓ Make a column graph. ✓ Solve a multi-step problem with area.

Mathseeds Year 3 Workbook © 3P Learning ISBN 978-1-923253-14-8

Critical thinking and problem-solving

Mathseeds encourages children to solve problems and use higher-level thinking throughout the program. These critical thinking and problem-solving activities provide a growing toolkit of different strategies, using a simple structure that helps children grow in skills and confidence. The more experience children have with higher-level thinking, the more confidence they gain to think logically, take risks, ask questions and apply reason. In turn, this encourages them to communicate, explain and justify their mathematical reasoning.

Children should tackle each problem using this simple structure:

1. **Read the question.** Encourage children to read the question carefully.
   a. **Underline the question.** What is the question asking them to do? Children can ask their own questions, such as: *Is this an addition problem? Do I need to draw a shape? Am I being asked to measure something?*
   b. **Highlight the facts.** Focus on the important facts needed to solve the problem. These might be numbers, words or phrases that are key to understanding and interpreting the problem.
2. **Plan a strategy.** Choose an appropriate method to solve this problem. Many Mathseeds activities will guide children in the use of a specific strategy. In other activities, children will need to choose a strategy based on operation, size of numbers or type of problem.
3. **Work the strategy.** Children use the strategy they chose to solve the problem. The next two pages explain the most common problem-solving strategies.
4. **Answer the question.** Encourage students to write a sentence based on the wording of the question, to be sure they have answered the question actually being asked.
5. **Check the answer.** Encourage children to think about how they solved the problem, to check their answer, and to share their solutions with a partner. Consider other strategies they could have used to find a solution. This encourages children to reflect, to analyse, to ask questions and to explore options.

Write an Equation or Algorithm

1. **Read** the problem.
   Underline the question.
   Highlight the facts.
2. **Plan** a strategy. Identify the operation and numbers.
3. **Work** the strategy.
4. **Answer** the question.
5. **Check** the answer.
   Does the answer make sense?
   Use another strategy to check.

Ruby has four shoe boxes. Each box holds two shoes. How many shoes in total?

Equation
+ – × ÷
4 and 2 $4 \times 2 = \mathbf{8}$

Ruby has **8** shoes in total.

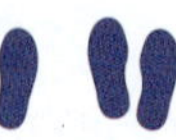

2 + 2 + 2 + 2 = **8** ✓

Waldo caught 136 fish and Mango caught 241 fish. How many fish altogether?

Algorithm
+ – × ÷
136 and 241

$$\begin{array}{r} 136 \\ +\,241 \\ \hline \mathbf{377} \end{array}$$

They have **377** fish altogether.

136 + 200 = 336 + 40 = 376
376 + 1 = **377** ✓

Draw a Diagram

1. **Read** the problem.
2. **Plan** a strategy.
   Decide on a diagram, such as a bar diagram, array, number line and so on.
3. **Work** the strategy.
4. **Answer** the question.
5. **Check** the answer.
   Use the inverse operation.

Mrs T bought 85 tea bags. She used 13 this week. How many left?

85 – 13 = ?

Number line

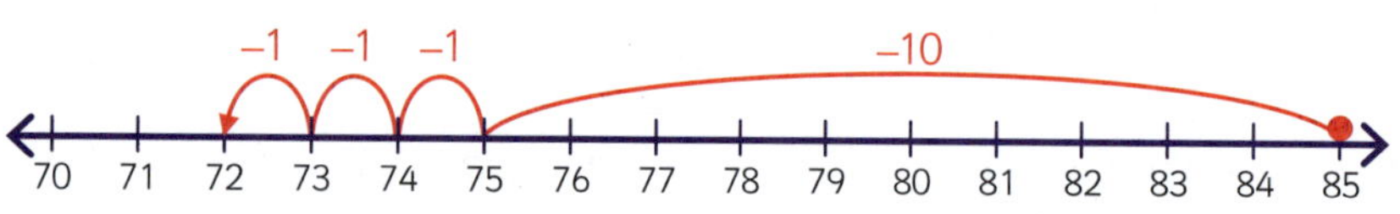

Mrs T has **72** tea bags left.

72 + 13 = 70 + 10 + 2 + 3 = 80 + 5 = 85 ✓

Work Backwards

1. **Read** the problem.
2. **Plan** a strategy.
   Start with the information given. Work backwards using inverse operations.
3. **Work** the strategy.
4. **Answer** the question.
5. **Check** the answer.
   Use the original equation.

Doc has some books. He lends 33 to Dizzy. He has 472 left.
How many books did Doc have to start with?

? – 33 = 472

472 + 33 = 472 + 30 + 3 = 502 + 3 = **505**

Doc had **505** books to start with.

505 – 33 = 505 – 30 – 3 = 502 – 30 = 472 ✓

Look for Patterns

1. **Read** the problem.
2. **Plan** a strategy.
   Look for patterns in the given information. Use a diagram or a table to make it easier to see. Is there a rule?
3. **Work** the strategy.
4. **Answer** the question.
5. **Check** the answer.
   Finish the table.

Mango eats 9 bananas a week. How many bananas does she eat in 5 weeks? How many will she eat in 9 weeks?

Week	1	2	3	4	5
Bananas	9	18	27	36	**45**

Mango eats **45** bananas in 5 weeks. Rule: number of weeks ×9.

9 × 9 = **81** Mango eats **81** bananas in 9 weeks.

Week	5	6	7	8	9
Bananas	**45**	54	63	72	**81** ✓

Mathseeds Year 3 Workbook © 3P Learning ISBN 978-1-923253-14-8

Make an Organised List

1. **Read** the problem.
2. **Plan** a strategy.
   Find **all the possibilities** by writing a list using a system. Start with 1, then work through all the digits one by one.
3. **Work** the strategy.
4. **Answer** the question.
5. **Check** the answer is complete.

Dizzy has four number cards: 1, 2, 3 and 4.
How many 4-digit numbers can he make?

1234, 1243, 1342, 1324, 1423, 1432,
2134, 2143, 2314, 2341, 2413, 2431,
3124, 3142, 3214, 3241, 3412, 3421,
4123, 4132, 4213, 4231, 4312, 4321

Dizzy can make **24** numbers. ✓

Mrs T and her friends tallied how many glasses of water they drank in one day. Who drank the most? Who drank the least?

Mrs T: 𝍸 I Waldo: 𝍸 Doc: 𝍸 I Ruby: 𝍸 II

	1	2	3	4	5	6	7	8
Mrs T	■	■	■	■	■	■		
Waldo	■	■	■	■				
Doc	■	■	■	■	■	■		
Ruby	■	■	■	■	■	■	■	

Ruby drank the most. **Waldo** drank the least.

Mrs T: 6 Waldo: **4** Doc: 6 Ruby: **7** ✓

Use a Graph or Table

1. **Read** the problem.
2. **Plan** a strategy.
   Use a **graph** or a **table** to make the **given information** easier to read.
3. **Work** the strategy.
4. **Answer** the question.
5. **Check** the tallies and numbers are right.

Guess and Check

1. **Read** the problem.
2. **Plan** a strategy.
   Guess an answer. Check it against the **given information**. If it doesn't work, guess again.
3. **Work** the strategy.
4. **Answer** the question.
5. **Check** the answer.
   Draw a picture.

Dizzy has a number of birds and lizards. There are 9 heads and 30 legs altogether. How many of each animal does Dizzy have?

Guess: 6 birds + 3 lizards = 9 heads
Check: 6 × 2 legs + 3 × 4 legs = 12 + 12 = 24 legs ✗

Guess: 3 birds + 6 lizards = 9 heads
Check: 3 × 2 legs + 6 × 4 legs = 6 + 24 = 30 legs ✓

Dizzy has 3 birds and 6 lizards.

= 24 legs

= 6 legs 6 + 24 = 30 ✓

My 4-digit number ends with an odd number under 5. The first digit is even. There are as many hundreds as ones. There are no tens. There are no digits over 2. What is my number?

Thou	Hund	Tens	Ones
2/4/6/8	1/3	0	1/3
2	1	0	1

My number is 2101.

4 digits ✓ ends with odd number < 5 ✓ first digit even ✓
hundreds = ones ✓ no tens ✓ no digits > 2 ✓

Use Logical Reasoning

1. **Read** the problem.
2. **Plan** a strategy.
   Write **possible answers** and eliminate incorrect options based on the **given information**.
3. **Work** the strategy.
4. **Answer** the question.
5. **Check** the answer fits all the **information given**.

Counting 1000-5000

1 Write the thousands in order on the number line.

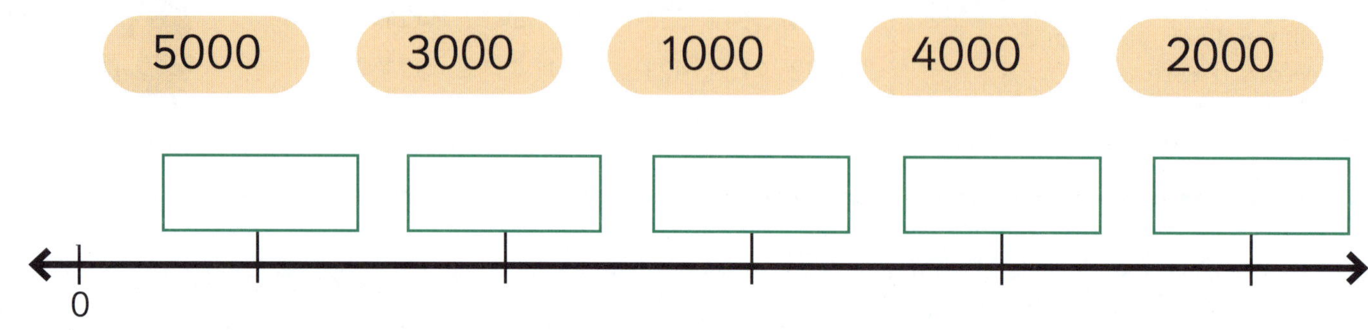

2 Write the numbers in words.

a 2000 ______

b 5000 ______

c 1000 ______

d 4000 ______

e 3000 ______

3 Write these numbers in order from **smallest** to **largest**.

a 3000 4 50 200

______

b 500 4000 1 20

______

c 3 1000 4000 10

______

Mathseeds Year 3 Workbook © 3P Learning ISBN 978-1-923253-14-8

4 Fill in the missing numbers.

100	200	300	400				800	900	
1100	1200	1300	1400	1500	1600				2000
2100			2400	2500	2600	2700			
		3300				3700	3800	3900	4000
4100	4200	4300		4500	4600	4700	4800	4900	

5 Put these numbers in order on the number line.

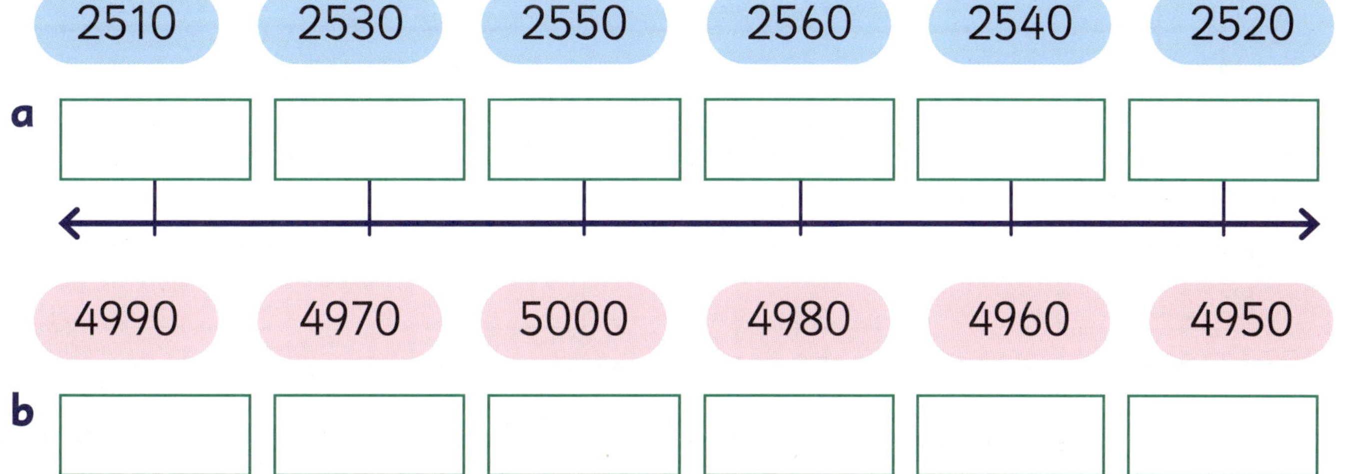

6 Put the correct symbol in the box: **< >**

a 1000 ☐ 4000 **b** 3400 ☐ 2900 **c** 1100 ☐ 1700

d 4250 ☐ 2070 **e** 1400 ☐ 1900 **f** 3560 ☐ 3760

g 3500 ☐ 3600 **h** 4440 ☐ 4410 **i** 2110 ☐ 2010

j 2930 ☐ 2970 **k** 3870 ☐ 3880 **l** 1950 ☐ 1780

LESSON 151 COUNTING 1000–5000

7 Put these numbers in order on the number line.

a

b

c

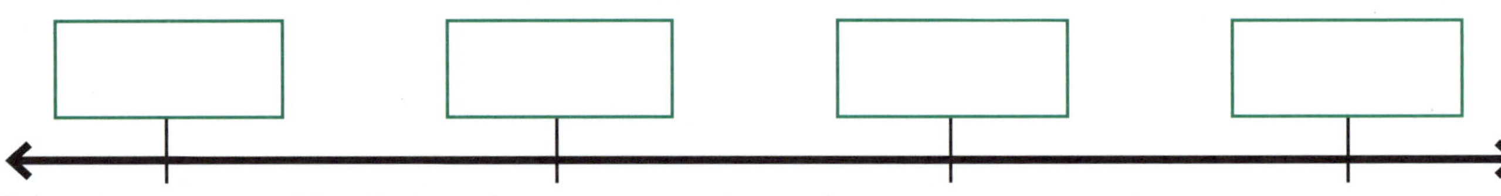

8 Write these numbers in order from **smallest** to **largest**.

3429 4930 2316 3781 4213

____

9 Write these numbers in numerals.

a two thousand, five hundred and thirty-nine ____________

b four thousand, eight hundred and ninety ____________

Mathseeds Year 3 Workbook © 3P Learning ISBN 978-1-923253-14-8

10 Dizzy has four number cards: 1, 2, 4 and 5.
How many 4-digit numbers can he make?

1 2 4 5

a Underline the question. **b** Circle the facts.

c Make a list of all the 4-digit numbers that can be made.

____

____

____

____

d There are __________ 4-digit numbers.

11 Mango has some questions.

a What is the largest number on the list? __________

b What is the largest number starting with 1? __________

c What is the largest number starting with 2? __________

d What is the largest number starting with 4? __________

12 How do you find the largest number in a list? Write the steps.

____

____

I finished this lesson online.

151

I can

- Order numbers to 5000 from smallest to largest and on a number line. ☐
- Count to 5000 by hundreds and compare numbers to 5000. ☐
- Write numbers to 5000 in words and vice versa. ☐
- Make all 4-digit numbers given 4 digits. ☐

We went to

LESSON 152 SYMMETRY

1 Colour the symmetrical items.

2 Draw a line of symmetry on the symmetrical shapes.

 Mathseeds Year 3 Workbook © 3P Learning ISBN 978-1-923253-14-8

3 Circle the symmetrical things.

4 Colour the symmetrical halves in matching colours.

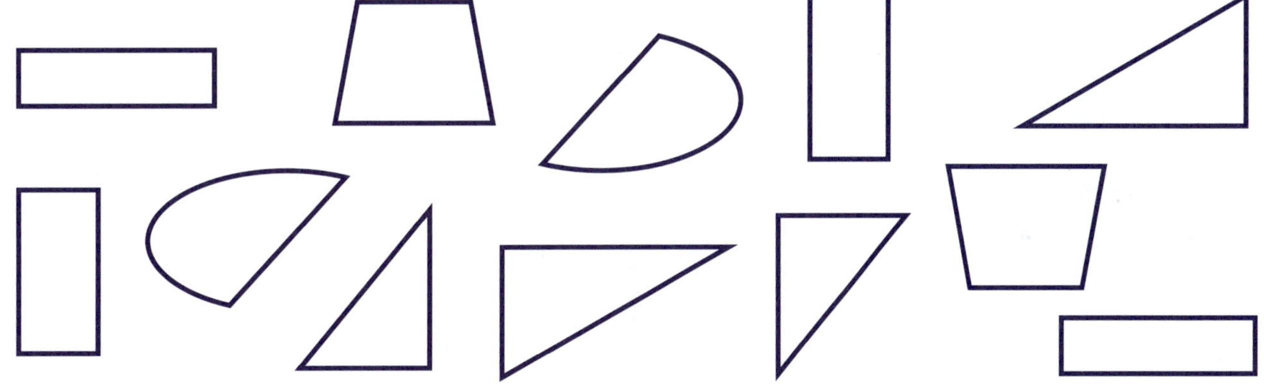

5 Complete the symmetrical patterns.

  ISBN 978-1-923253-14-8

6 Complete the symmetrical pictures.

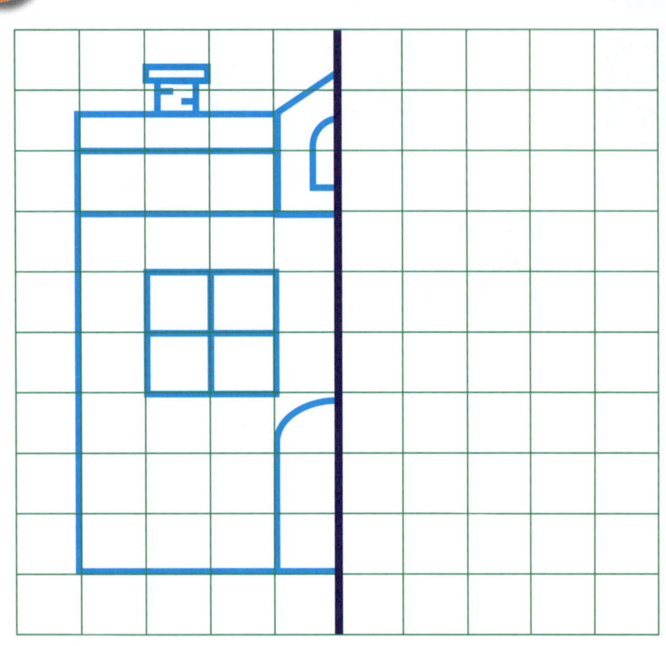

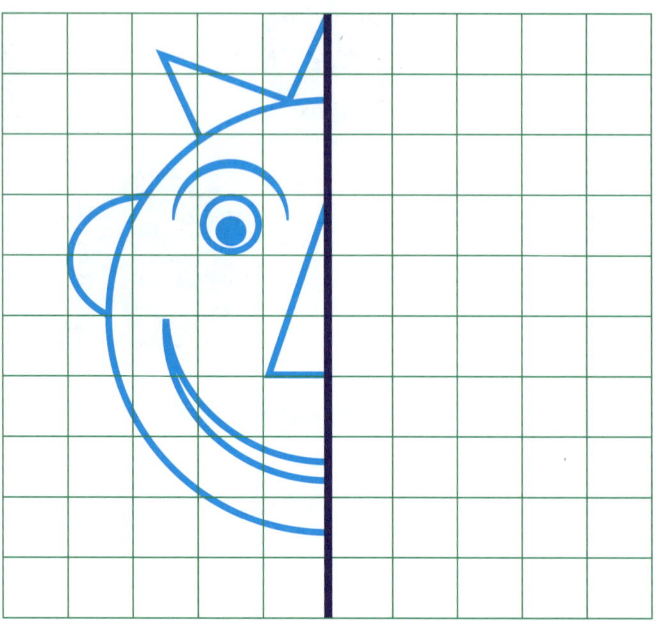

7 Draw your own symmetrical picture.

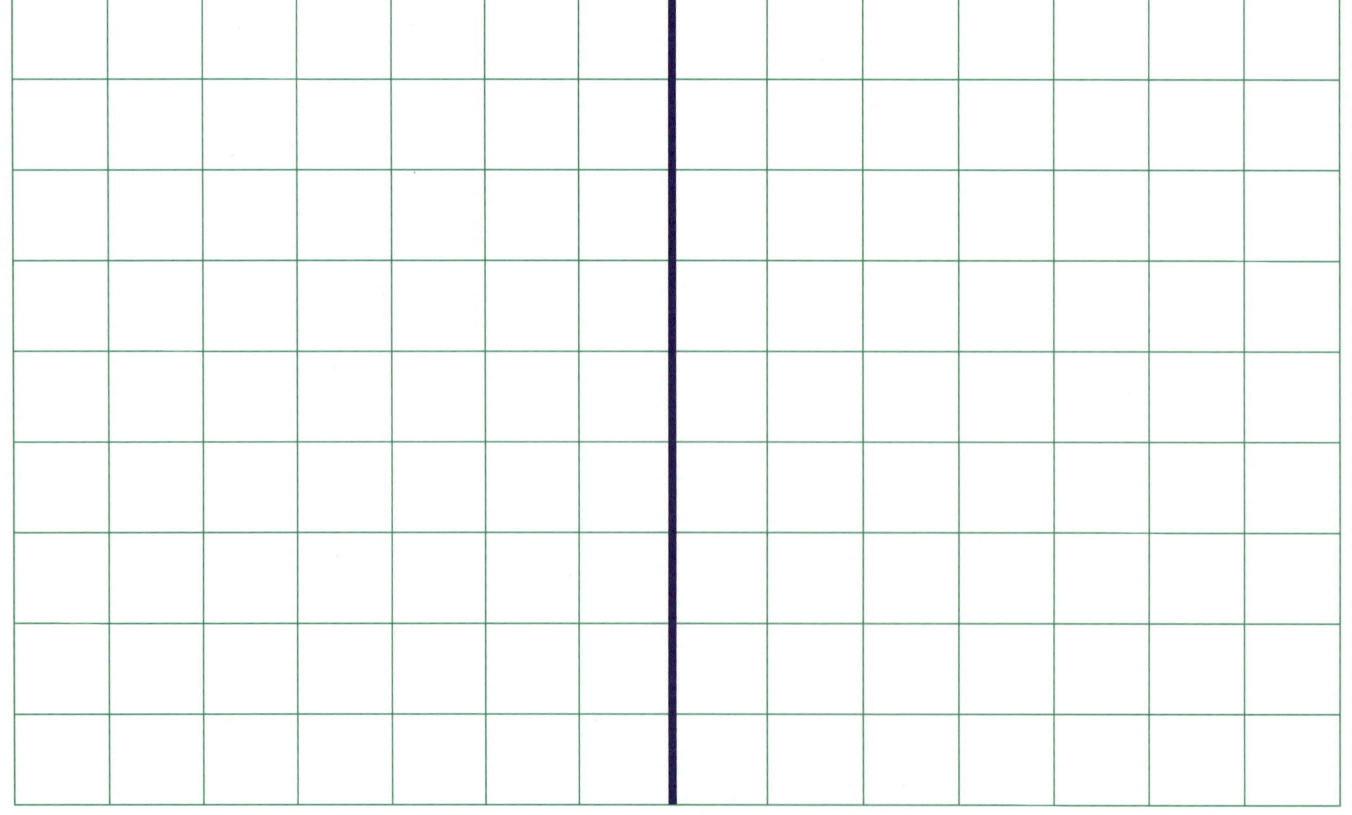

Mathseeds Year 3 Workbook © 3P Learning ISBN 978-1-923253-14-8

Symmetry

8 Ruby is investigating upper-case letters. She is looking for letters that are symmetrical. Can you finish the list?

a Underline the question. **b** Circle the facts.

c Tick symmetrical shapes. Draw in the lines of symmetry.

A	✓	H		O		V	
B	✓	I		P		W	
C		J	✗	Q		X	
D		K		R		Y	
E		L		S	✗	Z	
F		M		T			
G		N		U			

9 Look at the letters that are not symmetrical. Can you change them to make a symmetrical shape?

I finished this lesson online.

I can
- Identify images that are symmetrical. ☐
- Draw vertical and horizontal lines of symmetry. ☐
- Draw symmetrical patterns and images. ☐

We went to

1 Complete these sums.

1 + 1 =

1 + 2 =

2 + 3 =

3 + 5 =

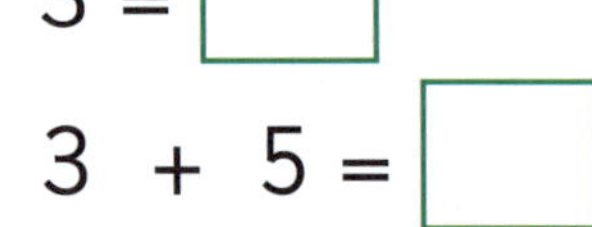

2 Find the next four numbers in the Fibonacci sequence.

1, 1, 2, 3, 5, 8, , , ,

3 Complete the sums for the numbers you added to the sequence.

5 + 8 =

8 + =

\+ =

\+ =

4 Find the next four numbers in the Fibonacci sequence.

34 + 55 =

55 + =

\+ =

\+ =

Mathseeds Year 3 Workbook © 3P Learning ISBN 978-1-923253-14-8

5 Explain the rule for the Fibonacci sequence.

____

____

6 Follow the rule to complete the pattern.

	Rule										
a	+3	1	4	7							
b	–5	61	56	51							
c	+2, –1	1	3	2	4						
d	–3, +5	7	4	9	6						
e	+3, +6	13	16	22	25						
f	–2, –4	55	53	49	47						
g	+10, –5	4	14	9	19						
h	–9, +10	18	9	19	10						
i	+10, +15	5	15	30	40						
j	–5, –4	99	94	90	85						

  ISBN 978-1-923253-14-8

7 What comes next? What is the rule?

a 15, 25, 20, 30, 25, 35, ____, ____, ____ + ______, – ______

b 23, 15, 25, 17, 27, 19, ____, ____, ____ ______, ______

c 35, 37, 40, 42, 45, 47, ____, ____, ____ ______, ______

d 99, 90, 96, 87, 83, 74, ____, ____, ____ ______, ______

e 181, 185, 184, 188, 187, ____, ____, ____ ______, ______

f 462, 460, 467, 465, 472, ____, ____, ____ ______, ______

g 854, 857, 861, 864, 868, ____, ____, ____ ______, ______

h 576, 476, 466, 366, 356, ____, ____, ____ ______, ______

8 Now try these trickier ones. What is the rule?

a 1, 2, 4, 7, 11, 16, ____, ____, ____

____

b 1, 2, 12, 112, 113, 123, 223, ____, ____, ____

____

c 1, 2, 4, 8, 16, 32, ____, ____, ____

____

Mathseeds Year 3 Workbook © 3P Learning ISBN 978-1-923253-14-8

9 Mango wrote out some addition and subtraction patterns. She made a mistake in each one. Can you find the mistakes and fix the patterns?

a Underline the question. **b** Circle the facts.

10 Work out the rule. Cross out the mistake. Write in the correct number.

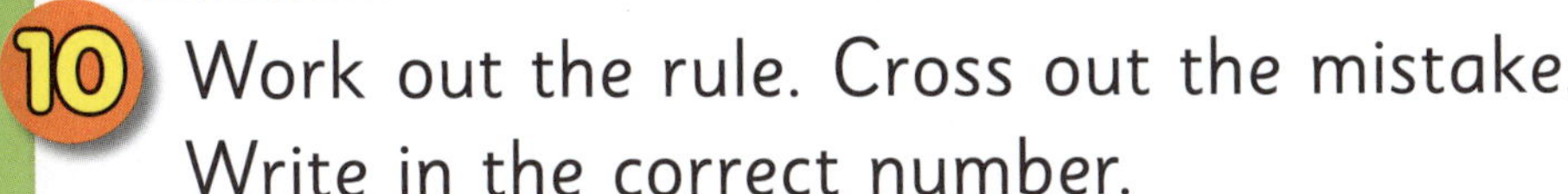

a 1, 6, 11, 16, 21, 26, 30, 36 Rule: ____________

b 46, 43, 40, 37, 33, 31, 28, 25 Rule: ____________

c 102, 112, 110, 120, 118, 128, 126, 124 Rule: ____________

11 **a** Write three of your own patterns. Add a mistake to each one.

____

____

____

b Swap with a partner. Write the rules they used and try to fix each other's patterns.

12 Describe the pattern you think is the most interesting and why.

____

____

I finished this lesson online.

153

I can
- Explore the Fibonacci sequence. ☐
- Identify and follow a rule to continue a number pattern. ☐
- Correct mistakes in a given number pattern. ☐

We went to

  ISBN 978-1-923253-14-8

LESSON 154 LITRES & MILLILITRES

1 Match the correct label to each jug.

a

b

c
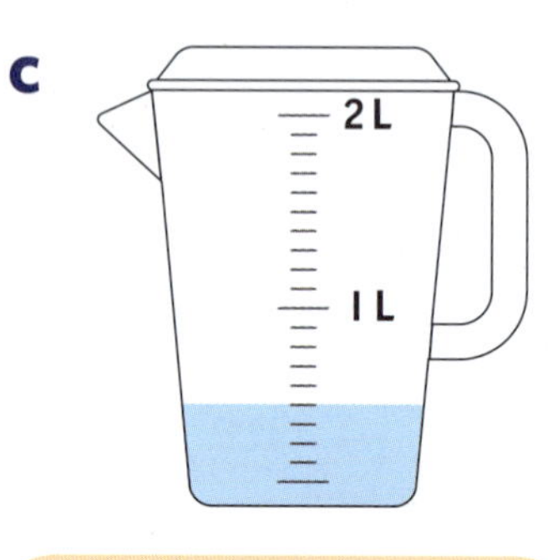

more than 1 L | 1 L | less than 1 L

2 Write the measurement in litres, eg 1 L.

a ______

b ______

c ______

3 Colour the jugs to show the amounts.

a

more than 1 L

b

1 L

c
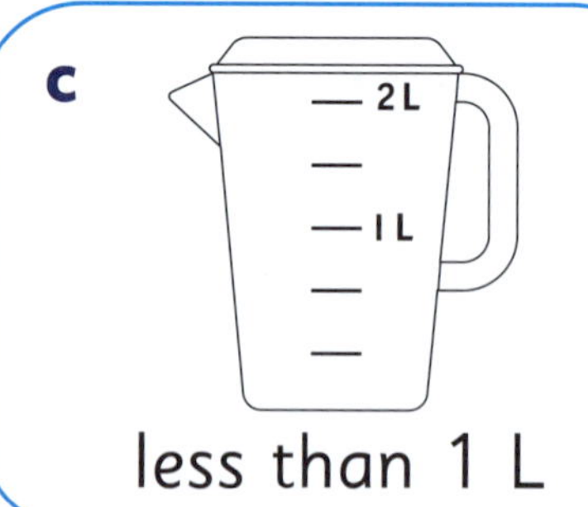

less than 1 L

d

three litres

e

five litres

f

two litres

Mathseeds Year 3 Workbook ISBN 978-1-923253-14-8

4 Match the correct label to each jug.

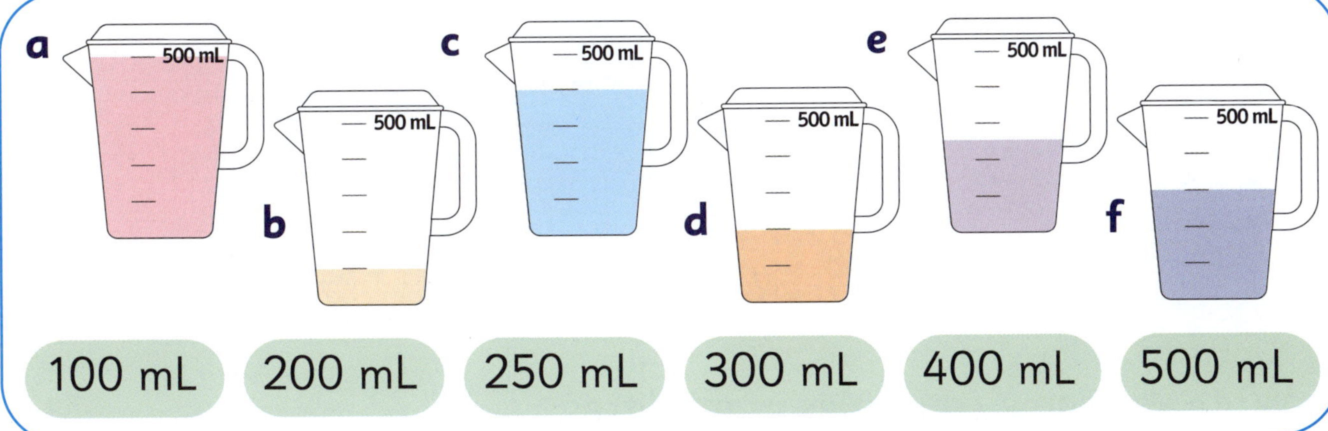

5 Write the measurement in millilitres, eg 200 mL.

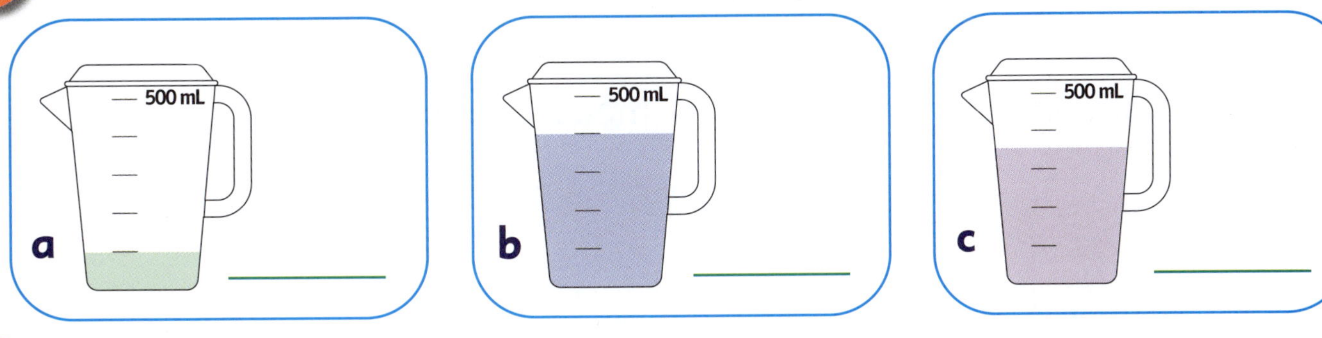

6 Colour the jugs to show the amounts.

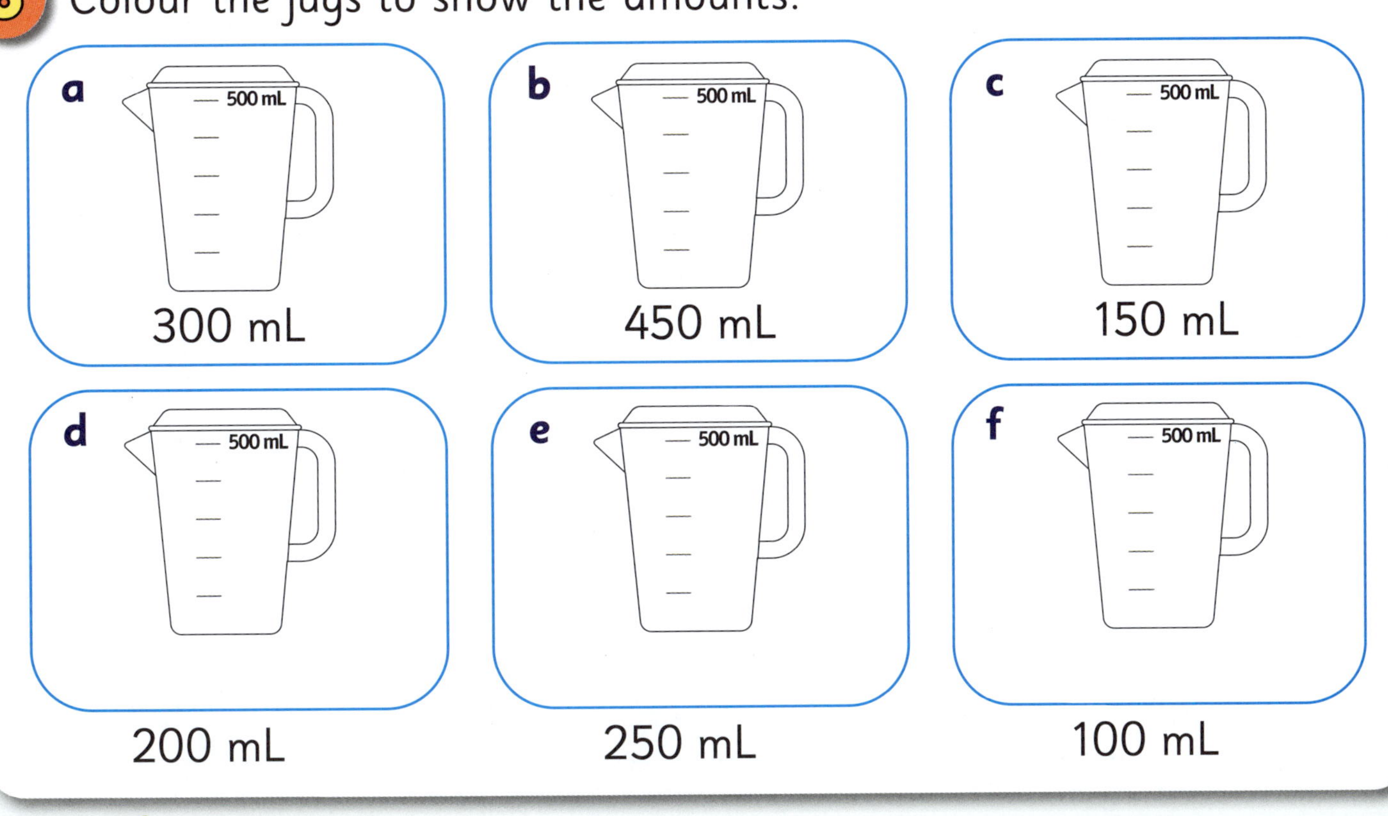

7 Write the capacity of each jug in litres.

_______ L

_______ L

_______ L

8 Write the same capacities in millilitres.

a _______ mL
b _______ mL
c _______ mL

9 Which units should you write the measurement in: mL or L?

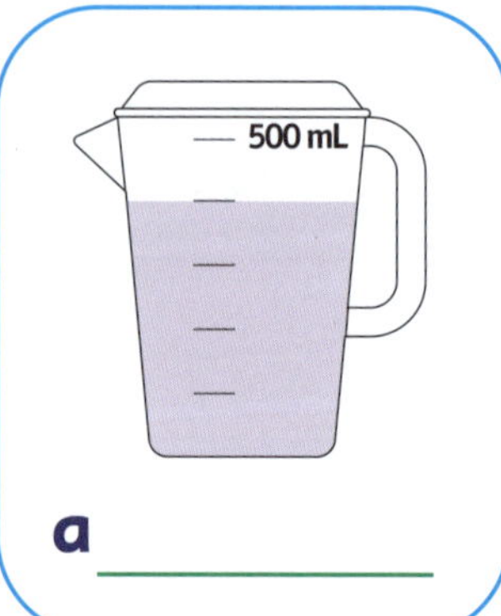

a _______

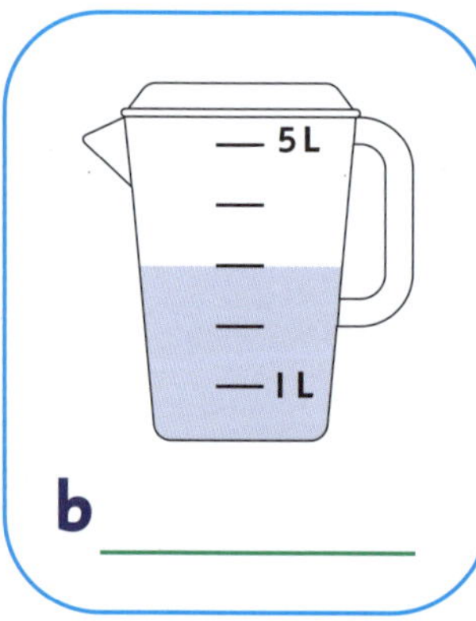

b _______

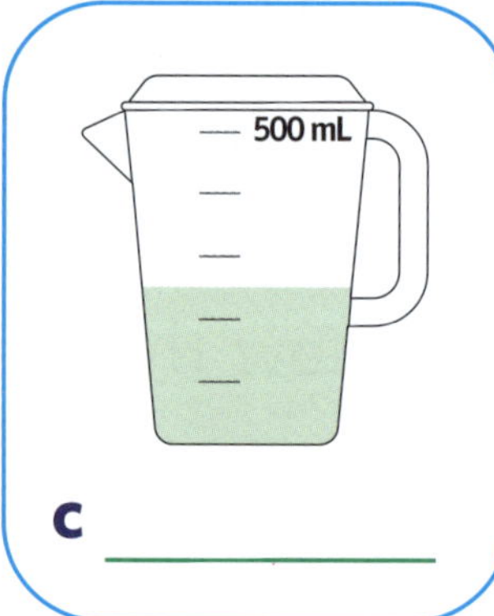

c _______

d _______

10 Match the correct label to each jug.

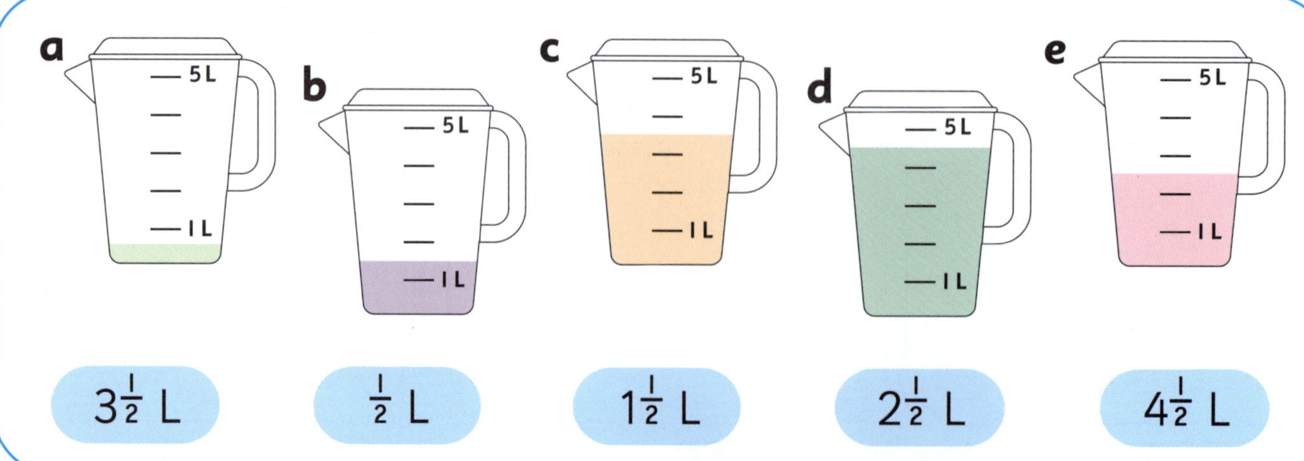

$3\frac{1}{2}$ L $\frac{1}{2}$ L $1\frac{1}{2}$ L $2\frac{1}{2}$ L $4\frac{1}{2}$ L

Mathseeds Year 3 Workbook © 3P Learning ISBN 978-1-923253-14-8

Litres & Millilitres

11 Dizzy bought two cartons of milk. Each carton holds 2 L of milk. How much milk did Dizzy buy?

_______ × _______ = _____________

12 Waldo has three glasses of water. Each glass holds 300 mL of water. How much water altogether?

_______ × _______ = _____________

13 Ruby has a 400 mL bottle of cleaning spray. She uses 50 mL a week. How many weeks will the bottle last? _______

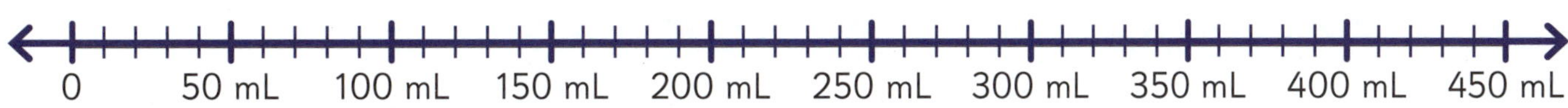

14 Mango makes a special juice. She uses 200 mL of orange juice, 300 mL of apple juice, 100 mL of carrot juice and 50 mL of lime juice. How much special juice does she end up with? _____________

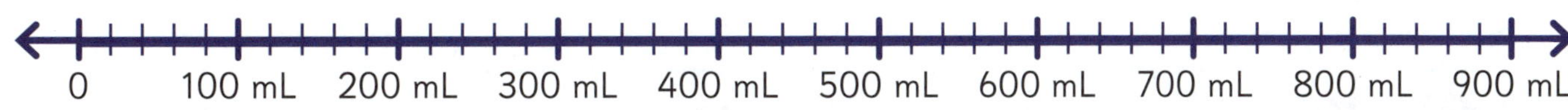

15 Mrs T drank two enormous cups of tea. Each cup had 500 mL of tea in it. How much tea is that in litres?

_______ + _______ = _______ mL = _______ L

I finished this lesson online.

I can

- Determine if a vessel holds >, < or = to 1 L. ☐
- Use increments on measuring vessels in mL and L. ☐
- Convert between litres and millilitres and solve capacity word problems. ☐

We went to

LESSON 155 MULTIPLICATION REVISION

1 How many? Fill in the repeated addition.

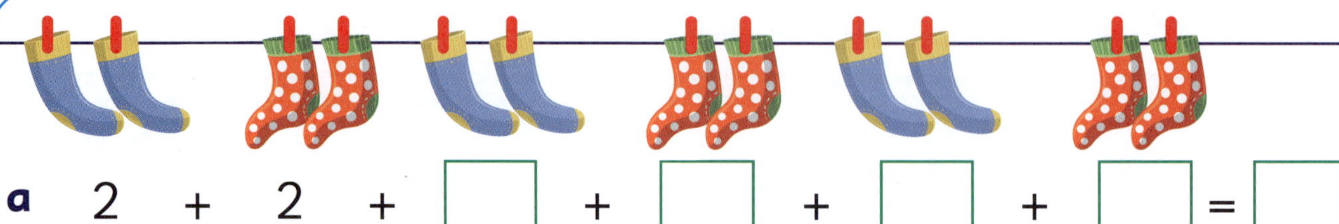

a 2 + 2 + ☐ + ☐ + ☐ + ☐ = ☐

b 3 + ☐ + ☐ = ☐

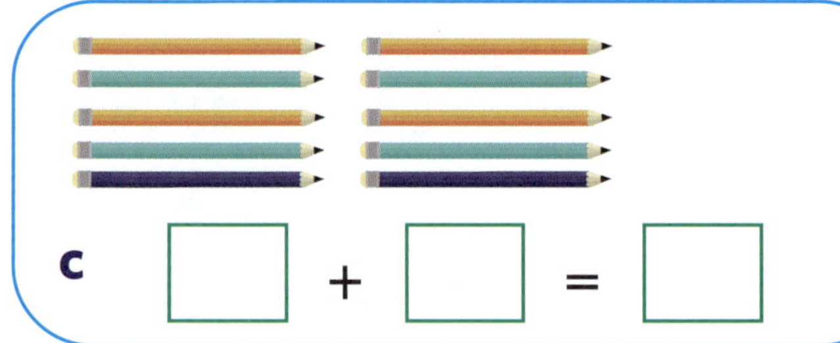

c ☐ + ☐ = ☐

2 How many? Skip count to find the answer.

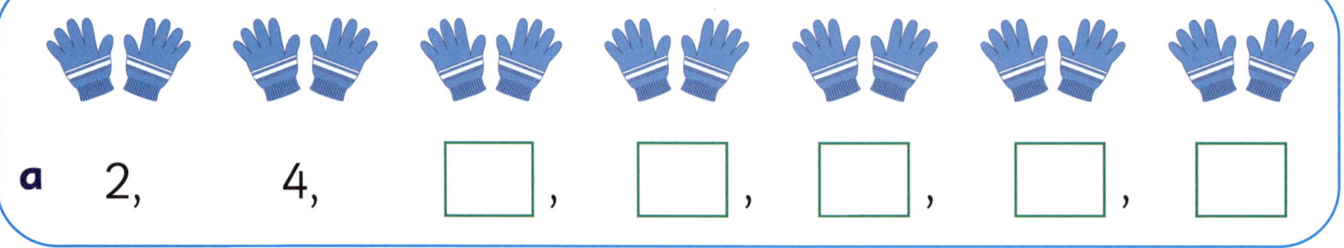

a 2, 4, ☐, ☐, ☐, ☐, ☐

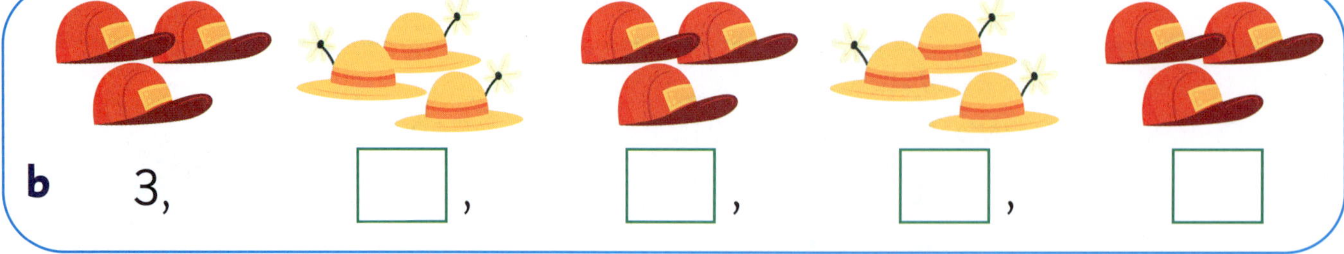

b 3, ☐, ☐, ☐, ☐

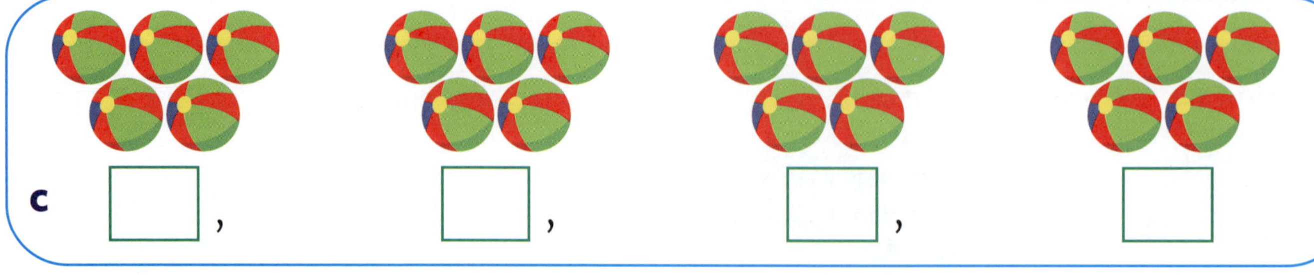

c ☐, ☐, ☐, ☐

Mathseeds Year 3 Workbook © 3P Learning ISBN 978-1-923253-14-8

Multiplication Revision

Jump along the number line to find how many.

3 I buy 8 pairs of shoes. How many shoes altogether? ______

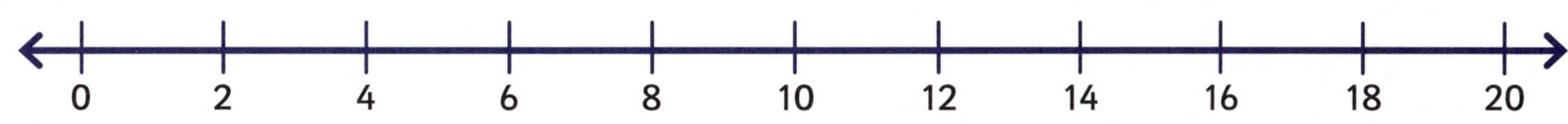

4 You have 5 packs of 5 pens each.

How many pens altogether? ______

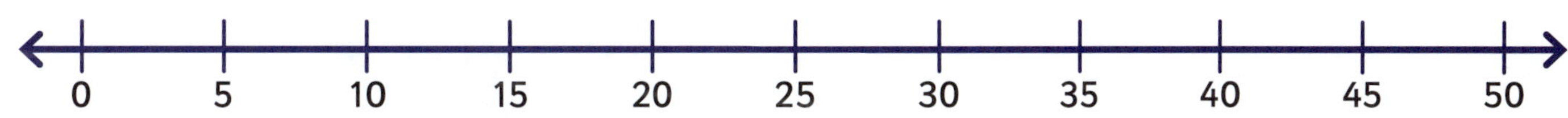

5 We have 7 baskets with 3 dumplings in each.

How many dumplings altogether? ______

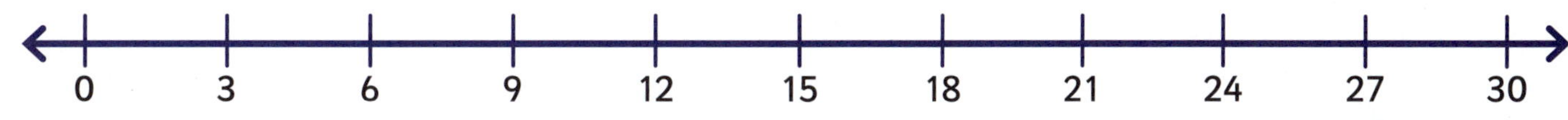

6 $7 \times 5 =$ ______

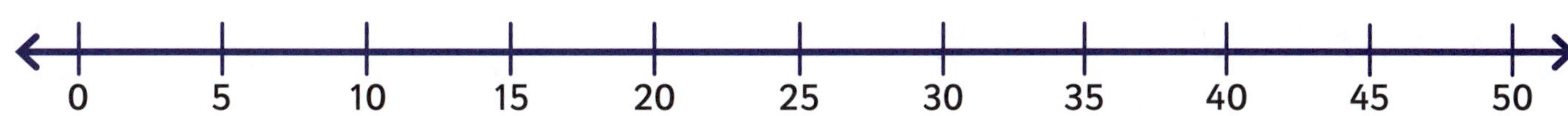

7 $9 \times 10 =$ ______

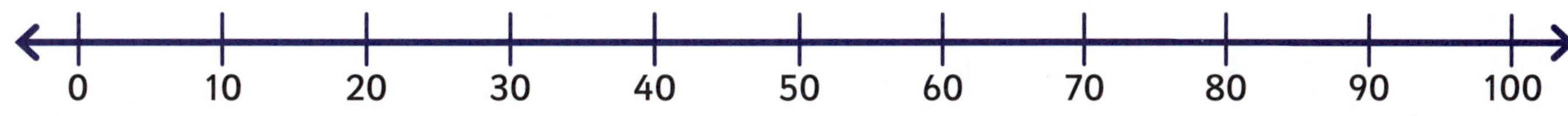

8 $5 \times 2 =$ ______

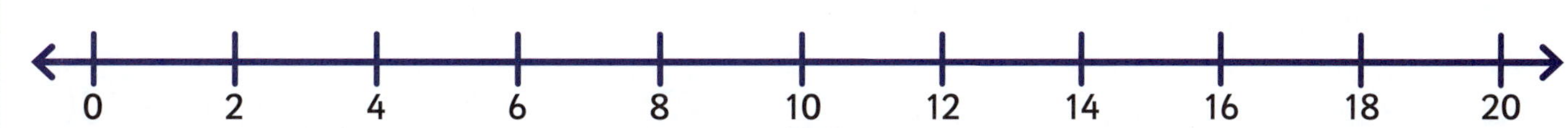

  ISBN 978-1-923253-14-8

9 Write the equation to match the array.

a ☐ × ☐ = ☐

b ☐ × ☐ = ☐

c ☐ × ☐ = ☐

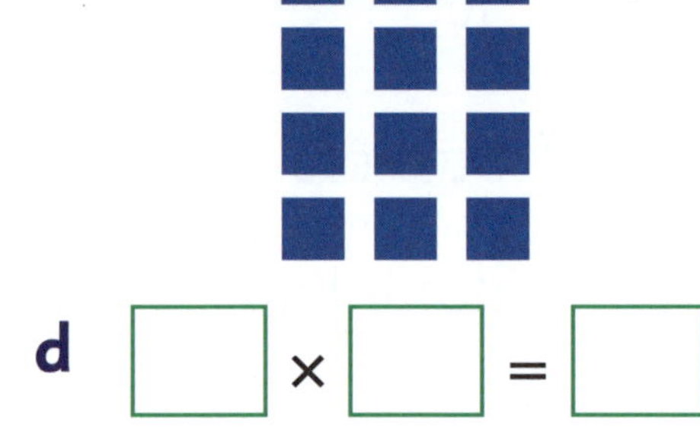

d ☐ × ☐ = ☐

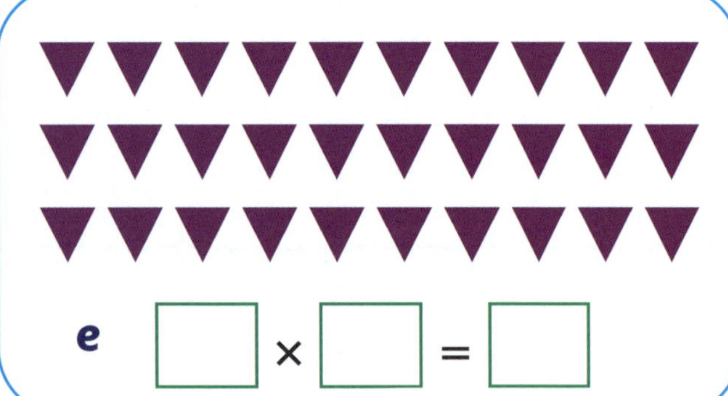

e ☐ × ☐ = ☐

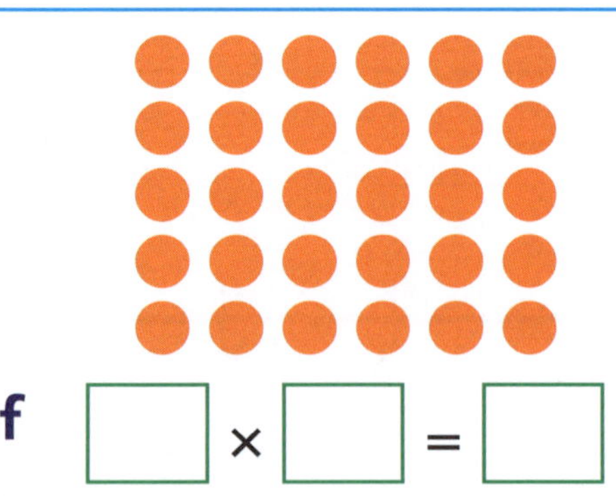

f ☐ × ☐ = ☐

10 What is the missing number?

a 10 × 2 = ______

b 5 × ______ = 50

c ______ × 5 = 45

d 9 × 3 = ______

e 3 × ______ = 6

f ______ × 2 = 4

g 8 × 5 = ______

h 7 × ______ = 70

i ______ × 10 = 100

Mathseeds Year 3 Workbook ISBN 978-1-923253-14-8

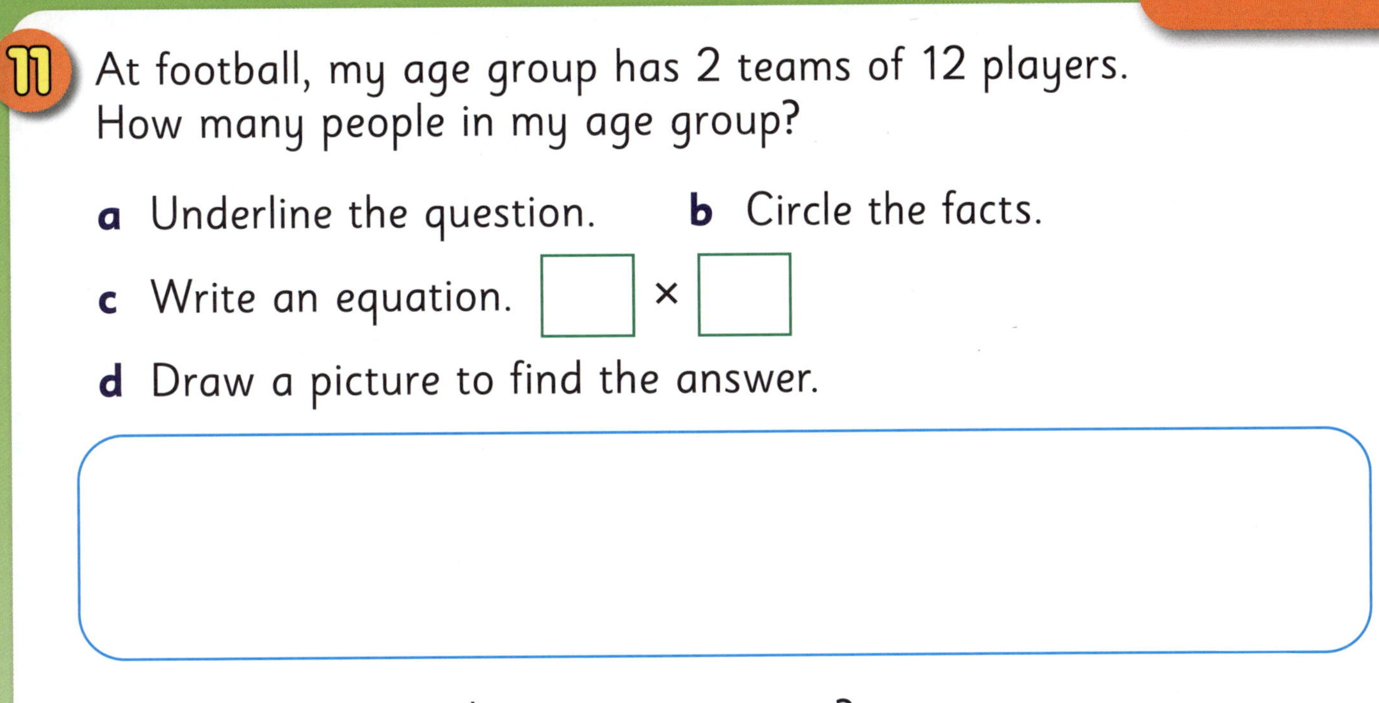

11 At football, my age group has 2 teams of 12 players. How many people in my age group?

a Underline the question. **b** Circle the facts.

c Write an equation. ☐ × ☐

d Draw a picture to find the answer.

e How many people in my age group? ____________

12 At basketball, we have 3 teams of 6 players. How many people in my age group?

a Underline the question. **b** Circle the facts.

c Write an equation. ☐ × ☐

d Draw a number line to find the answer.

e How many people in my age group? ____________

I finished this lesson online.	I can		We went to
155	• Use repeated addition, skip counting and the number line to multiply.	☐	
	• Write equations for arrays and find missing numbers in equations.	☐	
	• Solve multiplication word problems.	☐	

QUIZ

END OF MAP 31 QUIZ

1 Write these numbers in order from smallest to largest.

2834 | 2438 | 4378 | 4387 | 3743

____

2 Write the numbers in words.

a 5786 ______________________________

b 1203 ______________________________

3 Which is the line of symmetry? Trace it.

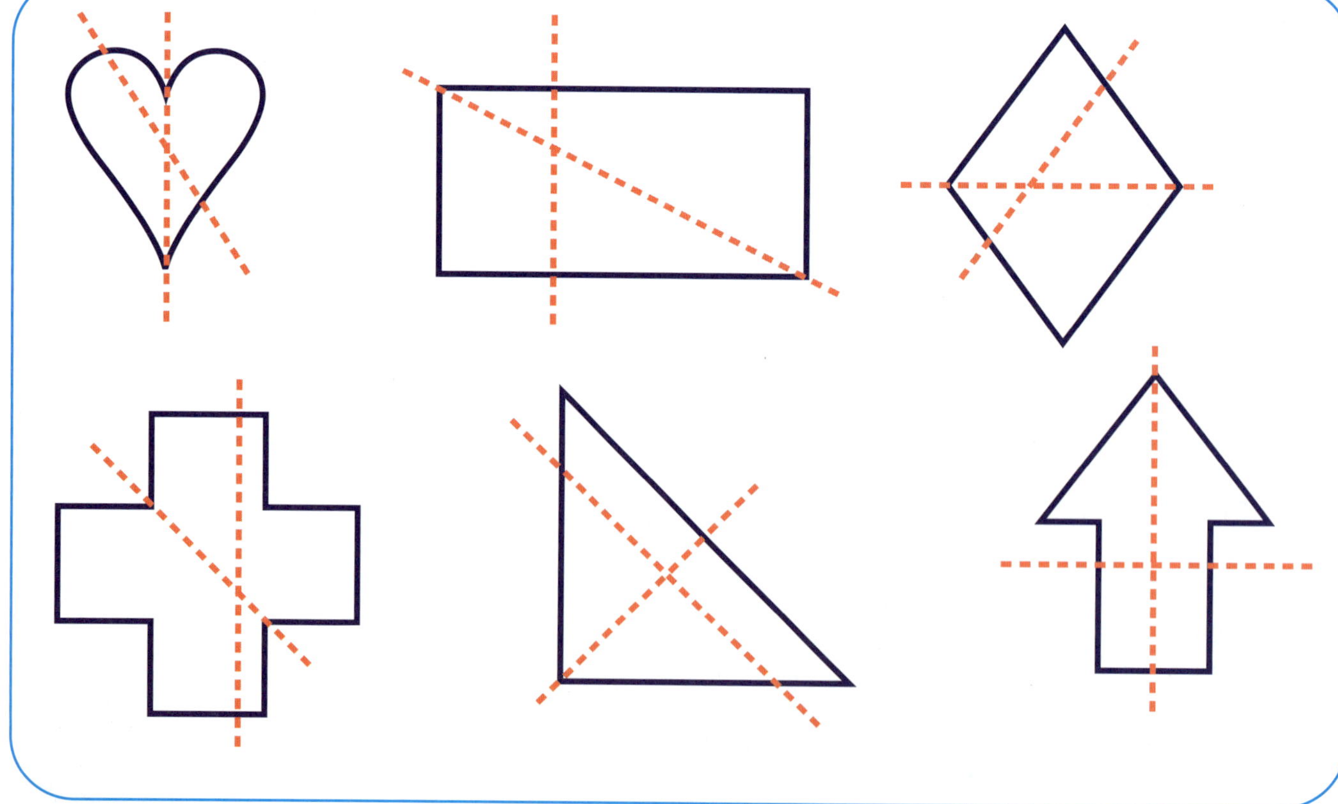

Mathseeds Year 3 Workbook © 3P Learning ISBN 978-1-923253-14-8

4 What comes next? What is the rule?

a 3, 6, 10, 13, 17, ____, ____, ____, ____ ________

b 3, 13, 113, 123, 223, ____, ____, ____, ____ ________

c 300, 290, 295, 285, ____, ____, ____, ____ ________

d 3, 4, 6, 9, 13, 18, ____, ____, ____, ____ ________

5 Write the amount.

a ________

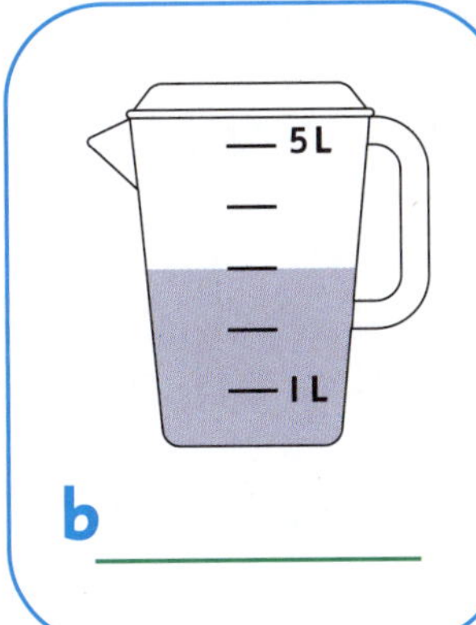

b ________

c ________

d ________

6 Mango ate 4 tubs of yoghurt in a week. Each tub had 250 mL of yoghurt.

How much yoghurt is that in litres?

____ + ____ + ____ + ____ = ____ mL = ____ L

7

a $10 \times 4 =$ ____ b $3 \times 5 =$ ____ c $5 \times 6 =$ ____

d $2 \times 9 =$ ____ e $3 \times 4 =$ ____ f $5 \times 7 =$ ____

  ISBN 978-1-923253-14-8

YOU COMPLETED

YOU CAN:

- **Order** numbers to **5000** and **write** numbers in words.
- Choose the **line of symmetry** on a shape.
- Identify and follow a **rule** to continue a **number pattern**.
- Read increments on measuring vessels in **mL** and **L**.
- Solve a multiplication **word problem** and answer **multiplication equations**.

Signed:

Dated:

Mathseeds Year 3 Workbook © 3P Learning ISBN 978-1-923253-14-8

SUMS MAZE

1. Colour the path that leads to <u>51</u>.

◯ + 8 = ◯ + 9 = ◯ + 8 = ☐

+ 7 =

19 + 9 = ◯ + 4 = ◯ + 8 = ☐

+ 8 =

◯ + 7 = ◯ + 9 = ◯ + 7 = ☐

+ 8 =

◯ + 9 = ◯ + 8 = ◯ + 8 = ☐

1 Draw each number in blocks.

	Thousands	Hundreds	Tens	Ones
a 4353				
b 6229				
c 2801				

2 Write the numbers in words.

a 7857 ______________________

b 9803 ______________________

c 5491 ______________________

d 3890 ______________________

Mathseeds Year 3 Workbook © 3P Learning ISBN 978-1-923253-14-8

3 Put these numbers in order on the number lines.

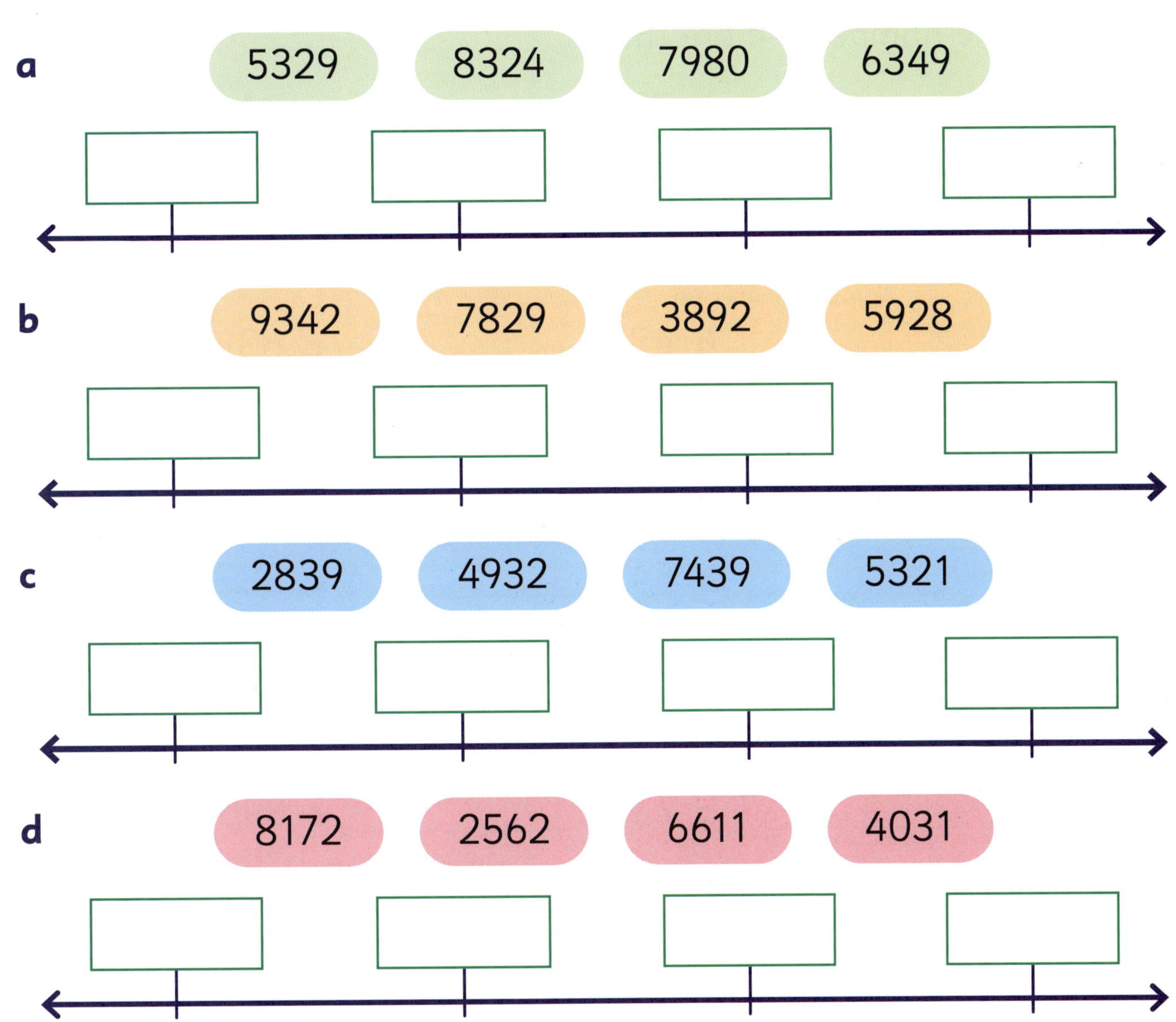

4 Write these numbers in order from **smallest** to **largest**.

9928, 1347, 3946, 8230, 6394

5 Write these numbers in order from **largest** to **smallest**.

5720, 7305, 2934, 8294, 4897

  ISBN 978-1-923253-14-8

6 Write the number 1 more than:

a 3984 ______ b 7826 ______ c 2409 ______

d 8274 ______ e 5129 ______ f 6710 ______

7 Write the number 10 more than:

a 9273 ______ b 4820 ______ c 6394 ______

d 1000 ______ e 5789 ______ f 3210 ______

8 Write the number 100 more than:

a 5395 ______ b 6474 ______ c 8828 ______

d 4927 ______ e 9051 ______ f 1010 ______

9 Write the number 1000 more than:

a 1749 ______ b 7352 ______ c 3957 ______

d 9372 ______ e 622 ______ f 5891 ______

10 Complete.

a 2856 = 2000 + ______ + ______ + ______

b 5937 = ______ + ______ + ______ + 7

c 8360 = ______

d 4023 = ______

e 7804 = ______

f 914 = ______

g 1743 = ______

Mathseeds Year 3 Workbook © 3P Learning ISBN 978-1-923253-14-8

11 **a** Pick 4 different numbers between 1 and 9 and make a 4-digit number.

b Add 1 to the number.

c Add 100 to the number.

d Add 1000 to the number.

e Add 10 to the number.

12 From the five numbers you made:

a Circle the largest number.

b Highlight the smallest number.

c Put the numbers in order on this number line.

13 **a** Share your numbers with a partner. Were any of your numbers the same?

b Put all ten numbers in order from smallest to largest.

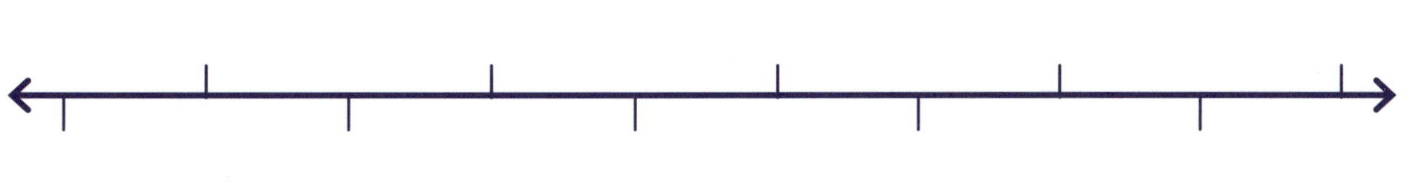

I finished this lesson online. 156

I can

- Model 4-digit numbers in base ten blocks, words and expanded form.
- Order 4-digit numbers forwards and backwards, and on a number line.
- Add 1, 10, 100, 1000 to a 4-digit number.

We went to

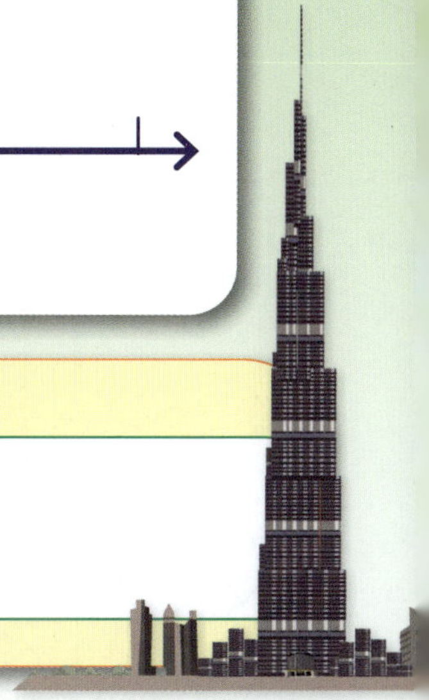

1 What is the area?

a

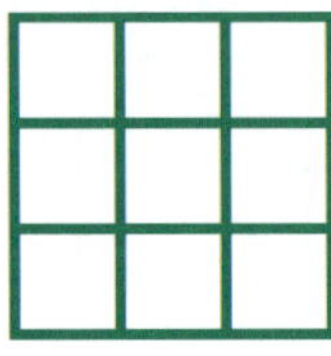

area = ____ squares

b

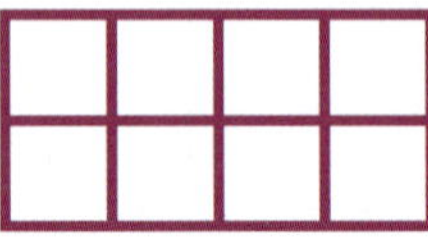

area = ____ squares

c

area = ____ squares

d

area = ____ squares

2 Calculate the area.

a

____ × ____ = ____ squares

b

____ × ____ = ____ squares

c

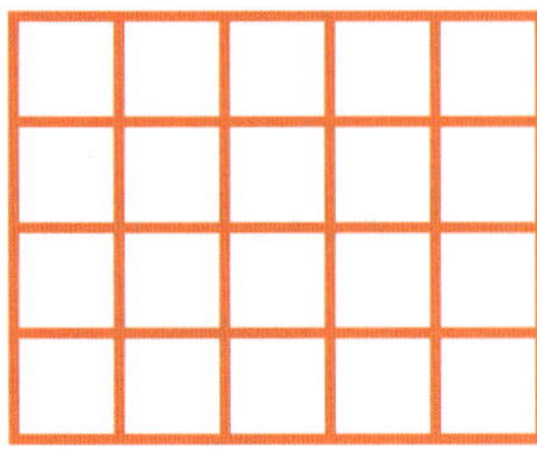

____ × ____ = ____ squares

d

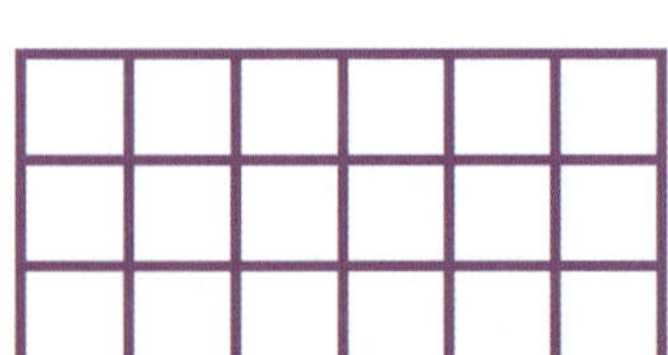

____ × ____ = ____ squares

Mathseeds Year 3 Workbook © 3P Learning ISBN 978-1-923253-14-8

3 Calculate the area.

a

6 m

2 m

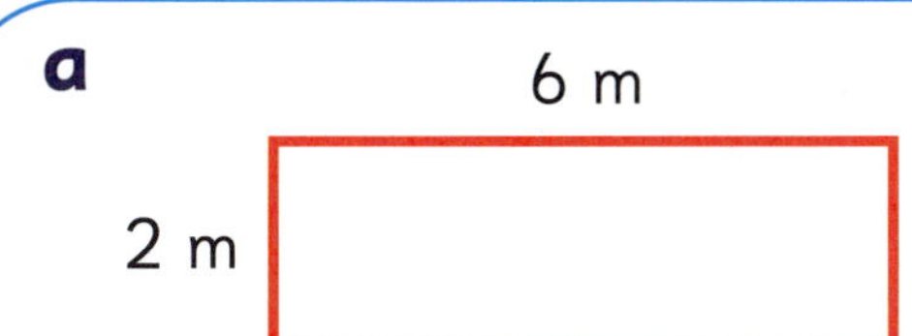

____ × ____ = ____ m^2

b

5 m

5 m

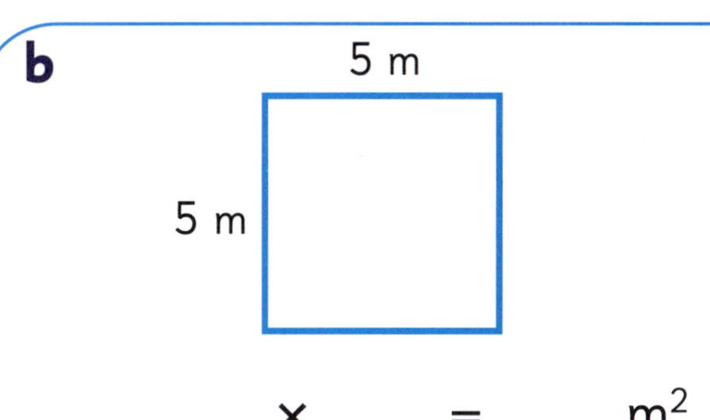

____ × ____ = ____ m^2

c

3 m

2 m

____ × ____ = ____ m^2

d

6 m

4 m

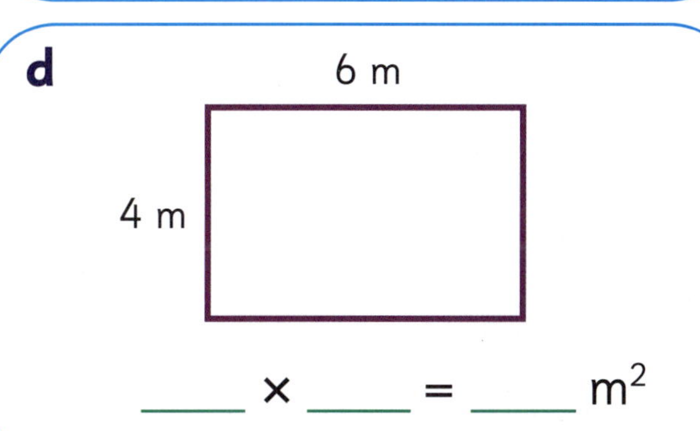

____ × ____ = ____ m^2

4 What is the area?

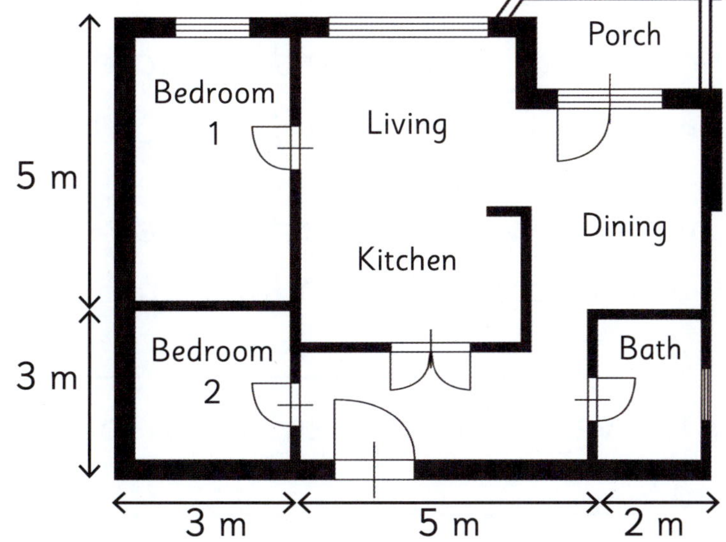

a Bedroom 1 is ____ m^2.

b Bedroom 2 is ____ m^2.

c The bathroom is ____ m^2.

d The house is ____ m^2.

Answer the questions. Don't forget to use square units!

5 Farmer Helen has a vegetable garden.
Each row is 5 m long and 1 m wide.

a She plants 1 row of lettuce. What is the area? ____________

b She plants 2 rows of capsicums. What is the area? ____________

c She plants 5 rows of tomatoes. What is the area? ____________

6 Farmer Helen also has an orchard.
Each fruit tree takes up a 2 m^2 space.

a She has 4 apple trees. What is the area? ____________

b She has 6 orange trees. What is the area? ____________

c She has 9 peach trees. What is the area? ____________

7 Farmer Helen wants to get some sheep.
Each sheep needs 5 m^2 in the yard.

a If she gets 3 sheep, what area should the yard be? ____________

b If she gets 6 sheep, what area should the yard be? ____________

c If she gets 7 sheep, what area should the yard be? ____________

8 Farmer Helen plans to build a new barn in one of three places.

a The space next to the stables is 6 m long and 6 m wide.
What is the area? ____________

b The space near the vegetable garden is 7 m long and 7 m wide.
What is the area? ____________

c The space behind the farmhouse is 8 m long and 8 m wide.
What is the area? ____________

d Which is the biggest area? ____________

Mathseeds Year 3 Workbook © 3P Learning ISBN 978-1-923253-14-8

Area 3

Ruby is making furniture for her dollhouse living room. The room is 10 cm long by 10 cm wide. Ruby wants to know how much furniture she can fit into the living room.

9 What is the area of the room? ________ × ________ = ________

Remember: length × width = area

10 Draw in a couch, bookcase, dining table and 4 dining chairs.

11 Find the area of each piece of furniture.

a couch ________ × ________ = ________

b bookcase ________ × ________ = ________

c table ________ × ________ = ________

d chair ________ × ________ = ________ × 4 chairs = ________

I finished this lesson online.

I can

- Count squares and multiply length × width to measure area. ☐
- Measure area in m^2 and solve area word problems. ☐

We went to

  ISBN 978-1-923253-14-8

Times Tables
×2 ×4

LESSON 158 TIMES TABLES: ×2, ×4

1 How many wings? Fill in the equations.

a _____ × 2 = _____

b _____ × 2 = _____

c _____ × 2 = _____

d _____ × 2 = _____

e _____ × 2 = _____

f _____ × 2 = _____

2 Find the answers.

×	0	1	2	3	4	5	6	7	8	9	10
2											

3 Complete.

a 2 × 4 = _____ × 2 = 8

b 2 × 7 = _____ × 2 = _____

c 2 × 3 = _____ × _____ = _____

d 2 × 9 = _____ × _____ = _____

e 2 × 5 = _____ × _____ = _____

f 2 × 8 = _____ × _____ = _____

Mathseeds Year 3 Workbook © 3P Learning ISBN 978-1-923253-14-8

4 Complete the table.

		1 × 4	4 × 1	4
A	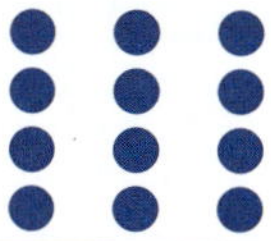			
B	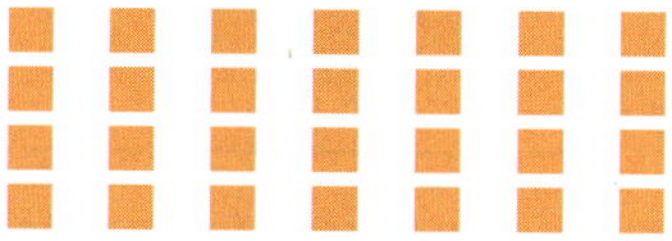			
C	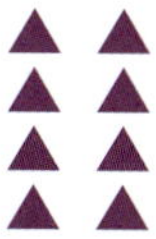			
D				
E				
F	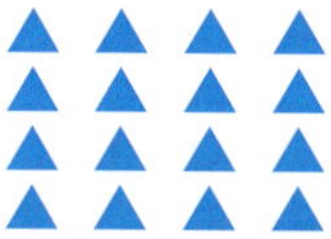			
G	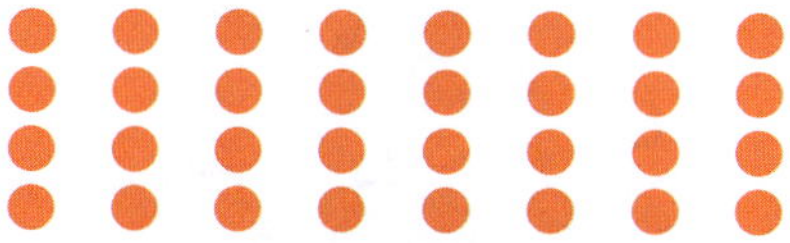			
H				
I				

5 Find the answers.

×	0	1	2	3	4	5	6	7	8	9	10
4											

  ISBN 978-1-923253-14-8

LESSON 158 TIMES TABLES: ×2, ×4

6 Double these numbers.

0	1	2	3	4	5	6	7	8	9	10

7 What times table are these answers for? ______________________

8 Now double the numbers again.

9 What times table are these answers for? ______________________

10 Complete.

×2
2 5
6 9
0 3

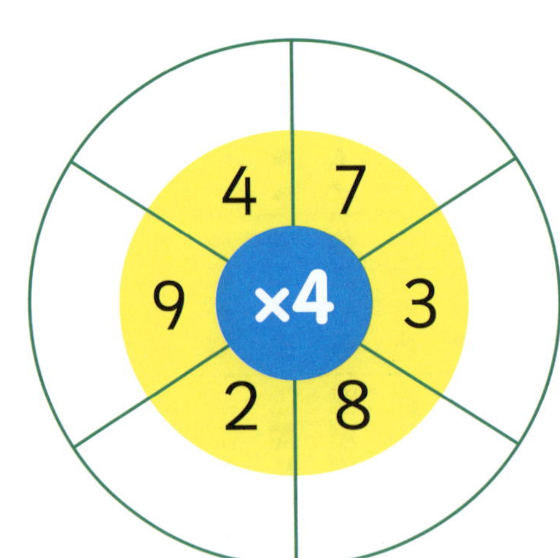

11 Fill in the gaps.

a 2 × ____ = 8 **b** 3 × ____ = 6 **c** 4 × ____ = 16

d 5 × ____ = 20 **e** 6 × ____ = 12 **f** 7 × ____ = 14

g 8 × ____ = 32 **h** 9 × ____ = 36 **i** 10 × ____ = 20

Mathseeds Year 3 Workbook © 3P Learning ISBN 978-1-923253-14-8

12 In Africa, Doc saw a herd of ostriches and zebras. He counted 18 heads and 56 legs altogether. How many of each animal were in the herd?

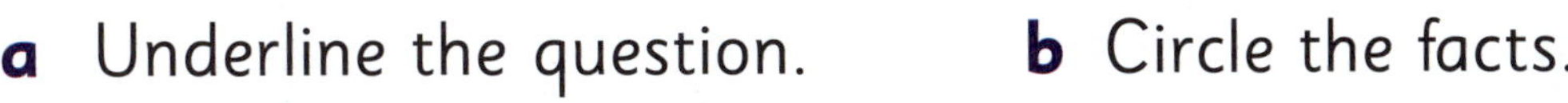

a Underline the question. **b** Circle the facts.

c Guess: how many ostriches and how many zebras.

d Check: does this add to 18 heads? Yes No

e Calculate the number of legs. An ostrich has 2 legs, a zebra has 4. ______

f Check: does this add to 56 legs? Yes No

13 Keep guessing until you find the correct answer.

How many of each animal were in the herd?

Ostriches = ______ Zebras = ______

14 Can you write your own heads and legs problem? Swap with a partner.

I finished this lesson online.

I can

- Write multiplication equations based on groups and arrays. ☐
- Fill in a multiplication table for ×2 and ×4. ☐
- Use the commutative property of multiplication to write equations. ☐
- Explore ×2 and ×4 using doubling. ☐

We went to

LESSON 159 MONEY: EQUIVALENT AMOUNTS 2

	1 How much?	2 Write or draw another way to make this amount.
a 		
b 		
c 		
d 		
e 		

Mathseeds Year 3 Workbook © 3P Learning ISBN 978-1-923253-14-8

3 Circle the change from $5.

a $4.65      

b $1.85      

c $3.50      

d $4.15      

e $2.45      

f $1.30      

4 Find the change from $20.

a $20 – $15.60 = ____________ **b** $20 – $12.35 = ____________

c $20 – $19.95 = ____________ **d** $20 – $10.50 = ____________

e $20 – $8.05 = ____________ **f** $20 – $3.85 = ____________

  ISBN 978-1-923253-14-8

LESSON 159 MONEY: EQUIVALENT AMOUNTS 2

Fill in the algorithms to find the totals.

5 bike + socks

$
+ $
$

6 gloves + cap

$
+ $
$

7 ball + book

$
+ $
$

8 socks + gloves

$
+ $
$

9 cap + book

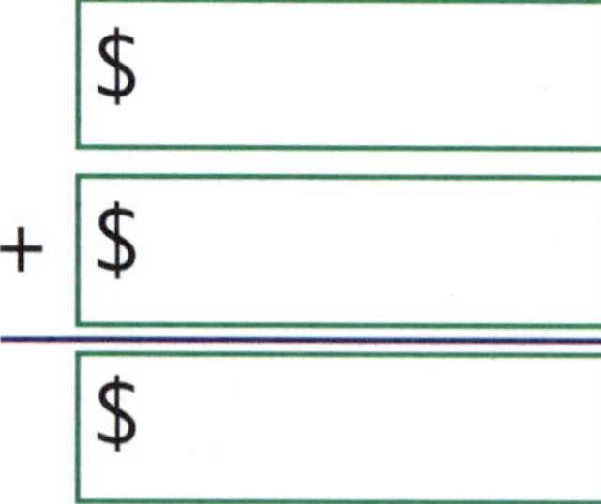

$
+ $
$

10 book + socks

$
+ $
$

11 ball + gloves

$
+ $
$

12 socks + cap

$
+ $
$

13 book + gloves

$
+ $
$

Mathseeds Year 3 Workbook © 3P Learning ISBN 978-1-923253-14-8

14 Dizzy wants to buy a new pot for his cactus. The pot costs $18.50. How can he make the right amount in notes and coins?

a Underline the question.

b Circle the facts.

c How can Dizzy make exactly $18.50 with notes and coins?

15 Dizzy has no $10 notes. Find another way to make $18.50.

16 Dizzy has no 50c coins. Find another way to make $18.50.

17 Dizzy ends up paying with a $20 note. Show his change.

I finished this lesson online.

I can

- Identify amounts of currency and make equivalent amounts.
- Find change from $5 and $20 using dollars and cents.
- Use an algorithm to add amounts of money in dollars and cents.

We went to

  ISBN 978-1-923253-14-8

1 Circle the larger fraction. Colour that fraction of the food.

a $\frac{1}{4}$ $\frac{3}{4}$

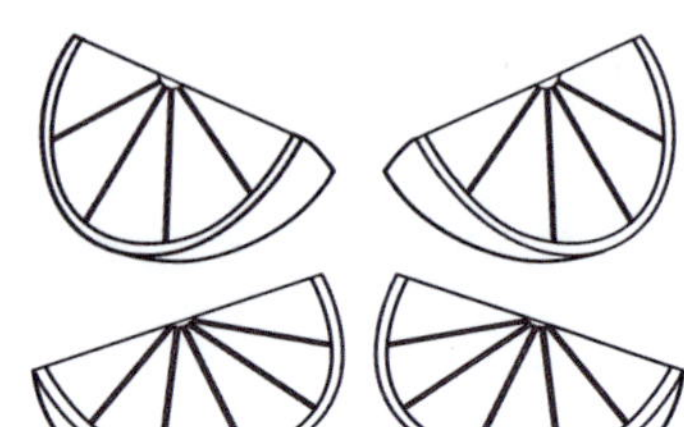

b $\frac{1}{3}$ $\frac{2}{3}$

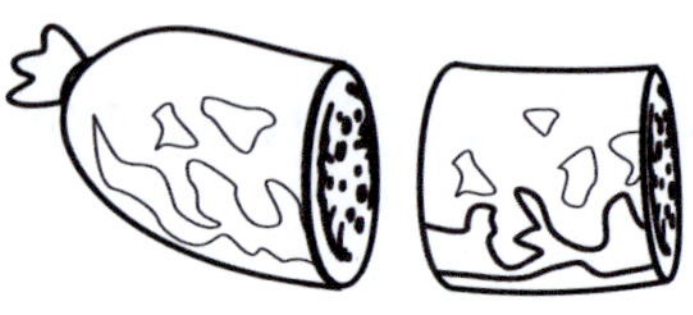

c $\frac{6}{8}$ $\frac{2}{8}$

d $\frac{5}{8}$ $\frac{3}{8}$

e $\frac{4}{6}$ $\frac{2}{6}$

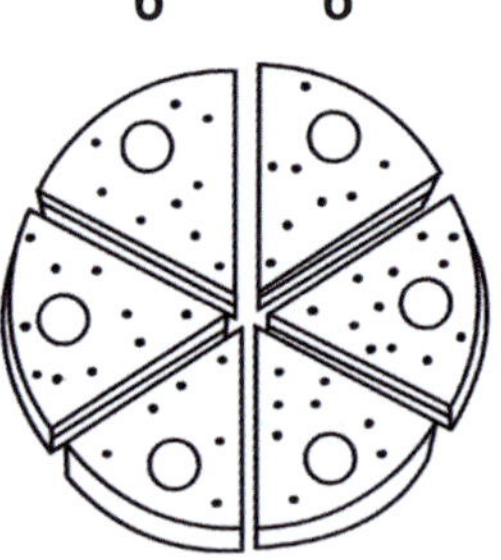

f $\frac{3}{5}$ $\frac{2}{5}$

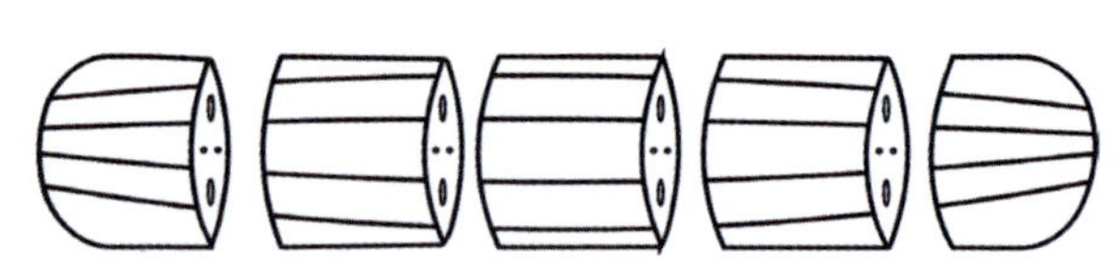

2 Use the correct symbol: $<$ or $>$.

a $\frac{1}{2}$ ☐ $\frac{1}{4}$

b $\frac{3}{4}$ ☐ $\frac{1}{4}$

c $\frac{2}{3}$ ☐ $\frac{1}{3}$

d $\frac{1}{5}$ ☐ $\frac{4}{5}$

e $\frac{5}{6}$ ☐ $\frac{1}{6}$

f $\frac{1}{8}$ ☐ $\frac{7}{8}$

g $1\frac{2}{3}$ ☐ $1\frac{1}{3}$

h $1\frac{2}{4}$ ☐ $1\frac{3}{4}$

i $1\frac{3}{5}$ ☐ $1\frac{4}{5}$

Mathseeds Year 3 Workbook ISBN 978-1-923253-14-8

3 Put these in order from **smallest** to **largest**.

a $\frac{1}{5}, \frac{2}{5}, \frac{4}{5}, \frac{3}{5}, \frac{5}{5}$ ______________________

b $\frac{6}{6}, \frac{1}{6}, \frac{3}{6}, \frac{5}{6}, \frac{4}{6}, \frac{2}{6}$ ______________________

c $1, \frac{3}{8}, \frac{1}{4}, \frac{7}{8}, \frac{1}{2}, \frac{1}{8}, \frac{5}{8}, \frac{3}{4}$ ______________________

4 Fill in the fraction number lines.

a

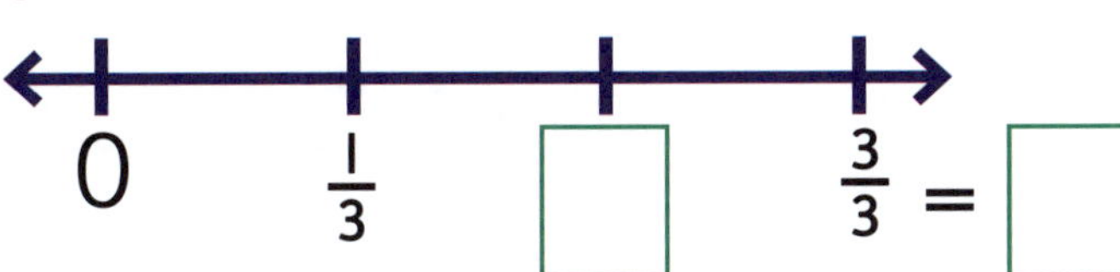

b

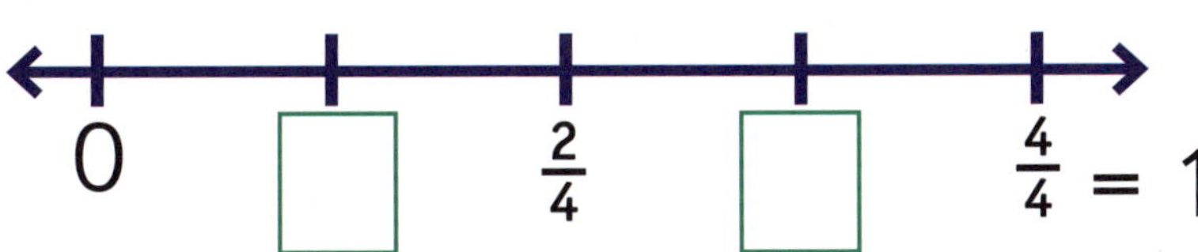

c

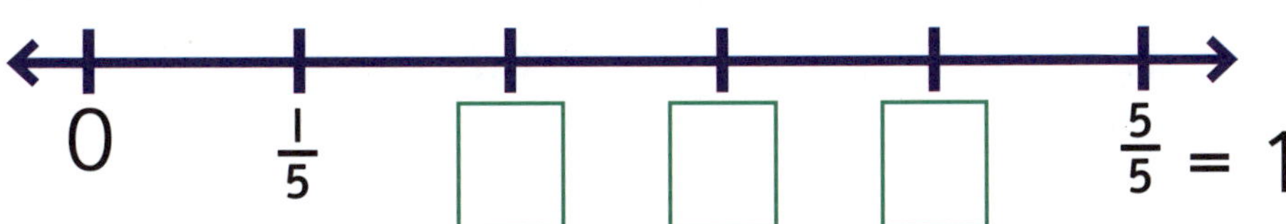

d

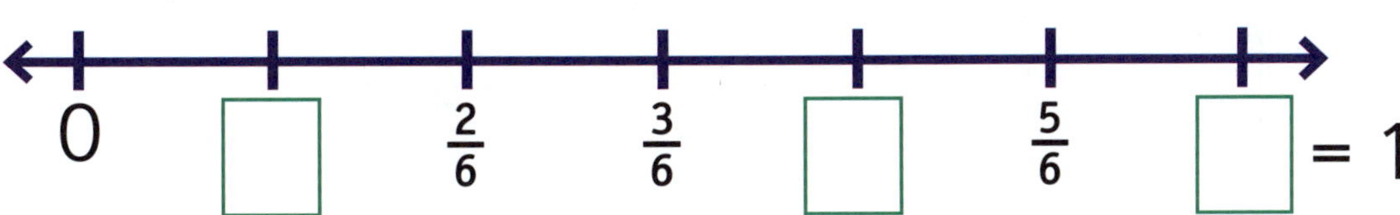

e

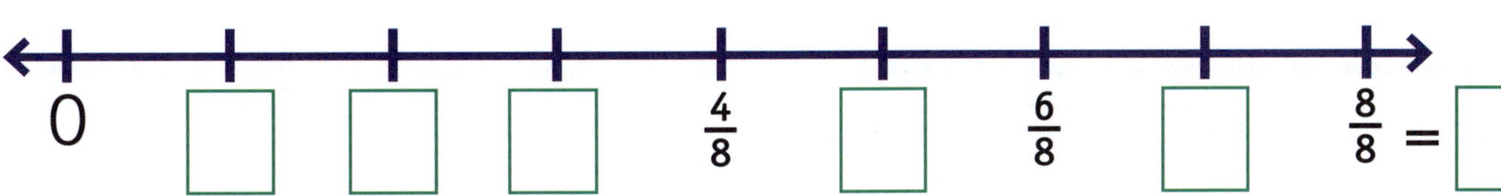

  ISBN 978-1-923253-14-8

5 Colour the fractions.

a $1\frac{3}{4}$

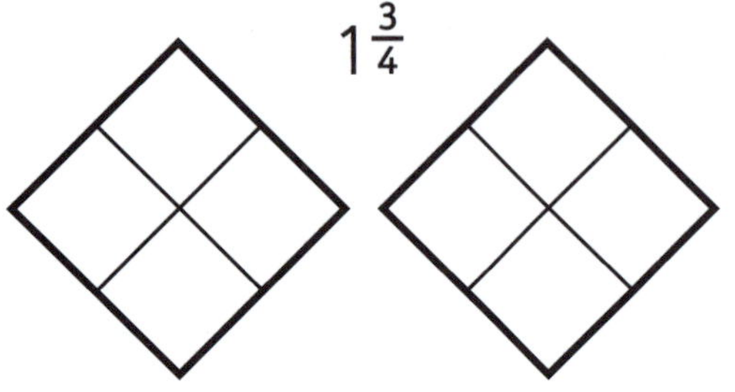

b $1\frac{3}{8}$

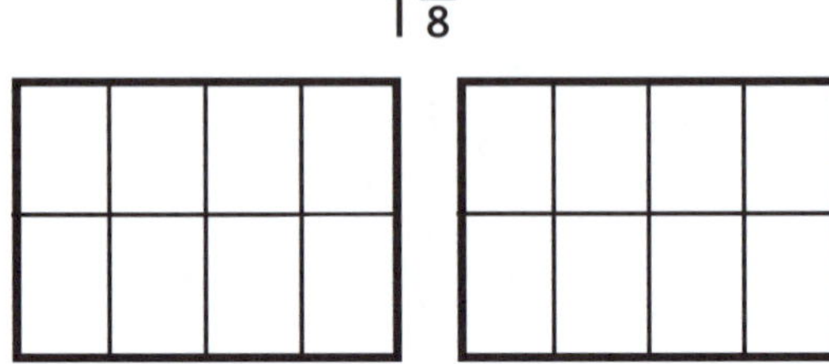

c $1\frac{5}{6}$

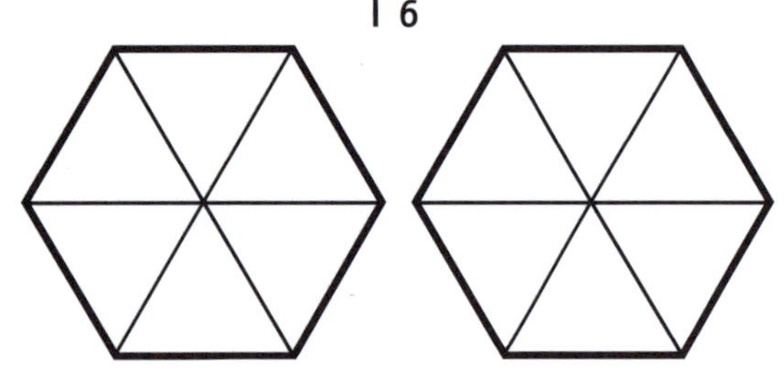

d $1\frac{3}{5}$

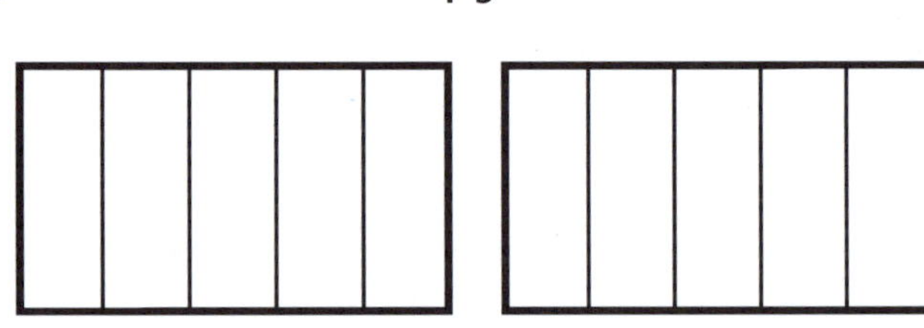

Fill in the fraction number lines.

6

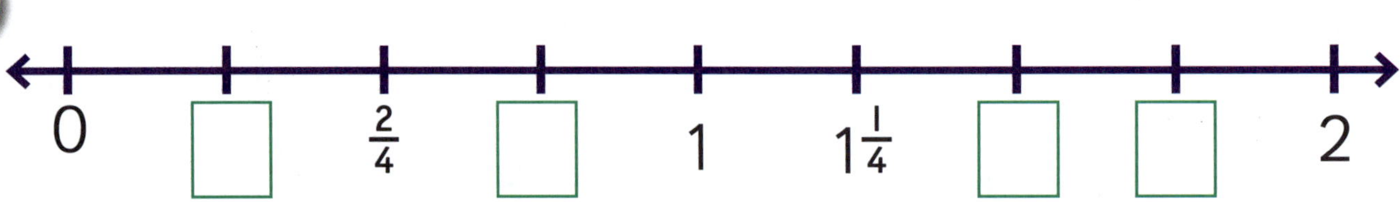

7

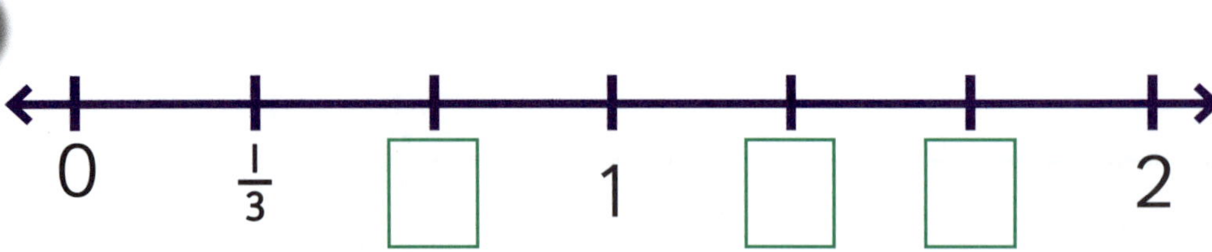

8

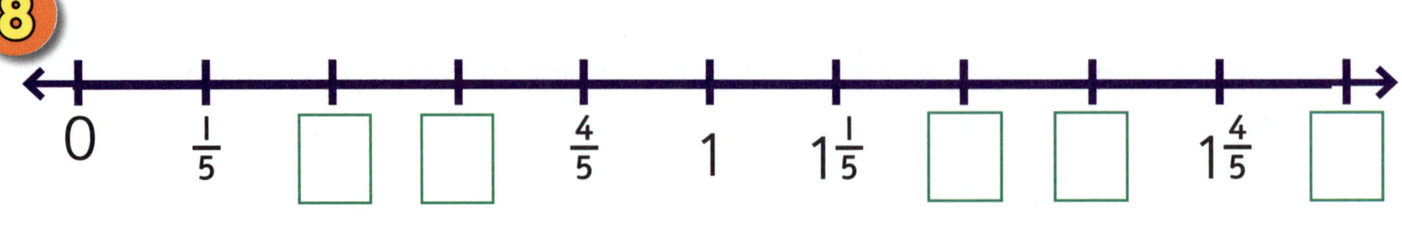

Mathseeds Year 3 Workbook © 3P Learning ISBN 978-1-923253-14-8

9 Waldo tells Doc that four sixths is more than one half. Is he correct?

a Underline the question.

b Circle the facts.

c Draw the fractions.

d Write the two fractions and choose the correct symbol.

< > =

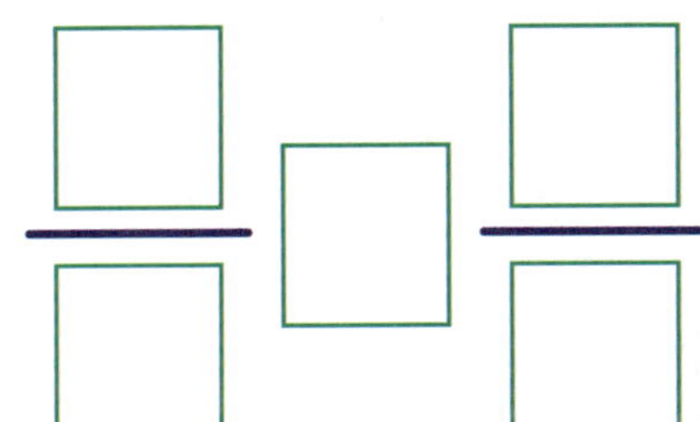

e Is Waldo correct? ____________

10 Mrs T tells Waldo that one and a half is less than one and three eighths. Is she correct?

a Underline the question.

b Circle the facts.

c Draw the fractions.

d Write the two fractions and choose the correct symbol.

< > =

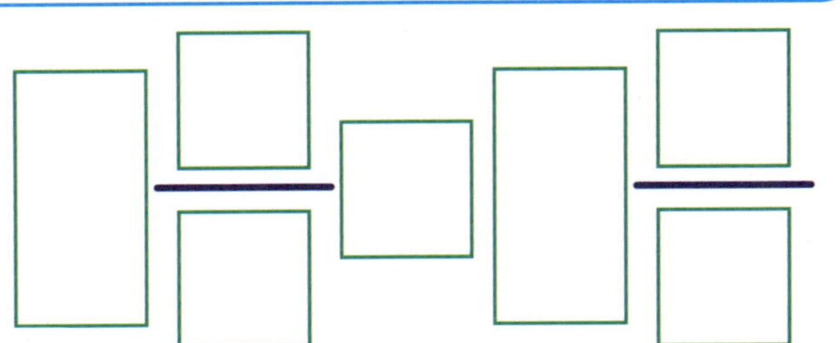

e Is Mrs T correct? ____________

I finished this lesson online.

I can

- Work with fractions and mixed numbers with the same denominators. ☐
- Work with the equivalencies between halves, quarters and eighths. ☐
- Compare the sizes of fractions with and without models. ☐
- Order fractions and fill in fraction number lines. ☐

We went to

  ISBN 978-1-923253-14-8

QUIZ

END OF MAP 32 QUIZ

1 Write the number: 1 more than | 10 more than | 100 more than

a 6789 ______ ______ ______

b 5932 ______ ______ ______

2 Complete.

a 7320 = ______ + ______ + ______ + ______

b 9843 = ______ + ______ + ______ + ______

3 Calculate the areas. Show your working. Don't forget the units.

5 m

2 m

4 m

4 m

a ______ b ______

4 Complete.

a $4 \times 4 =$ ______ b $2 \times 7 =$ ______ c $4 \times 6 =$ ______

d $2 \times 8 =$ ______ e $4 \times 5 =$ ______ f $4 \times 7 =$ ______

Mathseeds Year 3 Workbook © 3P Learning ISBN 978-1-923253-14-8

5 Write or draw 2 ways to make this amount.

$7.65

6 Mango buys a sandwich for $8.95 and a drink for $3.50. She pays with a $20 note.

a How much does this cost in total?

$ ______
\+ $ ______
$ ______

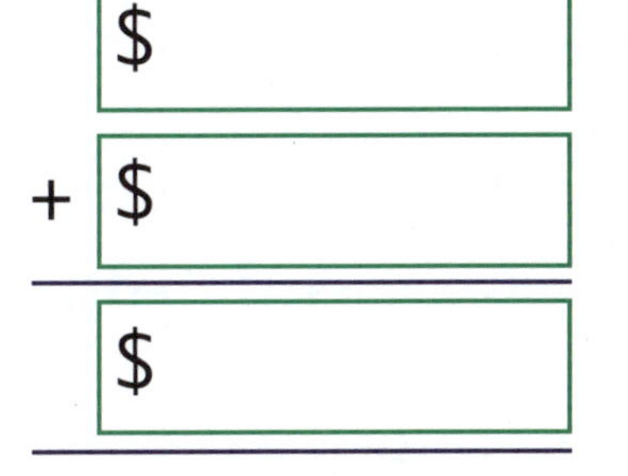

b How much change does she get? ______

7 Put these in order from smallest to largest.

$\frac{2}{3}$, 1, $1\frac{1}{3}$, 2, $1\frac{2}{3}$, $\frac{1}{3}$ ______

8 Use the correct symbol: < or >.

a $\frac{1}{2}$ ☐ $\frac{3}{4}$ **b** $\frac{2}{5}$ ☐ $\frac{1}{5}$ **c** $1\frac{5}{8}$ ☐ $1\frac{7}{8}$

  ISBN 978-1-923253-14-8

Well Done!

YOU COMPLETED

MAP 32

YOU CAN:

- ☐ **Add 1, 10, 100** to a 4-digit number and write numbers in **expanded form**.
- ☐ Multiply **length × width** to find **area** and answer **multiplication equations**.
- ☐ Identify 2 ways to make an **equivalent** amount of **money**.
- ☐ Use an **algorithm** to add money and then calculate **change** from $20.
- ☐ Order and compare **fractions**.

Signed:

Dated:

Mathseeds Year 3 Workbook © 3P Learning ISBN 978-1-923253-14-8

FUN SPOT 2

WHO AM I?

1. I am an odd number but three of my four digits are even.
My tens digit is larger than my ones digit. I have a zero.
My thousands digit is double my tens digit, and four times my ones digit.

Who am I? ____________

2. I have only 1 odd digit. My other 3 digits are the same.
My thousands digit is 1 larger than my hundreds digit.
My tens digit is the same as my hundreds digit.
My ones digit is the smallest it can be.

Who am I? ____________

3. All four of my digits are even. None of my digits are the same.
My ones digit is twice my thousands digit. I have no zeroes.
My hundreds digit is two more than my tens digit.

Who am I? ____________

LESSON 161 PARTITIONING NUMBERS

1 What is the value of the bold digit in each number?

a 829**4** ________ **b** 72**5**1 ________ **c** 6**3**05 ________

d **5**021 ________ **e** 49**7**2 ________ **f** **3**564 ________

g 214**8** ________ **h** 1**7**16 ________ **i** 948**0** ________

2 Colour the place values which make up each number.

a 9472

9000	900	90	9
7000	700	70	7
4000	400	40	4
2000	200	20	2

b 3329

9000	900	90	9
3000	300	30	3
2000	200	20	2
1000	100	10	1

c 8415

8000	800	80	8
5000	500	50	5
4000	400	40	4
1000	100	10	1

d 9737

9000	900	90	9
7000	700	70	7
3000	300	30	3
1000	100	10	1

e 1603

6000	600	60	6
5000	500	50	5
3000	300	30	3
1000	100	10	1

f 2880

8000	800	80	8
3000	300	30	3
2000	200	20	2
1000	100	10	1

3 Fill in the expanded notation.

1188 = 1000 + 100 + 80 + 8

a 5640 = ____________________

b 2806 = ____________________

c 7033 = ____________________

4 Fill in the expanded notation. Then add one.

a 3441 = ______ + ______ + ______ + ______ + 1 = ______

b 8965 = ______ + ______ + ______ + ______ + 1 = ______

c 6399 = ______ + ______ + ______ + ______ + 1 = ______

5 Fill in the expanded notation. Then add ten.

a 4727 = ______ + ______ + ______ + ______ + 10 = ______

b 9254 = ______ + ______ + ______ + ______ + 10 = ______

c 2572 = ______ + ______ + ______ + ______ + 10 = ______

6 Fill in the expanded notation. Then add a hundred.

a 1802 = ______ + ______ + ______ + ______ + 100 = ______

b 5448 = ______ + ______ + ______ + ______ + 100 = ______

c 9120 = ______ + ______ + ______ + ______ + 100 = ______

7 Fill in the expanded notation. Then add a thousand.

a 8353 = ______ + ______ + ______ + ______ + 1000 = ______

b 3695 = ______ + ______ + ______ + ______ + 1000 = ______

c 7066 = ______ + ______ + ______ + ______ + 1000 = ______

LESSON 161 PARTITIONING NUMBERS

Town	Population
Wee Waa	1653
Roma	6906
Tanunda	4153
Esperance	9919

8 Which town has the largest population? ____________

9 Which town has the smallest population? ____________

10 Write the town names in order from largest population to smallest.

____

11 If one thousand people move into the town of Wee Waa, what will the population be?

____

12 If one hundred people move to the town of Roma, what will the population be?

____

13 If ten people move into Tanunda, what will the population be?

____

14 If one person moves to Esperance, what will the population be?

____

15 Circle the town with the larger population.

a Wee Waa (pop. 1653) or Harden (pop. 1877)

b Roma (pop. 6906) or Nambucca Heads (pop. 6222)

c Tanunda (pop. 4153) or Kadina (pop. 4470)

d Esperance (pop. 9919) or Longford (pop. 930)

Mathseeds Year 3 Workbook © 3P Learning ISBN 978-1-923253-14-8

Partitioning Numbers

16 Ruby has four number cards: 0, 3, 6 and 8.
How many 4-digit numbers can she make?

8 6 3 0

a Underline the question. b Circle the facts.

c Make a list of all the **4-digit** numbers that can be made.

____

____

____

____

d There are ________ 4-digit numbers.

e Which number card **cannot** go in the thousands place? ______

f Why? ______________________________

17 Mango has some questions about these numbers.

a What is the largest number? ________ b Smallest? ________

c Write all the numbers **starting with 3** in order on the number line.

d Write all the numbers with **0 on the end** in order on the number line.

I finished this lesson online.

161

I can
- Recognise digit place values in 4-digit numbers. ☐
- Write 4-digit numbers in expanded form then add 1, 10, 100, 1000. ☐
- Order and compare 4-digit numbers. ☐
- Make all 4-digit numbers given 4 digits and explain placement of 0. ☐

We went to

LESSON 162 TIME TO THE MINUTE

1 Write the time in words.

a

b
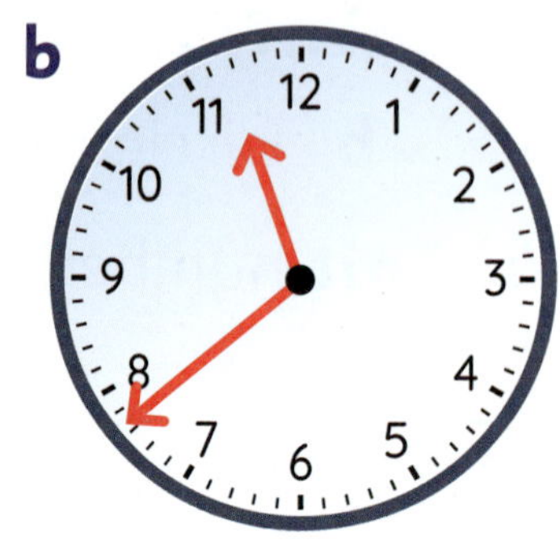

c
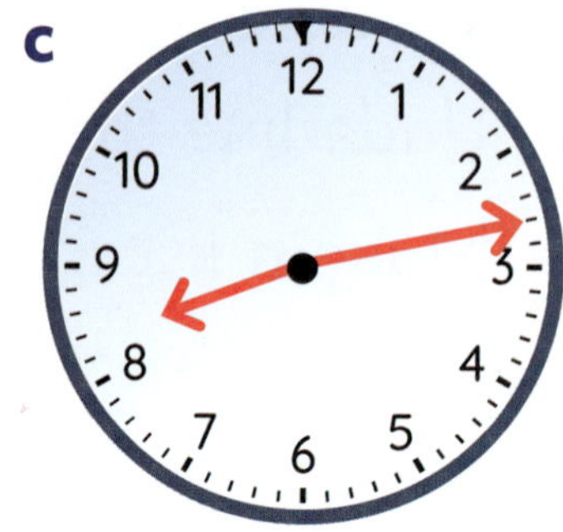

d

e

f

2 Match the times.

a

b

c 4:44

d 12:31

e 6:28

f 2:19

- thirty-one past twelve
- two past ten
- nineteen past two
- fifty-six past one
- forty-four past four
- twenty-eight past six

Mathseeds Year 3 Workbook © 3P Learning ISBN 978-1-923253-14-8

Time to the Minute

3 Draw the hands on the clocks to match the times.

a

7:08

b

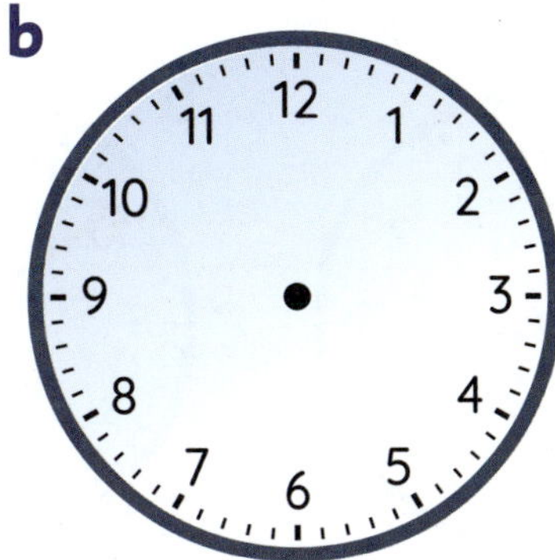

10:11

c

5:53

d

3:34

e

1:22

f

12:47

g

9:06

h

4:39

i

8:24

  ISBN 978-1-923253-14-8

4 How much time has passed?

a

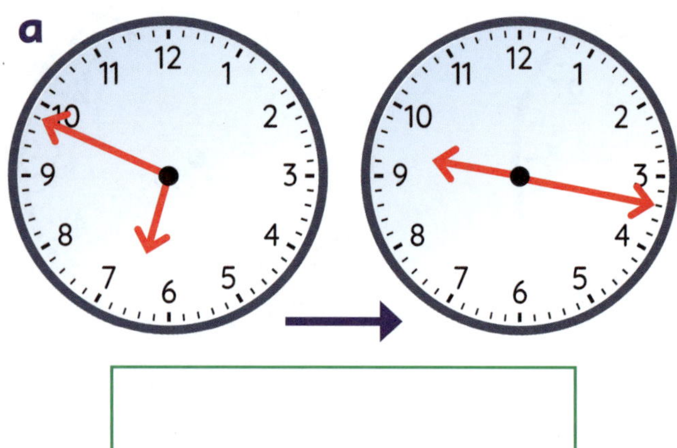

b

c

d

5 How much time has passed?

a

2:43 → 4:09

c

7:32 → 8:21

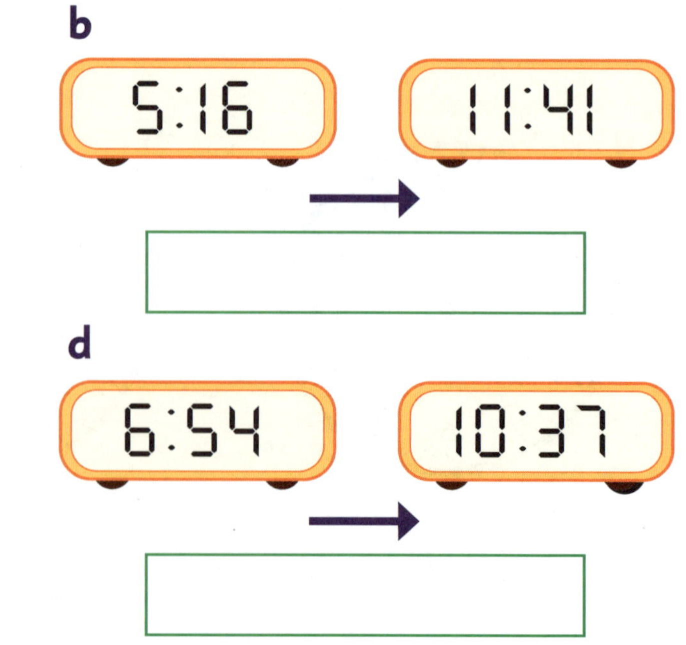

Mathseeds Year 3 Workbook © 3P Learning ISBN 978-1-923253-14-8

Time to the Minute

Ruby had a list of jobs to get through. She started at 9:00. As she finished each job she looked at her watch and noted the time.

6 Work out how long each job took.

a

b

c

d
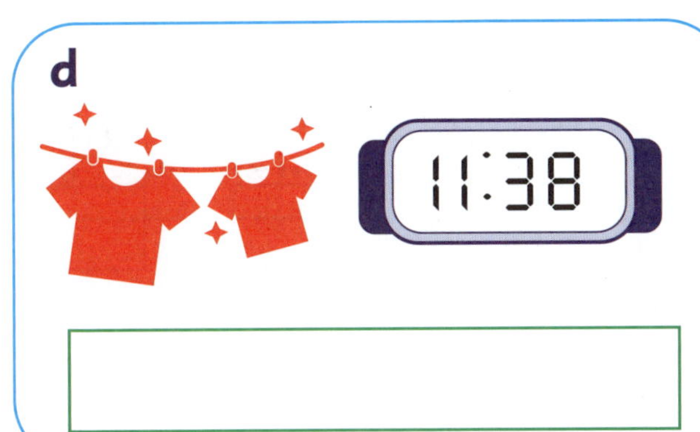

e

7 How long did Ruby spend doing jobs altogether?

I finished this lesson online.

I can

- Read and show time to the nearest minute on analog clocks. ☐
- Read and write time in words and in digital format. ☐
- Calculate the amount of time passed between two times. ☐

We went to

LESSON 163 EQUIVALENT NUMBER SENTENCES

1 Fill in the second number sentence.

a 23 + 45 = 68
45 + 23 = ☐

b 72 + 13 = 85
13 + ☐ = ☐

c 69 + 25 = 94
☐ + ☐ = ☐

d 35 – 17 = 18
35 – 18 = ☐

e 59 – 36 = 23
59 – ☐ = ☐

f 91 – 43 = 48
☐ – ☐ = ☐

2 Find the answer. Complete the related number sentence.

a 55 + 29 = ☐
☐ – 29 = ☐

b 82 – 41 = ☐
☐ + 41 = ☐

c 31 + 58 = ☐
☐ – 58 = ☐

d 75 – 38 = ☐
☐ + 38 = ☐

e 64 + 15 = ☐
☐ – 15 = ☐

f 97 – 53 = ☐
☐ + 53 = ☐

3 Complete the number fact families.

a 32 + 46 = ☐
☐ + ☐ = ☐
☐ – ☐ = ☐
☐ – ☐ = ☐

b 11 + 62 = ☐
☐ + ☐ = ☐
☐ – ☐ = ☐
☐ – ☐ = ☐

c 75 + 23 = ☐
☐ + ☐ = ☐
☐ – ☐ = ☐
☐ – ☐ = ☐

d 54 + 34 = ☐
☐ + ☐ = ☐
☐ – ☐ = ☐
☐ – ☐ = ☐

Mathseeds Year 3 Workbook © 3P Learning ISBN 978-1-923253-14-8

4 Are these equivalent number sentences? ✓ for yes. ✗ for no.

a $8 + 7 = 20 - 5$ ☐

b $19 - 8 = 6 + 6$ 

c $13 + 5 = 18 + 1$ ☐

d $22 - 8 = 30 - 16$ ☐

e $32 + 25 = 60 - 3$ ☐

f $87 - 43 = 22 + 23$ 

5 Make these number sentences equivalent.

a $13 + 22 = 40 - \square$

b $29 - 13 = 15 + \square$

c $49 + \square = 60 + 19$

d $84 - \square = 79 - 15$

e $56 + 15 = \square - 22$

f $96 - 24 = \square + 42$

6 Write an equivalent number sentence.

a $9 + 23 =$ ____________

b $49 - 17 =$ ____________

c $14 + 52 =$ ____________

d $95 - 33 =$ ____________

e $29 + 26 =$ ____________

f $78 - 39 =$ ____________

g $64 + 17 =$ ____________

h $81 - 45 =$ ____________

7 Make these number sentences equivalent.

a $41 + \square = 71 - \square$

b $29 - \square = 11 + \square$

c $23 + \square = 32 + \square$

d $88 - \square = 95 - \square$

e $\square + 16 = \square - 20$

f $\square - 31 = \square + 10$

  ISBN 978-1-923253-14-8

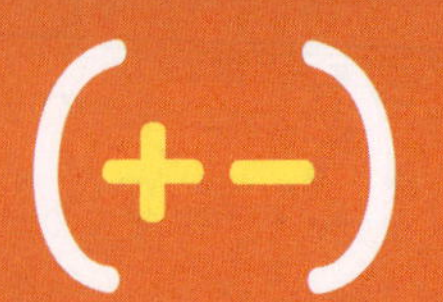

8 Complete the equivalent equations to find the answers.

a Gina and Maria picked the same number of pieces of fruit. Gina picked five apples and seven oranges. Maria picked two apples and some oranges.

How many oranges did Maria pick? ______

5 + 7 = 2 + ☐

b Max and Bella each get 30 minutes of screen time a day. Today Max had 14 minutes in the morning and Bella had 21. How much time does each child have in the afternoon?

14 + ☐ = 21 + ☐ Max ______ Bella ______

c Lim had 40 chocolates. Yee had 32. They each ate some of their chocolates. Then they both had 25 left. How many chocolates did they each eat?

40 – ☐ = 32 – ☐ Lim ______ Yee ______

9 Find the equivalent number sentences.

a Roshi had nine cards and Adit had three. They were supposed to both have five cards. Write equivalent number sentences to show how they end up with five cards each.

______________________ = ______________________

b Abdul and Issy have two jobs each, taking the same amount of time. Abdul vacuums for 17 minutes and dusts for 8 minutes. Issy mops for 13 minutes and cleans the sinks. How long does Issy take to clean the sinks? ______ minutes

______________________ = ______________________

Mathseeds Year 3 Workbook © 3P Learning ISBN 978-1-923253-14-8

10 Ruby writes this number sentence: **7 + 9 =**
She asks Doc to write an equivalent number sentence.
Doc says, "There are too many to choose from!"
How many equivalent number sentences are there?

a Underline the question. **b** Circle the facts.

c Write as many equivalent addition number sentences as you can.

7 + 9 = _____

d Compare your list with a partner's. Write in any sums you don't have.

e Have you found every addition number sentence that is equivalent to 7 + 9? ________

11 Write as many equivalent subtraction number sentences as you can.

7 + 9 = _____

I finished this lesson online.

I can

- Complete number fact families. ☐
- Calculate equivalent addition and subtraction equations. ☐
- Use equivalent equations to solve word problems. ☐
- Compare options in equivalent addition and subtraction equations. ☐

We went to

  ISBN 978-1-923253-14-8

Maps

1. Label the points on the compass: North, South, East, West.

2. Use this map of the world and the compass to answer these questions.

   a Which continent is south of Europe? ____________

   b Which continent is west of Europe? ____________

   c Which continent is north of Australia? ____________

   d Which continent is west of Australia? ____________

   e Which continent is east of Australia? ____________

   f Which continent is south of North America? ____________

   g Which continent is east of North America? ____________

   h Which continent is west of North America? ____________

   i Which ocean is east of the Americas and west of Africa?

   ____

   j Which ocean is south of Asia and east of Africa? ____________

   k Which ocean is east of Asia and west of the Americas?

   ____

Mathseeds Year 3 Workbook © 3P Learning ISBN 978-1-923253-14-8

Zoo

6						
5						
4						
3						
2						
1						
	A	B	C	D	E	F

3 Write the coordinates for these items.

a monkey _____ _____ **b** owl _____ _____

c fox _____ _____ **d** bear _____ _____

e lion _____ _____ **f** koala _____ _____

4 What is at these coordinates?

a A4 _______________ **b** B6 _______________

c C3 _______________ **d** D6 _______________

e B1 _______________ **f** F4 _______________

5 Where are the restrooms located? _____ _____ & _____ _____

6 Where can you go for first aid? _____ _____ & _____ _____

7 Where can you go to eat? _____ _____ & _____ _____

8 Where are the hippos? _____ _____ & _____ _____

9 What are the empty squares for?

(a) more animals (b) a path (c) it's a mistake

  ISBN 978-1-923253-14-8

10 Draw Sara's usual walking route on the map.
Start at home in A4 and go east to the corner shop.
Turn right and head south to the stadium.
Turn left and head east to the lighthouse.
Turn right and walk to the hotel, then turn right and go to the bridge.
Head north to the factory and then walk west to the airport.

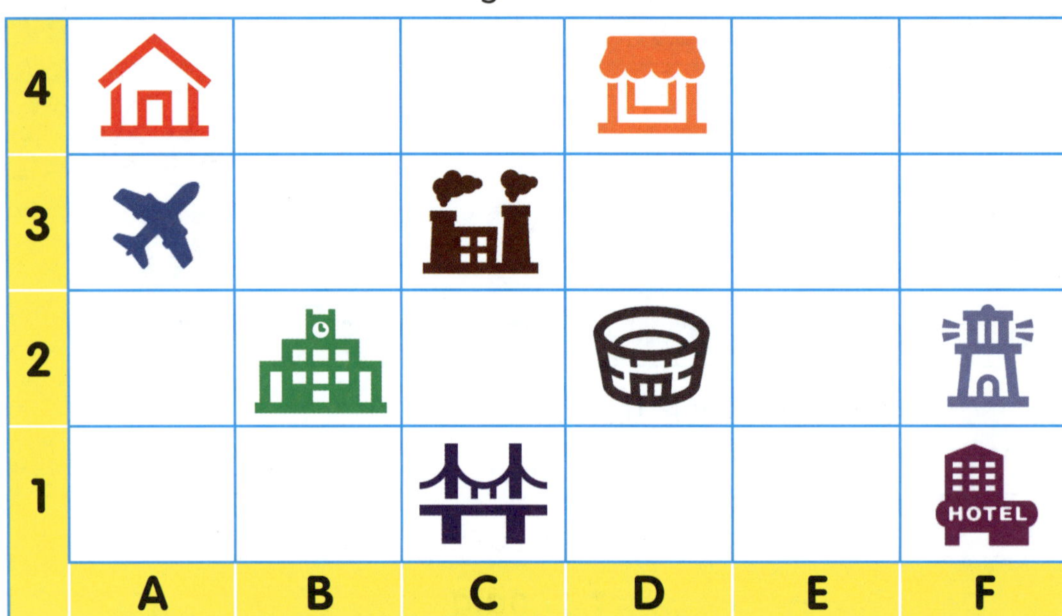

11 Write the coordinates for Sara's walking route.

_____ _____ → _____ _____ → _____ _____ → _____ _____ →
_____ _____ → _____ _____ → _____ _____ → _____ _____

12 Use the map to answer these questions.

a Which compass direction does Sara walk in to get home from the airport? __________

b How many squares on the map does Sara walk through? __________

c If each square is 100 m, how far does Sara walk? __________

d What are the coordinates for the school? _____ _____

e Draw a park in the square at A1.

Mathseeds Year 3 Workbook ISBN 978-1-923253-14-8

13 You have a Puppy-Bot 3000. You can program it to move using coordinates. Program Puppy-Bot to get to the gate on this map. Can you find two different paths?

5					Gate
4			Pool	Pool	
3					
2		Sand pit			
1			Puppy-Bot		
	A	**B**	**C**	**D**	**E**

Key: = Puppy-Bot = Gate

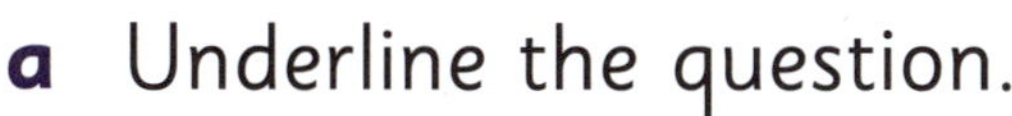

a Underline the question.

b Circle the facts.

c Where is the gate?

_____ _____

d Where is Puppy-Bot?

_____ _____

e Act it out by tracing two paths.

14 Now fill in the table with the coordinates. *One path has been done for you.*

Path 1	C1, C2, C3, B3, B4, B5, C5, D5, E5
Path 2	C1,
Path 3	C1,

I finished this lesson online. 164

I can

- Label the directions on a compass and use it to answer questions. ☐
- Use grid coordinates to identify places and features on a map. ☐
- Use grid coordinates and compass directions to map a route. ☐
- Calculate distance on a map. ☐

We went to

LESSON 165 DIVISION

1 Share the shapes into groups and answer the equation.

a

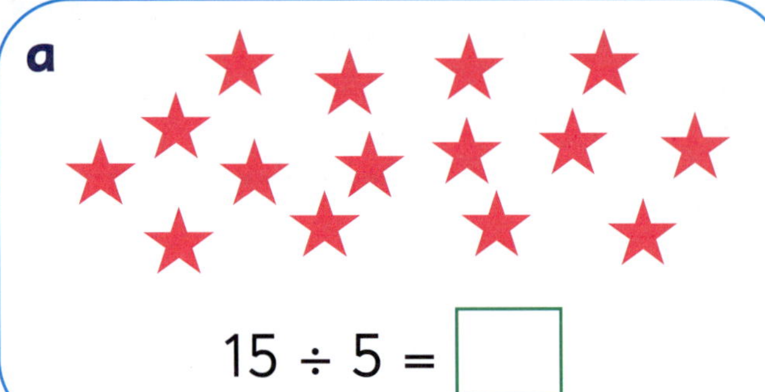

$15 \div 5 =$ ☐

b

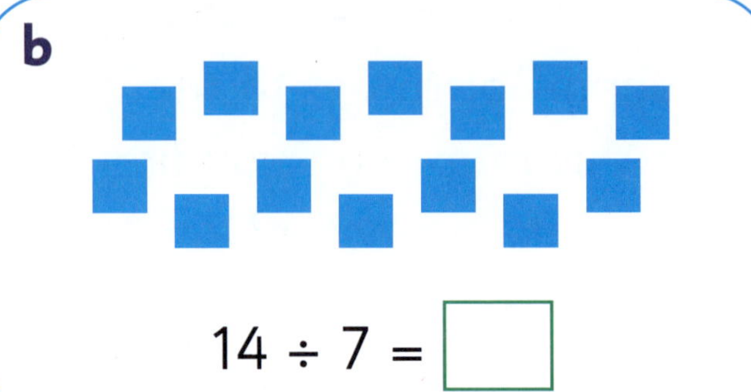

$14 \div 7 =$ ☐

c

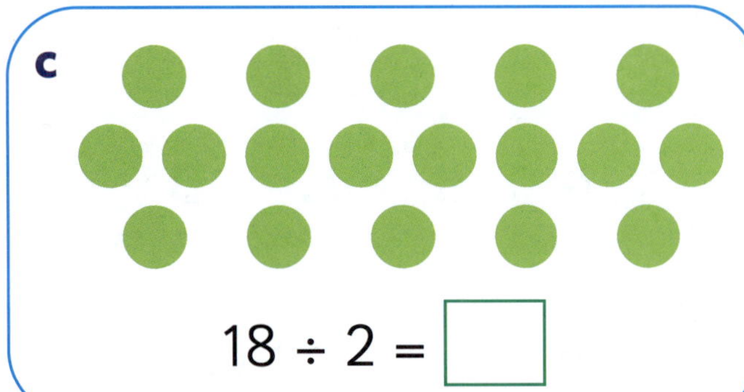

$18 \div 2 =$ ☐

d

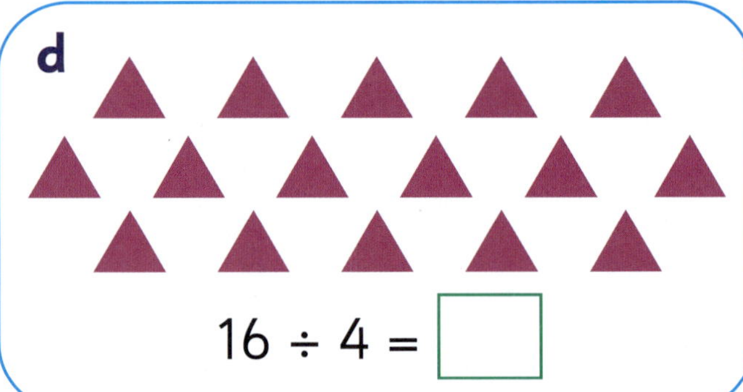

$16 \div 4 =$ ☐

2 Share the shapes into groups and find the missing number.

a

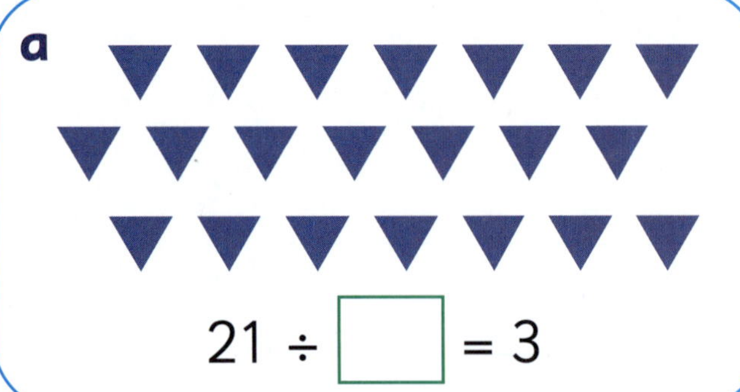

$21 \div$ ☐ $= 3$

b

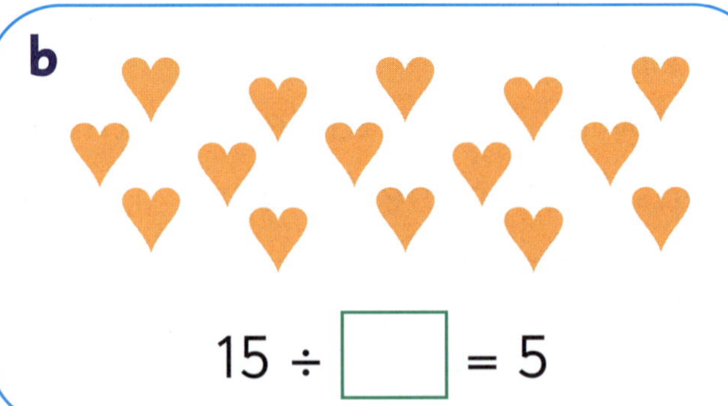

$15 \div$ ☐ $= 5$

c

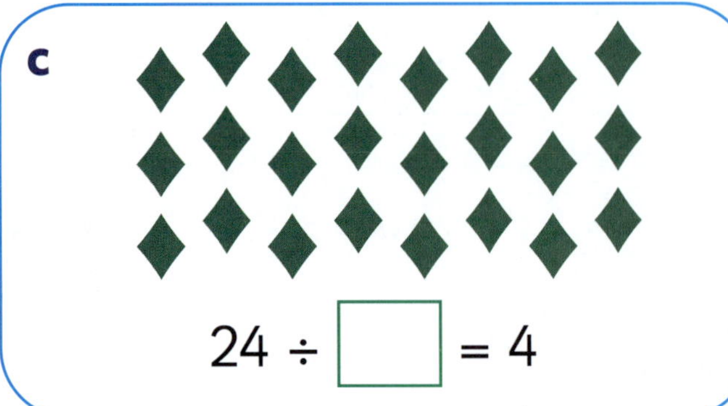

$24 \div$ ☐ $= 4$

d

$12 \div$ ☐ $= 2$

  ISBN 978-1-923253-14-8

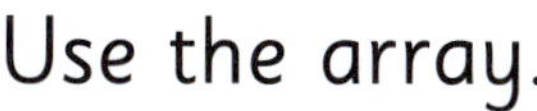
Use the array.

③ Answer the sum.

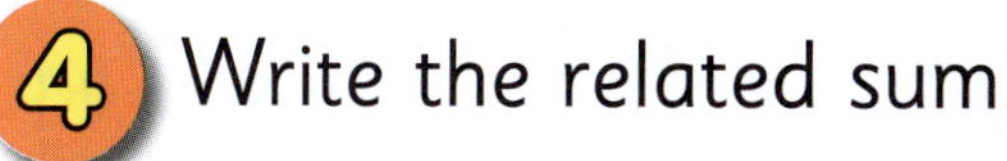
④ Write the related sum.

	Use the array.	③ Answer the sum.	④ Write the related sum.
a		18 ÷ 3 = ☐	☐ ÷ ☐ = ☐
b		12 ÷ 3 = ☐	☐ ÷ ☐ = ☐
c		16 ÷ 2 = ☐	☐ ÷ ☐ = ☐
d		20 ÷ 2 = ☐	☐ ÷ ☐ = ☐
e		24 ÷ 3 = ☐	☐ ÷ ☐ = ☐
f		28 ÷ 4 = ☐	☐ ÷ ☐ = ☐

  ISBN 978-1-923253-14-8

5 Answer the division equations.

a $18 \div 9 =$ ☐
b $14 \div 2 =$ ☐
c $24 \div 4 =$ ☐
d $12 \div 2 =$ ☐
e $15 \div 5 =$ ☐
f $30 \div 10 =$ ☐
g $32 \div 8 =$ ☐
h $21 \div 3 =$ ☐

6 Are these equations correct? ✓ for yes. ✗ for no.

a $12 \div 3 = 4$ ☐
b $16 \div 8 = 3$ ☐
c $24 \div 4 = 4$ ☐
d $18 \div 6 = 3$ ☐
e $28 \div 4 = 9$ ☐
f $25 \div 5 = 5$ ☐
g $36 \div 6 = 6$ ☐
h $42 \div 7 = 7$ ☐

7 Complete the equation and write the related division sum.

a $20 \div 4 =$ ☐ ____________________
b $36 \div 9 =$ ☐ ____________________
c $63 \div 7 =$ ☐ ____________________
d $48 \div 6 =$ ☐ ____________________
e $27 \div$ ☐ $= 3$ ____________________
f $54 \div$ ☐ $= 9$ ____________________
g $40 \div$ ☐ $= 4$ ____________________
h $72 \div$ ☐ $= 8$ ____________________

Mathseeds Year 3 Workbook © 3P Learning ISBN 978-1-923253-14-8

8 Mrs T knitted 30 socks each for Mango, Doc and Dizzy. She told them to put their socks neatly in rows. How could each of them arrange their 30 socks differently?

a Underline the question. **b** Circle the facts.

9 Show each of their sock drawers as an array.

a Mango

b Doc

c Dizzy

10 Write a division equation for each of them.

a Mango 30 ÷ ________ = ________

b Doc 30 ÷ ________ = ________

c Dizzy 30 ÷ ________ = ________

I finished this lesson online.

I can

- Answer division equations, with and without groups of shapes. ☐
- Find missing divisors, with and without groups of shapes. ☐
- Write related division equations, with and without arrays. ☐
- Find multiple arrays and equations for division into 30. ☐

We went to

  ISBN 978-1-923253-14-8

QUIZ

END OF MAP 33 QUIZ

1

a 9213 = 9000 + ________ + ________ + ________

b 4508 = ________ + ________ + ________ + ________

2

a Make the biggest **odd** number possible.

0 6 7 3 ________

b Make the smallest **even** number possible

0 6 7 3 ________

3 Write or draw the matching times.

a twenty-four past three

b ________

c ________

4 Make these number sentences equivalent.

a 78 – 35 = ________

b 51 + 26 = ________

c 13 + ______ = 68 + ______

d 94 – ______ = 42 + ______

5 Complete the number fact family.

629 + 131 = ______

______ + ______ = ______

______ – ______ = ______

______ – ______ = ______

Mathseeds Year 3 Workbook © 3P Learning ISBN 978-1-923253-14-8

4						
3						
2						
1						
	A	B	C	D	E	F

6 Deb is shopping for a party. First she went to the donut shop, then she picked up some bubble tea. Next she got some pizzas and popcorn. And finally the birthday cake! Write the coordinates for each shop in the order she visited them.

A4 → ____ ____ → ____ ____ → ____ ____ → ____ ____ → ____ ____

7

a 16 ÷ 2 = ______ **b** 18 ÷ 3 = ______ **c** 32 ÷ 4 = ______

d 45 ÷ 5 = ______ **e** 24 ÷ 8 = ______ **f** 70 ÷ 10 = ______

Nice Work!

YOU COMPLETED

MAP 33

YOU CAN:

- [ ] Write 4-digit numbers in **expanded form**.
- [ ] Make the largest odd and smallest even numbers **given 4 digits**.
- [ ] Make matching **times to the minute** on analog and digital clocks and in words.
- [ ] Complete **equivalent equations** and **number fact families**.
- [ ] Use **grid coordinates** to map a route.
- [ ] Answer **division equations**.

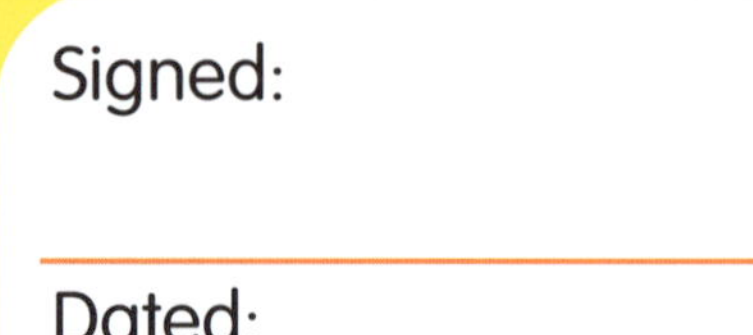

Signed:

Dated:

Mathseeds Year 3 Workbook © 3P Learning ISBN 978-1-923253-14-8

FUN SPOT 3

READ THE CODE

1. Match each answer to a letter.

10	40	30	4	9	6	5	2	14
A	**C**	**E**	**F**	**I**	**K**	**S**	**T**	**X**

1 × 5 = _____		18 ÷ 2 = _____		7 × 2 = _____	
40 ÷ 10 = _____		2 × 5 = _____		20 ÷ 10 = _____	
4 × 10 = _____		100 ÷ 10 = _____		1 × 2 = _____	
25 ÷ 5 = _____		3 × 10 = _____		50 ÷ 5 = _____	
10 ÷ 5 = _____		1 × 10 = _____		8 × 5 = _____	
5 × 2 = _____		12 ÷ 2 = _____		6 × 5 = _____	

2. What is the message?

____

____

  ISBN 978-1-923253-14-8

Odd & Even Numbers 2

LESSON 166 ODD AND EVEN NUMBERS · PART 2

1 Tick ✓ the even numbers. Cross ✗ the odd numbers.

a 43 ☐	**b** 87 ☐	**c** 93 ☐	**d** 22 ☐
e 38 ☐	**f** 92 ☐	**g** 547 ☐	**h** 342 ☐
i 900 ☐	**j** 901 ☐	**k** 653 ☐	**l** 294 ☐

2 Fill in the ones digits to make even numbers.

a 8☐	**b** 9☐	**c** 48☐	**d** 73☐
e 835☐	**f** 213☐		

3 Fill in the ones digits to make odd numbers.

a 3☐	**b** 5☐	**c** 76☐	**d** 81☐
e 912☐	**f** 201☐		

4 Colour the odd numbers red and the even numbers blue.

241

  ISBN 978-1-923253-14-8

5 Find the answer. Is it odd or even? Circle.

a $2 + 8 =$ _____ odd even
b $14 + 4 =$ _____ odd even
c $26 + 12 =$ _____ odd even
d $38 + 18 =$ _____ odd even
e $40 + 14 =$ _____ odd even
f $54 + 26 =$ _____ odd even

6 Find the answer. Is it odd or even? Circle.

a $3 + 5 =$ _____ odd even
b $11 + 7 =$ _____ odd even
c $29 + 13 =$ _____ odd even
d $35 + 17 =$ _____ odd even
e $49 + 19 =$ _____ odd even
f $51 + 27 =$ _____ odd even

7 Find the answer. Is it odd or even? Circle.

a $8 + 5 =$ _____ odd even
b $16 + 7 =$ _____ odd even
c $22 + 13 =$ _____ odd even
d $30 + 17 =$ _____ odd even
e $44 + 19 =$ _____ odd even
f $58 + 27 =$ _____ odd even

8 Find the answer. Is it odd or even? Circle.

a $3 + 2 =$ _____ odd even
b $11 + 4 =$ _____ odd even
c $29 + 18 =$ _____ odd even
d $35 + 16 =$ _____ odd even
e $49 + 20 =$ _____ odd even
f $51 + 22 =$ _____ odd even

9 Finish the rules. Write the word **odd** or **even**.

a even + even = __________
b odd + odd = __________
c even + odd = __________
d odd + even = __________

  ISBN 978-1-923253-14-8

10 Is the answer odd or even? Circle.

a 72 + 15 = ______ odd even

b 24 + 38 = ______ odd even

c 31 + 55 = ______ odd even

d 91 + 6 = ______ odd even

e 53 + 40 = ______ odd even

f 86 + 13 = ______ odd even

11 Will the answer be odd or even? Circle, then find the answer.

a odd even

$$\begin{array}{r} 266 \\ +\ 142 \\ \hline \end{array}$$

b odd even

$$\begin{array}{r} 175 \\ +\ 317 \\ \hline \end{array}$$

c odd even

$$\begin{array}{r} 427 \\ +\ 284 \\ \hline \end{array}$$

d odd even

$$\begin{array}{r} 342 \\ +\ 928 \\ \hline \end{array}$$

e odd even

$$\begin{array}{r} 985 \\ +\ 256 \\ \hline \end{array}$$

f odd even

$$\begin{array}{r} 674 \\ +\ 245 \\ \hline \end{array}$$

12 Is the answer odd or even? Complete the sums.

a 423 + 987 = ________ odd + odd = ________

b 829 + 392 = ________ odd + even = ________

c 7394 + 3650 = ________ even + even = ________

d 98 321 + 83 650 = ________ odd + even = ________

e 38 390 + 32 894 = ________ even + even = ________

Mathseeds Year 3 Workbook © 3P Learning ISBN 978-1-923253-14-8

Odd & Even Numbers 2

13 Mrs T has four number cards: 3, 5, 6 and 9.
How many odd 4-digit numbers can she make?

3 5 9 6

a Underline the question. **b** Circle the facts.

c Make a list of all the 4-digit numbers that can be made.

____

____

____

____

____

____

d Circle the odd numbers.

e There are __________ odd 4-digit numbers.

14 Ruby wants to know if the number of even numbers is the same.

a There are __________ even 4-digit numbers in the list.

b Is this number the same as for odd numbers? **Yes** **No**

c Why do you think this is so?

____

____

____

I finished this lesson online. 166

I can

- Identify and make odd and even numbers. ☐
- Find rules in odd and even number patterns with addition and use them to predict if answers to additions will be odd or even. ☐
- Explore odd and even numbers given 4 digits – 3 odd and 1 even. ☐

We went to

1 Tick the box to show the chance of this happening.

a Landing on heads or tails when you flip a coin.

☐ impossible ☐ equal chance ☐ certain

b Landing on heads when you flip a coin.

☐ impossible ☐ equal chance ☐ certain

c The coin spinning forever when you flip it.

☐ impossible ☐ equal chance ☐ certain

2 Colour the items to match the chance.

a You are certain to select a yellow marble.

b It is impossible to pick a blue flower.

c You have an equal chance of choosing a red or black card.

d It is impossible to select a green pencil.

e You have an equal chance of picking a pink or purple bow.

f You are certain to choose an orange lolly.

Mathseeds Year 3 Workbook © 3P Learning ISBN 978-1-923253-14-8

3 What are the possible outcomes when you roll a six-sided die?

a 

b 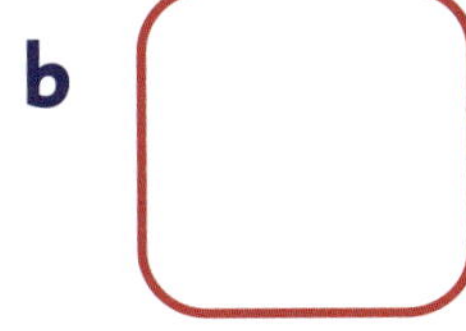

c 

d ☐

e ☐

f ☐

4 What is the chance of rolling:

a an odd number on a six-sided die?

☐ impossible ☐ equal chance ☐ certain

b a 7 or an 8 on a six-sided die?

☐ impossible ☐ equal chance ☐ certain

c a number from 1 to 6 on a six-sided die?

☐ impossible ☐ equal chance ☐ certain

5 What is the chance of rolling a:

a 1? _____ in 6 **b** 2? _____ in 6 **c** 3? _____ in 6

d 4? _____ in 6 **e** 5? _____ in 6 **f** 6? _____ in 6

6 If a six-sided die was rolled 24 times, how many rolls do you predict for each outcome?

Outcomes	1	2	3	4	5	6
Predictions						

  ISBN 978-1-923253-14-8

7 If this spinner is spun 20 times, how many spins do you predict will land on each outcome?

Outcomes	Red	Blue	Green	Yellow
Predictions				

R B Y G

8 Complete the experiment.

Use a paper plate, coloured pencils, cardboard arrow and split pin to make this spinner.
Spin the spinner 20 times and record each result.

Outcomes	Red	Blue	Green	Yellow
Predictions				

9 Did the results match the predictions? ________ Why or why not?

____

10 If this spinner is spun 24 times, how many spins do you predict will land on each outcome?

Outcomes	Red	Blue	Green	Yellow
Predictions				

R B Y G

11 Complete the experiment.

Use a paper plate, coloured pencils, cardboard arrow and split pin to make this spinner.
Spin the spinner 24 times and record each result.

Outcomes	Red	Blue	Green	Yellow
Predictions				

12 Did the results match the predictions? ________ Why or why not?

____

Mathseeds Year 3 Workbook © 3P Learning ISBN 978-1-923253-14-8

13 Waldo has a new spinner. It has sections for scoring 10, 20, 50 and 100. Waldo knows these chance words:

certain **impossible** **likely**
unlikely **equal chance**

What is the possibility of landing on each score?

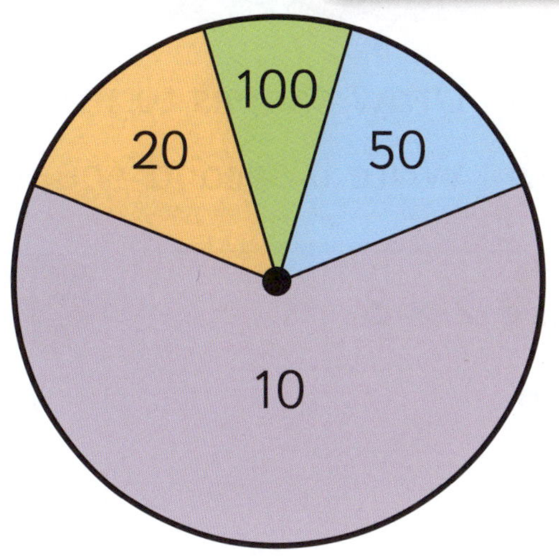

a Underline the question. **b** Circle the facts.

c Choose a chance word to label each score. Explain why you chose this word.

Score	Chance word	Why did you choose this word?
10		
100		
20 & 50		

14 Design your own spinners to match these possibilities:

a You are certain to score 100 every time.

b It is impossible to score 100.

c It is likely you will score 100, and unlikely you will score 1.

d You have an equal chance of scoring 100 or 1.

I finished this lesson online. 167

I can
- Revise 'certain', 'impossible' and 'equal chance'. ☐
- Write probability as a ratio, eg 1 in 6. ☐
- Identify outcomes for chance experiments and predict frequency. ☐
- Record results for chance experiments and compare to predictions. ☐

We went to

a Draw shapes to make an array for each equation.

b Write a second equation for the array. Find the product.

1 2 × 8

a

b ___ × ___ = ___

2 4 × 5

a

b ___ × ___ = ___

3 5 × 3

a

b ___ × ___ = ___

4 6 × 4

a

b ___ × ___ = ___

5 3 × 7

a

b ___ × ___ = ___

6 9 × 2

a

b ___ × ___ = ___

7 5 × 5

a

b ___ × ___ = ___

8 3 × 2

a

b ___ × ___ = ___

9 4 × 10

a

b ___ × ___ = ___

Mathseeds Year 3 Workbook © 3P Learning ISBN 978-1-923253-14-8

Multiplication Word Problems 2

a Draw an array for each question.
b Complete the equation and find the product.

10 Ruby has 10 hats with 5 feathers on each hat. How many feathers are there altogether?

a

b ___ × ___ = ___

11 Mango's muffin tray holds 8 muffins. She makes 3 trays of muffins. How many muffins in total?

a

b ___ × ___ = ___

12 Doc has 5 tie racks. Each rack holds 6 ties. How many ties does Doc have altogether?

a

b ___ × ___ = ___

13 Mrs T eats 7 cactus plants in a day. How many plants does she eat in a week?

a

b ___ × ___ = ___

a Solve the first step. **b** What is the next step?
c Draw an array and solve the problem.

14 Dottie played 2 games of Scrabble with her dad 3 nights a week for 4 weeks. How many games of Scrabble did she play?

a 2 × ____ = ____ **b** ____ × _____ **c** ____ games of Scrabble

15 Robby eats 2 sandwiches for lunch every school day. The school term goes for 10 weeks. How many sandwiches does Robby eat at school in one term?

a 2 × ____ = ____ **b** ____ × _____ **c** ____ sandwiches

16 Lottie played 2 games of soccer every Saturday and 2 games of netball every Sunday. Over 8 weeks, how many games of sport did she play?

a 2 × ____ = ____ **b** ____ × _____ **c** ____ games of sport

17 Write your own word problem and solve it.

a ________________ buys ____ packets of ______________________.
Each pack holds ______.
How many ______________ altogether?

b

Mathseeds Year 3 Workbook © 3P Learning ISBN 978-1-923253-14-8

Multiplication Word Problems 2

18 A box of tea bags is packed in three rows. Each row has 20 tea bags. The box has two layers of tea bags. How many tea bags in a box?

a Underline the question. **b** Circle the facts.

c Draw arrays to show the tea bags.

d How many tea bags in total? ________

19 **a** Complete this problem with your own numbers:

A box of tea bags is packed in ________ rows.

Each row has ________ tea bags.

The box has two layers of tea bags.

How many tea bags in the box?

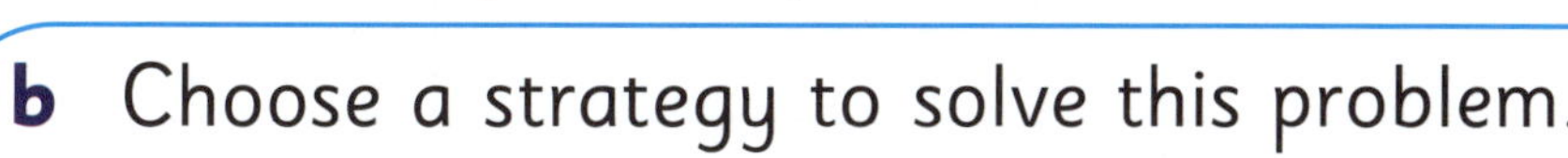

b Choose a strategy to solve this problem.

I finished this lesson online.

I can
- Write commutative multiplication equations with arrays. ☐
- Solve multiplication problems using arrays and equations. ☐
- Solve multiplication problems with 3 multipliers. ☐

We went to

  ISBN 978-1-923253-14-8

LESSON 169 PRISMS AND PYRAMIDS

1 Colour the end faces of these prisms.

2 Name each prism.

a

b

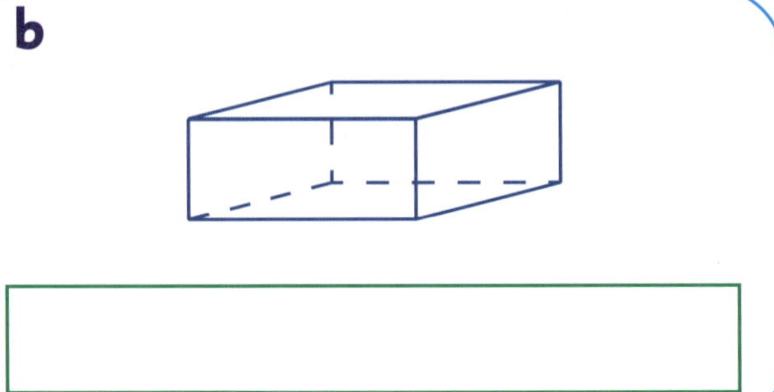

c

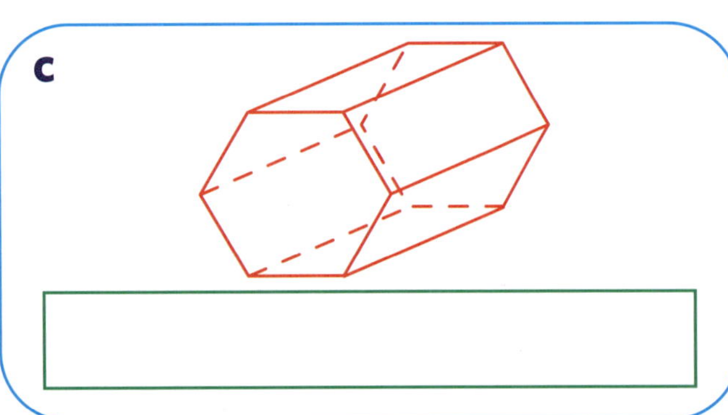

d

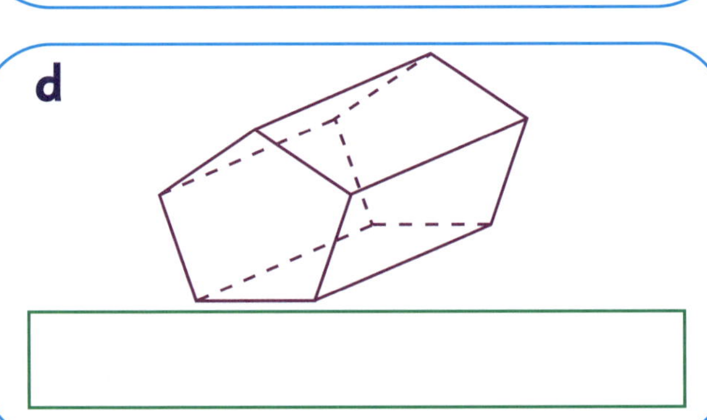

3 Draw all the faces for each prism.

Prism	Faces							
a triangular								
b rectangular								
c hexagonal								
d pentagonal								

Mathseeds Year 3 Workbook © 3P Learning ISBN 978-1-923253-14-8

4 Colour the bases of these pyramids.

5 Name each pyramid.

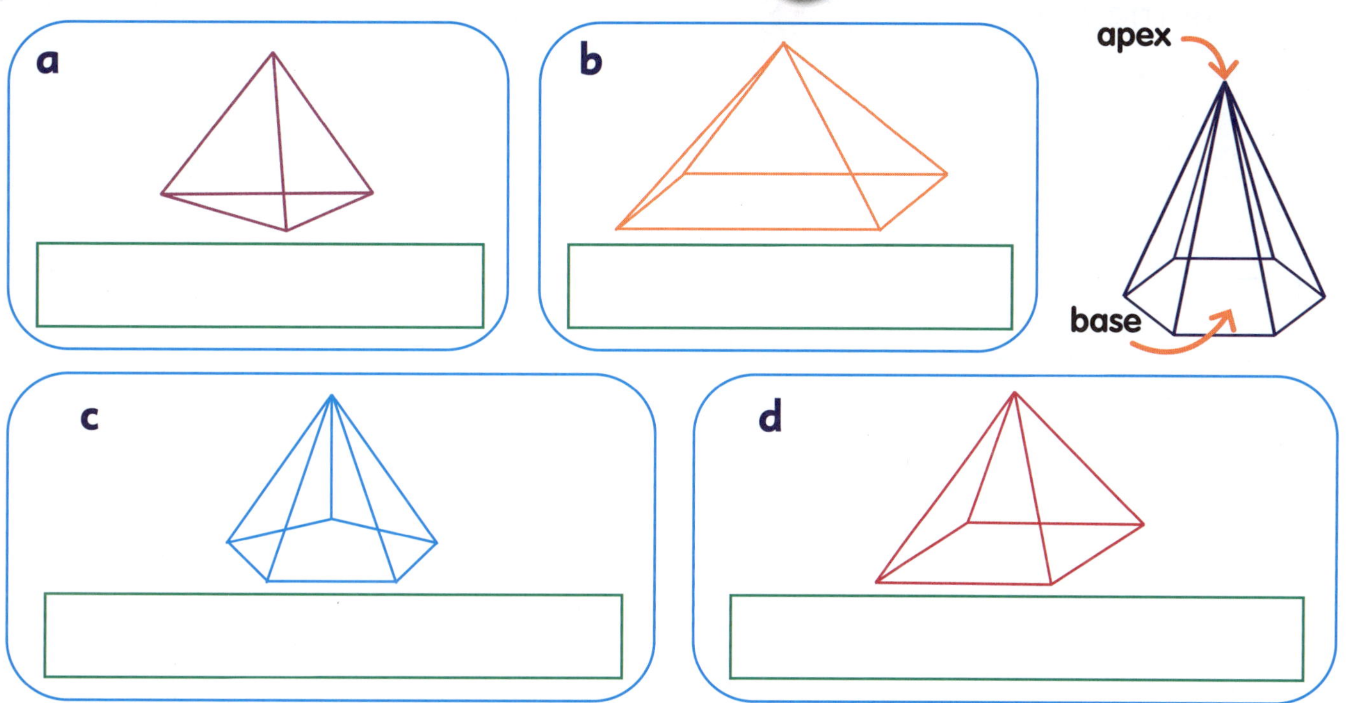

6 What does a pyramid have that a prism does not? ____________

7 Draw all the faces for each pyramid.

Pyramid	Faces							
a triangular								
b rectangular								
c pentagonal								
d square								

8 Name the 3D objects.

9 Match the 3D objects to their nets.

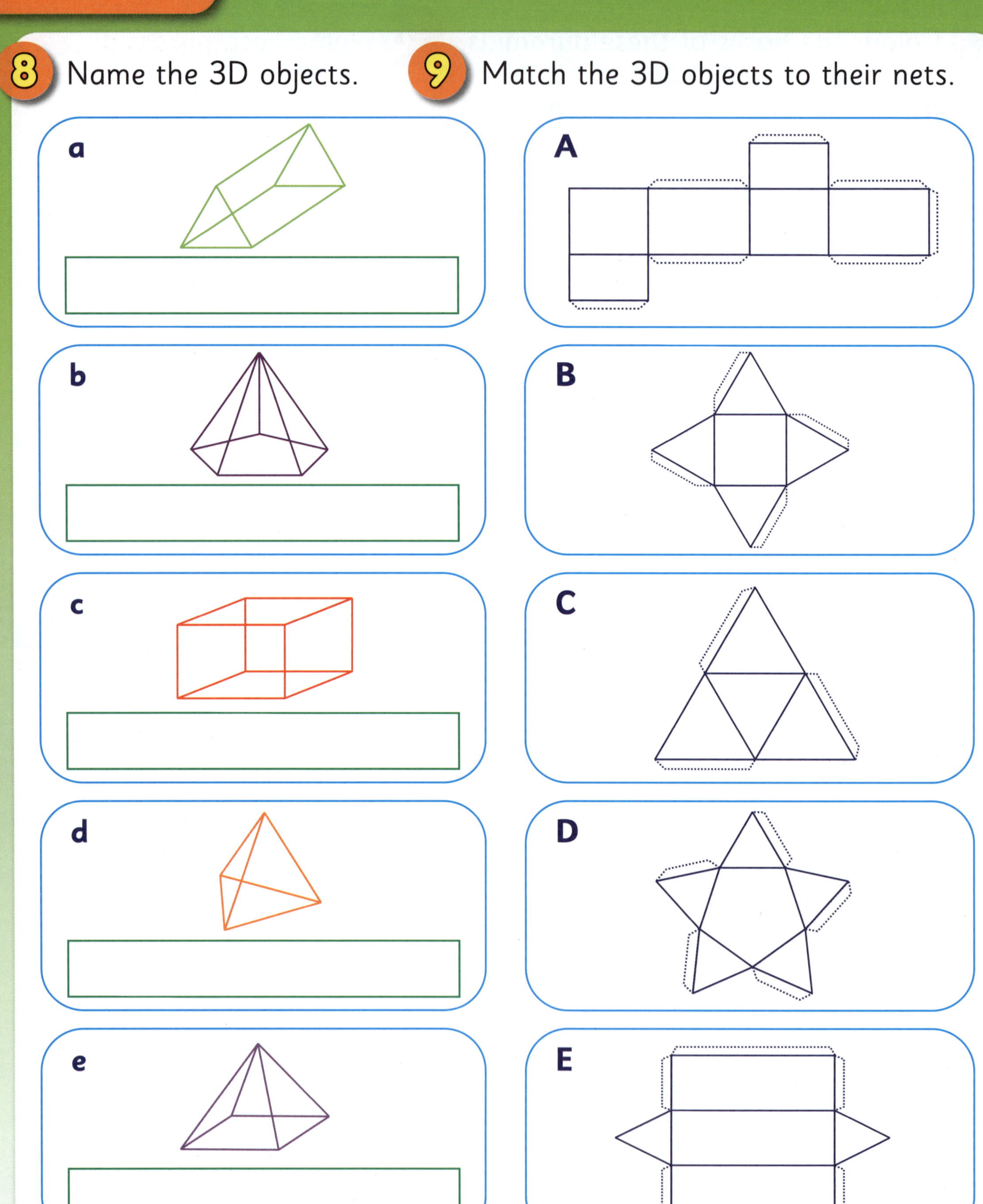

Mathseeds Year 3 Workbook © 3P Learning ISBN 978-1-923253-14-8

Prisms and Pyramids

10 Write a description of a 3D object. If your partner can guess your shape without you saying its name, you win.

a Name a 3D object. ______________________________

b Draw it.

c Draw its net.

d List the features of your shape.

Edges	Vertices	Faces — number and shape	Apex? Bases?

11 Write a description of your 3D object.

____

____

____

I finished this lesson online.

169

I can

- Identify prisms and pyramids and describe their key features. ☐
- Name prisms for their end faces and identify all their faces. ☐
- Name pyramids for their base, identify the apex and draw all faces. ☐
- Match prisms and pyramids to their nets. ☐

We went to

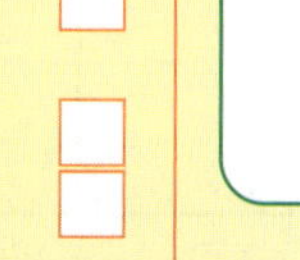

  ISBN 978-1-923253-14-8

a Draw blocks to show the sums.

b Regroup and trade by crossing out 10 ones or 10 tens and drawing the extra ten or hundred in the next column.

c Then find the total.

1. 257 + 135

	Hundreds	Tens	Ones
a b			
	+		
c			

2. 465 + 371

	Hundreds	Tens	Ones
a b			
	+		
c			

3. 359 + 263

	Hundreds	Tens	Ones
a b			
	+		
c			

Mathseeds Year 3 Workbook © 3P Learning ISBN 978-1-923253-14-8

4 Calculate the answer. Don't forget to trade.

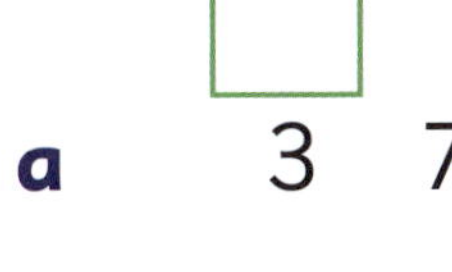

a 37 + 27

b 24 + 18

c 38 + 49

d 44 + 36

e 59 + 37

f 25 + 17

g 72 + 19

h 48 + 26

5 Write the algorithm and find the answer.

a 75 + 15 =

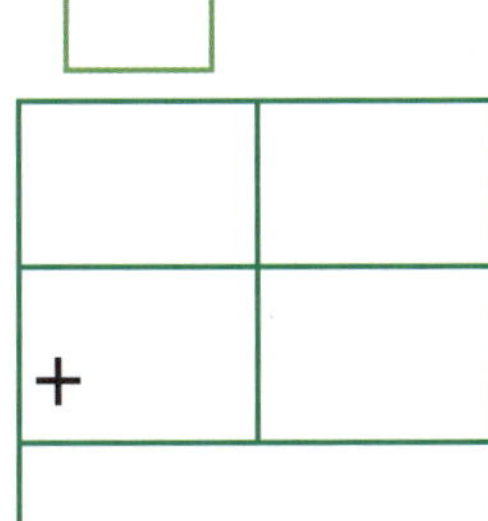

b 44 + 37 =

c 68 + 22 =

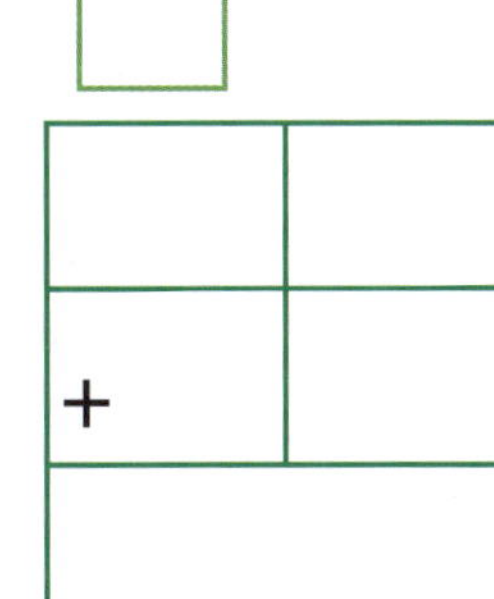

d 63 + 19 =

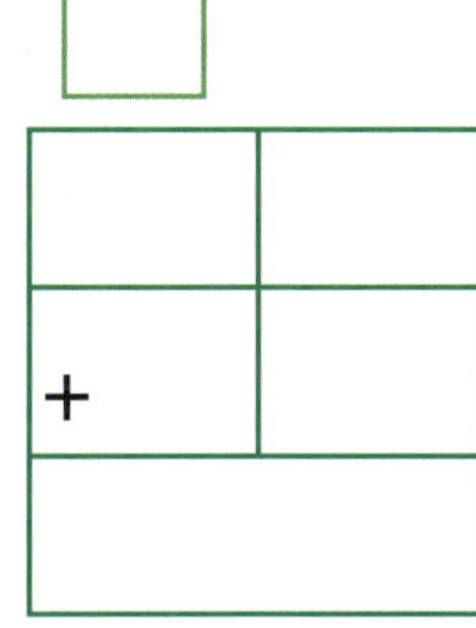

e 51 + 29 =

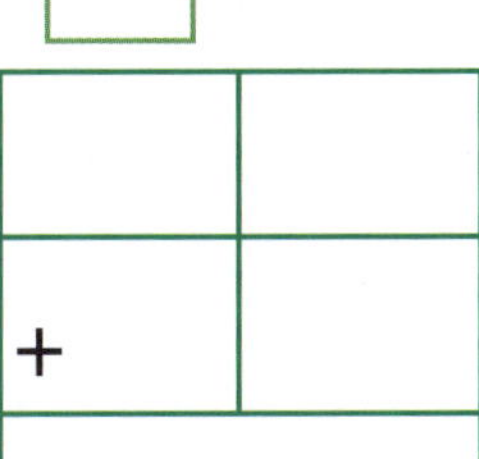

f 48 + 43 =

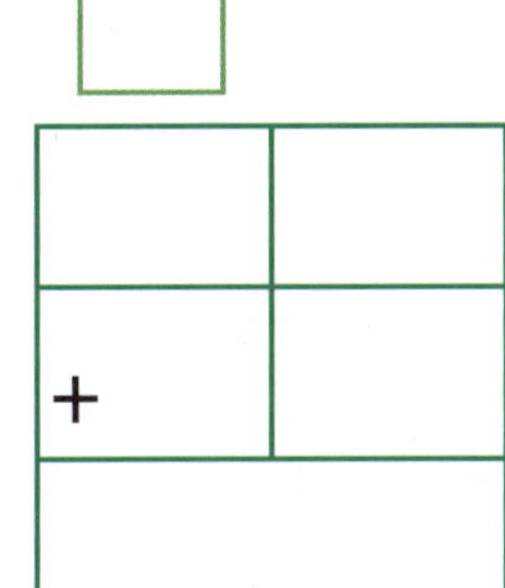

g 46 + 19 =

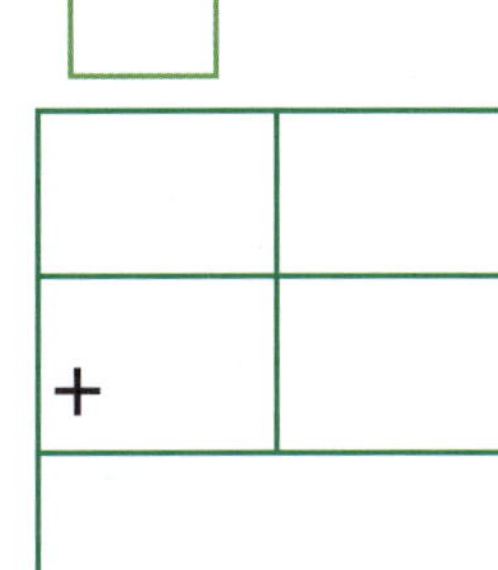

h 27 + 56 =

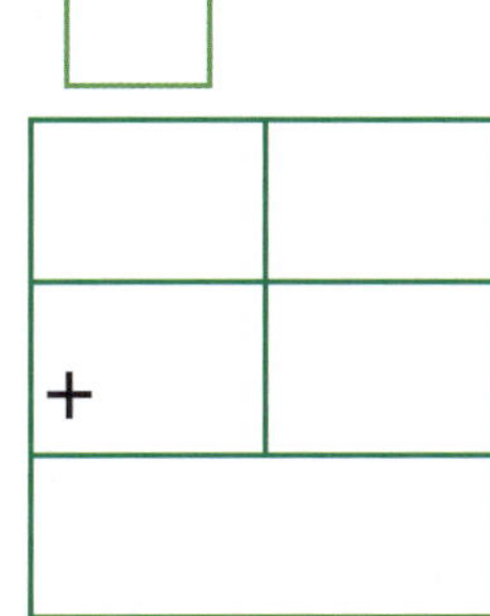

  ISBN 978-1-923253-14-8

6 Calculate the answer. Don't forget to trade.

a
```
  5 5 9
+ 2 3 7
```

b
```
  2 7 5
+ 1 7 1
```

c
```
  3 8 2
+ 4 0 9
```

d
```
  4 6 8
+ 3 6 1
```

e
```
  5 5 6
+ 1 2 7
```

f
```
  2 4 5
+ 5 9 4
```

g
```
  3 5 5
+ 5 0 9
```

h
```
  3 5 4
+ 3 6 1
```

7 Write the algorithm and find the answer.

a 739 + 106 =

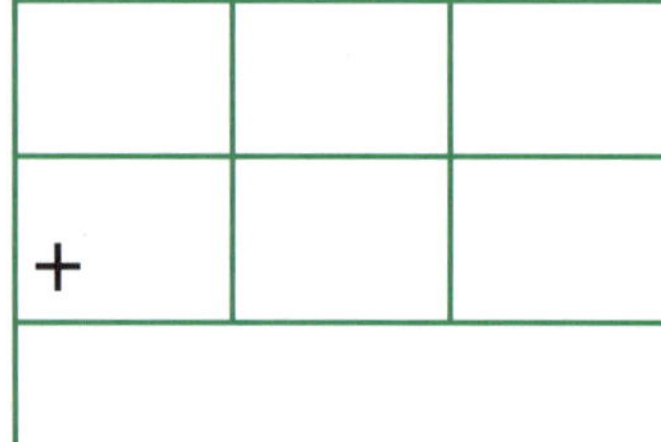

b 473 + 227 =

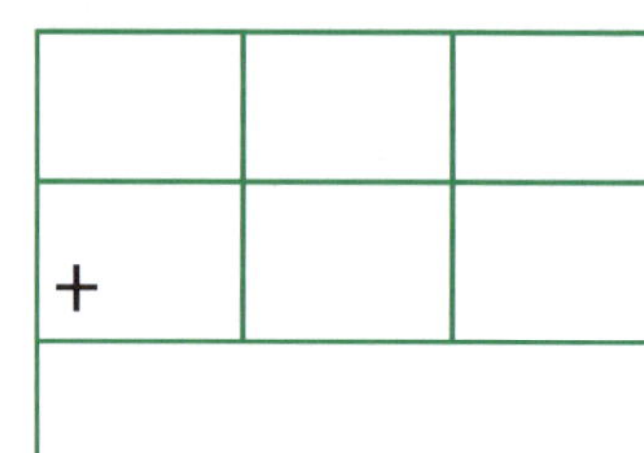

c 628 + 217 =

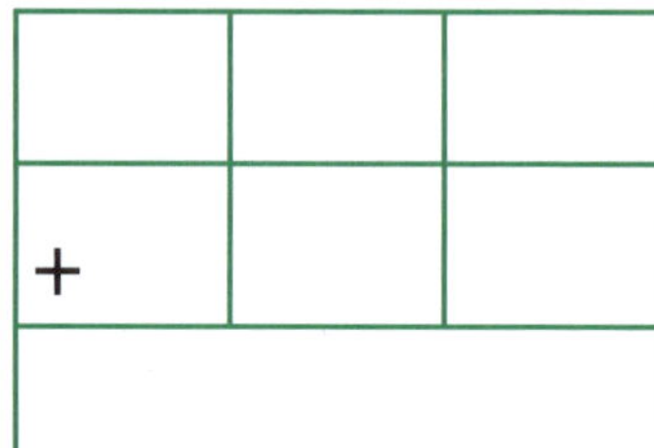

d 683 + 191 =

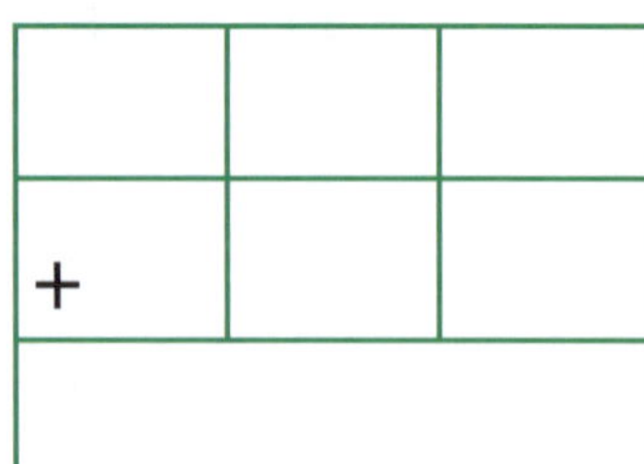

e 582 + 352 =

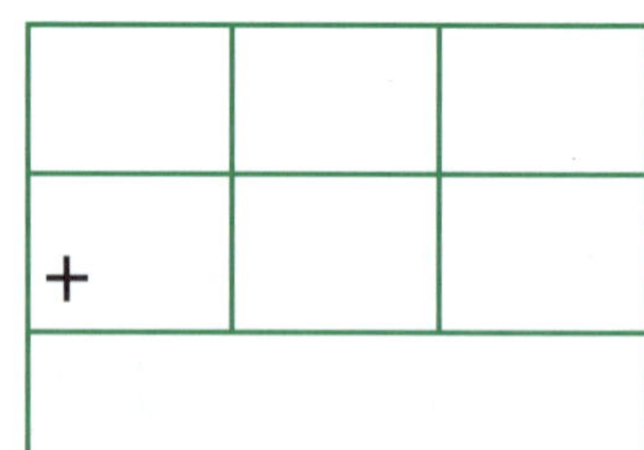

f 496 + 491 =

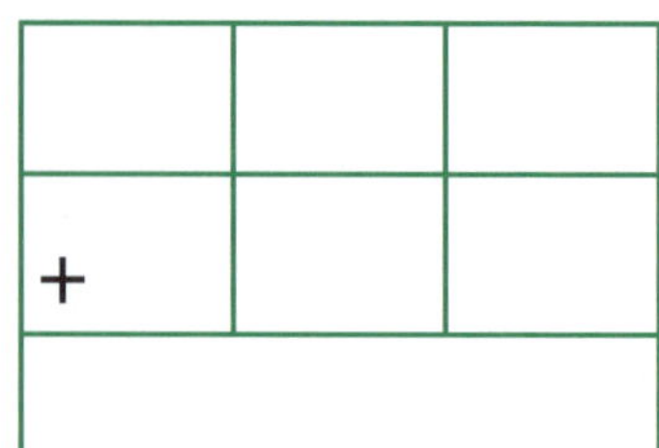

g 134 + 298 =

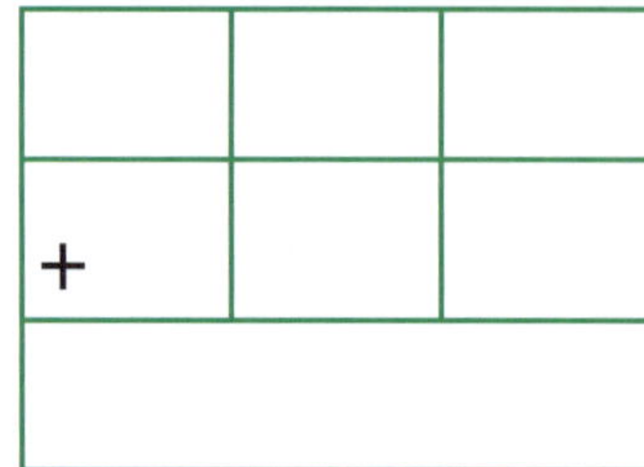

h 365 + 285 =

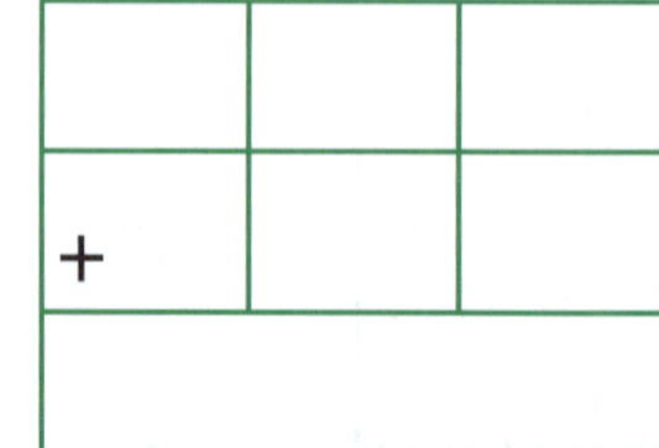

i 178 + 453 =

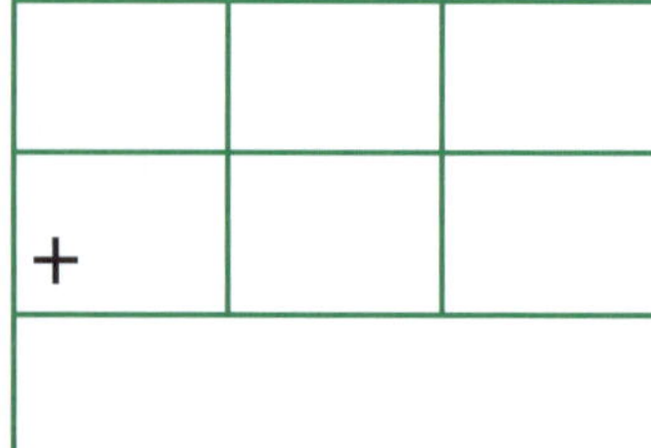

Mathseeds Year 3 Workbook © 3P Learning ISBN 978-1-923253-14-8

Write the algorithm and find the answer.

8 Mango has 24 eggs in one box and 37 eggs in another box. How many eggs altogether?

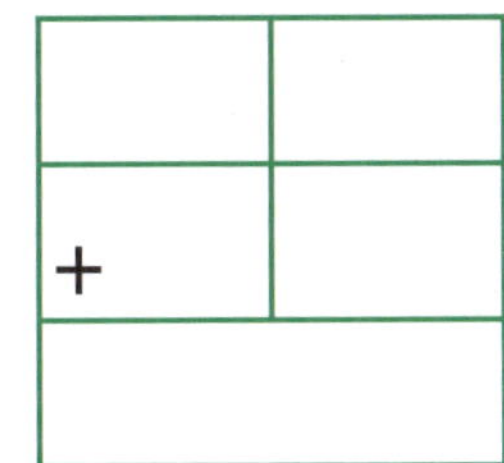

9 Doc sees 49 cocoons on one branch and 33 on another branch. How many cocoons in total?

10 Mrs T counts 157 butterflies in one cage and 371 in the other cage. How many butterflies in total?

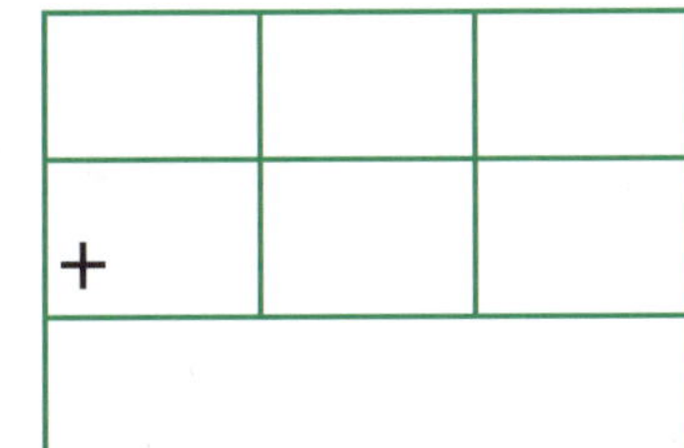

11 Ruby walks down one path for 236 steps, then down another for 166 steps. How many steps altogether?

12 Waldo finds 428 empty cocoons in one area and 319 in another area. How many empty cocoons?

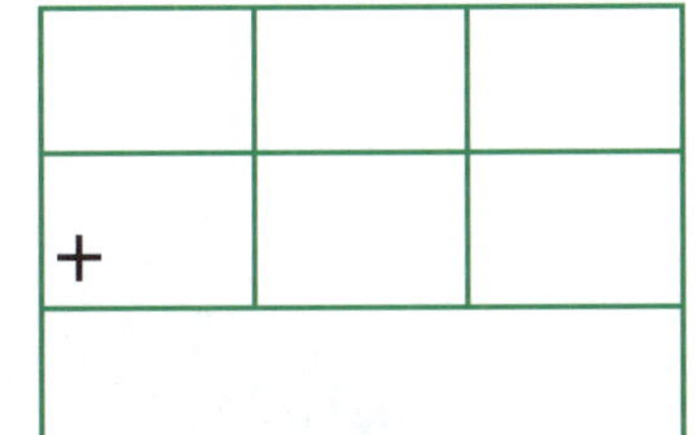

13 Dizzy buys a new cage for the butterflies for $690 and a box for more eggs for $150. How much did he spend?

I finished this lesson online.

I can

- Explore regrouping or trading with base ten blocks and algorithms. ☐
- Use vertical algorithms to add 2- and 3-digit numbers. ☐
- Solve problems using vertical addition algorithms. ☐

We went to

QUIZ

END OF MAP 34 QUIZ

1 Is the answer odd or even? Circle. Find the answer.

a 17 + 25 = ______ odd even

b 34 + 59 = ______ odd even

c 46 + 48 = ______ odd even

d 63 + 20 = ______ odd even

2 What is the chance of pulling out a:

a blue marble? ______ in ______

b green marble? ______ in ______

c red marble? ______ in ______

3 Bobby has 5 shelves of shoes.
Each shelf holds 4 shoe boxes.
Each box holds a pair of shoes.
How many shoes in total?

a 5 × ______ = ______ b ______ × ______ c ______ shoes

Mathseeds Year 3 Workbook © 3P Learning ISBN 978-1-923253-14-8

4 Label the features of these shapes.

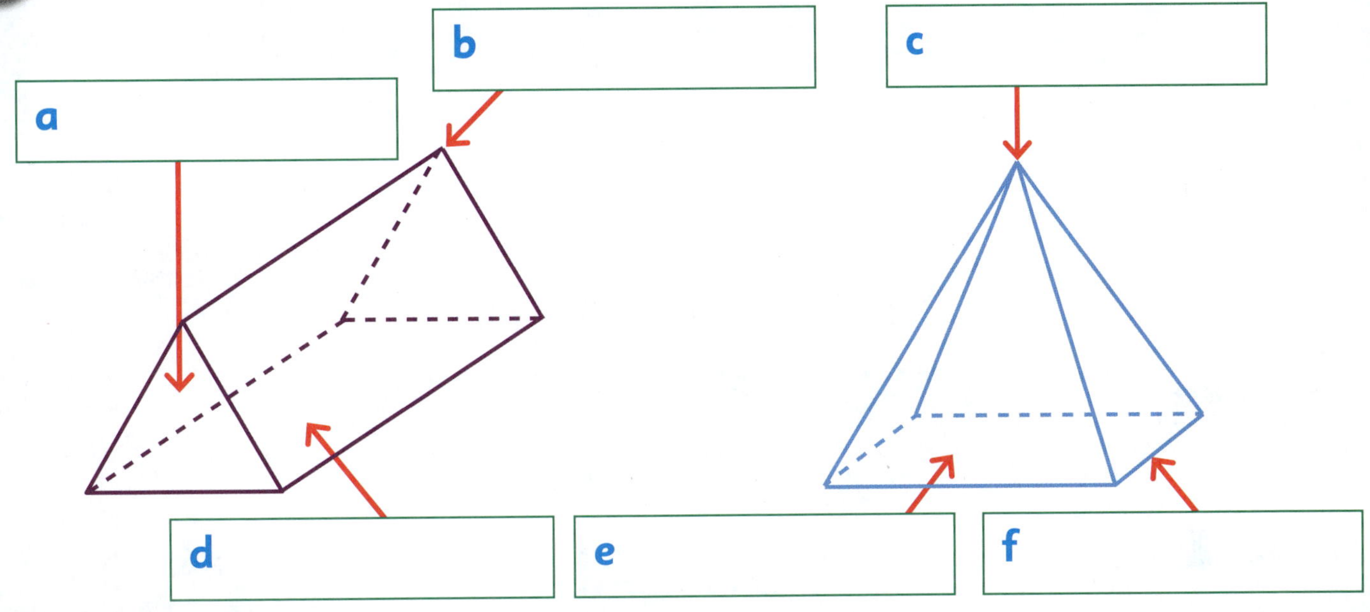

5 Name the above shapes. Draw a net for each.

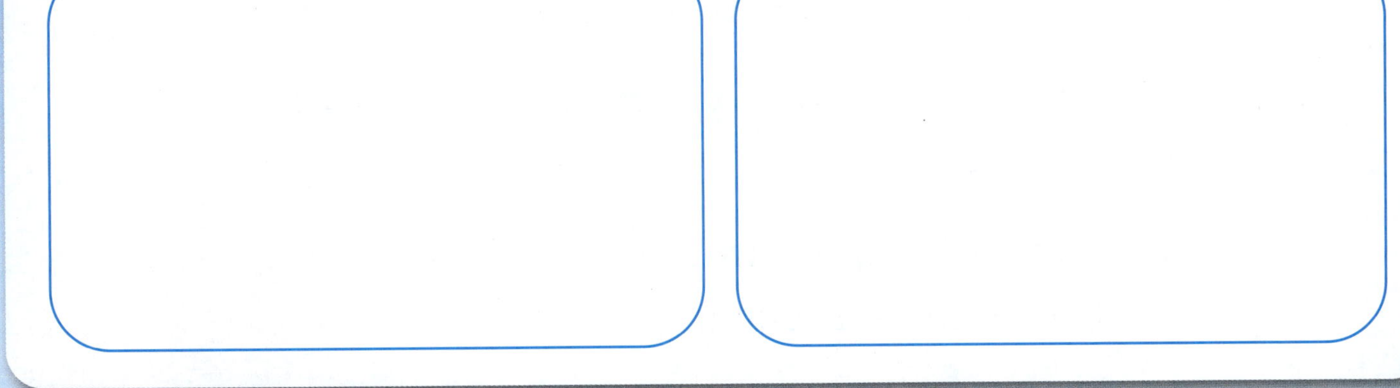

6 Calculate the answer. Don't forget to trade.

a 175 + 782 = ____

b 342 + 590 = ____

c 468 + 307 = ____

d 939 + 281 = ____

  ISBN 978-1-923253-14-8

Good Job!

YOU COMPLETED

MAP 34

YOU CAN:

- ☐ Use rules to predict if answers to **additions** will be **odd or even**.
- ☐ Write **probability as a ratio**, eg 1 in 6.
- ☐ Solve **multiplication problems** with 3 multipliers.
- ☐ Label the features of a **prism** and a **pyramid** and draw a **net** for each.
- ☐ Use **vertical algorithms** to add 3-digit numbers with regrouping.

Signed:

Dated:

Mathseeds Year 3 Workbook © 3P Learning ISBN 978-1-923253-14-8

FUN SPOT 4

WHO AM I? PROBLEMS

1 Use the clues to name and draw each 3D object.

a I have an apex and a base.
I have 1 curved surface
and 1 flat face.

I am a ______________________.

b I have 6 flat faces.
They are all the same shape and size.
I have 8 vertices.

I am a ______________________.

c I have one curved surface.
I also have 2 flat faces
and 2 edges.

I am a ______________________.

d I have an apex and a base.
My sides are all triangles
and there are 4 of them.

I am a ______________________.

1. How many legs? Complete the equations.

a ______ × 4 = ______

b ______ × 4 = ______

c ______ × 4 = ______

d ______ × 4 = ______

e ______ × 4 = ______

f ______ × 4 = ______

2. Find the answers.

×	0	1	2	3	4	5	6	7	8	9	10
4											

3. Complete.

a 4 × 2 = 2 × 4 = ______

b 4 × 5 = ______ × 4 = ______

c 4 × 7 = ______ × ______ = ______

d 4 × 8 = ______ × ______ = ______

e 4 × 3 = ______ × ______ = ______

f 4 × 6 = ______ × ______ = ______

Mathseeds Year 3 Workbook © 3P Learning ISBN 978-1-923253-14-8

×8

4 Find the answers.

×	0	1	2	3	4	5	6	7	8	9	10
8											

5 How many legs? Fill in the equations.

a $1 \times 8 = 8 \times 1 =$ _____

b $10 \times 8 = 8 \times$ _____ = _____

c $4 \times 8 =$ _____ × _____ = _____

d $6 \times 8 =$ _____ × _____ = _____

e _____ × 8 = _____ × _____ = _____

f _____ × 8 = _____ × _____ = _____

g _____ × _____ = _____ × _____ = _____

h _____ × _____ = _____ × _____ = _____

i _____ × _____ = _____ × _____ = _____

j _____ × _____ = _____ × _____ = _____

6 Complete.

a $8 \times$ _____ = 16

b $8 \times$ _____ = 40

c $8 \times$ _____ = 32

d $8 \times$ _____ = 56

e $8 \times$ _____ = 24

f $8 \times$ _____ = 48

7 Match the items to their boxes. Fill in the equations.

a 3 stacks of 4 books each

_____ × _____ = _____

b 4 piles with 4 t-shirts in each pile

_____ × _____ = _____

c 5 packets each holding 4 bags of 10 pencils

_____ × _____ × _____ = _____

d 4 crates with 2 bundles of 7 carrots in each crate

_____ × _____ × _____ = _____

e 2 sacks each with 3 bags holding 8 balls

_____ × _____ × _____ = _____

f 20 cartons holding 4 rows of 2 cans each

_____ × _____ × _____ = _____

200

12

56

16

160

48

8 Complete.

a 2 × 5 × _____ = 60

b 3 × _____ × 4 = 120

c _____ × 2 × 4 = 64

d 4 × 5 × _____ = 40

e 5 × _____ × 5 = 100

f _____ × 8 × 8 = 640

Mathseeds Year 3 Workbook © 3P Learning ISBN 978-1-923253-14-8

9 Dizzy has five treasure chests. Each chest has eight bags of coins in it. Each bag has two gold coins in it. How many gold coins does Dizzy have?

a Underline the question. **b** Circle the facts.

c Write a multiplication equation for this problem: ☐ × ☐ × ☐

d Solve the problem.

e How many gold coins does Dizzy have? ____________

10 Mango also has two treasure chests. Each chest has five bags of coins. Each bag has eight gold coins in it. How many gold coins does Mango have?

a Underline the question. **b** Circle the facts.

c Write a multiplication equation for this problem: ☐ × ☐ × ☐

d Solve the problem.

e How many gold coins does Mango have? ____________

I finished this lesson online.

I can
- Write multiplication equations based on groups. ☐
- Fill in a multiplication table for ×4 and ×8. ☐
- Use the commutative property of multiplication to write equations. ☐
- Find missing factors in multiplication equations. ☐
- Solve multiplication problems with 3 multipliers. ☐

We went to

LESSON 172 KILOGRAMS AND GRAMS

= 50 kg

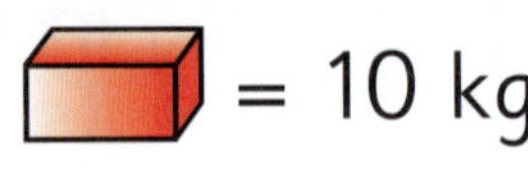
= 10 kg

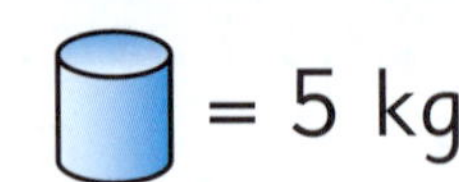
= 5 kg

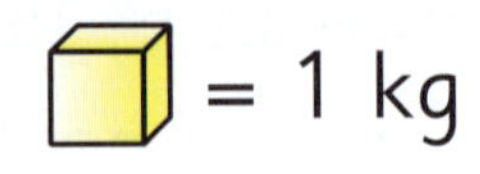
= 1 kg

1 Write the mass in kilograms.

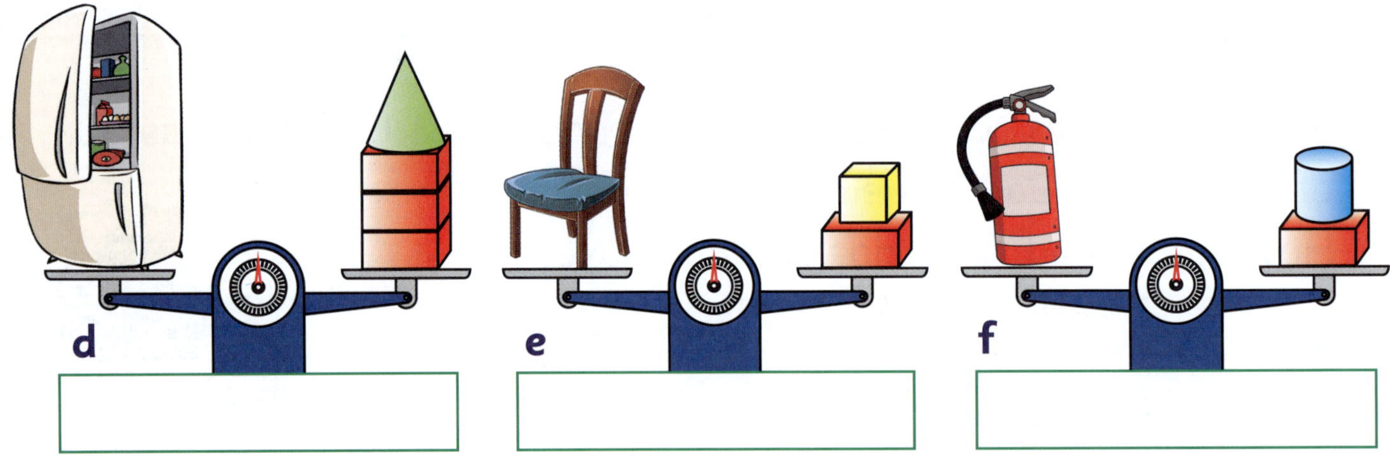

2 Number these items from 1 to 5, heaviest to lightest.

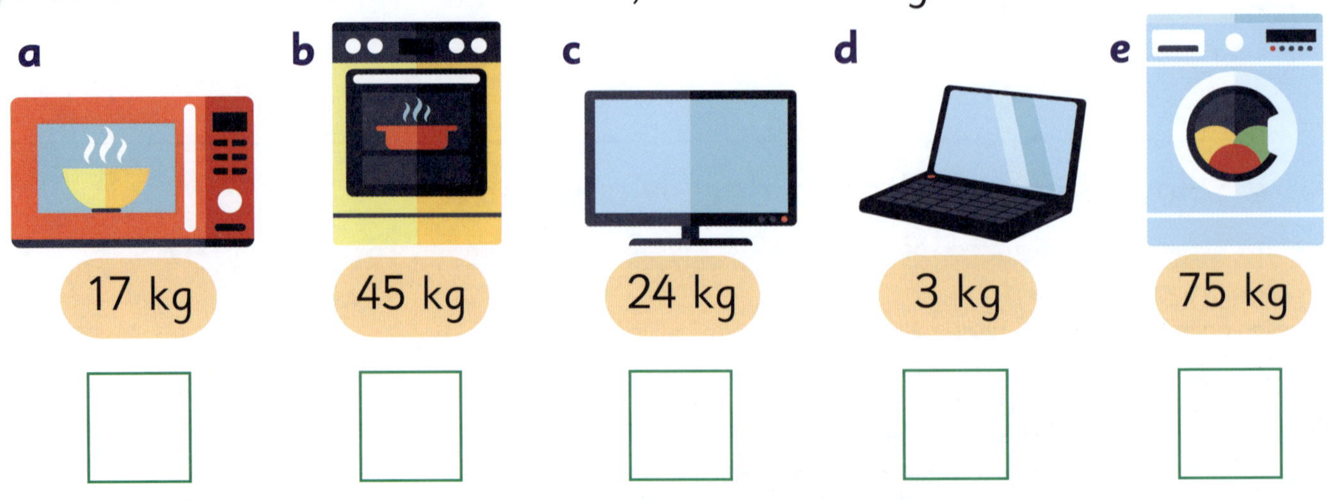

Mathseeds Year 3 Workbook © 3P Learning ISBN 978-1-923253-14-8

3 Write the mass in grams.

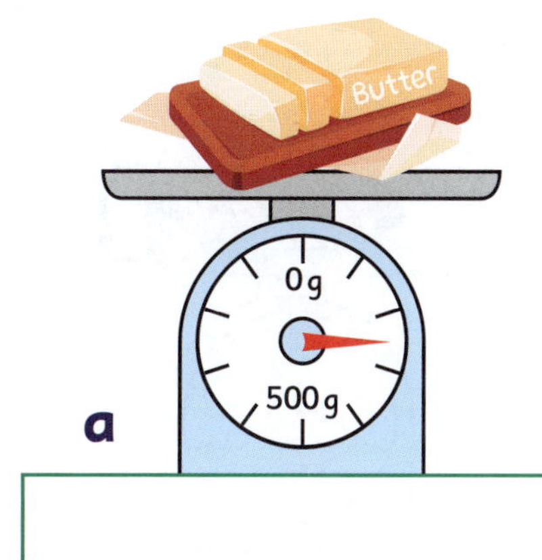

a

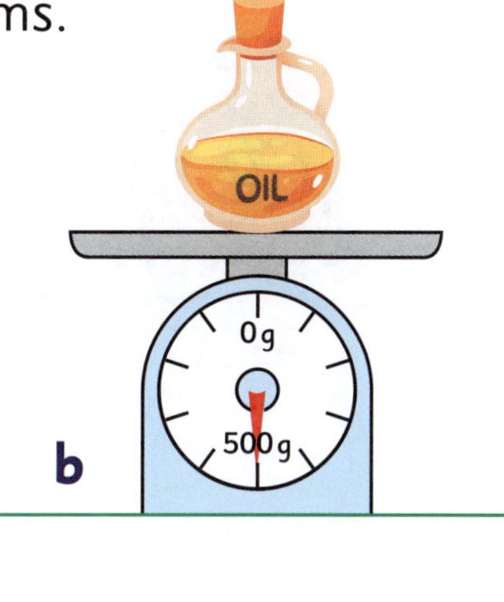

b

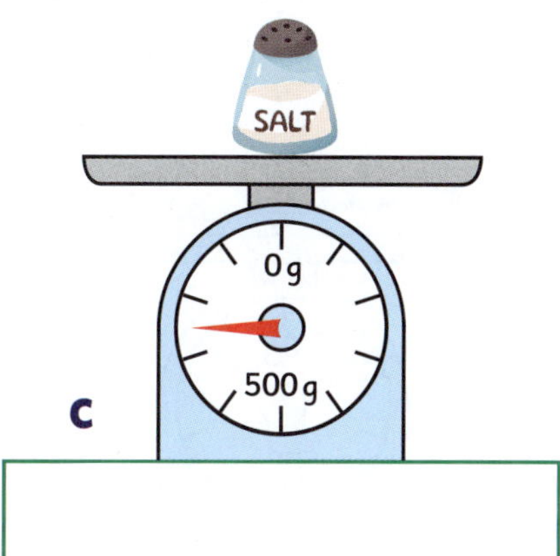

c

d

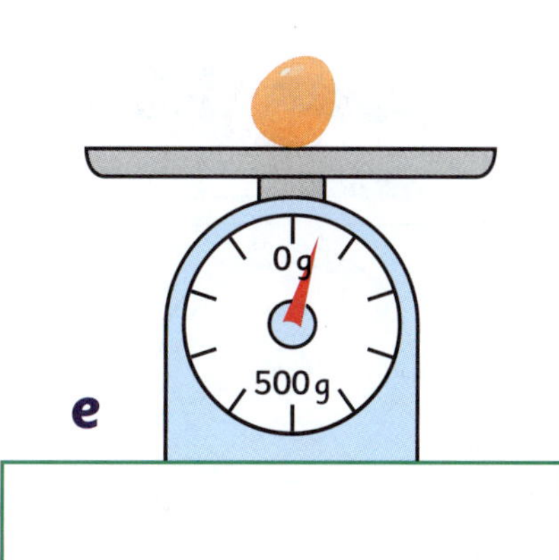

e

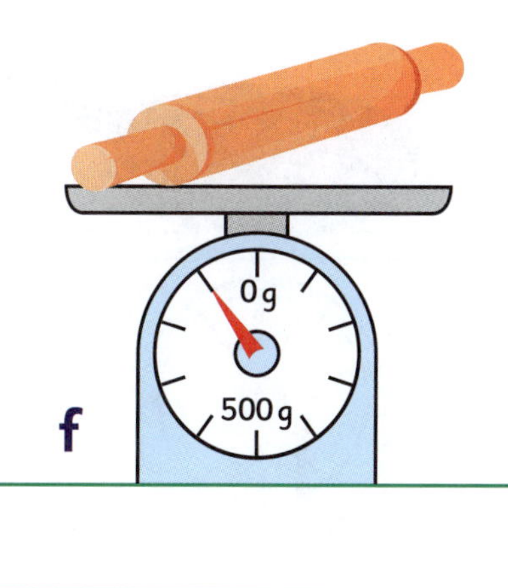

f

4 Number these trophies from 1 to 5, heaviest to lightest.

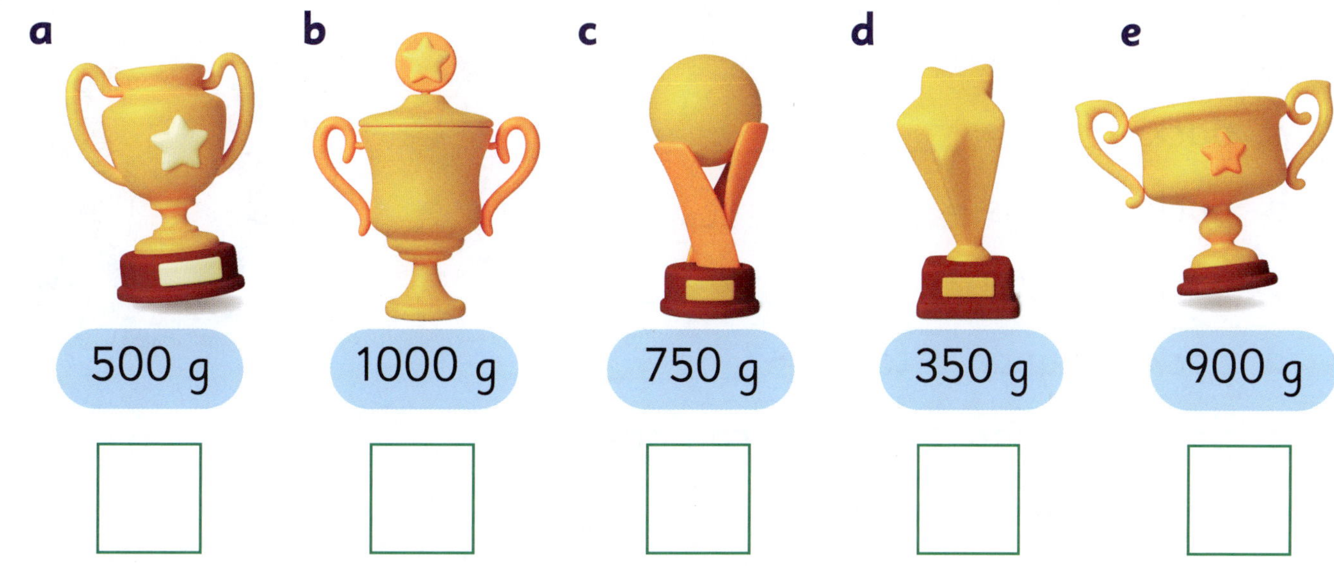

  ISBN 978-1-923253-14-8

5 Write the mass of each item.

a

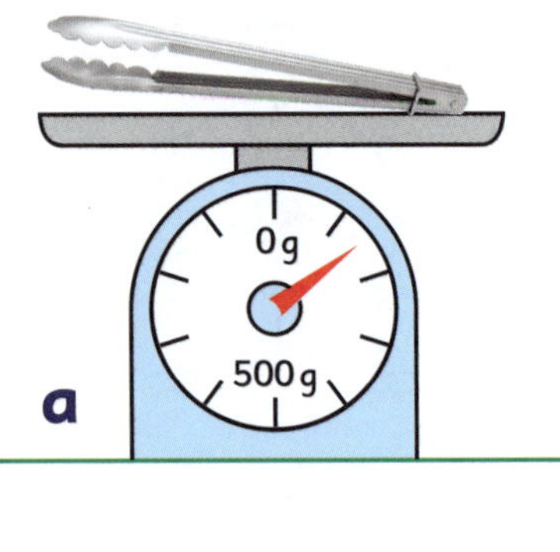

b

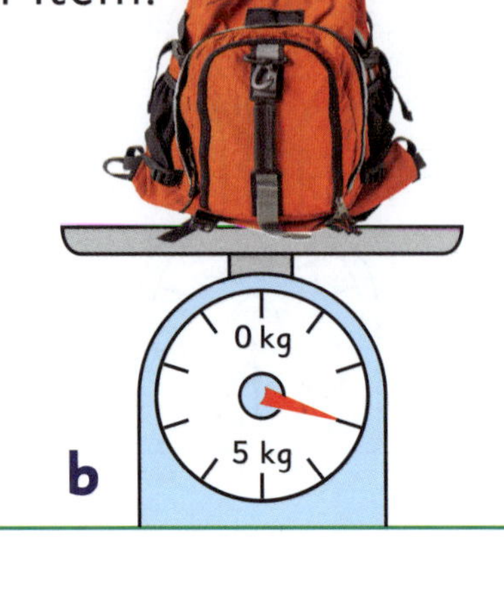

c

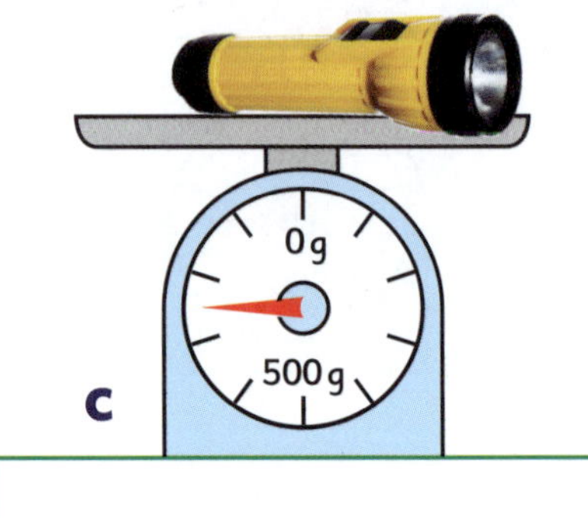

d

e

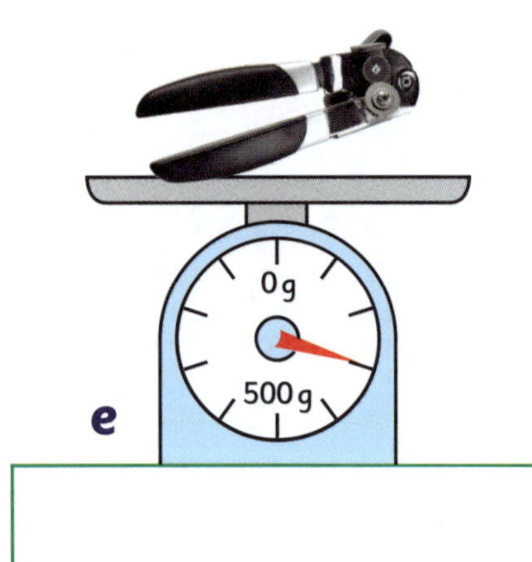

f

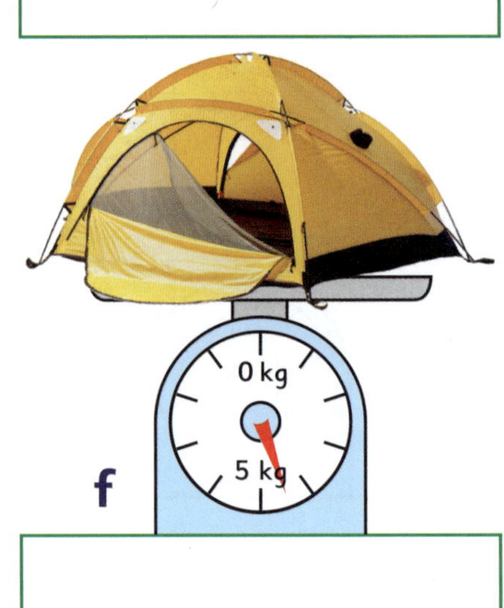

6 Work out the weight of each pack and its contents in kilograms.

a pack + tent = ____________

b pack + tongs = ____________

c pack + tent + torch = ____________

d pack + frypan + tongs = ____________

e pack + frypan + tongs + can opener = ____________

f pack + everything = ____________

Mathseeds Year 3 Workbook ISBN 978-1-923253-14-8

7 Waldo can only take 1 kg of snacks on the plane. Help Waldo get his snack bag down to 1 kg.

a Underline the question. b Circle the facts.

c You need to know: 1 kg = ____________ grams

8 This is what's in Waldo's snack bag.

a Work out the total mass for each fruit.

b Work out the total mass of Waldo's snack bag.

Fruit	Number	Mass each	Total mass of each fruit
apple	3	200 g	
apricot	4	100 g	
strawberry	10	25 g	
pear	1	250 g	
		Total mass of the snacks:	

9 a Is Waldo's snack bag too heavy? ____________

b By how much? ____________

10 Repack Waldo's snack bag so that it weighs 1 kg. Show your thinking.

I finished this lesson online.

I can
- Use balance scales to measure mass in kilograms kg.
- Order items from heaviest to lightest.
- Read a dial scale to measure mass in grams g and kilograms kg.
- Add and subtract masses to solve problems.

We went to

  ISBN 978-1-923253-14-8

LESSON 173 MENTAL + – STRATEGIES

1 Complete.

a 45 + 37 = 45 + 40 = ☐ – 3 = ☐

b 67 + 24 = 67 + 20 = ☐ + 4 = ☐

c 56 + 29 = 56 + ☐ = ☐ – ☐ = ☐

d 78 + 13 = 78 + ☐ = ☐ + ☐ = ☐

e 46 + 47 = ______________________

f 59 + 32 = ______________________

2 Complete.

a 75 – 16 = 75 – 20 = ☐ + 4 = ☐

b 38 – 12 = 38 – 10 = ☐ – 2 = ☐

c 98 – 79 = 98 – ☐ = ☐ + ☐ = ☐

d 84 – 63 = 84 – ☐ = ☐ – ☐ = ☐

e 52 – 27 = ______________________

f 66 – 44 = ______________________

3 Find the answer mentally.

a 32 + 67 = ☐ b 78 – 23 = ☐ c 48 + 41 = ☐

d 55 – 37 = ☐ e 62 + 19 = ☐ f 99 – 65 = ☐

g 24 + 28 = ☐ h 92 – 54 = ☐ i 81 + 19 = ☐

Mathseeds Year 3 Workbook © 3P Learning ISBN 978-1-923253-14-8

4 Complete.

a 45 + 23 = 45 + 20 = ☐ + 3 = ☐

b 77 + 18 = 77 + 10 = ☐ + 8 = ☐

c 62 + 34 = 62 + ☐ = ☐ + ☐ = ☐

d 59 + 29 = 59 + ☐ = ☐ + ☐ = ☐

e 17 + 18 = ______________________

f 48 + 35 = ______________________

5 Complete.

a 88 – 16 = 88 – 10 = ☐ – 6 = ☐

b 94 – 68 = 94 – 60 = ☐ – 8 = ☐

c 52 – 28 = 52 – ☐ = ☐ – ☐ = ☐

d 78 – 42 = 78 – ☐ = ☐ – ☐ = ☐

e 63 – 16 = ______________________

f 49 – 24 = ______________________

6 Find the answer mentally.

a 18 + 47 = ☐ **b** 67 – 39 = ☐ **c** 53 + 32 = ☐

d 97 – 58 = ☐ **e** 33 + 49 = ☐ **f** 83 – 47 = ☐

g 67 + 28 = ☐ **h** 75 – 17 = ☐ **i** 59 + 29 = ☐

7 Complete these problems in your head and write the answer.

a River has 56 records and buys 19 more.
How many records does he own now? ______

b Blossom bakes 85 cookies, then eats 27.
How many cookies are left? ______

c Fern paints 43 pictures and sells 34 of them.
How many are left? ______

d Zen earns $65 for washing cars. His nan also gives him $28.
How much money does he have? ______

e Faith needs 100 g of flour. One bag had 73 g left in it.
How much more flour does she need? ______

8 Use mental strategies to work out the missing number in each story.

a Charles has 83 monster figurines. He has 57 good monsters.
He has ______ bad monsters.

b Dorothy spent $______ on cakes. She bought a chocolate cake for $49 and a sponge cake for $22.

c Doris took 17 minutes to walk to and from the shops and spent 68 minutes in there. She was out for ______ minutes altogether.

d Walter fills his bath with 72 L of hot water and 29 L of cold water. His bath now has ______ L of warm water in it.

e Albert counts 32 people in his class today. Yesterday there were only 19 people. That means ______ people were away yesterday.

Mathseeds Year 3 Workbook © 3P Learning ISBN 978-1-923253-14-8

9 Mrs T likes to add using the compensation strategy: round one number and adjust. For subtraction, she likes to use the jump strategy: break one number into parts. Which do you prefer?

a Underline the question.

b Circle the facts.

Solve the addition equation.

c Use compensation.

34 + 67 =

d Use the jump strategy.

34 + 67 =

10 Solve the subtraction equation.

a Use compensation.

83 – 48 =

b Use the jump strategy.

83 – 48 =

11 Which strategy do you prefer for each operation? Why?

____

____

____

I finished this lesson online.

I can

- Use the compensation strategy (round, adjust) to add and subtract. ☐
- Use the jump strategy (split by place value) to add and subtract. ☐
- Use mental strategies to solve problems or find the missing number. ☐
- Compare the compensation and jump strategies. ☐

We went to

  ISBN 978-1-923253-14-8

1 Fill in the missing part on each line of the frequency chart.

a	**Flavour**	**Tally**	
b	strawberry		15
c	chocolate	卌	10
d	vanilla	卌 卌 卌 卌	
e	caramel	卌 卌	25

2 Answer these questions about the frequency chart.

a What could this frequency chart be counting?

____

b What could be a good title for this data?

____

c How could this data have been collected?

____

d Who could this data have been collected from?

____

3 Answer these questions using the data from the frequency chart.

a What is the highest number of votes for a flavour? ________

b What is the flavour? ______________________________

c What is the lowest number of votes for a flavour? ________

d What is the flavour? ______________________________

e Calculate the difference in votes between those two flavours.

____

Mathseeds Year 3 Workbook ISBN 978-1-923253-14-8

Data 3

Brand of paint	Stayrite	Colour Brite	Hi Lite	Paint Delite
Total votes	10	14	12	13

4. Use the data in the table to fill in the picture graph.

a Decide on a scale and fill in the Key.

b Fill in the horizontal axis with the categories.

c Write a title at the top.

d Put pictures in the graph to show the numbers from the table.

  ISBN 978-1-923253-14-8

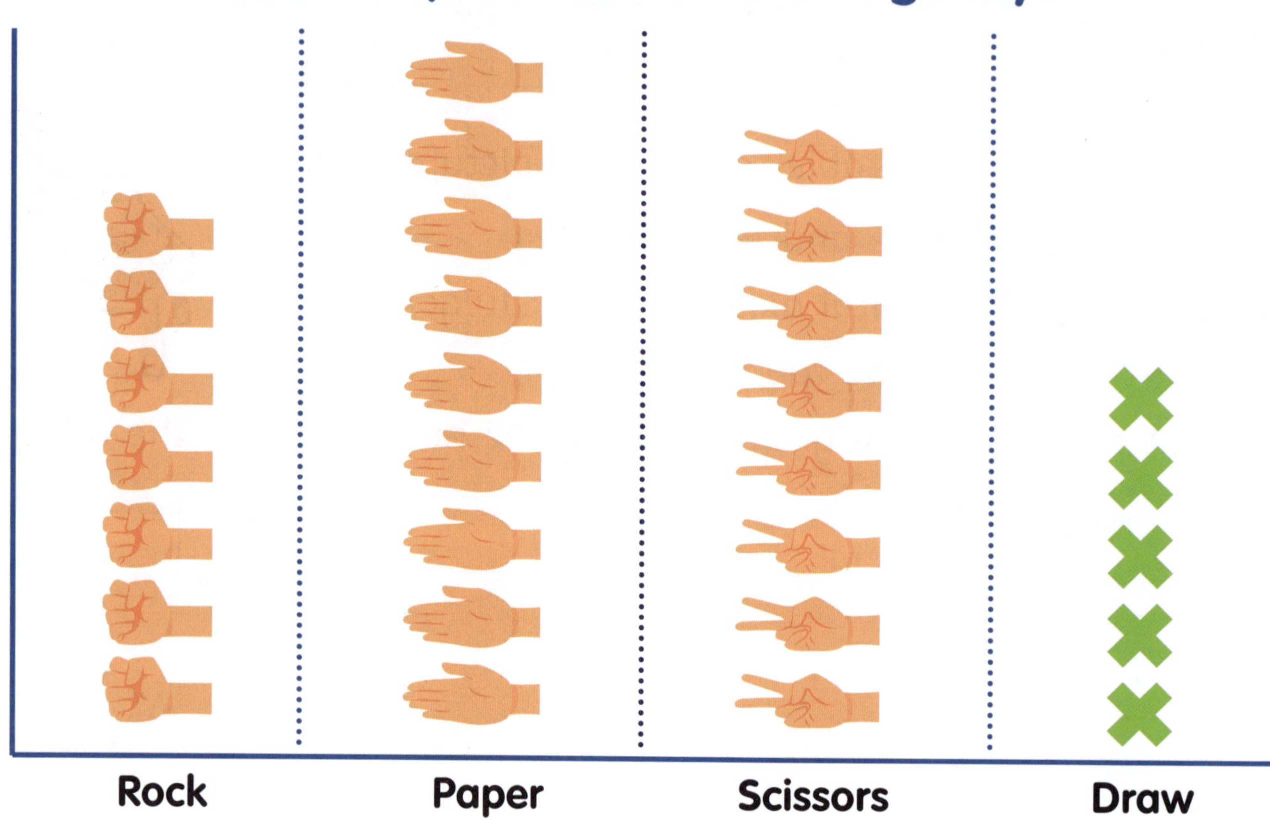

5 Answer these questions based on the picture graph above.

a How many games of Rock-Paper-Scissors were played? ______

b Which play won the most often? ○ rock ○ paper ○ scissors

c Which play was the least successful? ○ rock ○ paper ○ scissors

d What has happened when it is a draw? ______

e If you wanted to make the same play every time, which would you choose? ○ rock ○ paper ○ scissors

f Would this ensure you win 100% of the time? ○ yes ○ no

g Why or why not? ______

Mathseeds Year 3 Workbook © 3P Learning ISBN 978-1-923253-14-8

6 Conduct a survey with your friends or family. Keep your survey question simple, such as favourite foods, colours, pets, sports. Give them four answers to choose from.

a Underline the question. **b** Circle the facts.

c Survey question: ______________________________

d Ask your question. Record the answers using a frequency chart.

Answers	Tallies	Totals

7 Make a scaled picture graph of your data. Fill in:

a the title. **b** the key. **c** the 4 answers. **d** the pictures.

I finished this lesson online.

I can

- Explore how a frequency chart works and interpret its data. ☐
- Draw a scaled picture graph. ☐
- Interpret a scaled picture graph and apply the data to real life. ☐
- Conduct a survey: write a question, collect data, make a graph. ☐

We went to

  ISBN 978-1-923253-14-8

1. Draw a diagram to share the items equally.
2. What fraction of the collection does each person get?

a 2 people sharing 8 balloons.

$\frac{\square}{\square}$

b 3 people sharing 9 party hats.

$\frac{\square}{\square}$

c 4 people sharing 12 cupcakes.

$\frac{\square}{\square}$

d 5 people sharing 10 cups.

$\frac{\square}{\square}$

Mathseeds Year 3 Workbook © 3P Learning ISBN 978-1-923253-14-8

Comparing Fractions

	a What fraction of the collection is each group?	b What is the equivalent fraction?
Eg 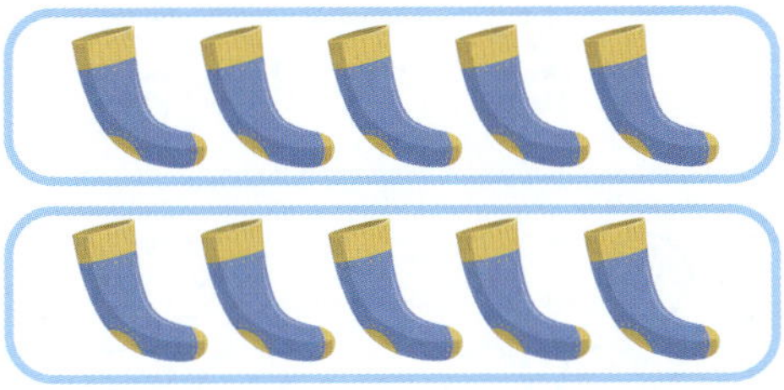	5/10	1/2 of the socks
3 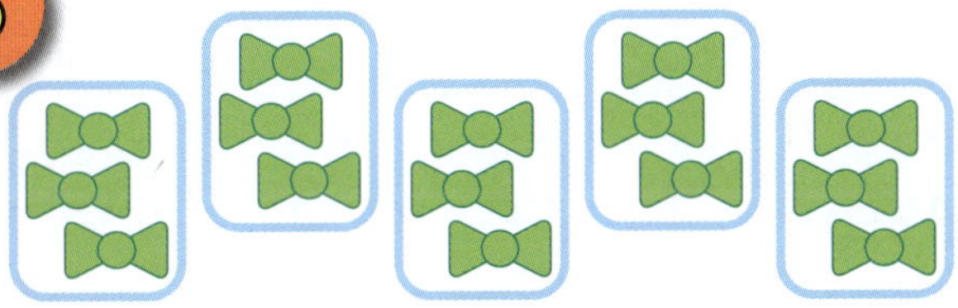	☐/☐	☐/☐ of the bows
4 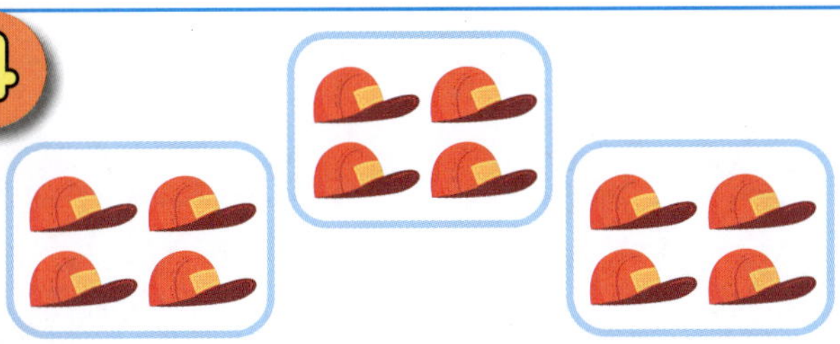	☐/☐	☐/☐ of the hats
5 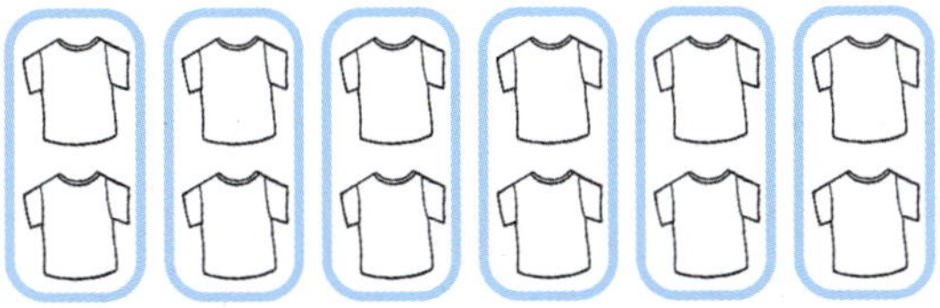	☐/☐	☐/☐ of the shirts
6 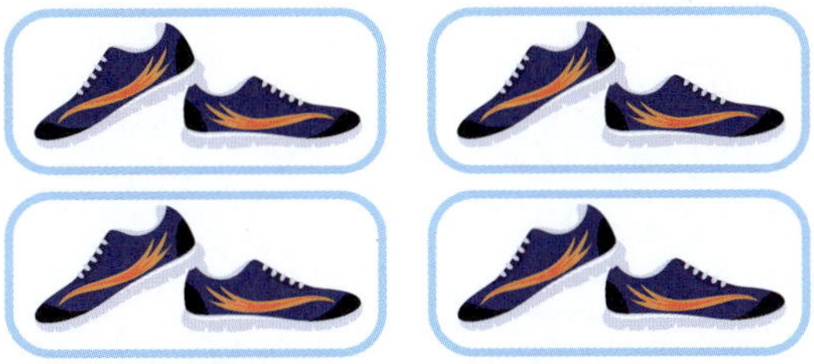	☐/☐	☐/☐ of the shoes
7 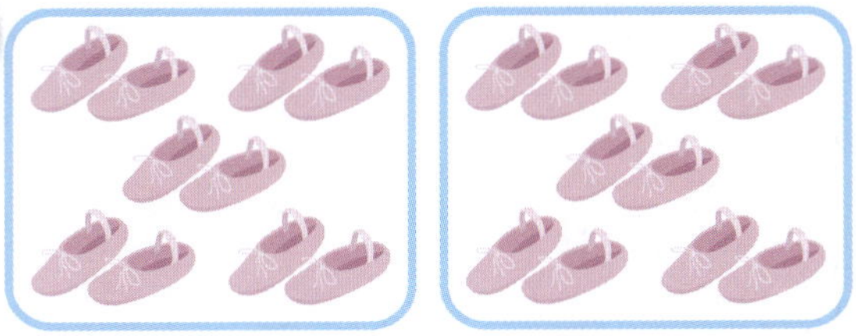	☐/☐	☐/☐ of the shoes

  ISBN 978-1-923253-14-8

8 Colour each fraction of the collection.

9 Write the correct symbol in the box > or < .

a $\frac{3}{6}$ ☐ $\frac{5}{6}$

b $\frac{9}{10}$ ☐ $\frac{6}{10}$

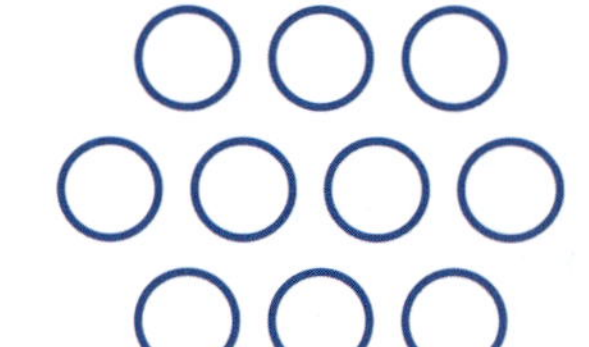

c $\frac{6}{8}$ ☐ $\frac{2}{8}$

d $\frac{1}{4}$ ☐ $\frac{3}{4}$

e $\frac{5}{5}$ ☐ $\frac{2}{5}$

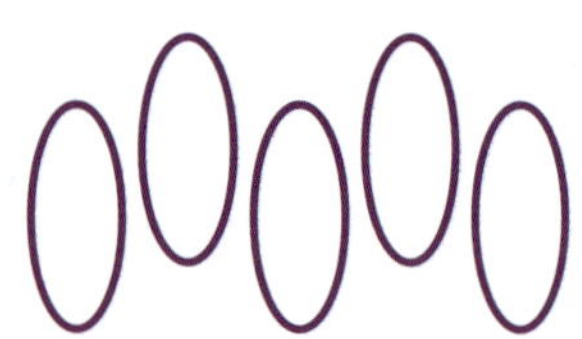
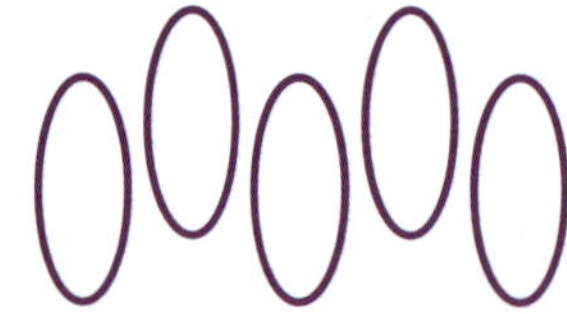

f $\frac{3}{6}$ ☐ $\frac{4}{6}$

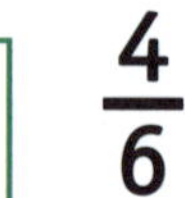
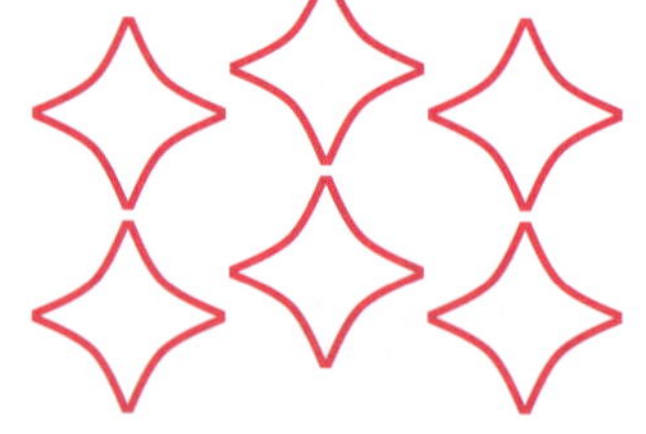
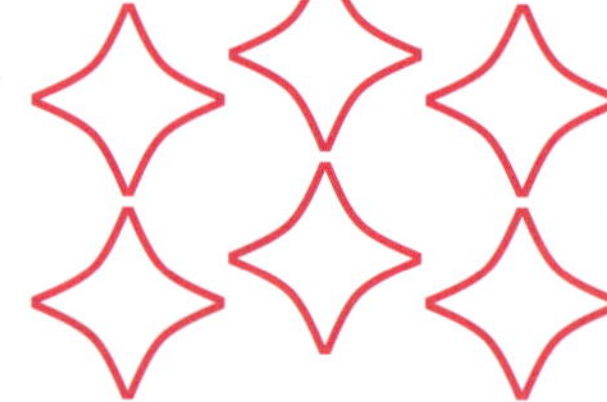

g $\frac{1}{8}$ ☐ $\frac{3}{8}$

h $\frac{4}{10}$ ☐ $\frac{2}{10}$

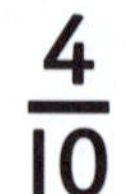
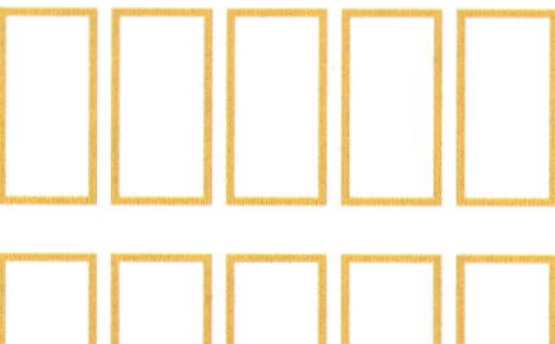

Mathseeds Year 3 Workbook © 3P Learning ISBN 978-1-923253-14-8

10 Ruby and Doc shared 8 balloons in different ways. What fractions could they have made?

a Underline the question. **b** Circle the facts.

c How many balloons are there? ________

d Share them equally between Ruby and Doc.

Ruby	Doc

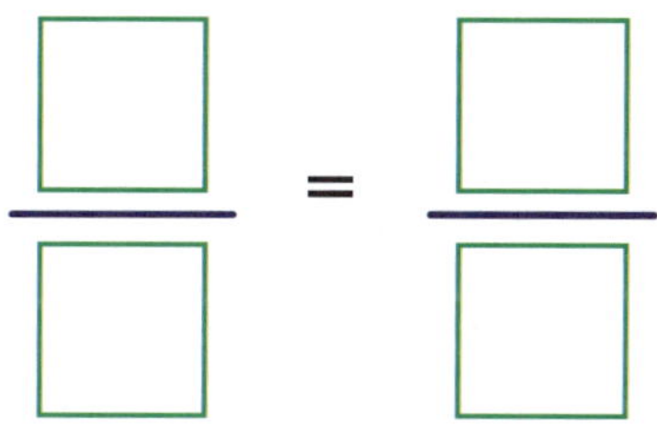

e Write these as fractions.

11 What if Ruby got more of the balloons than Doc?

a Write these as fractions. **b** Fill in the correct symbol. < > =

Ruby	Doc

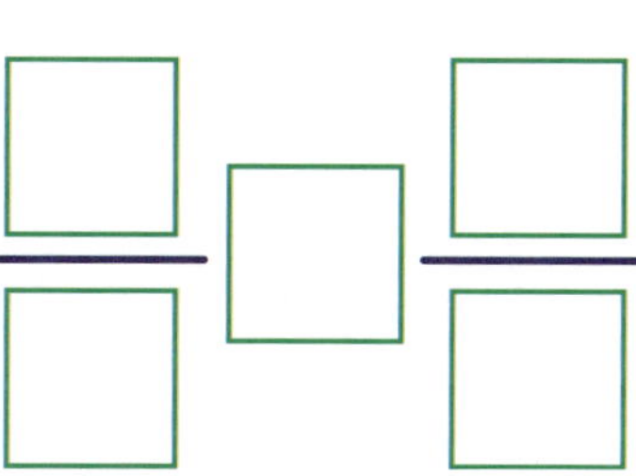

I finished this lesson online.

I can

- Link fractions to sharing groups (division).
- Find equivalent fractions of groups.
- Compare fractions using groups.

We went to

QUIZ

END OF MAP 35 QUIZ

1

a $4 \times 3 =$ ______ b $8 \times 5 =$ ______ c $4 \times 9 =$ ______

d $8 \times 8 =$ ______ e $4 \times 4 =$ ______ f $8 \times 9 =$ ______

2

a $4 \times 2 \times 5 =$ ______ b $2 \times 3 \times 8 =$ ______

3 Pinky is teaching a music lesson. She brings five guitars. How much do these instruments weigh altogether?

____

guitar

4 kg

4 Dash plays the trumpet and the saxophone. When she takes both to a concert, how much weight is she carrying?

____

trumpet

900 g

saxophone

3 kg

5 Write the mass.

Mathseeds Year 3 Workbook © 3P Learning ISBN 978-1-923253-14-8

QUIZ

6 Complete these problems in your head and write the answer.

a $73 + 29 =$ ______ b $33 + 56 =$ ______

c $49 + 18 =$ ______ d $67 + 27 =$ ______

7 Complete the totals.

	Genre		Total
a	sci-fi	卌 卌 卌 卌 卌 卌 卌 卌 卌 卌	
b	fantasy	卌 卌 卌 卌 卌 卌 卌	
c	comedy	卌 卌 卌 卌 卌 卌	
d	adventure	卌 卌 卌 卌 卌 卌 卌	

8 Answer these questions about the data.

a Which is the least popular genre? ______

b Which genres are equally as popular? ______

c How many more sci-fi than comedy books were counted? ______

d How many books were counted altogether? ______

e Where might you count books by genre? ______

9 Dahlia shares a bag of 20 bouncy balls between 5 people.

a How many balls does each person get? ______

b What fraction of the collection does each person get? ______

c What is the equivalent fraction? ______

  ISBN 978-1-923253-14-8

Hurray!

YOU COMPLETED

MAP 35

YOU CAN:

- [ ] Answer **multiplication equations** with 2 or 3 multipliers.
- [ ] Add and multiply **masses** to solve problems.
- [ ] Read a dial **scale** to measure mass in grams **g** and kilograms **kg**.
- [ ] Use mental strategies to answer **addition equations**.
- [ ] Complete a frequency chart and interpret the **data**.
- [ ] Solve a **sharing** problem using **fractions**.

IDEA

Signed:

Dated:

Mathseeds Year 3 Workbook © 3P Learning ISBN 978-1-923253-14-8

FUN SPOT 5

Write a number in each box.

Each row and column should have one each of 1, 2, 3 and 4.

In each outlined section write the numbers that use the operation to make the given answer. There could be more than one possibility, eg +5 could be 1 + 4 or 2 + 3.

1

+3		−1	+7
−1			
+5	1	+9	
			3

2

+6	−1		+3
	−3	2	
		+6	−1
4			

3

+9			+6
−1	+7		
	−3		
−1		+5	

4

2	+8	−2	
		+7	+5
+5	−1		
			4

1

9283 3982 8392 9823 3928

a Circle the odd numbers.

b Write in order from smallest to largest.

____

c Write the largest number in expanded form.

____

d Write the smallest number in words.

____

e If you add the largest and smallest numbers, will the answer be **odd** or **even**? Circle.

f Write the number: **1 more than** **10 more than** **100 more than**

The middle number __________ __________ __________

2 Continue these patterns.

3 What is the rule?

a 123, 234, 345, 456, 567, ______, ______, ______ ____________

b 500, 450, 475, 425, 450, ______, ______, ______ ____________

c 1, 1, 2, 3, 5, 8, ______, ______, ______, ______ ____________

4 Make these number sentences equivalent.

a 78 – 35 = 27 + ________

b 59 + 26 = 99 – ________

c 13 + 68 = ____________

d 94 – 42 = ____________

Mathseeds Year 3 Workbook © 3P Learning ISBN 978-1-923253-14-8

5 Complete the number fact families.

629 + 131 = ________ 275 + 432 = ________

________ + ________ = ________ ________ + ________ = ________

________ − ________ = ________ ________ − ________ = ________

________ − ________ = ________ ________ − ________ = ________

6 Write an algorithm to find the answer. Don't forget to trade.

a 378 + 527 = **b** 725 + 275 = **c** 118 + 697 =

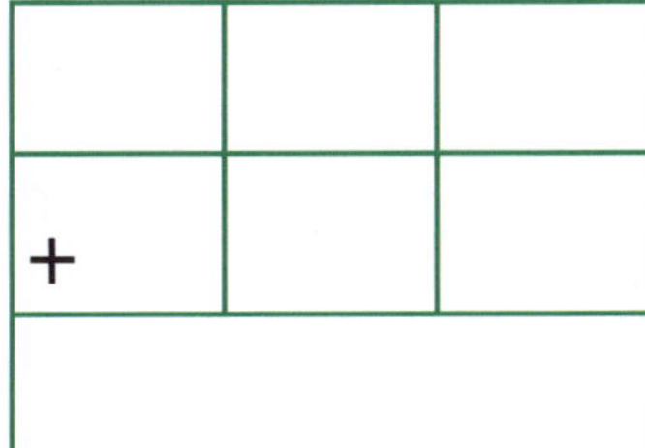

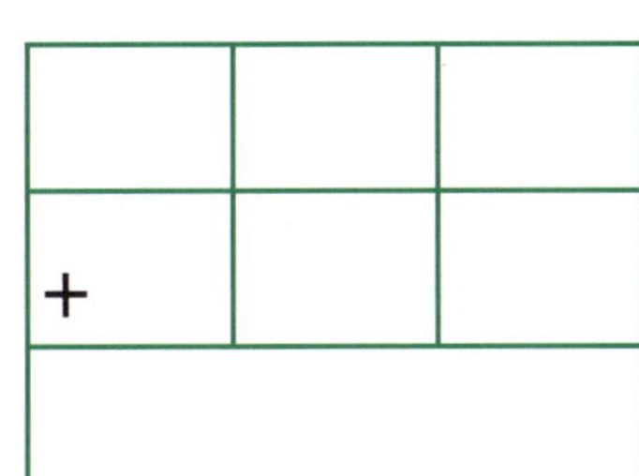

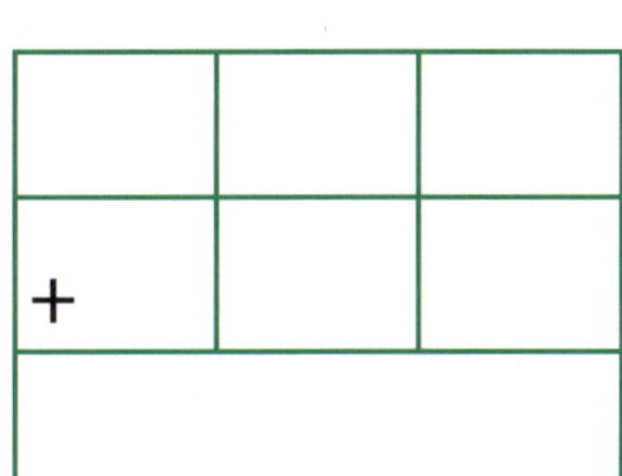

7 Katy buys a $7.85 sandwich and a $4.50 drink. She pays with a $20 note.

a What is her total cost? ________

b What is her change? ________

c How could this change be made in notes and coins?

____

d Show a different way this change could be made in notes and coins.

____

8

a $2 \times 9 =$ ______ b $3 \times 7 =$ ______ c $4 \times 8 =$ ______

d $5 \times 5 =$ ______ e $8 \times 7 =$ ______ f $10 \times 9 =$ ______

g $5 \times 2 \times 7 =$ ______ h $3 \times 3 \times 4 =$ ______

i $18 \div 2 =$ ______ j $18 \div 3 =$ ______ k $50 \div 4 =$ ______

l $45 \div 5 =$ ______ m $40 \div 8 =$ ______ n $60 \div 10 =$ ______

9 Draw an array and solve the problem.

Mark eats 2 apples, 3 days a week.
How many apples does he eat in 4 weeks?

a ______ × ______ = ______ b ______ × ______ = ______ apples

10 Fill in the fraction number line.

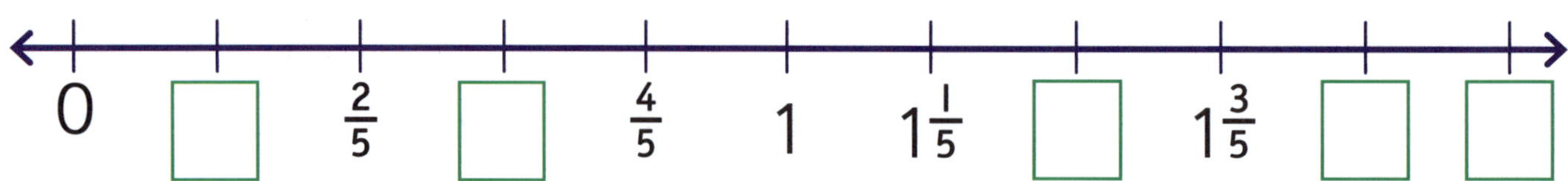

11 Use the correct symbol: < or >.

a $\frac{1}{2}$ ☐ $\frac{1}{4}$ b $\frac{3}{6}$ ☐ $\frac{4}{6}$ c $\frac{4}{8}$ ☐ $\frac{2}{8}$

12 Ash has 16 cards. He gives each person 4 cards and has none left.

a How many people does Ash share his cards with? ______

b What fraction of the collection does each person get? ______

c What is the equivalent fraction? ______

 Mathseeds Year 3 Workbook © 3P Learning ISBN 978-1-923253-14-8

13 Draw a line of symmetry on the patterns that are symmetrical.

14 Draw a net for these shapes.

a rectangular prism

b triangular prism

15 Convert between units of measurement.

a 1 L = ________ mL

b 4000 mL = ________

c $3\frac{1}{2}$ L = ________ mL

d 1000 g = ________ kg

e 2.5 kg = ________ g

f 3500 g = ________ kg

16 Jose's kitchen is 5 m long and 3 m wide. What is the area of his kitchen? ______________

17 Stacey worked from 8:55 am to 5:22 pm. How long did she work? ______________

18 There are 4 red, 5 black and 3 blue balls in a bag. What is the chance of drawing out a blue ball without looking?

_____ in _____

  ISBN 978-1-923253-14-8

LESSON 176 TIMES TABLES · 3 · MENTAL FACTS

1 How many leaves? Complete the equations.

a ______ × 3 = ______

b ______ × 3 = ______

c ______ × 3 = ______

d ______ × 3 = ______

e ______ × 3 = ______

f ______ × 3 = ______

2 Find the answers.

×	0	1	2	3	4	5	6	7	8	9	10
3											

3 Complete.

a 3 × 2 = 2 × 3 = ______

b 3 × 5 = ______ × 3 = ______

c 3 × 7 = ______ × ______ = ______

d 3 × 8 = ______ × ______ = ______

e 3 × 3 = ______ × ______ = ______

f 3 × 6 = ______ × ______ = ______

Mathseeds Year 3 Workbook © 3P Learning ISBN 978-1-923253-14-8

Times Tables
×3 ×6

4 Find the answers.

×	0	1	2	3	4	5	6	7	8	9	10
6											

5 How many legs? Complete the equations.

a ______ × 6 = ______

b ______ × 6 = ______

c ______ × 6 = ______

d ______ × 6 = ______

e ______ × 6 = ______

f ______ × 6 = ______

g ______ × 6 = ______

h ______ × 6 = ______

  ISBN 978-1-923253-14-8

6 Colour the arrays to show the two sums. Then fill in the answers.

a

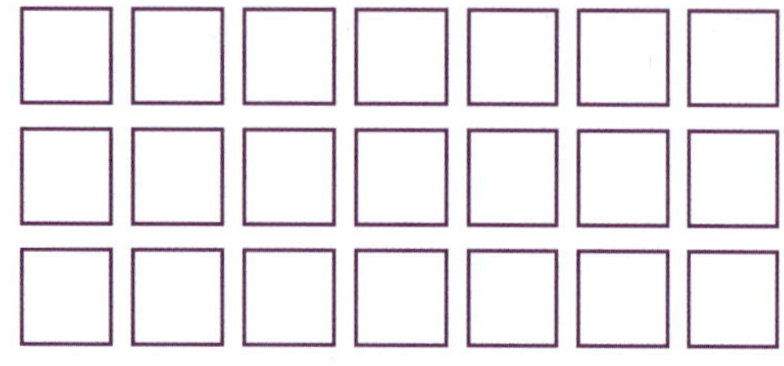

$5 \times 3 + 2 \times 3 =$

______ + ______ = ______

$7 \times 3 =$ ______

b

$5 \times 3 + 4 \times 3 =$

______ + ______ = ______

$9 \times 3 =$ ______

c

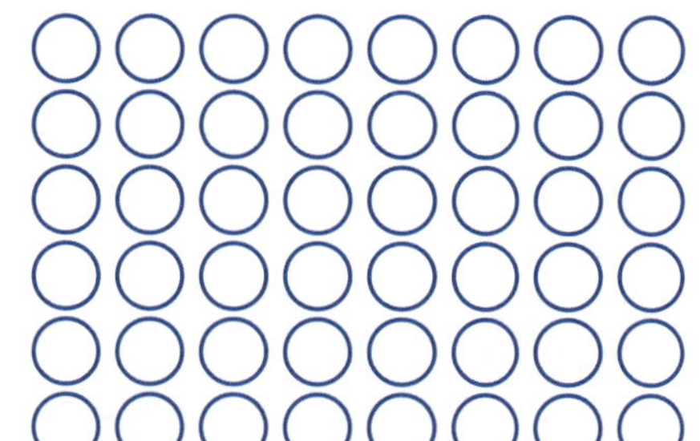

$4 \times 6 + 4 \times 6 =$

______ + ______ = ______

$8 \times 6 =$ ______

d

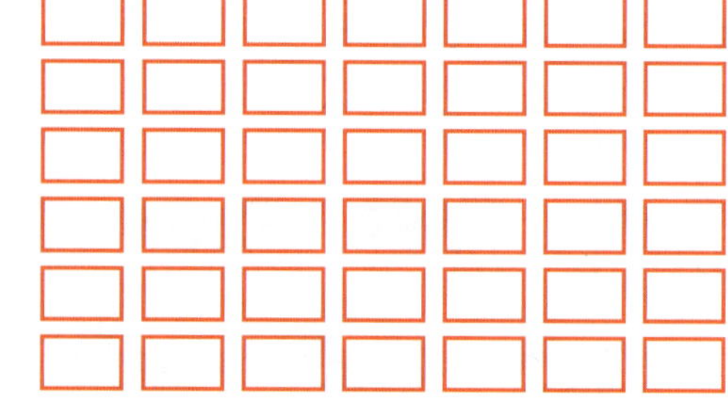

$5 \times 6 + 2 \times 6 =$

______ + ______ = ______

$7 \times 6 =$ ______

7 Complete the equations.

a $8 \times 9 =$

_____ × 9 + _____ × 9 =

_____ + _____ = _____

b $7 \times 9 =$

_____ × 9 + _____ × 9 =

_____ + _____ = _____

c $7 \times 8 =$

_____ × _____ + _____ × _____ =

_____ + _____ = _____

d $8 \times 8 =$

_____ × _____ + _____ × _____ =

_____ + _____ = _____

Mathseeds Year 3 Workbook © 3P Learning ISBN 978-1-923253-14-8

Times Tables ×3 ×6

8 Split one factor to make easier sums and find the answer.

a Ming scored 9 points on the dart board 9 times. How many points did he score altogether? ______

b Dale found 6 pens in 8 different places. How many pens does she have now? ______

c Gordon knocked down 8 bowling pins 7 times. How many pins did he knock down in total? ______

d Aura won 7 chests each with 6 gems in them. How many gems did she collect? ______

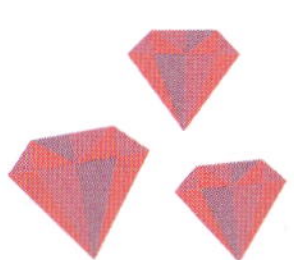

9 Find the answer.

a Hans ordered 7 pizzas. Each pizza had 9 olives on it. Hans picked them all off. How many was that? ______

b Vultan put 6 little tomatoes on each of 6 plates. How many tomatoes did he use in total? ______

I finished this lesson online.

I can
- Write multiplication equations based on groups. ☐
- Fill in a multiplication table for ×3 and ×6. ☐
- Use the commutative property of multiplication to write equations. ☐
- Use the distributive property to multiply larger numbers. ☐

We went to

1 Name the parts of the angle.

arm
angle
vertex
arm

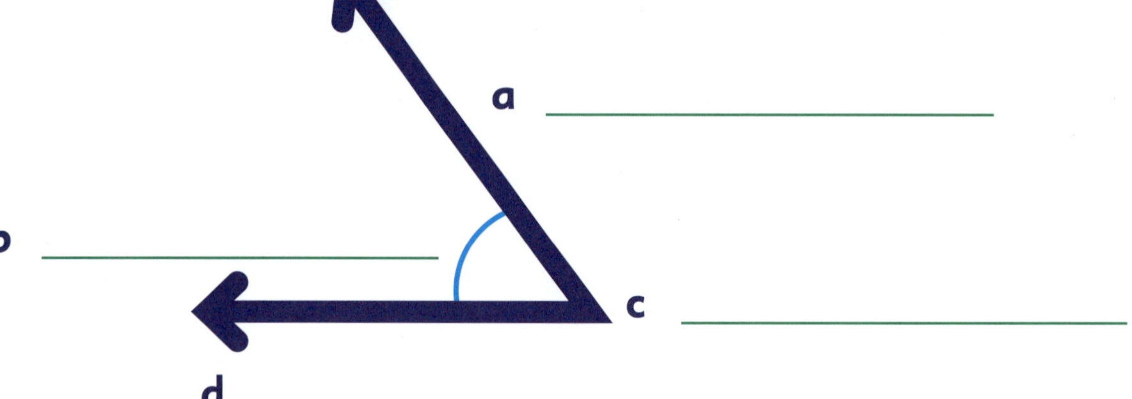

2 Which angles are the same size?

a

b

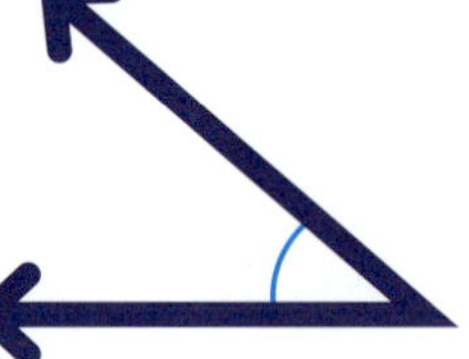

c

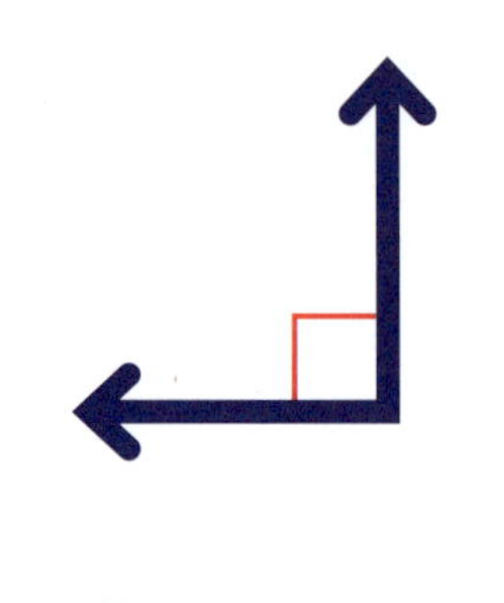

d

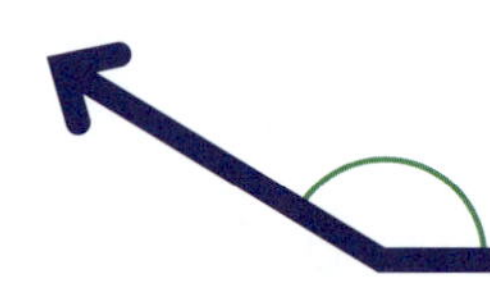

e

f

g

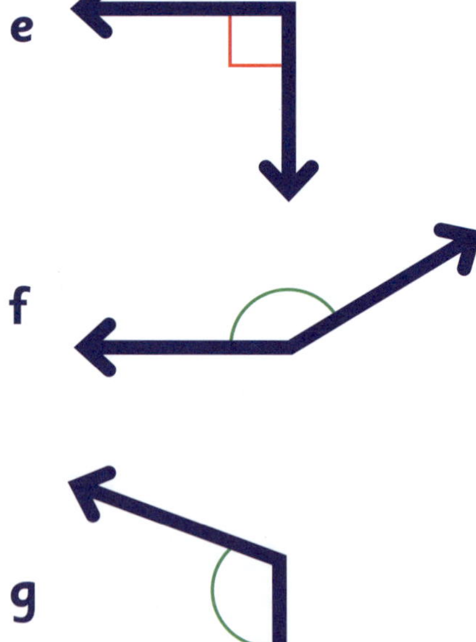

h

Mathseeds Year 3 Workbook © 3P Learning ISBN 978-1-923253-14-8

Angles

3 Colour the right angle red.

a
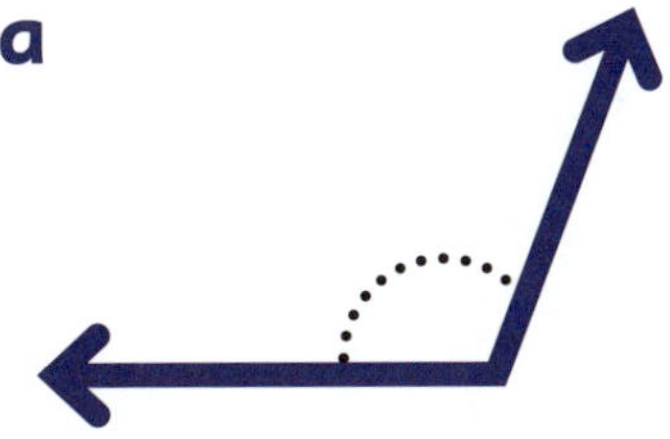

b
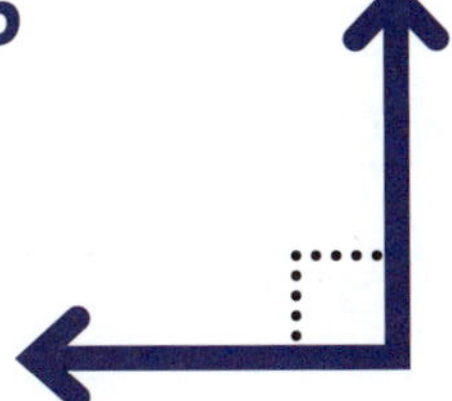

c
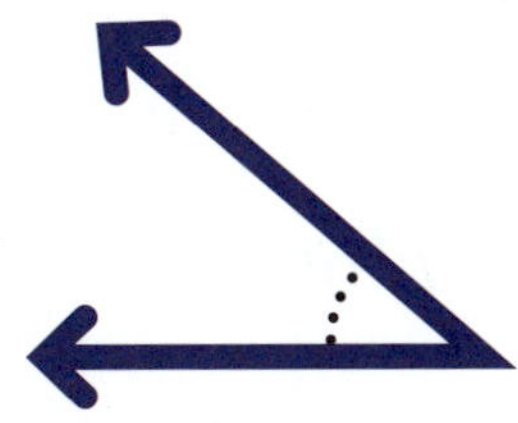

4 Draw the right angle symbols in red. Eg

a
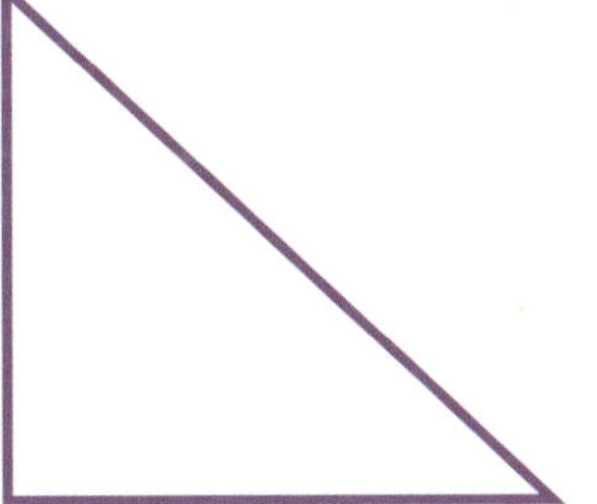

b

c

d

e
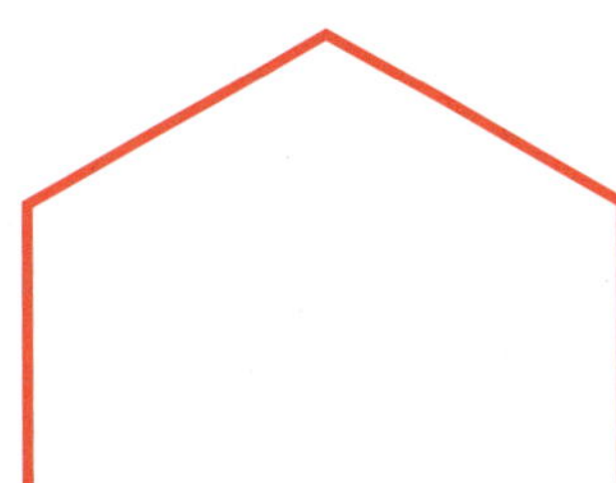

f

5 Complete these right angle triangles.

  ISBN 978-1-923253-14-8

LESSON 177 ANGLES

6

a Which is a right angle? ________

b Which is smaller than a right angle? ________

c Which is larger than a right angle? ________

A 

B 

C 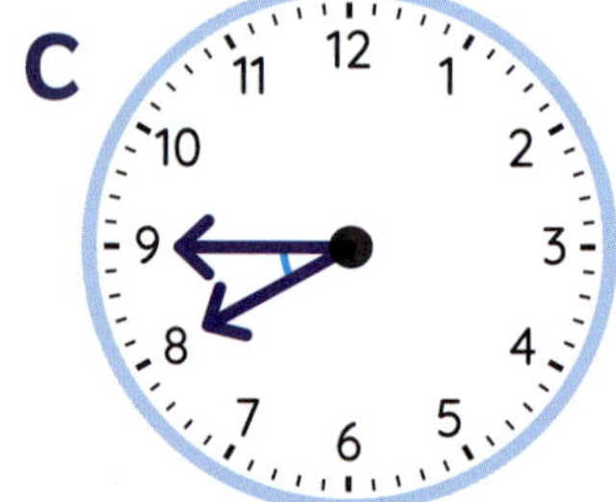

7 Draw the missing clock arms. Make 4 different right angles.

a 

b 

c 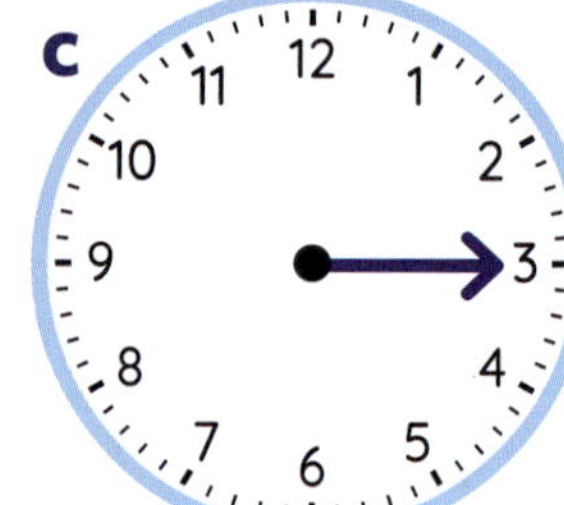

d 

8 Make 4 angles **smaller** than a right angle.

a 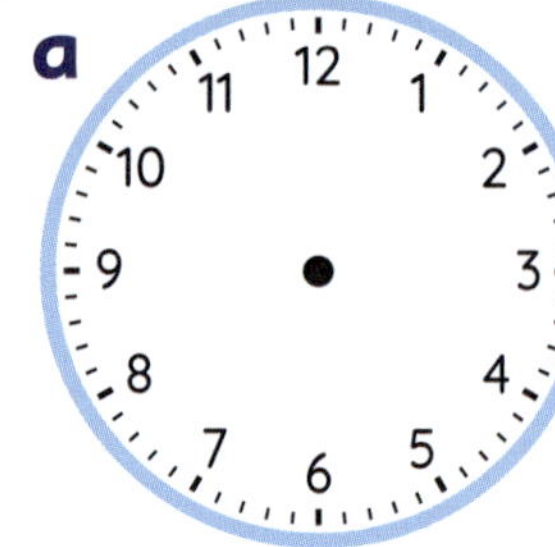

b 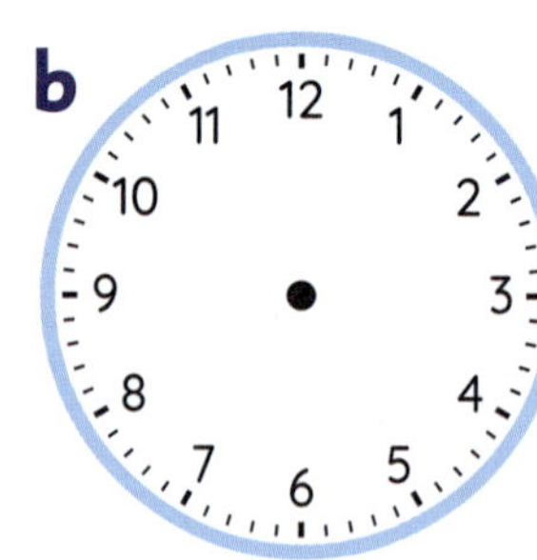

c 

d 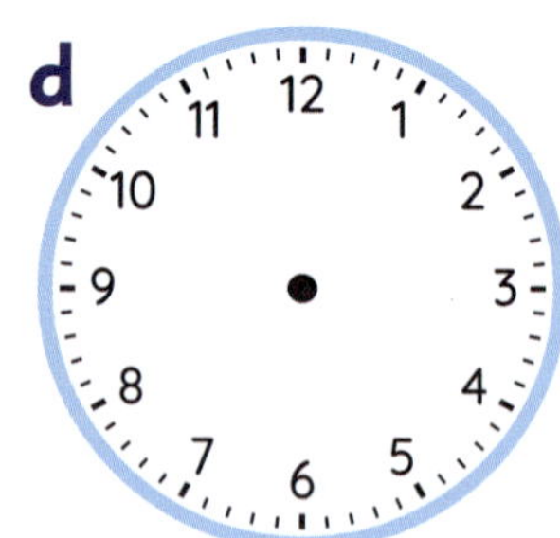

9 Make 4 angles **larger** than a right angle.

a 

b 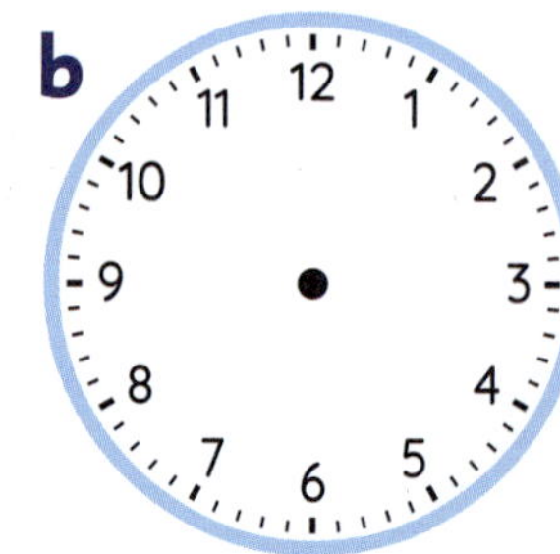

c 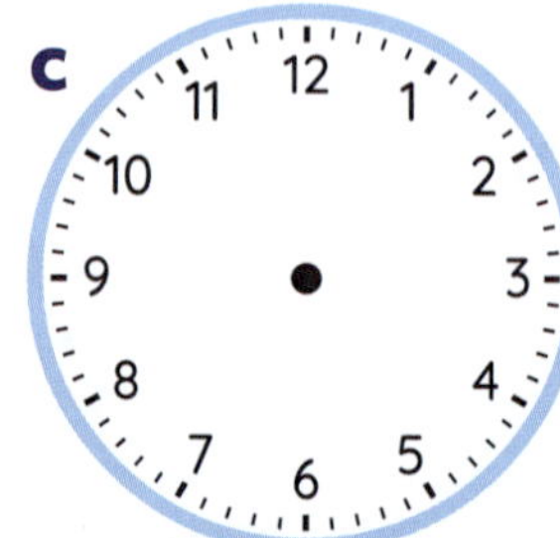

d 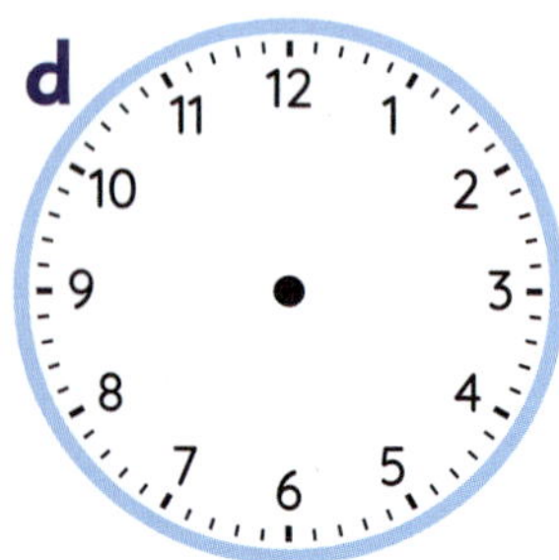

Mathseeds Year 3 Workbook © 3P Learning ISBN 978-1-923253-14-8

10 Use a set of pattern blocks to make the shape of an animal. Draw the outline and then classify the angles.

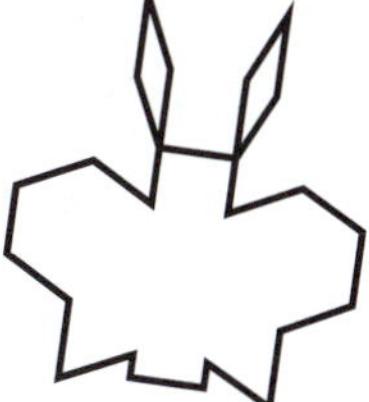

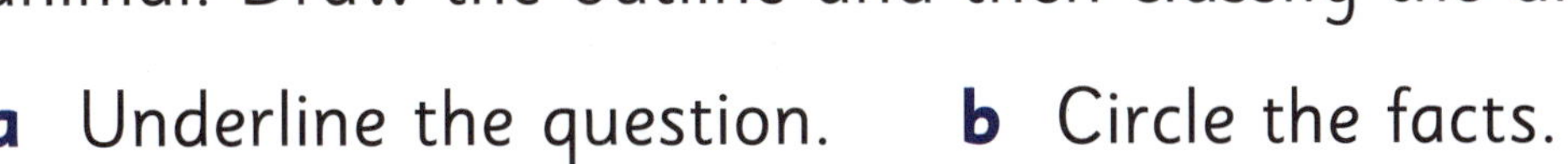

a Underline the question. b Circle the facts.

c What is an angle? ______________________

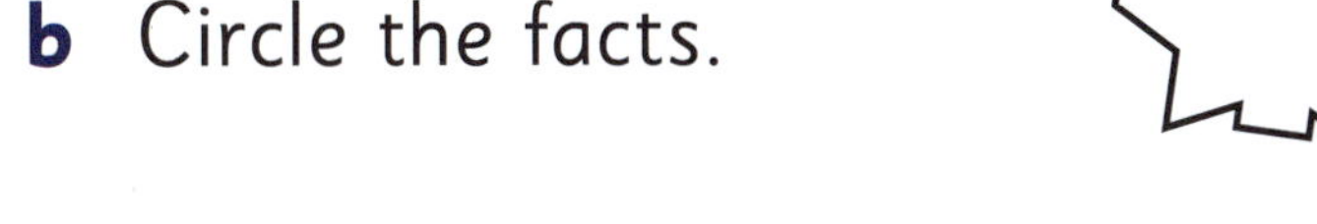

11 Draw your outline here.

12 a Put a red square in each right angle.

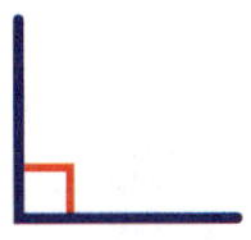

b Put a green arc in the angles which are larger than a right angle.

c Put a blue arc in the angles which are smaller than a right angle.

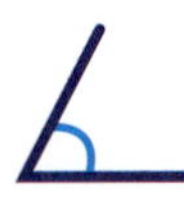

I finished this lesson online.

I can
- Name the parts of an angle and identify a right angle. ☐
- Compare angles visually. ☐
- Classify angles in relation to a right angle. ☐

We went to

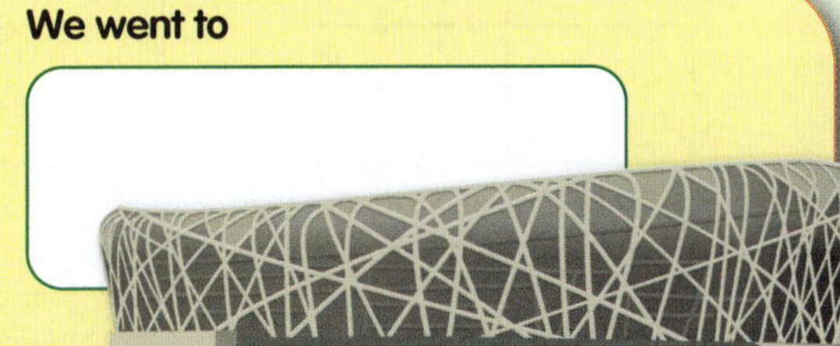

  ISBN 978-1-923253-14-8

Subtraction with Regrouping

LESSON 178 SUBTRACTION WITH REGROUPING

1 Calculate the answer. Use regrouping.

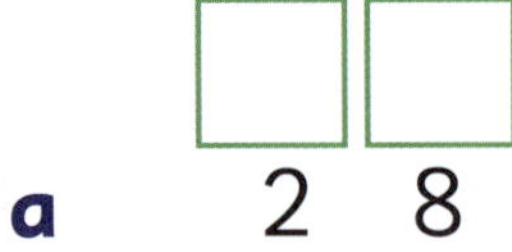

a 28 − 19 = ____

b 65 − 47 = ____

c 81 − 52 = ____

d 73 − 36 = ____

e 94 − 86 = ____

f 57 − 28 = ____

g 32 − 15 = ____

h 43 − 9 = ____

2 Write the algorithm and find the answer.

a 91 – 79 =

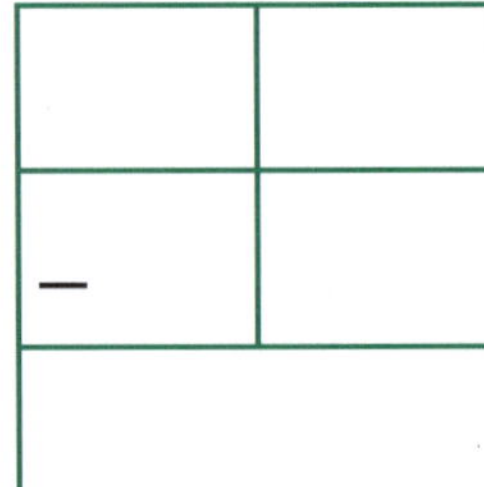

b 14 – 8 =

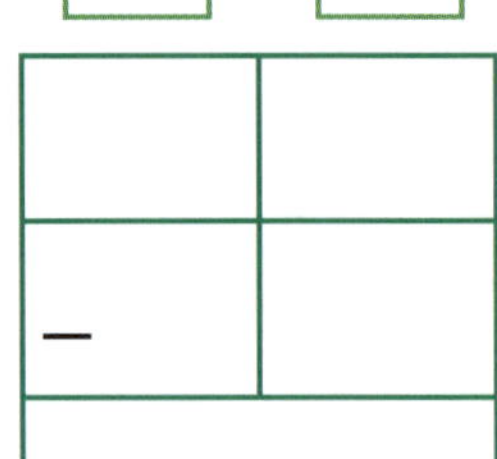

c 53 – 37 =

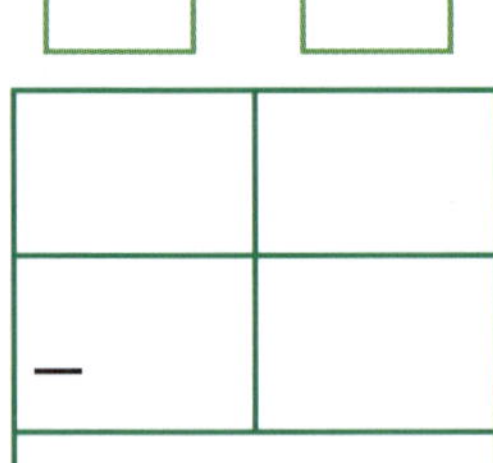

d 75 – 28 =

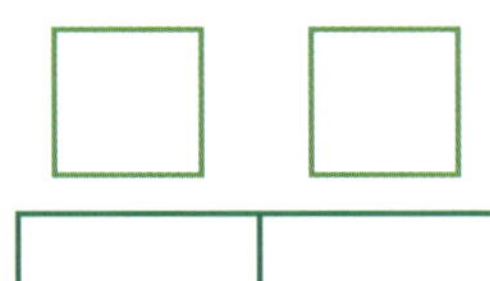

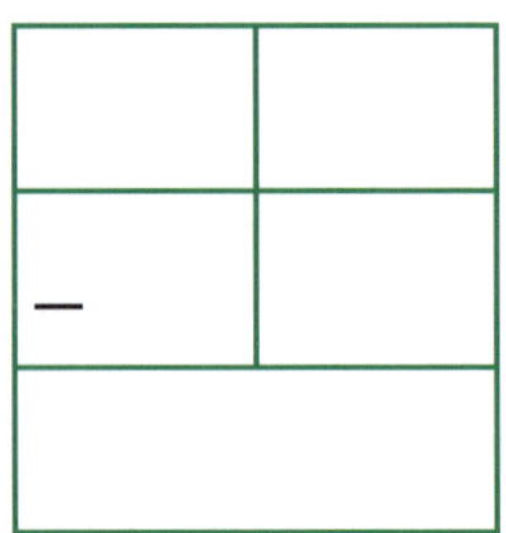

e 64 – 46 =

f 91 – 62 =

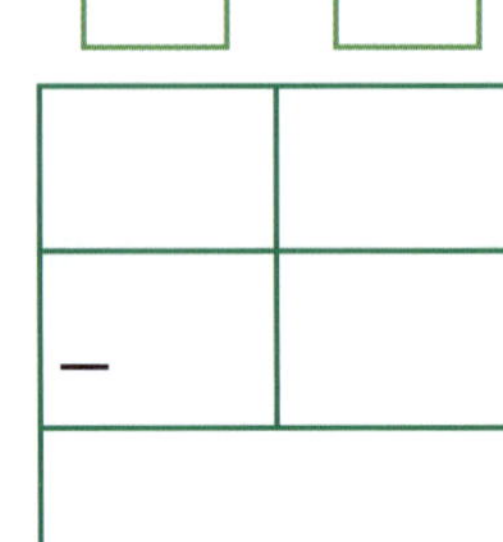

g 80 – 39 =

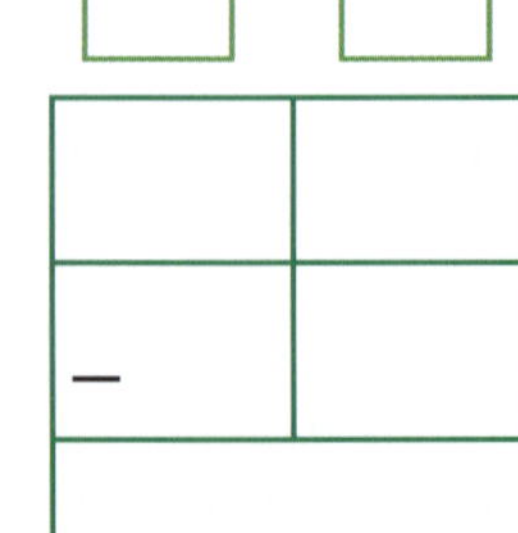

h 47 – 29 =

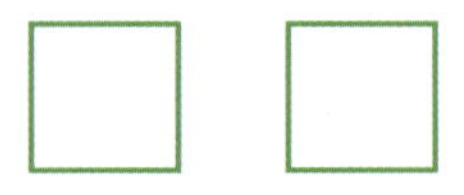

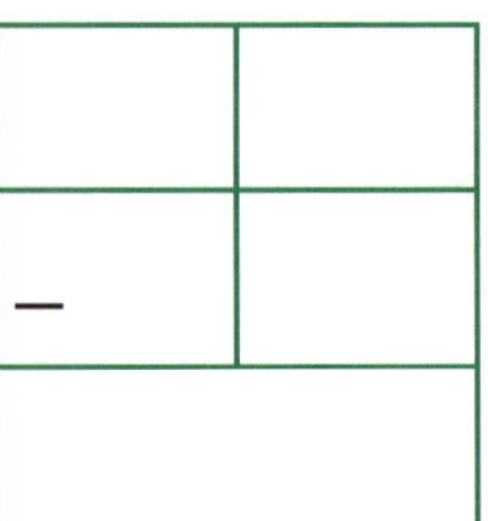

Mathseeds Year 3 Workbook © 3P Learning ISBN 978-1-923253-14-8

3 Calculate the answer. Use regrouping.

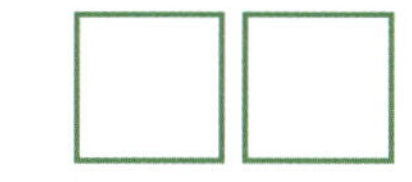

a 374 − 182 = ____

b 526 − 256 = ____

c 439 − 168 = ____

d 917 − 795 = ____

e 803 − 640 = ____

f 748 − 371 = ____

g 657 − 480 = ____

h 209 − 24 = ____

4 Write the algorithm and find the answer.

a 962 − 591 =

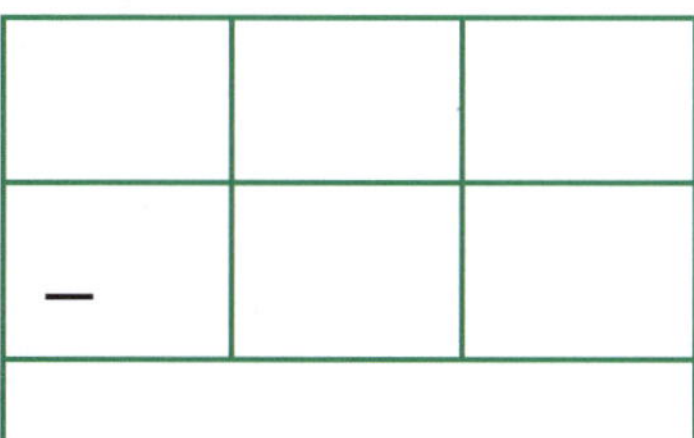

b 815 − 33 =

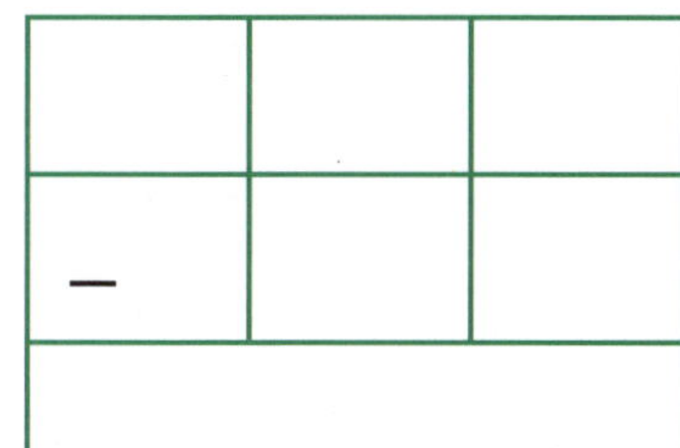

c 380 − 190 =

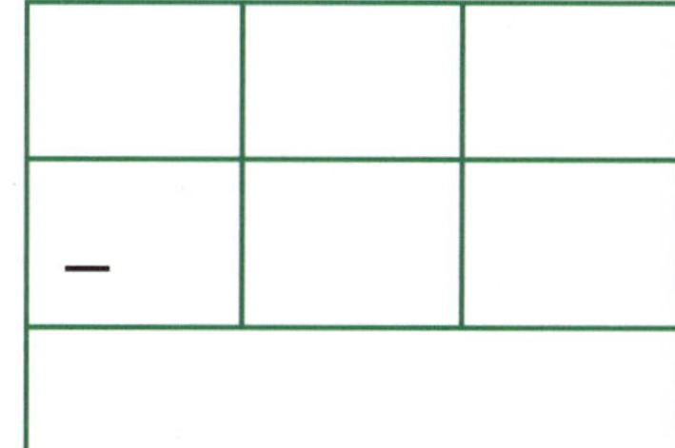

d 508 − 237 =

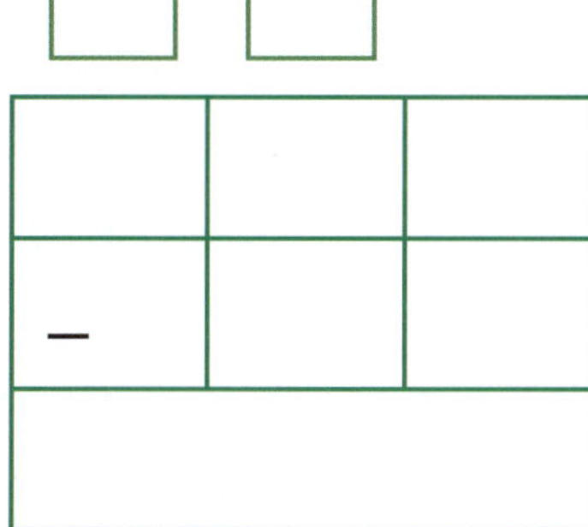

e 756 − 474 =

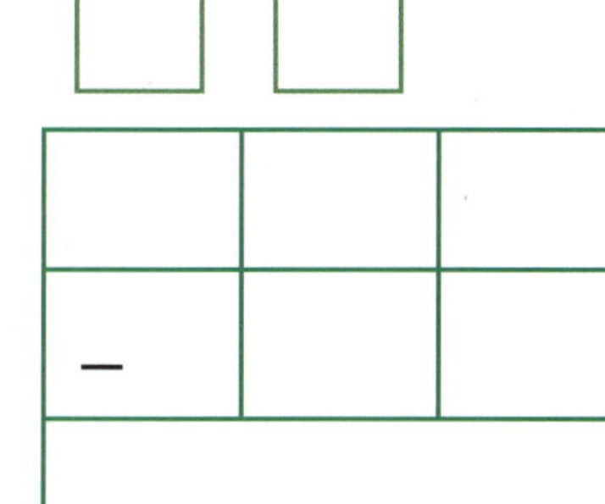

f 649 − 361 =

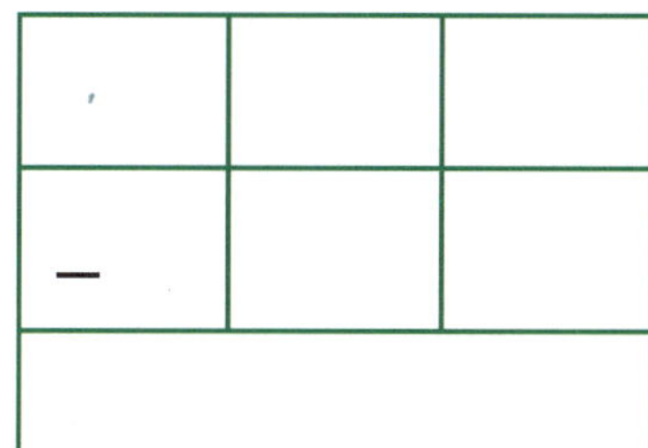

  ISBN 978-1-923253-14-8

5 Calculate the answer. Use regrouping.

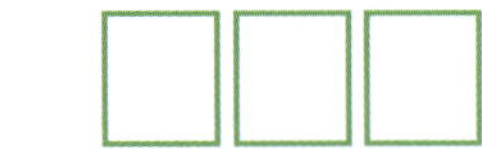

a $\begin{array}{r} 281 \\ -\ \ 95 \\ \hline \end{array}$

b $\begin{array}{r} 766 \\ -\ 487 \\ \hline \end{array}$

c $\begin{array}{r} 332 \\ -\ 163 \\ \hline \end{array}$

d $\begin{array}{r} 555 \\ -\ 278 \\ \hline \end{array}$

e $\begin{array}{r} 943 \\ -\ 757 \\ \hline \end{array}$

f $\begin{array}{r} 608 \\ -\ 319 \\ \hline \end{array}$

g $\begin{array}{r} 414 \\ -\ 336 \\ \hline \end{array}$

h $\begin{array}{r} 820 \\ -\ 624 \\ \hline \end{array}$

6 Write the algorithm and find the answer.

a 421 – 252 =

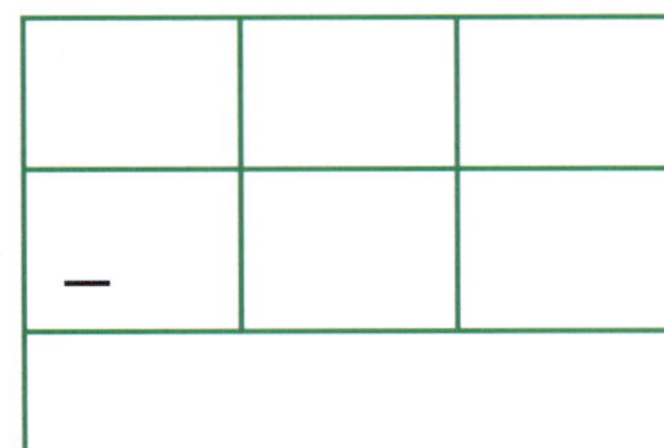

b 345 – 179 =

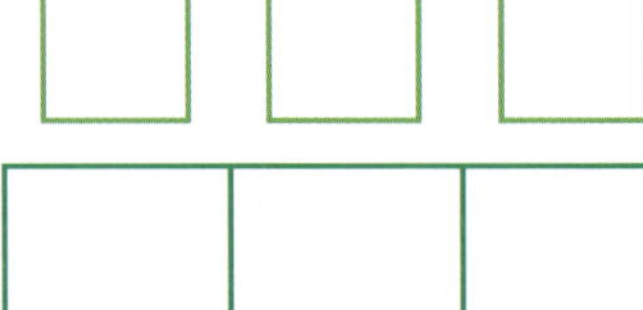

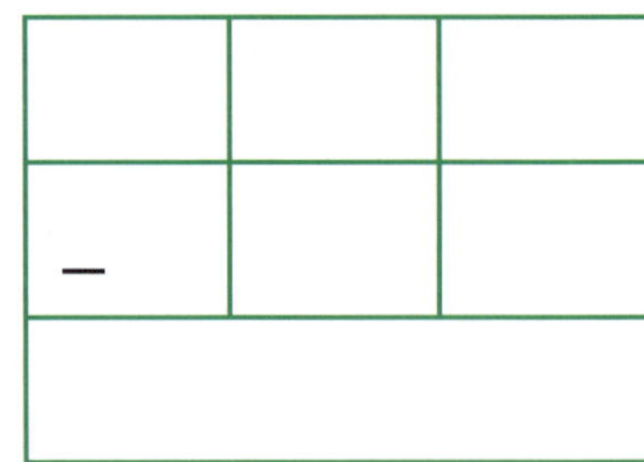

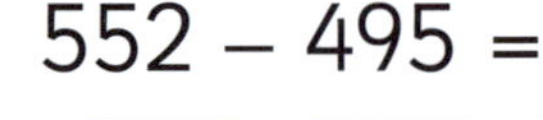

c 552 – 495 =

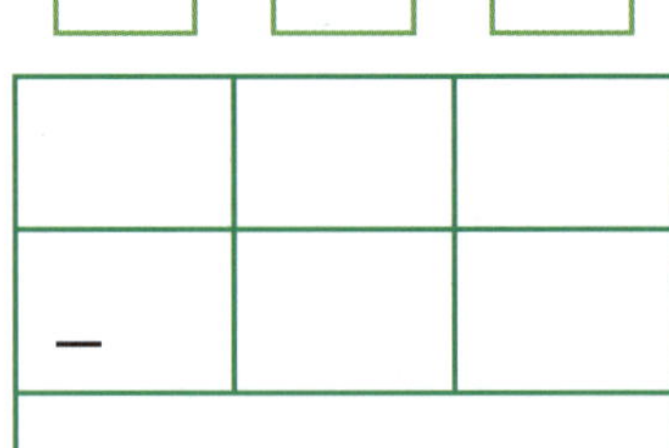

d 234 – 88 =

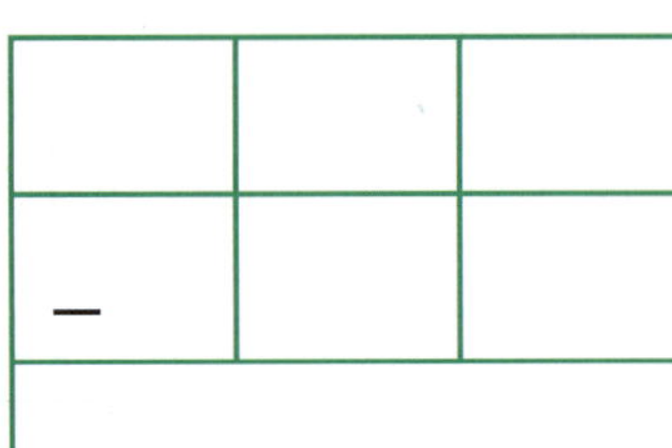

e 618 – 349 =

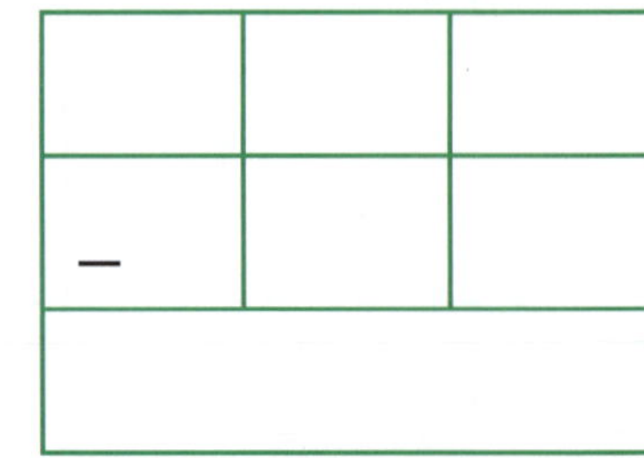

f 903 – 786 =

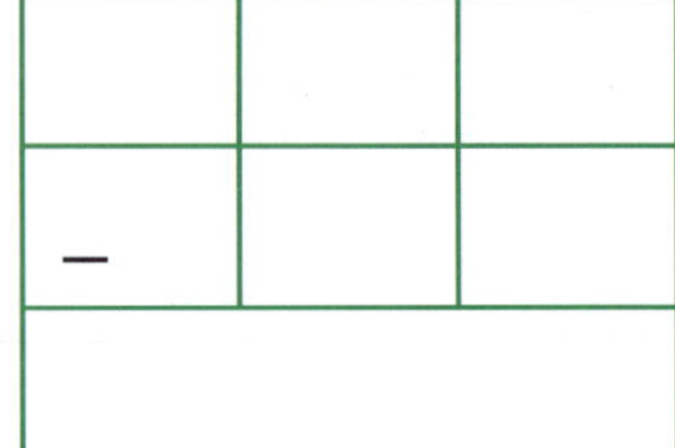

Mathseeds Year 3 Workbook © 3P Learning ISBN 978-1-923253-14-8

Write the algorithm and find the answer.

7. Mango makes 35 sandwiches. The team eats 17 of them! How many left? ____________

8. Doc packs 22 water bottles. He hands out 15 at lunch. How many left? ____________

9. Waldo counted 124 steps. Ruby counted 98 steps. What is the difference? ____________

10. Mrs T has to make it down 370 steps. She has done 259 steps so far. How many steps to go? ____________

11. Dizzy drove for 235 mins altogether. If the return trip only took 89 mins, how long did it take to get there?

____

12. Ruby packed 520 mL of sunscreen. They used 256 mL altogether. How much sunscreen is left? ____________

I finished this lesson online.

I can

- Explore regrouping or trading in subtraction algorithms. ☐
- Use vertical algorithms to subtract 2 and 3-digit numbers. ☐
- Solve problems using vertical subtraction algorithms. ☐

We went to

  ISBN 978-1-923253-14-8

LESSON 179 COMPARING TIMES

1 How much time is shown on each stopwatch?

a

______ minutes

b

______ hours +

______ minutes

c

______ hours +

______ minutes

d

e

f

2 Write the time on the stopwatch.

a one hour and forty-five minutes

b two hours and nineteen minutes

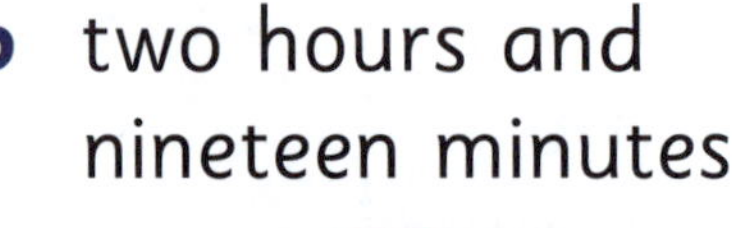

c thirty-one minutes

d four hours and fifty-two minutes

e eight minutes

f three hours and twenty-seven minutes

Mathseeds Year 3 Workbook © 3P Learning ISBN 978-1-923253-14-8

Comparing Times

Homework Times

Who?	Time
Mango	1:21
Ruby	1:18
Doc	0:58
Waldo	1:47
Dizzy	1:35

3. Compare the times and answer the questions.

a Who finished their homework fastest? ______________________

b Who took longest to complete their homework? ______________________

c Whose time was in the middle? ______________________

d Who was second fastest? ______________________

4. Write the names in order from shortest time to longest time.

______________________ ______________________ ______________________

______________________ ______________________

Bath Times

Who?	Time
Mango	0:59
Ruby	1:03
Doc	0:25
Waldo	1:31
Dizzy	0:47

5. Compare the times and answer the questions.

a Who was quickest in the bath? ______________________

b Who stayed longest in the bath? ______________________

c Which two times are closest in length? ______________________

d What is the difference between the longest and shortest times? ______________________

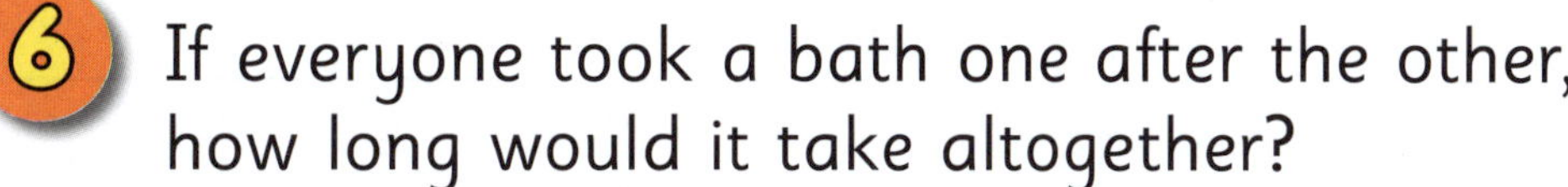

6. If everyone took a bath one after the other, how long would it take altogether? ______________________

  ISBN 978-1-923253-14-8

7 Use the number line.

a Add 35 minutes to 3:15.

b Add 42 minutes to 11:32.

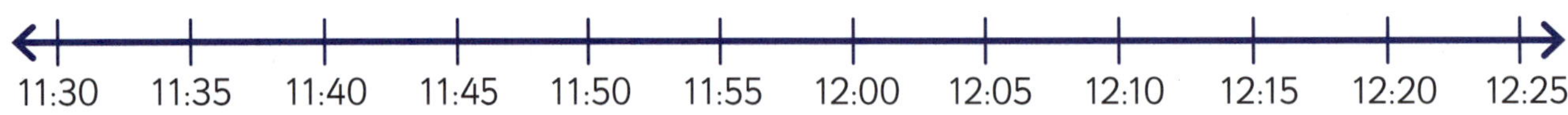

c Add 58 minutes to 8:24.

8 Use the number line.

a Add 1 hour and 23 minutes to 1:05.

b Add 3 hours and 17 minutes to 5:51.

c Add 2 hours and 9 minutes to 10:46.

9 Find the later time.

a 12:41 → 1 hr 39 mins → ____________

b 9:19 → 2 hrs 14 mins → ____________

c 2:58 → 45 mins → ____________

d 6:24 → 1 hr 55 mins → ____________

Mathseeds Year 3 Workbook ISBN 978-1-923253-14-8

10 Everyone was late for lunch today! Dizzy was 15 mins late. Doc was 6 mins late. Ruby was 12 mins late. Mango was 9 mins late. Waldo was 18 mins late. And Mrs T was 21 mins late. Mrs T had lunch at 12:51 pm. At what time did the others have lunch?

a Underline the question. **b** Circle the facts.

c Think about the facts. What time was lunch supposed to be?

____

11 Use a number line to work out everyone's late lunchtime.

a Dizzy's lunchtime: __________ **b** Doc's lunchtime: __________

c Ruby: __________ **d** Mango: __________ **e** Waldo: __________

12 Is there another way you could have solved this time problem? Try your other strategy here.

I finished this lesson online.

I can

- Read and write amounts of time in words and digital format. ☐
- Compare and order amounts of time in hours and minutes. ☐
- Add time with and without a number line. ☐
- Solve a complex word problem involving time. ☐

We went to

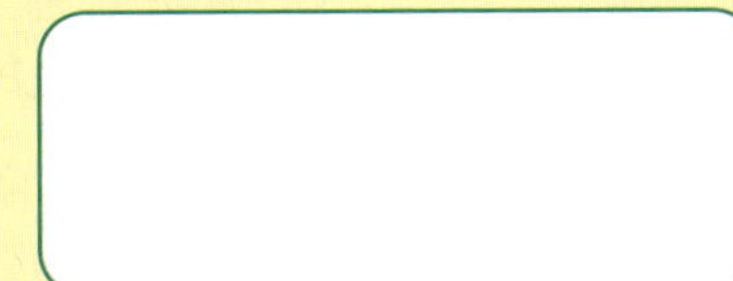

  ISBN 978-1-923253-14-8

LESSON 180 EQUIVALENT FRACTIONS

1 Colour $\frac{1}{2}$ of each shape. Label each fraction you coloured.

a 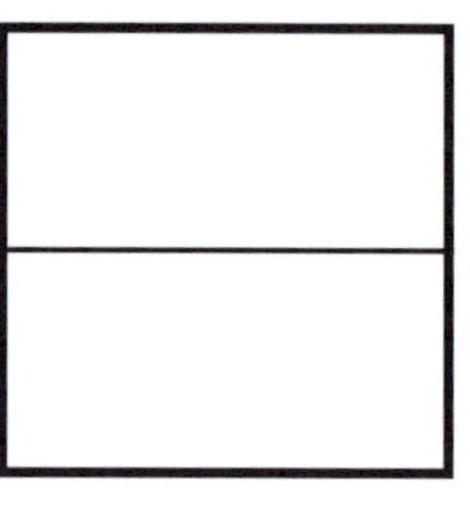

b 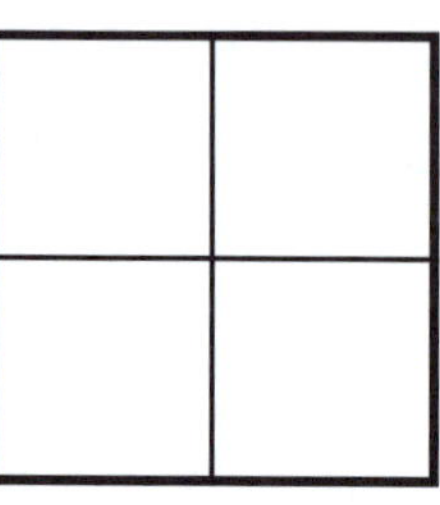

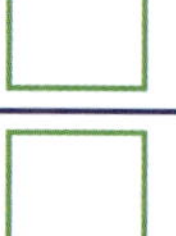

c 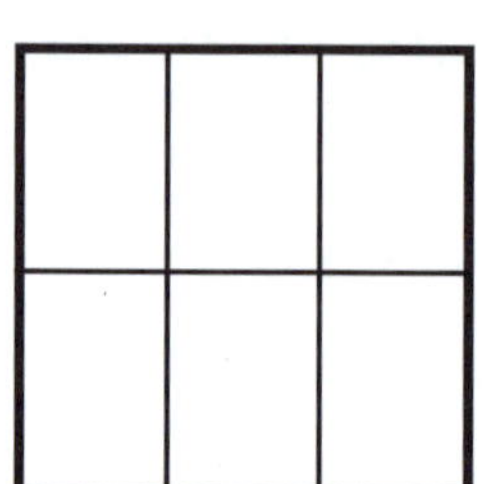

d 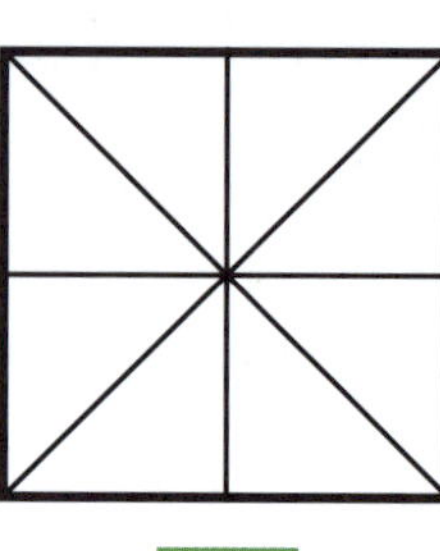

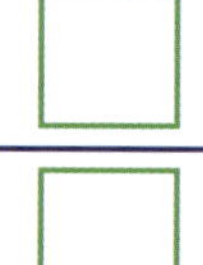

2 Colour equivalent fractions.

a 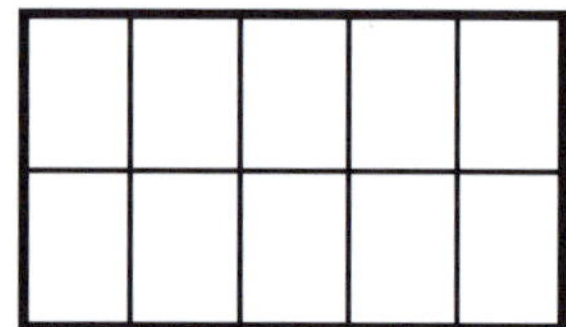

b 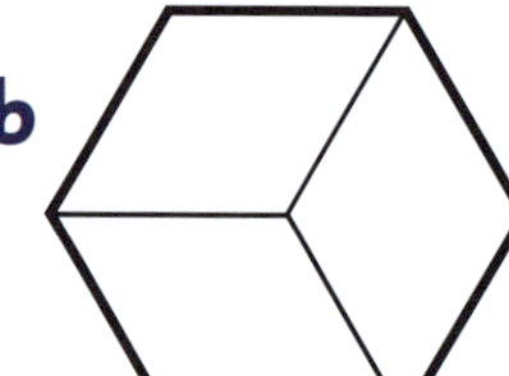 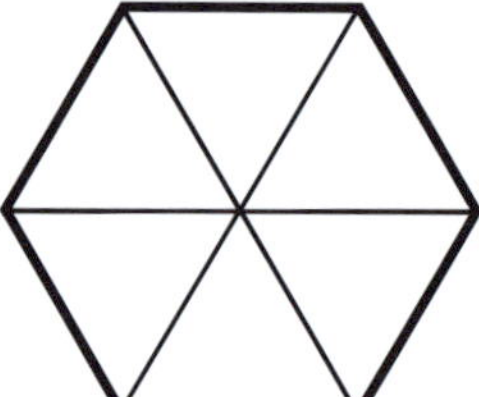

c  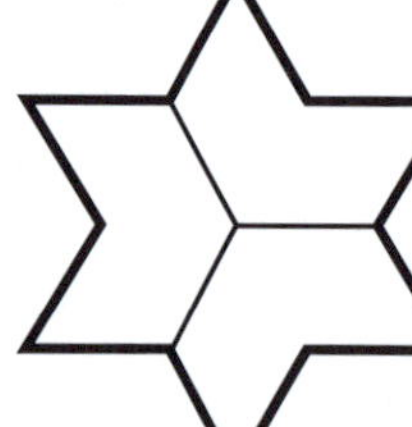

d 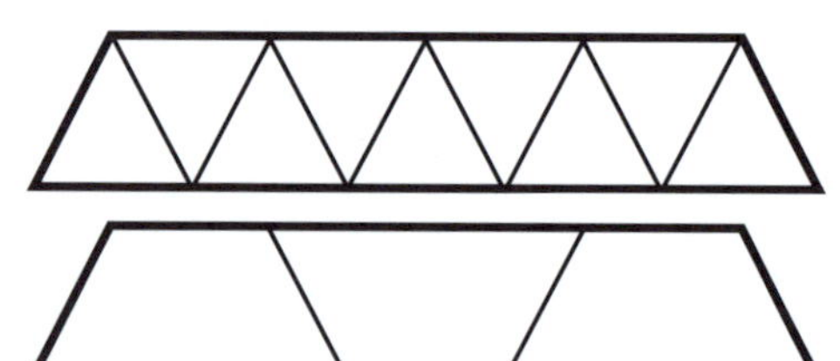

3 Write the equivalent fractions from question 2.

a 

b $\frac{\square}{\square} = \frac{\square}{\square}$

c 

d $\frac{\square}{\square} = \frac{\square}{\square}$

Mathseeds Year 3 Workbook © 3P Learning ISBN 978-1-923253-14-8

Equivalent Fractions

4 Label the fraction strips.

a
b
c
d

5 **a** How many quarters are the same as one half? $\frac{\square}{4}$

b How many eighths are the same as one half? $\frac{\square}{8}$

c How many eighths are the same as one quarter? $\frac{\square}{8}$

d How many eighths are the same as three quarters? $\frac{\square}{8}$

6 Label the fraction strips.

a
b
c

7 **a** How many sixths are the same as one third? $\frac{\square}{6}$

b How many sixths are the same as two thirds? $\frac{\square}{6}$

8 Write all the equivalent fractions for 1 whole that are shown on this page.

$1 = \frac{\square}{\square} = \frac{\square}{\square} = \frac{\square}{\square} = \frac{\square}{\square} = \frac{\square}{\square}$

  ISBN 978-1-923253-14-8

9 Complete the number lines.

a

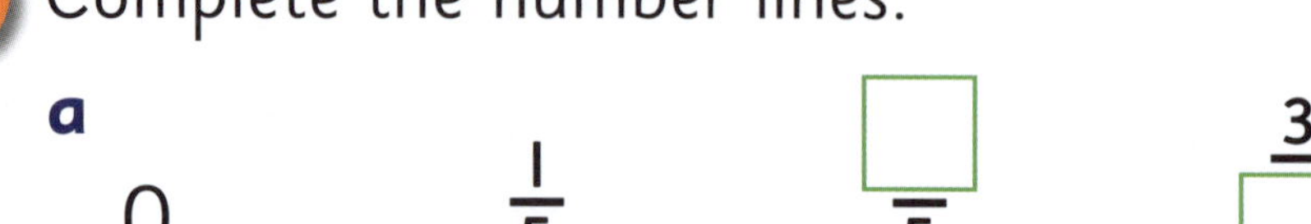

0 $\frac{1}{5}$ $\frac{\square}{5}$ $\frac{3}{\square}$ $\frac{\square}{\square}$ $\frac{5}{5}$

b

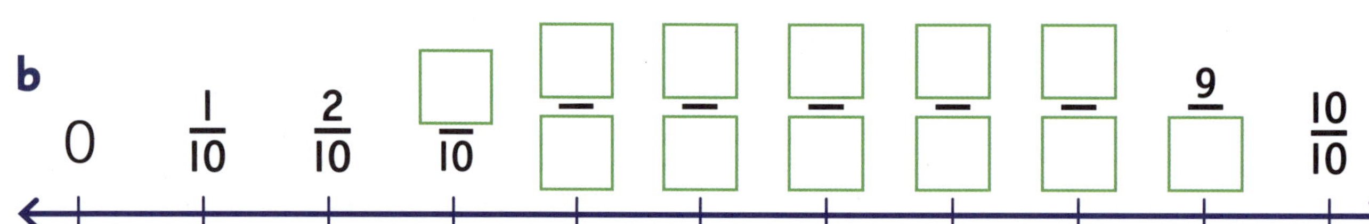

0 $\frac{1}{10}$ $\frac{2}{10}$ $\frac{\square}{10}$ $\frac{\square}{\square}$ $\frac{\square}{\square}$ $\frac{\square}{\square}$ $\frac{\square}{\square}$ $\frac{\square}{\square}$ $\frac{9}{\square}$ $\frac{10}{10}$

10 Complete the number lines.

a

0 $\frac{1}{3}$ $\frac{\square}{3}$ $\frac{3}{\square}$

b

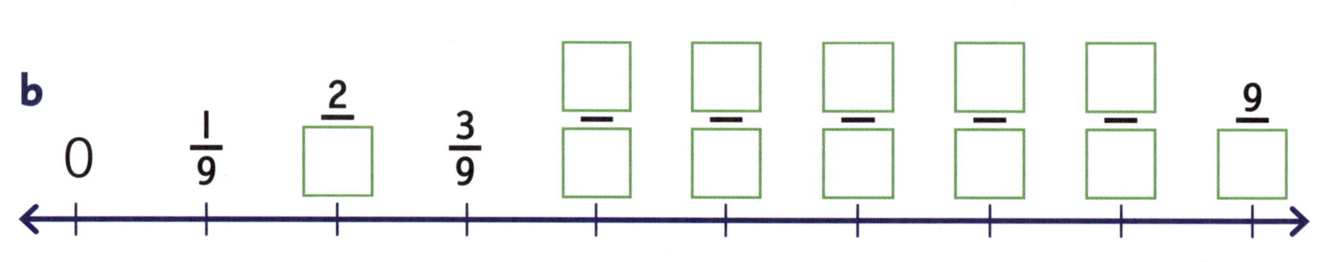

0 $\frac{1}{9}$ $\frac{2}{\square}$ $\frac{3}{9}$ $\frac{\square}{\square}$ $\frac{\square}{\square}$ $\frac{\square}{\square}$ $\frac{\square}{\square}$ $\frac{\square}{\square}$ $\frac{9}{\square}$

11 Use the number lines to complete the equivalent fractions.

a $\frac{\square}{5} = \frac{2}{10}$

b $\frac{2}{5} = \frac{\square}{10}$

c $1 = \frac{\square}{\square} = \frac{\square}{10}$

d $\frac{\square}{3} = \frac{3}{\square}$

e $\frac{2}{\square} = \frac{\square}{9}$

f $1 = \frac{\square}{\square} = \frac{\square}{9}$

Mathseeds Year 3 Workbook © 3P Learning ISBN 978-1-923253-14-8

12 Doc brought a bag of 6 apricots and a bag of 9 plums. He ate one third of each fruit. What are the equivalent fractions?

a Underline the question. **b** Circle the facts.

c Draw fraction strips to find the equivalent fractions.

d $\frac{1}{3} = \frac{\square}{6} = \frac{\square}{9}$

13 Ruby bought 5 chicken pies and 10 mushroom pies. She ate one fifth of each type of pie. What are the equivalent fractions?

a Underline the question. **b** Circle the facts.

c Use a number line to find the equivalent fractions.

d

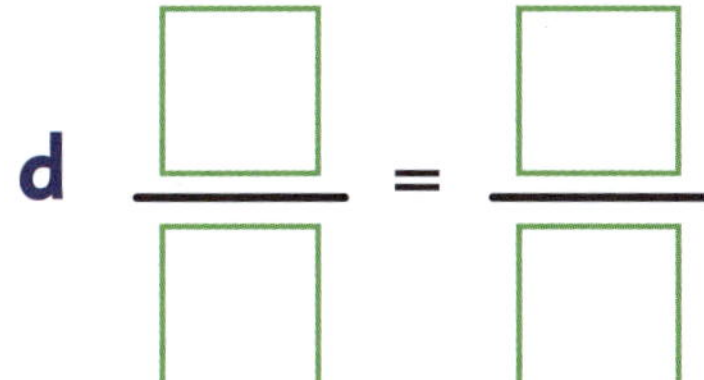

I finished this lesson online.

I can

- Make fractions in shapes and write equivalent fractions. ☐
- Use fraction walls or strips to identify equivalent fractions. ☐
- Fill in number lines and use them to identify equivalent fractions. ☐

We went to

QUIZ

END OF MAP 36 QUIZ

1

a $3 \times 5 =$ ______ b $3 \times 7 =$ ______ c $3 \times 8 =$ ______

d $6 \times 5 =$ ______ e $6 \times 7 =$ ______ f $6 \times 8 =$ ______

2 Split one factor to make easier sums and find the answer.

Mango has 13 cages with three bugs in each cage. How many bugs in total?

______ × ______ = ______ × ______ + ______ × ______

= ______ + ______

= ______

3 Colour right angles red. Colour smaller angles blue. Colour larger angles green.

a 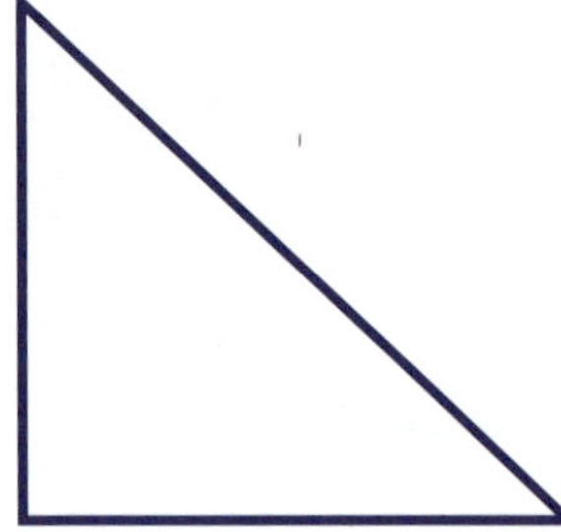

b 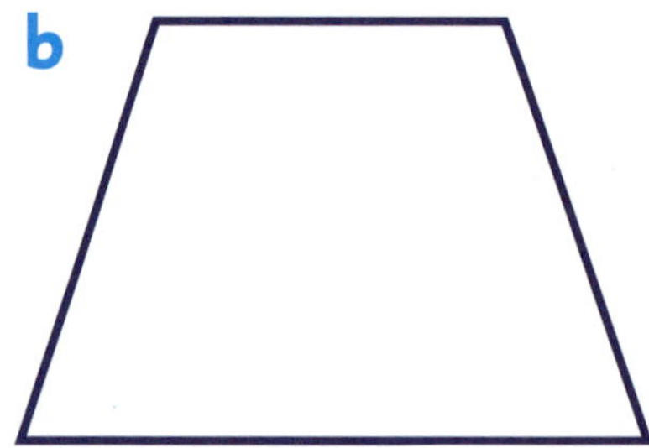

c 

4 Calculate the answer. Don't forget to regroup.

a
```
  7 8 5
– 3 5 8
_______
```

b
```
  4 3 0
– 1 9 0
_______
```

c
```
  4 6 8
– 3 0 9
_______
```

d
```
  9 3 1
– 2 8 2
_______
```


Mathseeds Year 3 Workbook © 3P Learning ISBN 978-1-923253-14-8

5 Fill in the missing parts of this table.

	Who?	Start	Finish	Time taken
a	Mango	9:02 am	10:21 am	
b	Ruby	10:27 am		1:26
c	Mrs T		2:13 pm	2:02
d	Waldo	2:25 pm		0:59
e	Dizzy	3:33 pm	5:27 pm	

6

a Who was fastest? ____________________

b Who was slowest? ____________________

7 Draw a diagram to solve these problems.

a Ruby, Dizzy, Mrs T and Mango need to share a length of ribbon. They need two pieces each.

  a What fraction of the ribbon is one piece? ________

  b What fraction of the ribbon is two pieces? ________

  c What is an equivalent fraction to this? ________

b Waldo has nine fish. He wants to divide the nine fish into three equal groups.

  a How many fish in one group? ________

  b What fraction of the larger group is this? ________

  c What is an equivalent fraction to this? ________

  ISBN 978-1-923253-14-8

Terrific!

YOU COMPLETED

MAP 36

YOU CAN:

- ☐ Answer equations and use the **distributive property** to multiply.
- ☐ **Classify angles** in shapes in relation to a right angle.
- ☐ Use **vertical algorithms** to subtract 3-digit numbers with regrouping.
- ☐ Add and subtract, **calculate amounts** and **compare times**.
- ☐ Solve **problems** with fractions and find **equivalent fractions**.

Signed:

Dated:

Mathseeds Year 3 Workbook © 3P Learning ISBN 978-1-923253-14-8

FUN SPOT 6

OPERATIONS PUZZLE

1 Can you work out which number each bug represents?

a = ________ **b** = ________

c = ________ **d** = ________

e = ________ **f** = ________

1 Fill in the related sums.

a 2 × 4 = 8

□ × □ = □

b 3 × 5 = 15

□ × □ = □

c 4 × 6 = 24

□ × □ = □

d 5 × 6 = 30

□ × □ = □

e 6 × 10 = 60

□ × □ = □

f 7 × 4 = 28

□ × □ = □

2 Fill in the related sums.

a 50 ÷ 5 = 10

□ ÷ □ = □

b 36 ÷ 9 = 4

□ ÷ □ = □

c 72 ÷ 8 = 9

□ ÷ □ = □

d 42 ÷ 7 = 6

□ ÷ □ = □

e 32 ÷ 4 = 8

□ ÷ □ = □

f 21 ÷ 7 = 3

□ ÷ □ = □

3 Complete the number fact families.

a

14

7 2

7 × 2 = 14

□ × □ = □

14 ÷ 7 = 2

□ ÷ □ = □

b

20

4 5

4 × 5 = 20

□ × □ = □

20 ÷ 4 = 5

□ ÷ □ = □

c

48

8 6

8 × 6 = 48

□ × □ = □

48 ÷ 8 = 6

□ ÷ □ = □

Mathseeds Year 3 Workbook © 3P Learning ISBN 978-1-923253-14-8

4 Complete the number fact families.

a

12

6 2

6 × 2 = ☐

2 × 6 = ☐

☐ ÷ 6 = 2

☐ ÷ 2 = 6

b

27

3 9

3 × ☐ = 27

☐ × 3 = 27

27 ÷ 3 = ☐

27 ÷ ☐ = 3

c

45

5 9

☐ × 9 = 45

9 × ☐ = 45

45 ÷ ☐ = 9

45 ÷ 9 = ☐

5 Fill in the related sums.

a 3 × 4 = ☐

4 × ☐ = 12

12 ÷ ☐ = 4

☐ ÷ 4 = 3

b 9 × 2 = ☐

2 × ☐ = 18

18 ÷ ☐ = 2

☐ ÷ 2 = 9

c 5 × 8 = ☐

8 × ☐ = 40

40 ÷ ☐ = 8

☐ ÷ 8 = 5

d 7 × 10 = ☐

☐ × 7 = 70

☐ ÷ 7 = 10

70 ÷ ☐ = 7

e 6 × 9 = ☐

☐ × 6 = 54

☐ ÷ 6 = 9

54 ÷ ☐ = 6

f 5 × 7 = ☐

☐ × 5 = 35

☐ ÷ 5 = 7

35 ÷ ☐ = 5

6 Complete the number fact families.

a

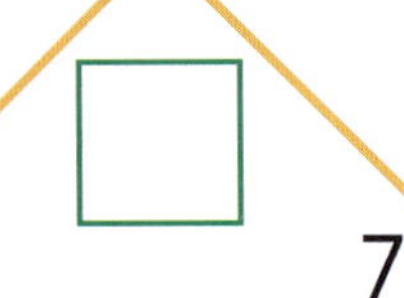

3 7

$3 \times 7 =$ □

$7 \times 3 =$ □

□ $\div 3 = 7$

□ $\div 7 = 3$

b

18

□ 2

□ $\times 2 = 18$

$2 \times$ □ $= 18$

$18 \div$ □ $= 2$

$18 \div 2 =$ □

c

40

4 □

$4 \times$ □ $= 40$

□ $\times 4 = 40$

$40 \div 4 =$ □

$40 \div$ □ $= 4$

7 Make each number fact family.

a

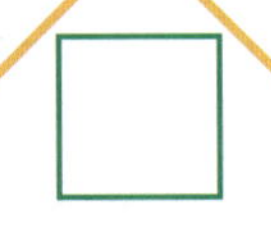

5 6

□ × □ = □

□ × □ = □

□ ÷ □ = □

□ ÷ □ = □

b

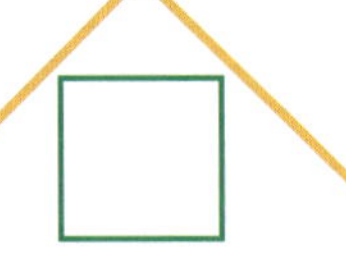

8 9

□ × □ = □

□ × □ = □

□ ÷ □ = □

□ ÷ □ = □

c

□

7 6

□ × □ = □

□ × □ = □

□ ÷ □ = □

□ ÷ □ = □

Mathseeds Year 3 Workbook © 3P Learning ISBN 978-1-923253-14-8

8 Mango rolled 2 dice. She used the numbers to make a multiplication and division fact family. What fact family could she make?

a Underline the question. **b** Circle the facts.

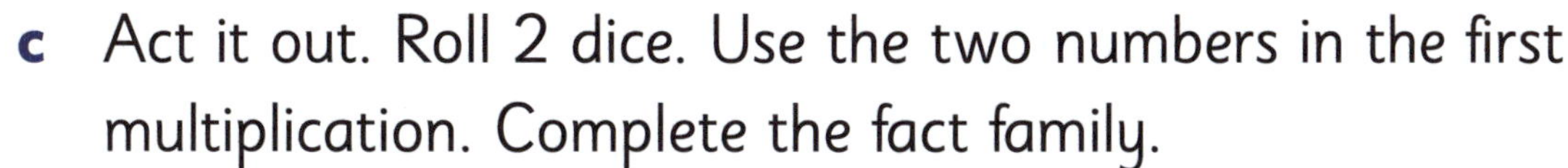

c Act it out. Roll 2 dice. Use the two numbers in the first multiplication. Complete the fact family.

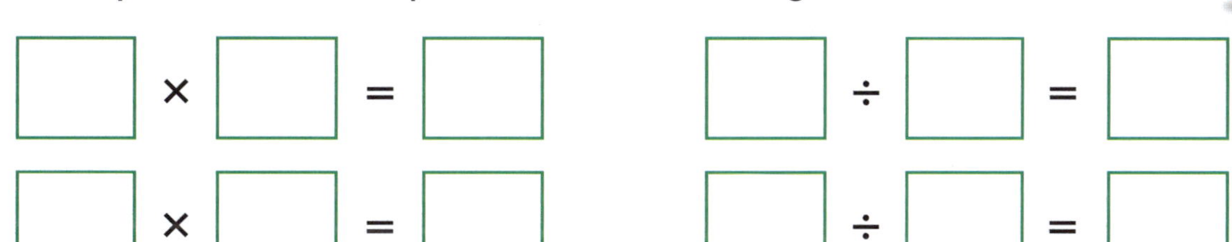

☐ × ☐ = ☐ ☐ ÷ ☐ = ☐

☐ × ☐ = ☐ ☐ ÷ ☐ = ☐

9 **a** What do you notice about the first number of each division sum?

____

b Does it matter if you swap the order of the first two numbers in division equations? Why?

____

10 Roll again. Write the new number fact family.

☐ × ☐ = ☐ ☐ ÷ ☐ = ☐

☐ × ☐ = ☐ ☐ ÷ ☐ = ☐

I finished this lesson online.

181

I can

- Complete commutative number sentences for multiplying. ☐
- Complete related number sentences for dividing. ☐
- Complete number fact families for multiplying and dividing. ☐

We went to

Nicobar Islands and Forests

Use your ruler to measure each ribbon.

1 

a ________ mm b ________ cm

2 

a ________ mm b ________ cm

3 

a ________ mm b ________ cm

4 

a ________ mm b ________ cm ________ mm

5 

a ________ mm b ________ cm ________ mm

6 

a ________ mm b ________ cm ________ mm

7

a ________ mm b ________ cm ________ mm

Mathseeds Year 3 Workbook ISBN 978-1-923253-14-8

8 Choose the measurement that matches.

a 356 cm
- ◯ 35 m 6 cm
- ◯ 3 m 56 cm

b 2 m 15 cm
- ◯ 215 cm
- ◯ 200 cm

c 460 cm
- ◯ 4 m 6 cm
- ◯ 4 m 60 cm

d 1 m 84 cm
- ◯ 184 m
- ◯ 184 cm

9 Which one is longer?

a	◯ 5 m 78 cm	◯ 587 cm
b	◯ 821 cm	◯ 8 m 31 cm
c	◯ 2 m 48 cm	◯ 199 cm
d	◯ 105 cm	◯ 1 m 50 cm
e	◯ 10 m 10cm	◯ 1001 cm
f	◯ 495 cm	◯ 4 m 59 cm

10 Which one is the same?

a 3 cm 2 mm
- ◯ 32 mm
- ◯ 320 mm

b 67 mm
- ◯ 67 cm
- ◯ 6 cm 7 mm

c 12 cm 2 mm
- ◯ 122 mm
- ◯ 1220 mm

d 99 mm
- ◯ 9 cm 9 mm
- ◯ 99 cm

11 Which one is shorter?

a	◯ 3 cm 8 mm	◯ 37 mm
b	◯ 97 mm	◯ 9 cm 9 mm
c	◯ 7 cm 1 mm	◯ 8 cm
d	◯ 5 cm 5 mm	◯ 56 mm
e	◯ 112 cm	◯ 12 cm 2mm
f	◯ 6 cm 6 mm	◯ 70 cm

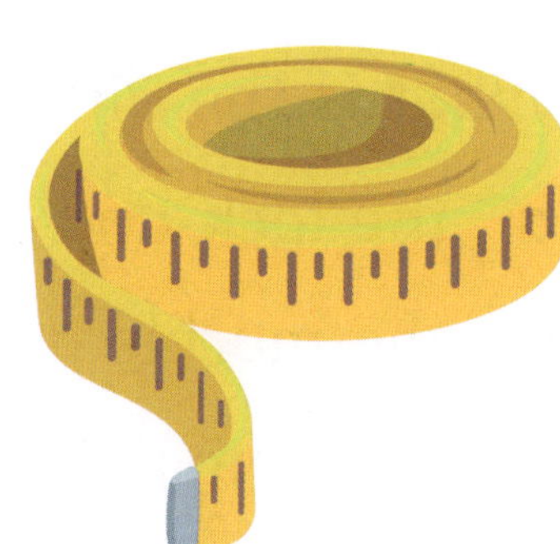

  ISBN 978-1-923253-14-8

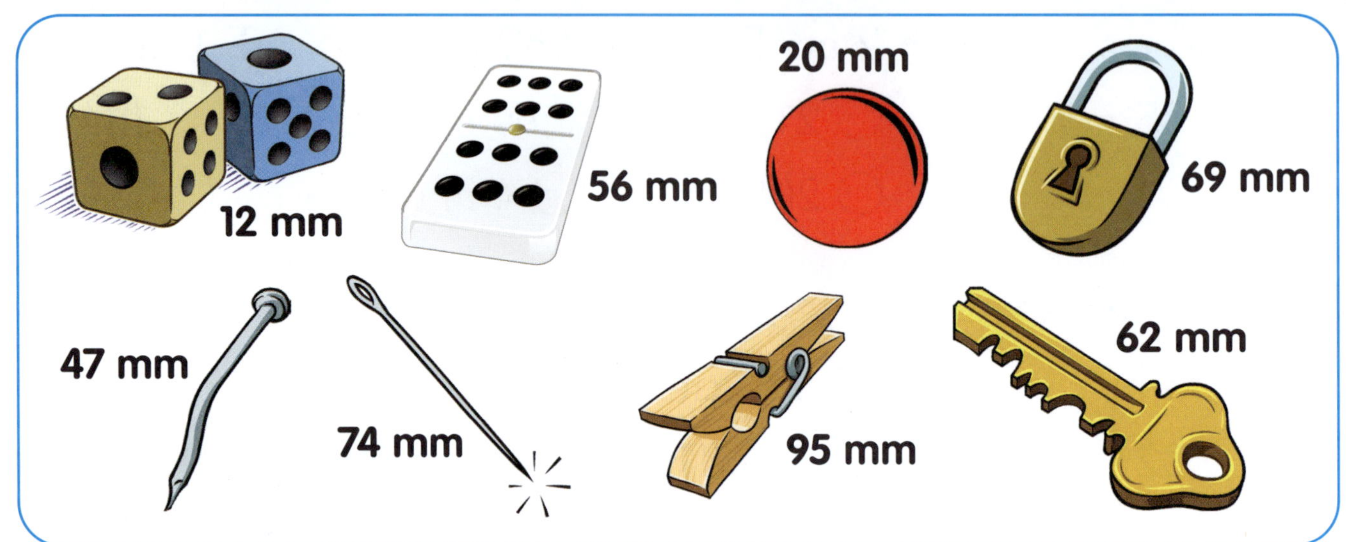

12 How long in centimetres and millimetres?

a dice ______ cm ______ mm **b** domino ______ cm ______ mm

c lock ______ cm ______ mm **d** nail ______ cm ______ mm

e needle ______ cm ______ mm **f** peg ______ cm ______ mm

13 What is the difference in millimetres between:

a the domino and the key? __________ mm

b the dice and the marble? __________ mm

c the nail and the needle? __________ mm

d the lock and the key? __________ mm

14 What is the difference in centimetres and millimetres between:

a the lock and the peg? ______ cm ______ mm

b the marble and the nail? ______ cm ______ mm

c the domino and the key? ______ cm ______ mm

d the dice and the key? ______ cm ______ mm

Mathseeds Year 3 Workbook © 3P Learning ISBN 978-1-923253-14-8

15 Dizzy says the length of the paperclip is 3 cm and Waldo says the length is 30 mm. Can they both be right?

a Underline the question. **b** Circle the facts.

c How can they both be right?

16 Measure a piece of paper. Record the measurements using mm and cm. Which unit of measure is more suitable? Why?

a Use a table to record your measurements.

Paper length	
mm	**cm**

b Which unit of measure is more suitable?

____

Why? _______________

____

I finished this lesson online.

I can

- Use a ruler to measure lengths in centimetres and millimetres. ☐
- Convert between metres m, centimetres cm and millimetres mm. ☐
- Compare lengths and find the difference. ☐
- Recognise the most appropriate unit of measure for an object. ☐

We went to

  ISBN 978-1-923253-14-8

LESSON 183 SOLVING WORD PROBLEMS

a Fill in the bar diagrams. **b** Use the equations to find the answers.

1 Maureen counted 247 girls and 256 boys at the assembly. How many students altogether?

a

Total students =	
Girls =	Boys =

b ☐ + ☐ = ☐

2 Marcel drove from the city to his farm. Between breakfast and lunch he drove 172 km. Between lunch and dinner he drove 156 km. After dinner he had 112 km left to go. How far did he travel altogether?

a

Total distance =		
1st drive =	2nd drive =	3rd drive =

b ☐ + ☐ + ☐ = ☐

3 Jimmy's basketball team scored 147 by the end of the game. Jimmy scored 35 points himself. How many points did the rest of the team score together?

a

Total score =	
Jimmy's points =	The rest of the team =

b ☐ – ☐ = ☐

Mathseeds Year 3 Workbook © 3P Learning ISBN 978-1-923253-14-8

4 Round the numbers, add and adjust.

a Sam has 121 t-shirts and 62 tank tops in his wardrobe. How many tops in all?

b Pam made 89 chocolate cupcakes and 42 vanilla ones for the cake sale. How many in total?

5 Add the tens and then the ones.

a Ying planted 16 lemon trees and 53 olive trees on the farm. How many trees planted altogether?

b Ming sold 31 buns and 45 hot dogs at the school fair. How many items did he sell in all?

6 Use the number line to add.

a Leah used 108 daisies and 39 roses in today's flower bouquets. How many flowers altogether?

b Mia had 227 sheep on her farm. Then 99 lambs were born. How many sheep in all now?

7 Round the numbers, subtract and adjust.

a Mina had 72 skirts in her wardrobe. She gave 29 of them away. How many skirts left?

____

b Deena baked 238 bread rolls and sold 89 by lunchtime. How many bread rolls still for sale?

____

8 Subtract the tens and then the ones.

a Harry counted 95 apples on the tree. He picked 73 apples. How many left on the tree?

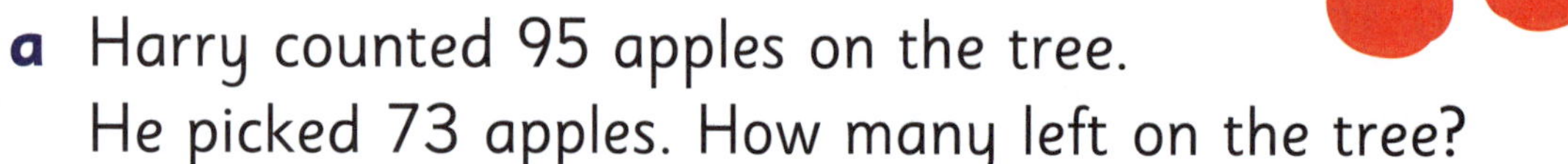

____

b Larry cooked 67 cookies. He ate 24 of them this afternoon. How many cookies left?

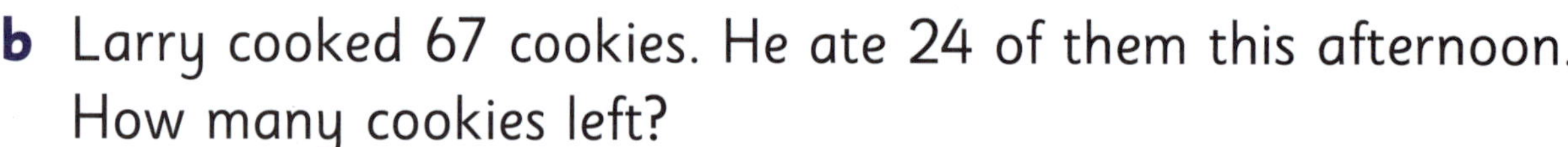

____

9 Use the number line to subtract.

a Akiko had 148 tomato plants in her garden but 89 died. How many tomato plants left now?

←――――――――――――――――――――――――――――→

b Kimko made 225 sandwiches. At the end of lunch there were 37 left. How many got eaten?

←――――――――――――――――――――――――――――→

Mathseeds Year 3 Workbook © 3P Learning ISBN 978-1-923253-14-8

10 Robin and Barbara are playing darts. On her first turn, Barbara hits 20, 5 and 14 points. On his first turn, Robin hits 9, 14 and 8. On her second turn, Barbara hits 1, 18 and double 20. On his second turn, Robin hits 11, double 15 and the outer bullseye for 25 points.

a Fill in the table.

	First turn	Second turn	Total so far
Barbara			
Robin			

b Who has scored the most points at this stage of the game? __________

11 Diana and Etta are practising their archery. With her first three arrows, Diana hits the 5, 4 and 6 point rings. Etta's first arrows hit the 6, 3 and 7 point rings. Next Diana hits 7, 7 and 8. Etta then hits 3, 4 and 9.

a Fill in the table.

	First turn	Second turn	Total so far
Diana			
Etta			

b Who has scored the most points so far? __________

I finished this lesson online.

I can

- Use bar diagrams to add and subtract up to 3-digit numbers. ☐
- Use rounding, place value and number lines to add and subtract. ☐
- Solve complex word problems using tables to organise information. ☐

We went to

  ISBN 978-1-923253-14-8

LESSON 184 PROPERTIES OF 2D SHAPES

1 Circle the correct words to define a polygon.

A polygon is a flat / solid shape with straight / curved, open / closed sides.

2 Colour the polygons.

3 Explain why each of these shapes is NOT a polygon.

a ______

f ______

g ______

k ______

p ______

q ______

Mathseeds Year 3 Workbook © 3P Learning ISBN 978-1-923253-14-8

4 Complete the definition of a quadrilateral.

solid flat closed open two three four five

A quadrilateral is a ________________, ________________ shape with ________________ sides and ________________ vertices.

5 Draw two quadrilaterals that fit each description.

	Description	Draw two quadrilaterals
a	Two pairs of parallel sides. Opposite sides are equal.	
b	Two pairs of parallel sides. All sides are equal.	
c	One pair of parallel sides.	

6 Draw this quadrilateral.

No parallel sides.
Adjacent sides
are equal.

7 Colour the right angles red. Colour the angles smaller than a right angle in blue. Colour the angles larger than a right angle in green.

a 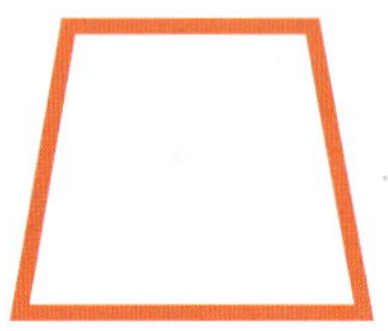

b 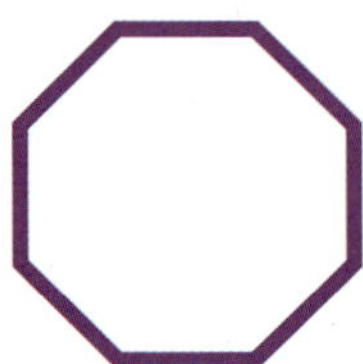

c 

d 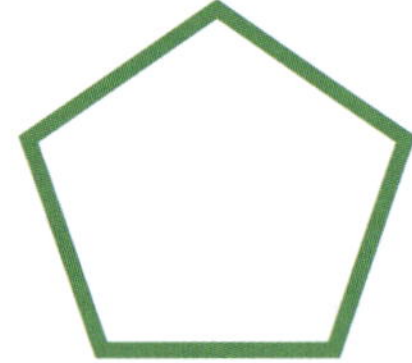

e 

f 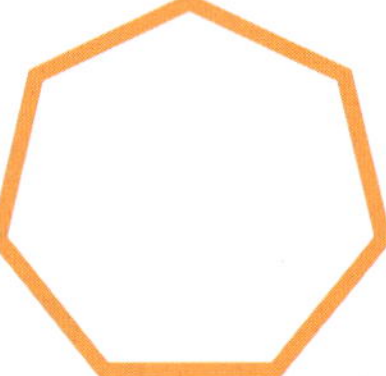

g 

h 

i 

8 Draw two other shapes with NO right angles.

a

b

9 Draw two other shapes with at least one right angle.

a

b

Mathseeds Year 3 Workbook © 3P Learning ISBN 978-1-923253-14-8

	Pair of shapes	a What is something they have in common?	b What is one difference between them?
10	square rhombus		
11	square rectangle		
12	square parallelogram		
13	parallelogram rectangle		
14	parallelogram rhombus		

I finished this lesson online.

I can

- Identify polygons and their features.
- Identify and compare quadrilaterals and their features.
- Draw shapes to match descriptions.
- Classify angles in shapes in relation to a right angle.

We went to

  ISBN 978-1-923253-14-8

1 Draw clock arms to show the time.

a 13 minutes past 5

b 26 minutes to 10

c 8 minutes past 4

d 2 minutes to 2

e 24 minutes past 1

f 18 minutes to 7

2 Write the time in words.

a

b

c

d

e

f

Mathseeds Year 3 Workbook © 3P Learning ISBN 978-1-923253-14-8

3 Match the times.

a 3 minutes past 3

b 21 minutes past 9

c 9 minutes to 6

d 16 minutes to 12

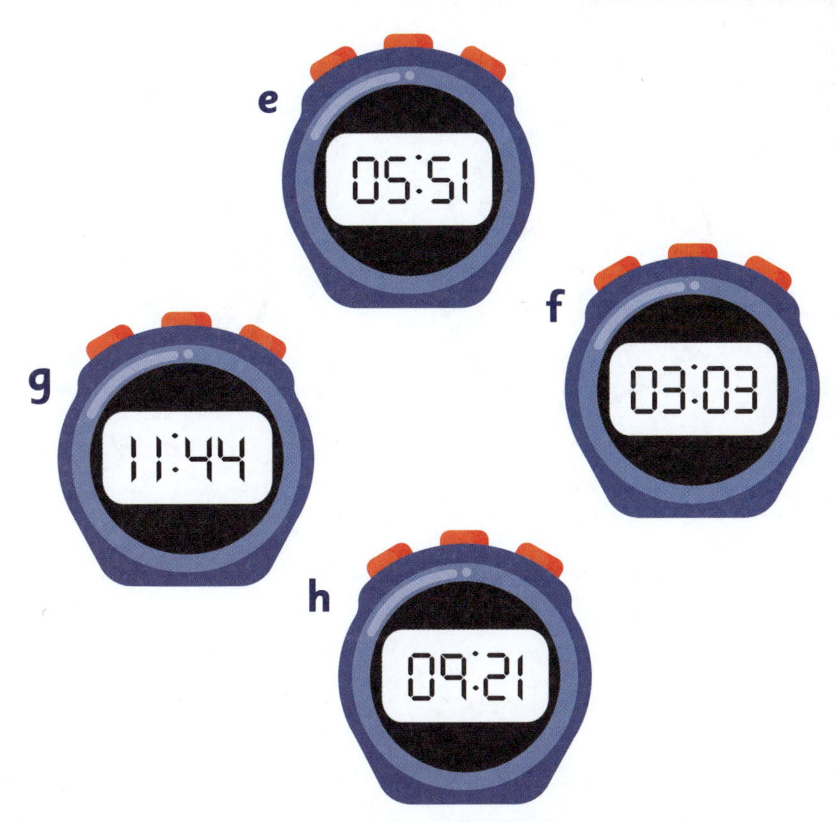

4 Write the time in words.

a

b

c

d

e

f

  ISBN 978-1-923253-14-8

5 Make the matching time on the second clock.

a

b

c

d

e

f

g

h

i

Mathseeds Year 3 Workbook © 3P Learning ISBN 978-1-923253-14-8

6 Show the start and finish times on the clocks.

a Rose started work at a quarter to nine in the morning. She headed home at twenty-five past five in the evening. Fill in the times for when Rose's work day started and ended.

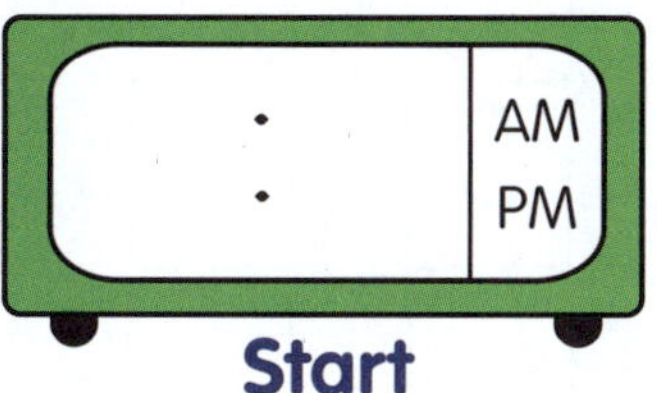

Start

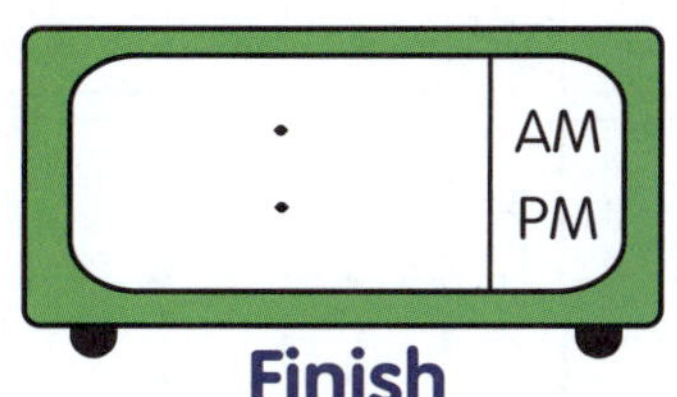

Finish

b Last night Rory went to sleep at eleven forty-one. He slept for eight hours and twenty minutes. Fill in the times for when Rory went to sleep and woke up.

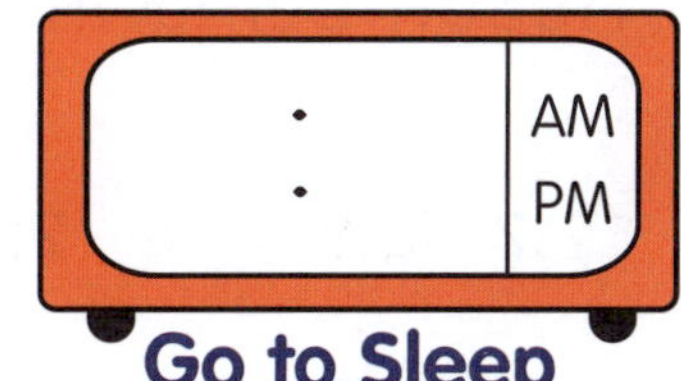

Go to Sleep

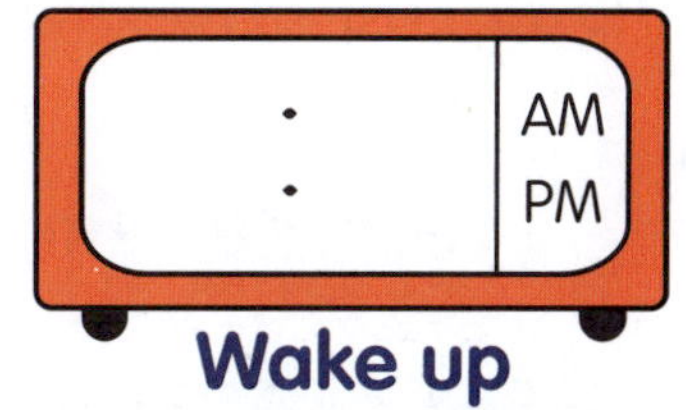

Wake up

c Amy spent five hours and twenty-two minutes driving home. She arrived home at thirteen minutes to two in the afternoon. Fill in the times for when Amy set out and when she got home.

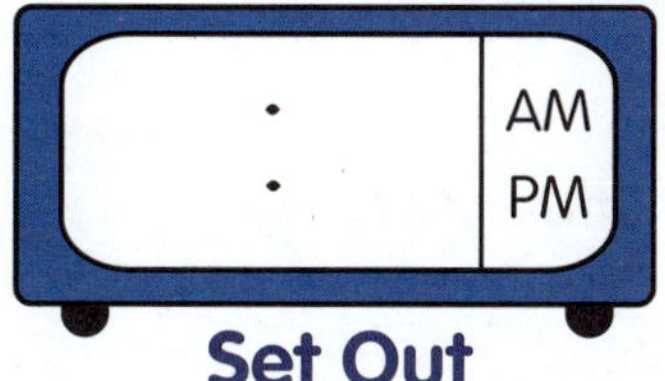

Set Out

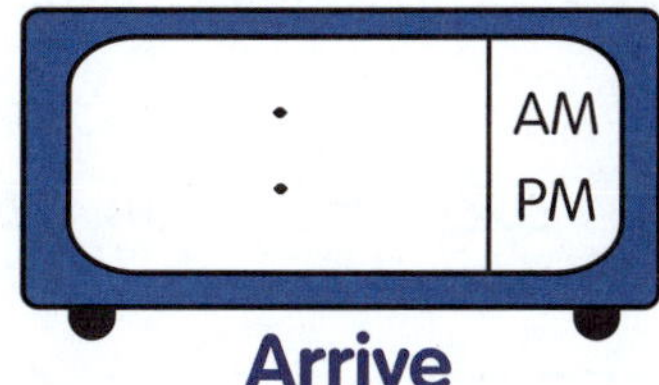

Arrive

I finished this lesson online.

I can

- Read and write time in words in minutes to and past the hour. ☐
- Tell and draw times in minutes on analog clocks. ☐
- Read and write digital times in minutes to and past the hour. ☐
- Add and subtract times to solve word problems. ☐

We went to

QUIZ

END OF MAP 37 QUIZ

1 Make each number fact family.

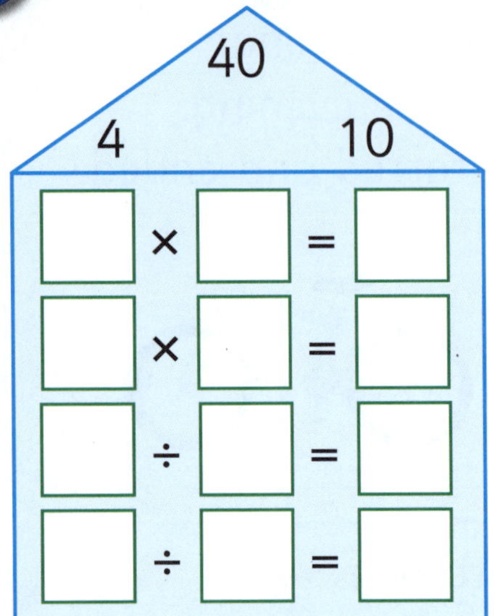

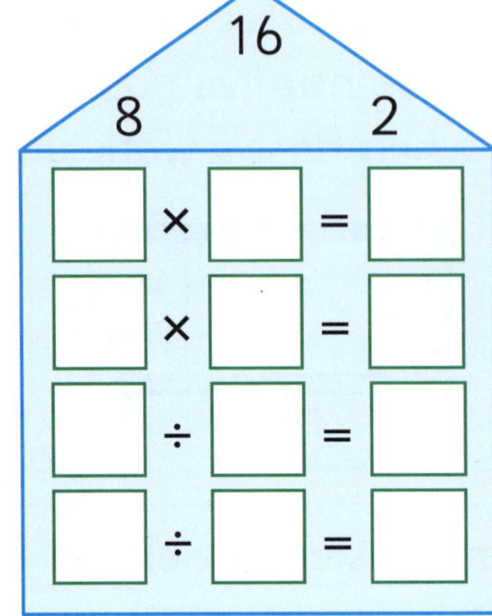

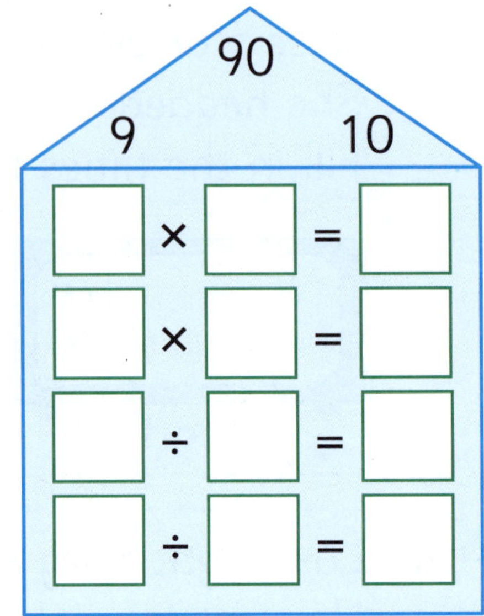

2 This is the end of each ribbon being measured. What is its length?

a 208 209 210 211 212 213 214 215 216 217 218 ______ cm

b 122 123 124 125 126 127 128 129 130 131 132 ______ cm

c 257 258 259 260 261 262 263 264 265 266 267 ______ cm

3 Convert between centimetres and millimetres.

a 3 cm = ________ mm

b 50 mm = ________ cm

c 2 cm 7 mm = ________ mm

Mathseeds Year 3 Workbook © 3P Learning ISBN 978-1-923253-14-8

4 Draw a bar diagram or a number line to solve this problem.

There are 500 students in the school. 323 are girls. How many are boys?

5 Round and adjust or add ones then tens to solve this problem. Show your thinking.

Sara owns 121 books and buys 35 more. How many books does Sara own now?

6 Complete the shape drawings.

Square	Parallelogram	Trapezium

7 Alex went to netball at twenty minutes to five. Netball goes for one hour and fifteen minutes.

Fill in the start and finish times.

: AM PM

Start

: AM PM

Finish

Yippee!

YOU COMPLETED

MAP 37

YOU CAN:

- [ ] Complete **number fact families** for multiplying and dividing.
- [ ] Interpret **lengths** and convert between units.
- [ ] Solve **add and subtract problems** with written and mental strategies.
- [ ] Draw **quadrilaterals**.
- [ ] **Add time** to solve a word problem.

Nicobar Islands and Forests

Signed:

Dated:

Mathseeds Year 3 Workbook © 3P Learning ISBN 978-1-923253-14-8

FUN SPOT 7

2D SHAPE SUDOKU

Each row, column and larger square must have 1 of each shape.

For example:

1 Can you complete these?

a

b

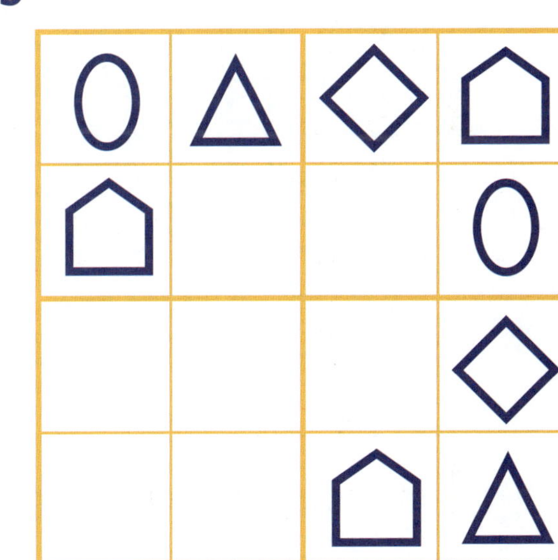

c

d

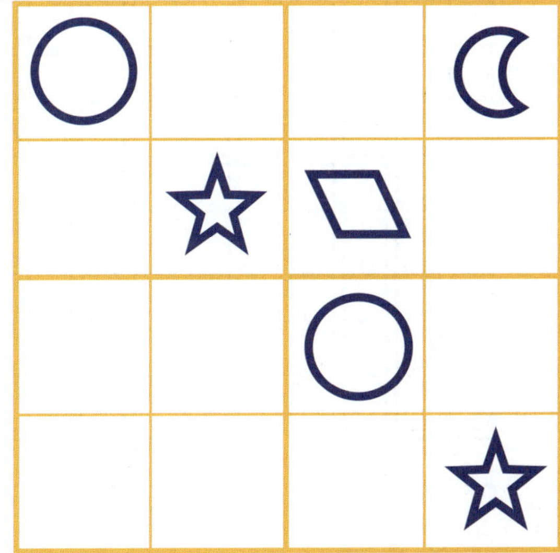

LESSON 186 MULTIPLICATION

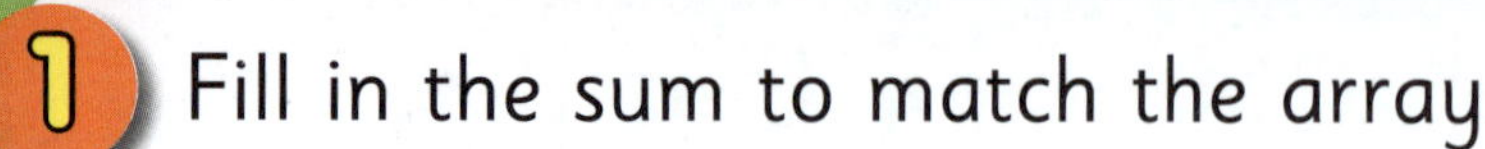

1 Fill in the sum to match the array.

a

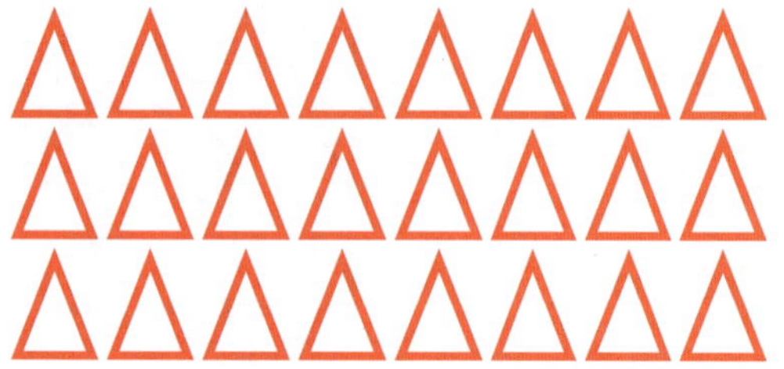

_____ × _____ = _____

b

_____ × _____ = _____

c

_____ × _____ = _____

d

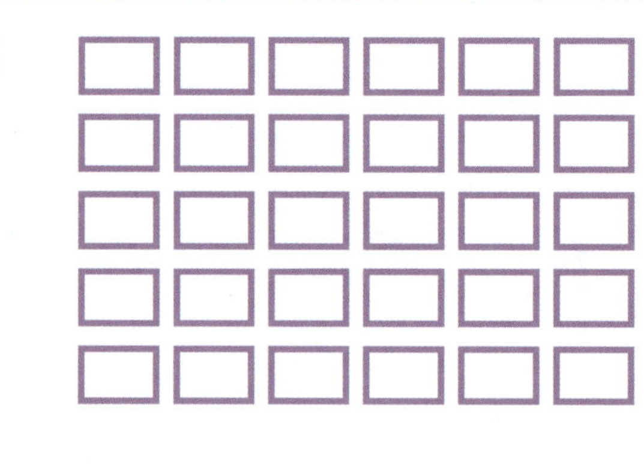

_____ × _____ = _____

2 Colour an array to match the sum and find the answer.

a

$7 \times 8 =$ _____

b

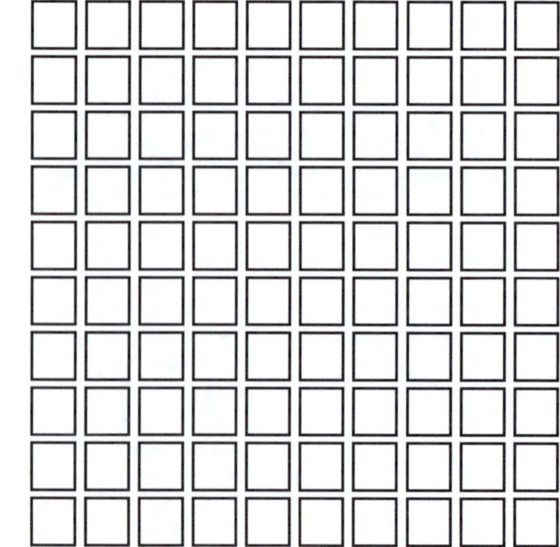

$6 \times 9 =$ _____

  ISBN 978-1-923253-14-8

3 Fill in the algorithm to match the array.

a

×

b

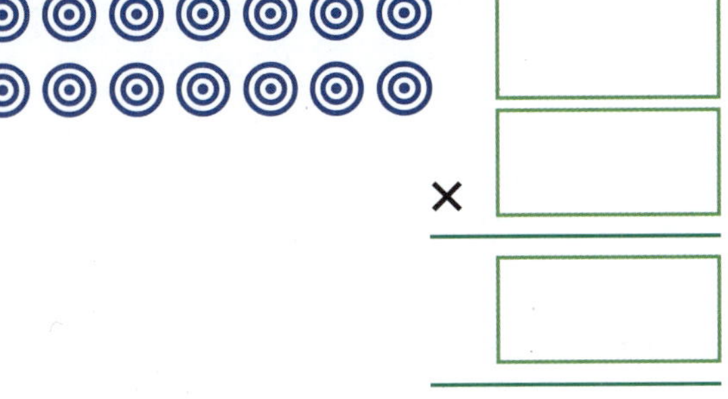

×

c

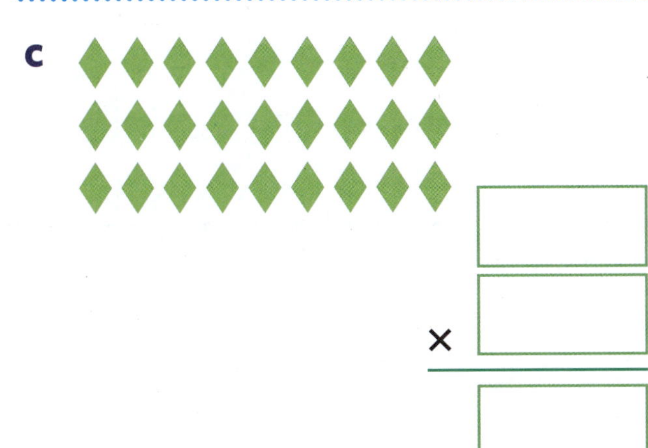

×

d

×

4 Answer the algorithms. Use times tables facts.

a 3×7

b 4×6

c 5×9

d 7×4

e 5×5

f 6×8

g 9×7

h 8×8

  ISBN 978-1-923253-14-8

5 Write an algorithm to match each number line.

a

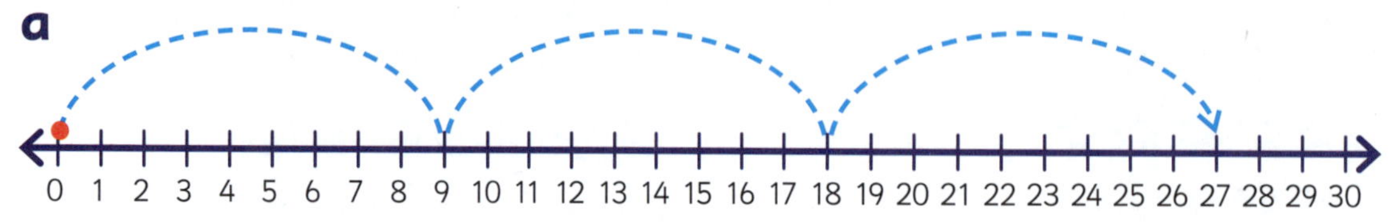

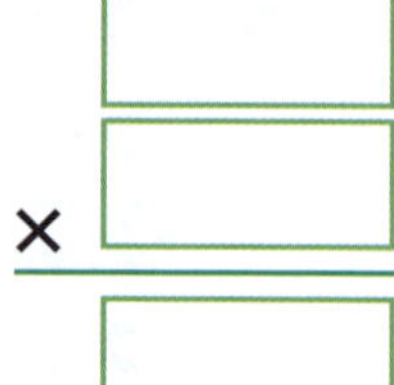

b

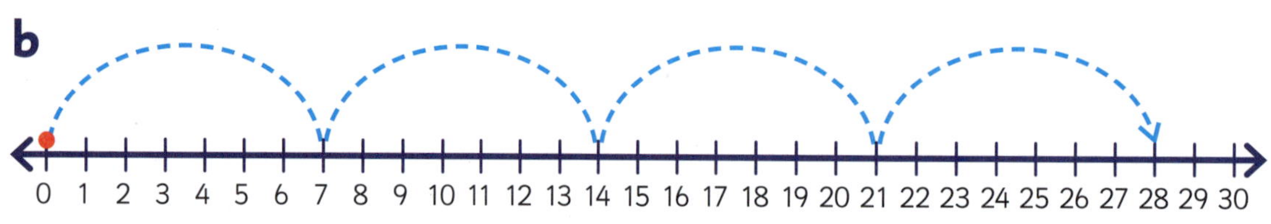

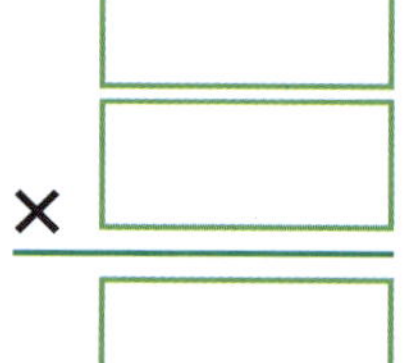

c

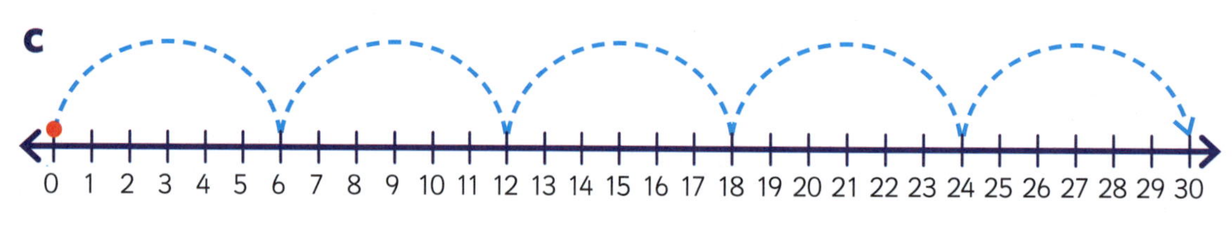

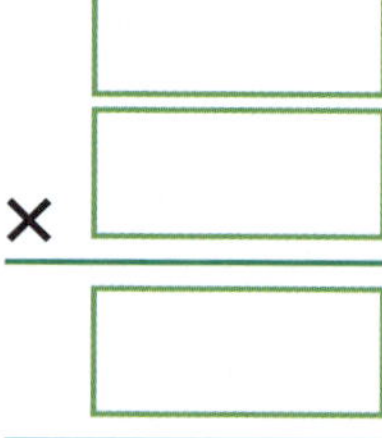

6 Use the empty number lines to find the answers.

a

$$\begin{array}{r} 3 \\ \times \quad 7 \\ \hline \\ \hline \end{array}$$

b

$$\begin{array}{r} 8 \\ \times \quad 4 \\ \hline \\ \hline \end{array}$$

c

$$\begin{array}{r} 9 \\ \times \quad 5 \\ \hline \\ \hline \end{array}$$

Mathseeds Year 3 Workbook © 3P Learning ISBN 978-1-923253-14-8

7 Write an algorithm to solve each problem.

a Chris books six taxis to take her and her friends to lunch. Four people get in each taxi. How many people are going to lunch?

×

b Naomi can fix five cars in a day. If she works all seven days one week, how many cars can she fix in that week?

×

c Amos buys nine boxes of biscuits. There are eight biscuits in each box. How many biscuits does Amos have?

×

d Alex bought six packets of beads for his daughter. Each packet holds nine beads. How many beads altogether?

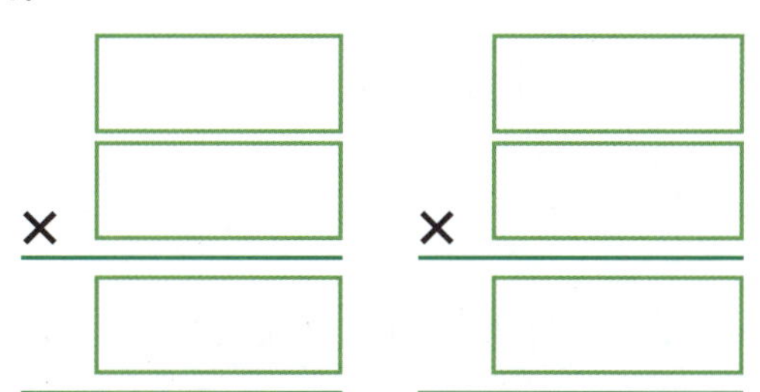

×

8 Write two algorithms to solve the problem.

James ordered three crates of apples. Each crate holds three trays. Each tray holds nine apples. How many apples altogether?

×

×

I finished this lesson online.

I can

- Use vertical algorithms to multiply 1 digit by 1 digit, and 2 digits by 1 digit. ☐
- Match multiplication equations and arrays. ☐
- Write vertical multiplication algorithms for arrays. ☐
- Answer vertical multiplication algorithms using times tables. ☐
- Match vertical multiplication algorithms and number lines. ☐
- Write vertical multiplication algorithms to solve problems. ☐

We went to

1 Fill in the missing totals on the tally chart.

Sales from Saturday		
Item	**Tally**	**Total**
t-shirts 	卌 卌 卌 卌 卌 |	**a**
jeans 	卌 卌 卌 卌 |||	**b**
jackets 	卌 卌 ||	**c**
shorts 	卌 卌 卌 |||	**d**
hats 	卌 ||||	**e**

2 Finish the sentences about the tally chart.

a This tally chart shows ______________________________

____.

b On Saturday, ________ jackets were sold.

c The most popular item on Saturday was ________________.

d The least popular item on Saturday was ________________.

e The total number of items sold on Saturday was ________.

f The difference between the number of t-shirts and jackets sold was ________.

g This is a tally chart from a ______________________.

Mathseeds Year 3 Workbook ISBN 978-1-923253-14-8

Item	T-shirts	Jeans	Jackets	Shorts	Hats
Sales	26	23	12	18	9

Use the data in the table to fill in the scaled column graph.

3 Write the title at the top.

4 Decide on a scale and fill in the numbers on the vertical axis.

5 Fill in the horizontal axis with the names of the items sold.

6 Colour the columns to show the number of sales for each item.

  ISBN 978-1-923253-14-8

Answer these questions about this graph.

7 How many races did:

a the unicorn win? ________ b the dragon win? ________

c the pegasus win? ________ d the phoenix win? ________

e the griffin win? ________

8 Which creature is the fastest? ____________________

9 Which creature is the slowest? ____________________

10 Which creature won half as many races as the pegasus?

____

11 Which creature won twice as many races as the unicorn?

____

12 How many races have been run altogether? ________

13 What is the scale? Each line on the graph represents ________ races.

Mathseeds Year 3 Workbook © 3P Learning ISBN 978-1-923253-14-8

14 Conduct a survey. Ask 4 people a question that will give you numbers over 10; eg, How many books do you own? How many meals do you eat in a week? Show your results in a scaled column graph.

a Underline the question.

b Circle the facts.

c Survey question: ______________________________

d Record the answers in this table.

Name				
Answer				

15 Make a scaled column graph of your data.

Scale	Title:			
Names:				

I finished this lesson online.

I can
- Complete the tally graph and interpret the data. ☐
- Draw a scaled column graph. ☐
- Interpret a scaled column graph. ☐
- Conduct a survey: write a question, collect data, make a column graph. ☐

We went to

  ISBN 978-1-923253-14-8

1. Alex has five good friends and she bought each of them four books. How many books did she buy in total?

   a Which operation? + − × ÷

   b ☐ ☐ ☐ = ☐

2. Juliet has ten stuffed toy cats and twelve soft dolls. How many soft toys altogether?

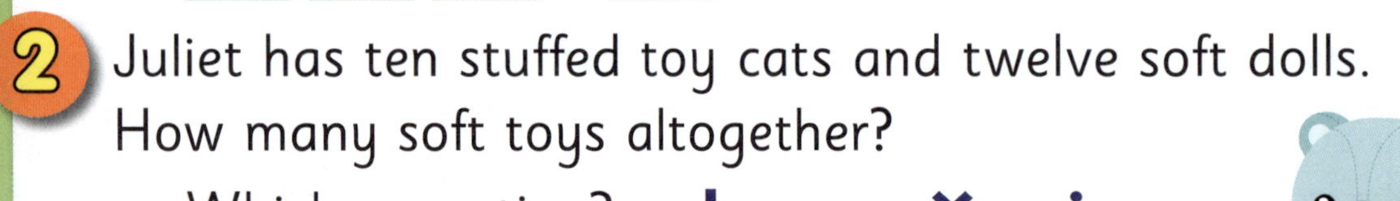

   a Which operation? + − × ÷

   b ☐ ☐ ☐ = ☐

3. Zahra cooked 24 pies. She shared them out to eight people. How many pies did each person get?

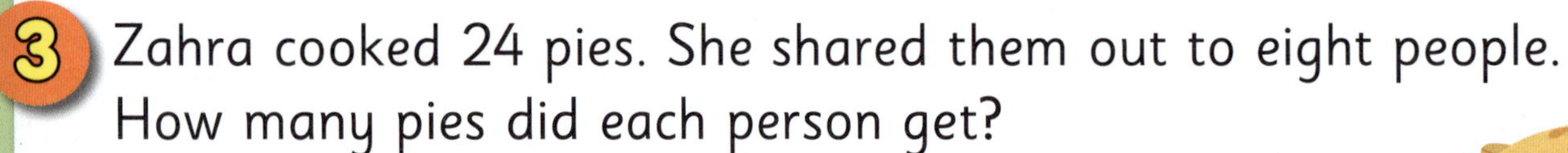

   a Which operation? + − × ÷

   b ☐ ☐ ☐ = ☐

4. Jake had forty toy trucks. He gave away eighteen. How many trucks left?

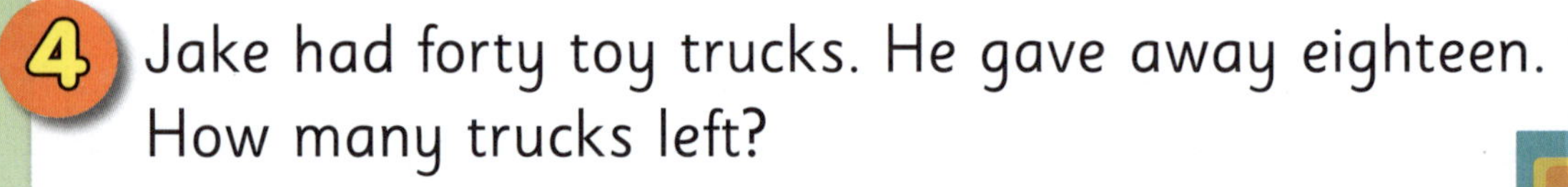

   a Which operation? + − × ÷

   b ☐ ☐ ☐ = ☐

5. Noah walks ten minutes to school every weekday morning. How much time does he spend walking to school in a week?

   a Which operation? + − × ÷

   b ☐ ☐ ☐ = ☐

6. Elijah needs fifty blocks to build his home. He has thirty-three so far. How many more does he need?

   a Which operation? + − × ÷

   b ☐ ☐ ☐ = ☐

Mathseeds Year 3 Workbook © 3P Learning ISBN 978-1-923253-14-8

7 Hannah has fourteen friends. She makes enough cupcakes so everyone gets two, including herself. How many cupcakes?

a Which operation? + − × ÷  Which operation? + − × ÷

b ☐ ☐ ☐ = ☐ 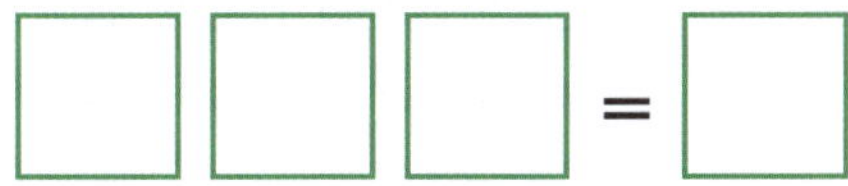 ☐ ☐ ☐ = ☐

8 Annabel made twenty bracelets. She sold three sets of five bracelets. How many bracelets are left?

a Which operation? + − × ÷ Which operation? + − × ÷

b ☐ ☐ ☐ = ☐  ☐ ☐ ☐ = ☐

9 Eden is in seven dances. Six of the dances are four minutes long and the final dance is five minutes. How long is she on stage for?

a Which operation? + − × ÷ Which operation? + − × ÷

b ☐ ☐ ☐ = ☐ ☐ ☐ ☐ = ☐

10 Zain rides three kilometres to school every morning and also back home in the afternoon. Today he spent sixty minutes riding. How long does each kilometre take?

a Which operation? + − × ÷ Which operation? + − × ÷

b ☐ ☐ ☐ = ☐ ☐ ☐ ☐ = ☐

11 Sam has $300. He shares it into ten equal amounts and puts one share into his pocket. Then he spends $19 of that money on lunch. How much money does he have left in his pocket?

a Which operation? + − × ÷ Which operation? + − × ÷

b ☐ ☐ ☐ = ☐ ☐ ☐ ☐ = ☐

Greg has a huge train set. He has three sets of four bridge pieces. He also has 21 straight pieces and 27 curved pieces of track. If he wants to divide it into three smaller but equally sized train sets, how many pieces will be in each smaller set?

12 Circle the answers.

a What do you need to find in the end?

one of three shares *total number of pieces*

b What do you need to find first?

difference between numbers of pieces *total number of pieces*

c How will you do that?

multiply & add *divide & subtract*

d What do you need to do in the end?

add *subtract* *multiply* *divide*

Write the sums and solve the problem.

e ☐ × ☐ = ☐ bridge pieces

f ☐ + ☐ + ☐ = ☐ total pieces

g ☐ ÷ ☐ = ☐ pieces in each smaller set

13 Complete this different approach to the same problem.

a straight pieces ☐ ÷ 3 = ☐

b curved pieces ☐ ÷ 3 = ☐

c bridge pieces in one set = ☐ +

d pieces in each smaller set = ☐

Mathseeds Year 3 Workbook © 3P Learning ISBN 978-1-923253-14-8

14 Carlotta needs tents for 24 people. The green tents cost $10 each and sleep 4 people. A purple tent costs $11 but it holds 6 people. Which type of tent will be cheaper for 24 people?

a Underline the question. **b** Circle the facts.

c How many of each type of tent sleeps 24 people?

Green: 24 ÷ ______ = ______ Purple: 24 ÷ ______ = ______

d How much will each set of tents cost? Show your working.

Green	**Purple**

e Which type of tent will be cheaper to buy? ____________

15 Carlotta now needs tents for 30 people. What mixture of green and purple tents will sleep exactly 30 people?

a Underline the question. **b** Circle the facts.

c Work out what tents Carlotta should buy.

d How much will that cost? Write equations.

____

I finished this lesson online.

188

I can

- Solve 1, 2 and multi-step problems using all operations. ☐
- Determine the appropriate operation/s and write equations. ☐

We went to

The Kalahari

  ISBN 978-1-923253-14-8

Time Word Problems

Fill in the number lines to find the end times.

1. Start at 10:15 am. Add 55 mins. End time? __________

2. Start at 2:20 pm. Add 1 hour and 35 mins. End time? __________

3. Start at 7:43 am. Add 3 hours and 12 mins. End time? __________

4. Start at 5:09 pm. Add 2 hours and 23 mins. End time? __________

5:09 pm

5. Start at 12:52 pm. Add 1 hour and 9 mins. End time? __________

Mathseeds Year 3 Workbook © 3P Learning ISBN 978-1-923253-14-8

Time Word Problems

Fill in the number lines to find how much time has passed.

6 Start at 4:45 pm. End at 6:25 pm. How long? ______________

7 Start at 11:35 am. End at 2:30 pm. How long? ______________

8 Start at 1:08 pm. End at 4:39 pm. How long? ______________

9 Start at 9:56 am. End at 10:40 am. How long? ______________

10 Start at 3:11 pm. End at 5:19 pm. How long? ______________

  ISBN 978-1-923253-14-8

a Fill in the missing numbers. **b** Answer the question.

11 **a**

Racer	Start	End	Race time
Mango	6:34 am		57 mins
Ruby	6:34 am	7:22 am	

b Who is faster? ______________________

12 **a**

Show	Start	End	Duration
Block Build	8:27 pm		1 hr 36 mins
Farm-a-go	9:03 pm		1 hr 21 mins

b Which show ends earlier? ______________________

13 **a**

Class	Start	End	Duration
Art	10:09 am		3 hrs 18 mins
Coding	10:09 am	1:42 pm	

b Which class is longer? ______________________

14 **a**

Bus	Departs	Arrives	Trip time
Bus 1234	2:40 pm	5:09 pm	
Bus 4321	2:55 pm	5:14 pm	

Mathseeds Year 3 Workbook © 3P Learning ISBN 978-1-923253-14-8

Time Word Problems

Solve these problems. Show your working.
You could use a number line, a table or equations.

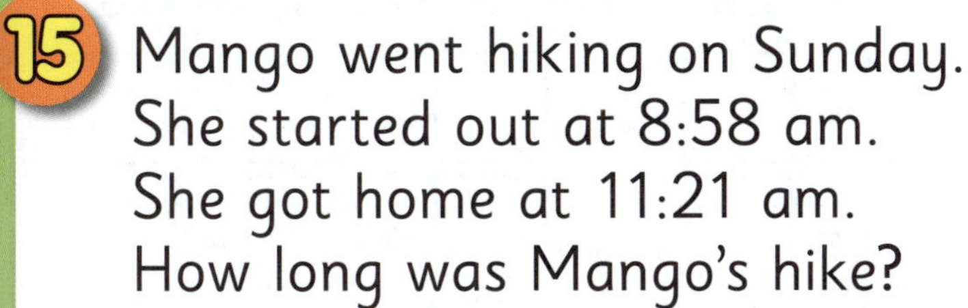

15 Mango went hiking on Sunday. She started out at 8:58 am. She got home at 11:21 am. How long was Mango's hike?

____

16 The movie started at 11:34 am. It ran for 1 hour and 47 mins. What time did it end?

____

17 Ruby started her homework at 3:41 pm. She finished at 4:56 pm. Doc started his homework at 5:05 pm. He finished at 6:27 pm. Who took longer to do their homework?

____

18 Waldo is roasting a chicken. He puts it in the oven at 9:26 am. It cooks for 2 hours and 35 mins. What time does he take it out?

____

I finished this lesson online.

189

I can

- Add and subtract, calculate amounts and compare times. ☐
- Use these skills to solve word problems. ☐

We went to

  ISBN 978-1-923253-14-8

1 Complete the number fact families.

a 5 × 6 = 30

___ × ___ = ___
___ ÷ ___ = ___
___ ÷ ___ = ___

b 4 × 7 = 28

___ × ___ = ___
___ ÷ ___ = ___
___ ÷ ___ = ___

c 8 × 9 = 72

___ × ___ = ___
___ ÷ ___ = ___
___ ÷ ___ = ___

2 Fill in the number fact families.

a 27
3 9

___ × ___ = ___
___ × ___ = ___
___ ÷ ___ = ___
___ ÷ ___ = ___

b 32
4 8

___ × ___ = ___
___ × ___ = ___
___ ÷ ___ = ___
___ ÷ ___ = ___

c

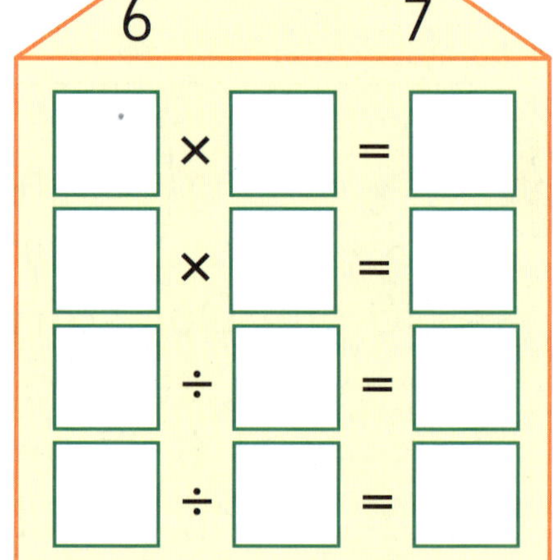

3 Make each number fact family.

a ___
5 9

___ × ___ = ___
___ × ___ = ___
___ ÷ ___ = ___
___ ÷ ___ = ___

b ___
6 8

___ × ___ = ___
___ × ___ = ___
___ ÷ ___ = ___
___ ÷ ___ = ___

c ___
7 10

___ × ___ = ___
___ × ___ = ___
___ ÷ ___ = ___
___ ÷ ___ = ___

Mathseeds Year 3 Workbook © 3P Learning ISBN 978-1-923253-14-8

4 Fill in the missing numbers in the number mountains.

a
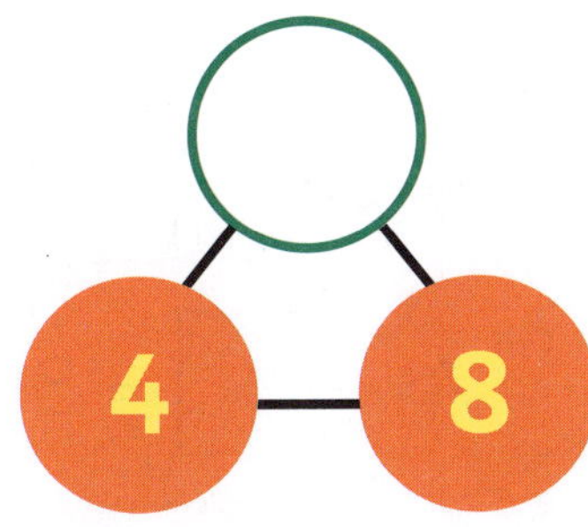

b
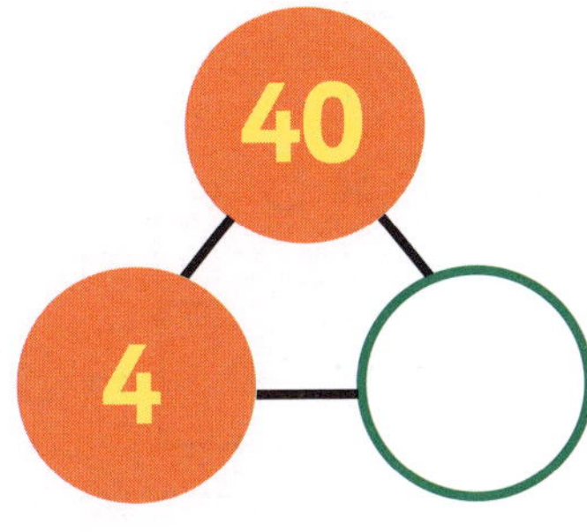

c
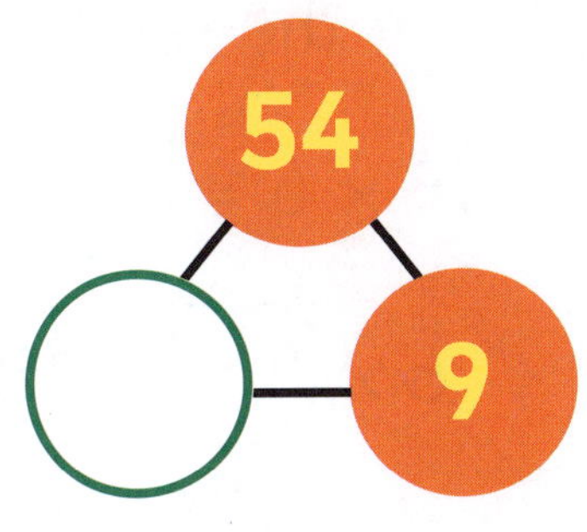

5 Write a number fact family for each number mountain above.

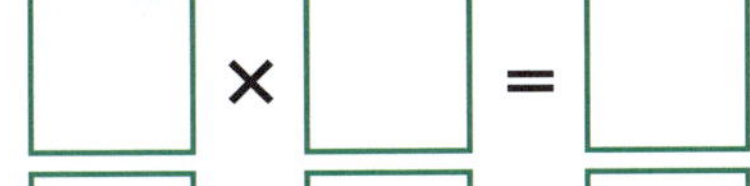

a
☐ × ☐ = ☐
☐ × ☐ = ☐
☐ ÷ ☐ = ☐
☐ ÷ ☐ = ☐

b
☐ × ☐ = ☐
☐ × ☐ = ☐
☐ ÷ ☐ = ☐
☐ ÷ ☐ = ☐

c
☐ × ☐ = ☐
☐ × ☐ = ☐
☐ ÷ ☐ = ☐
☐ ÷ ☐ = ☐

6 Fill in a number mountain to help you answer the equations.

a $42 \div 7 =$ ☐

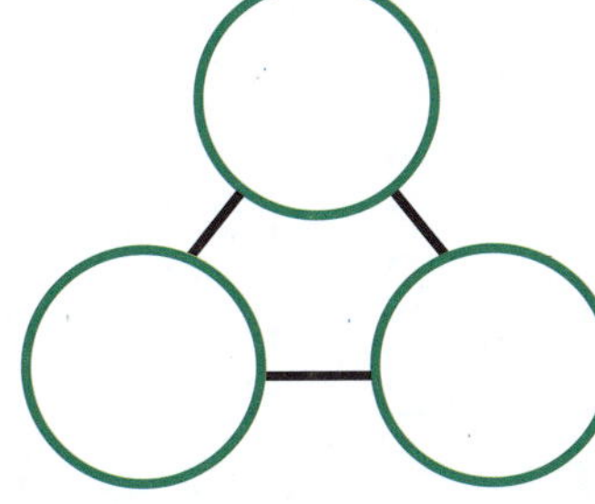

b $45 \div 9 =$ ☐

c $48 \div 8 =$ ☐

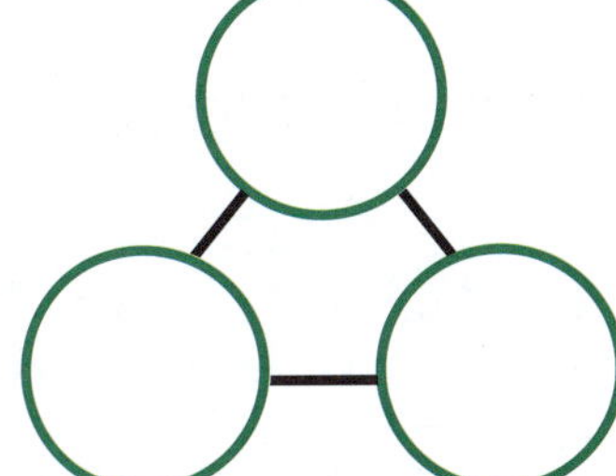

d $30 \div 6 =$ ☐

e $36 \div 9 =$ ☐

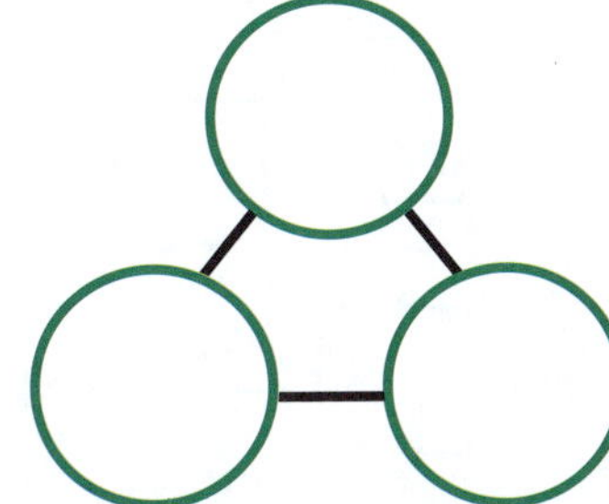

f $35 \div 7 =$ ☐

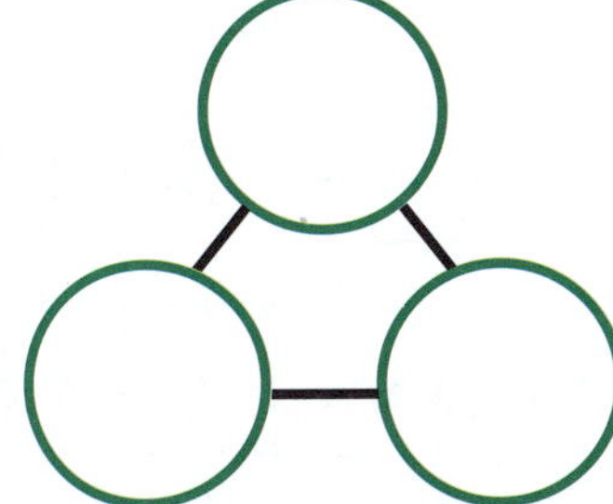

  ISBN 978-1-923253-14-8

7 Fill in the related sums.

a $3 \times 6 = \square$

$6 \times \square = 18$

$18 \div \square = 6$

$\square \div 6 = 3$

b $7 \times 5 = \square$

$5 \times \square = 35$

$35 \div \square = 5$

$\square \div 5 = 7$

c $9 \times 4 = \square$

$4 \times \square = 36$

$36 \div \square = 4$

$\square \div 4 = 9$

d $8 \times 7 = \square$

$7 \times \square = 56$

$56 \div \square = 7$

$\square \div 7 = 8$

e $5 \times 10 = \square$

$10 \times \square = 50$

$50 \div \square = 10$

$\square \div 10 = 5$

f $3 \times 8 = \square$

$8 \times \square = 24$

$24 \div \square = 8$

$\square \div 8 = 3$

8 Use related facts to work out the missing numbers.

a $63 \div \square = 9$

b $\square \div 4 = 6$

c $40 \div \square = 5$

d $\square \div 9 = 6$

e $21 \div \square = 3$

f $\square \div 9 = 10$

g $20 \div \square = 4$

h $\square \div 5 = 3$

i $30 \div \square = 3$

j $\square \div 9 = 8$

k $80 \div \square = 10$

l $\square \div 7 = 7$

m $64 \div \square = 8$

n $\square \div 7 = 4$

o $60 \div \square = 6$

  ISBN 978-1-923253-14-8

9 Doc made these number and symbol cards:

What equations could he write that include answer cards?

a Underline the question. **b** Circle the facts.

c What equations can you write with these cards?

____

____

____

____

____

d How many equations did you make? __________

10 **a** Did you write any related facts? __________

b Explain how they are related.

____

____

____

____

I finished this lesson online.

I can

- Complete number fact families for multiplying and dividing. ☐
- Use number mountains to write number fact families. ☐
- Use number mountains to find missing numbers in division equations. ☐

We went to

  ISBN 978-1-923253-14-8

QUIZ

END OF MAP 38 QUIZ

1 Write algorithms to solve the problems.

a Lisa has 5 packets of seeds. There are 9 seeds in each packet. How many seeds in total?

b Amy bought 4 boxes of strawberries. Each box holds 6 big strawberries. How many strawberries altogether?

2 Answer the questions using the bar graph.

Room Lengths (m)	2	4	6	8	10	12	14	16	18	20
Gym/Hall										
Office										
Staffroom										
Classroom										

a Which room is longest? ____________________

b How long is it? ______

c Which room is shortest? ____________________

d How long is it? ______

e What is the difference between the longest and shortest rooms? ______

f If two classrooms were joined together, how long would this room be? ______

Mathseeds Year 3 Workbook © 3P Learning ISBN 978-1-923253-14-8

3 Write equations to solve the problems.

a Mara spends 30 hours a week at school. Each day her lunch break is 40 mins and her recess break is 20 mins. How many hours a day are actually spent in class?

____

b Phil has a big collection of feathers. He has 32 seabird feathers, 19 eagle feathers and 15 finch feathers. He has six storage boxes, each holding an equal number of feathers. How many feathers in each box?

____

4 Solve these problems. Use a number line, a table or equations.

a Jarrah started work at 8:38 am.
He finished at 3:51 pm.
How long was Jarrah at work?

b Ariel played her game for 2 hours and 23 minutes. She finished at 9:09 pm. What time did she start?

c Daria went to a movie at 6:15 pm. The movie went for an hour and 56 minutes. What time did it end?

5 Fill in the missing numbers in the number mountains.

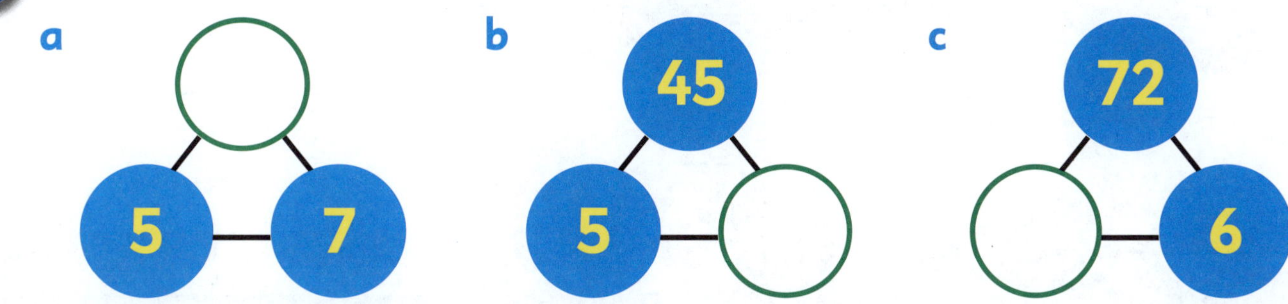

Amazing!

YOU COMPLETED

MAP 38

YOU CAN:

- [ ] Write **vertical algorithms** to solve multiplication problems.
- [ ] Interpret a **scaled bar graph**.
- [ ] Write equations to solve problems using **all operations**.
- [ ] Add and subtract and calculate amounts of time to **solve problems**.
- [ ] Find the **missing number** in number mountains.

Signed:

Dated:

Mathseeds Year 3 Workbook © 3P Learning ISBN 978-1-923253-14-8

FUN SPOT 8

1 Complete the pyramids using multiplication and division.

a
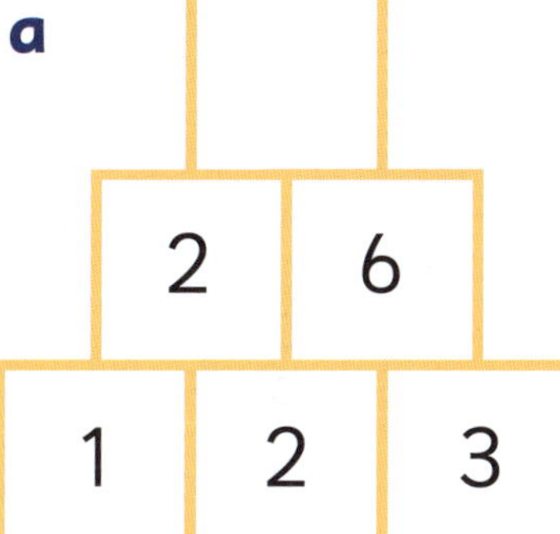

b
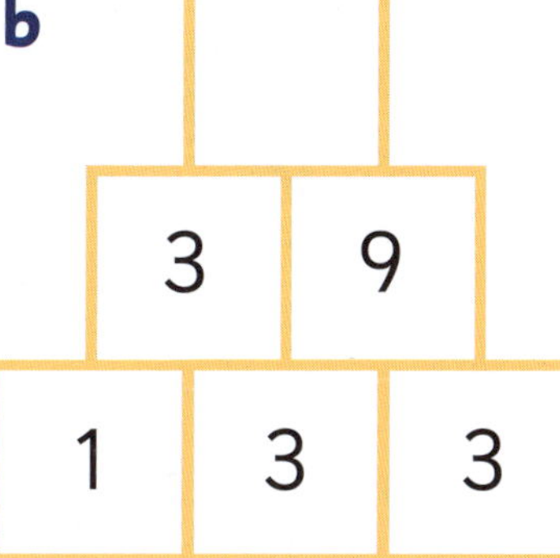

c
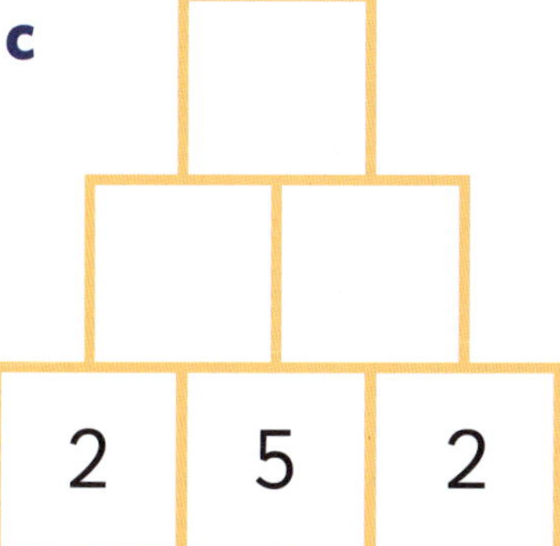

d
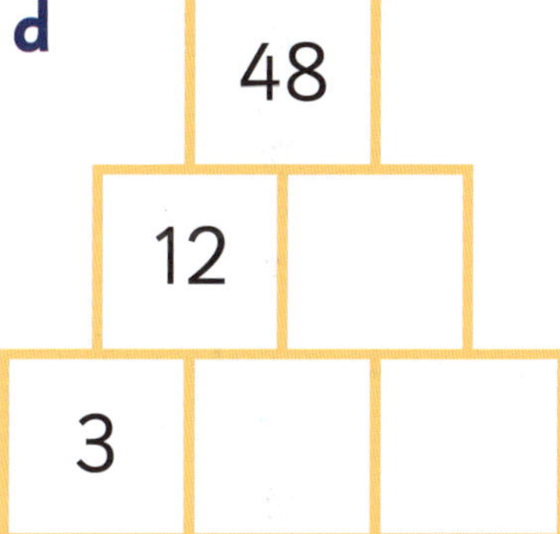

e
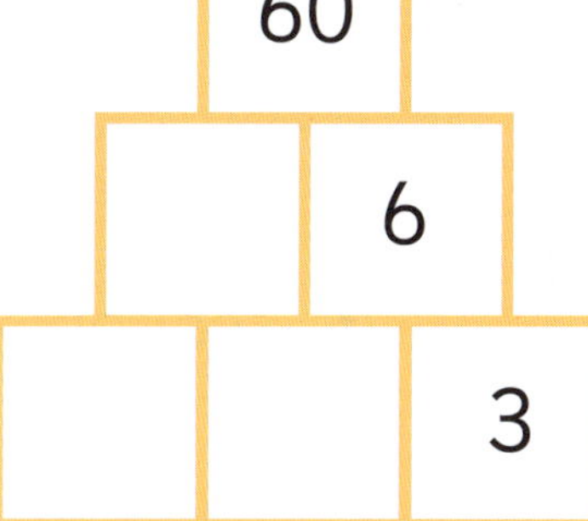

f
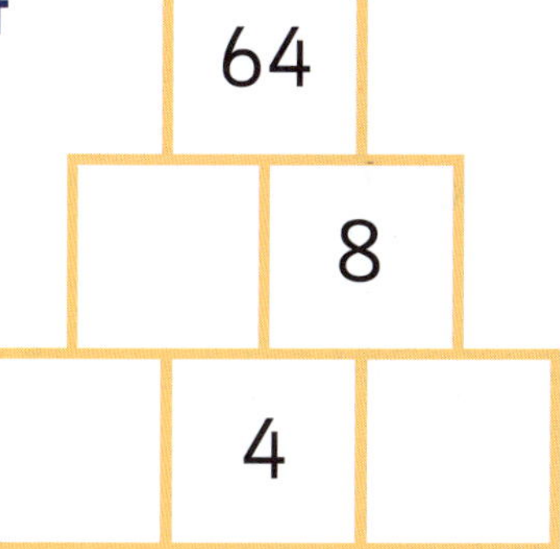

g
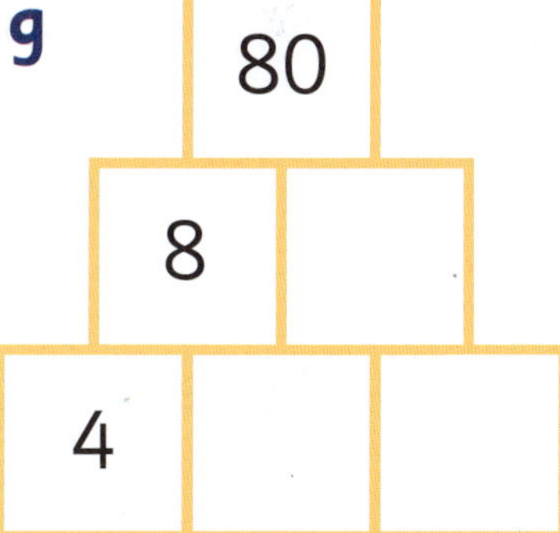

h
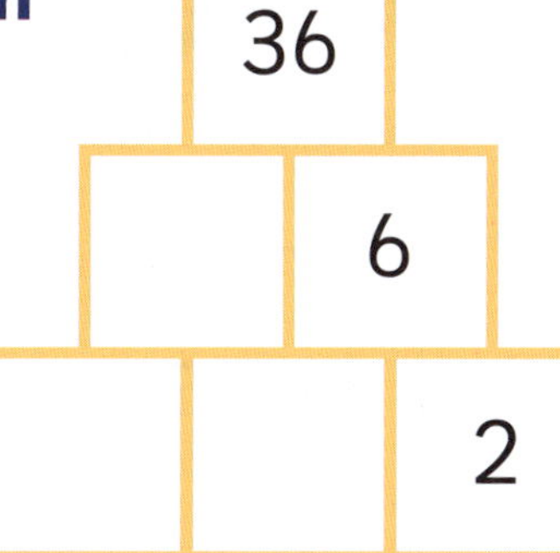

i
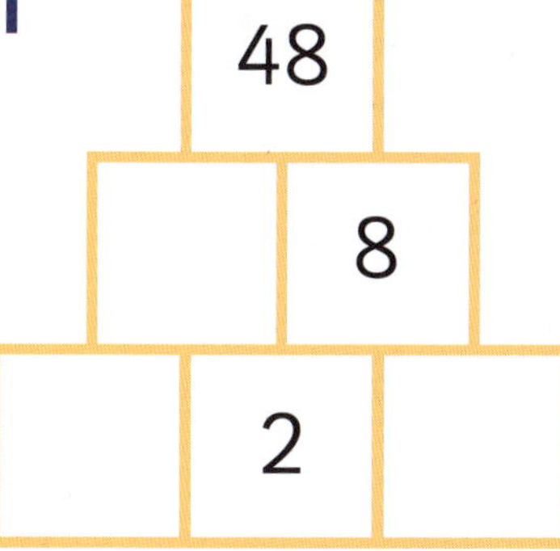

j
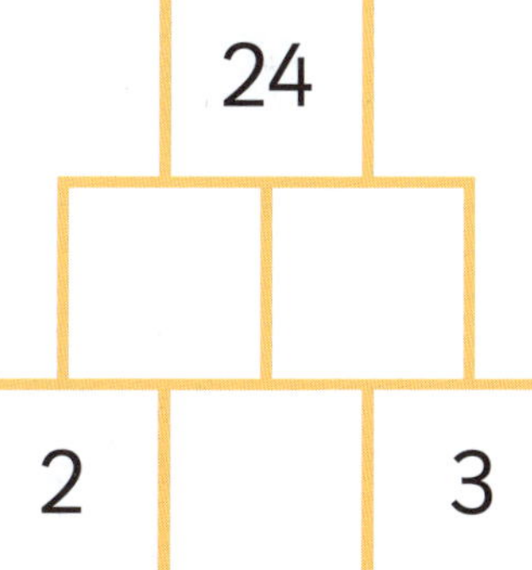

k

l
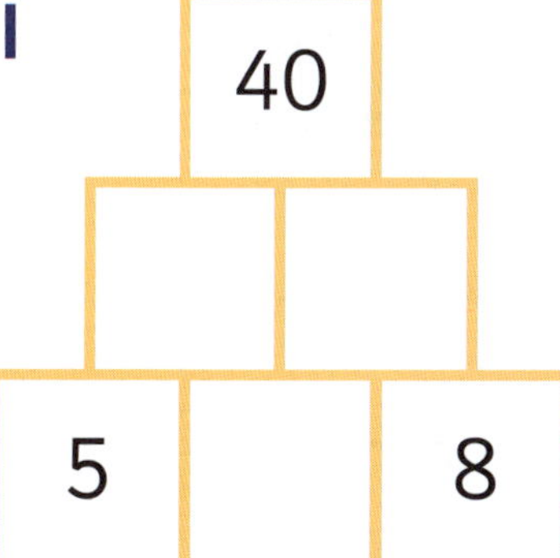

LESSON 191 FRACTION WORD PROBLEMS

1 a How many sea creatures are in this group? ______

b How many crabs? ______ c How many fish? ______

d How many seahorses? ______ e How many dolphins? ______

2 What fraction of the group are

a crabs? $\frac{\square}{\square}$ b fish? $\frac{\square}{\square}$ c seahorses? $\frac{\square}{\square}$ d dolphins? $\frac{\square}{\square}$

3 What fraction of the group are

a flowers? $\frac{\square}{\square}$ b sticks? $\frac{\square}{\square}$ c leaves? $\frac{\square}{\square}$

4 What fraction of the group are

a oranges? $\frac{\square}{\square}$ b apples? $\frac{\square}{\square}$ c pears? $\frac{\square}{\square}$

Mathseeds Year 3 Workbook © 3P Learning ISBN 978-1-923253-14-8

Colour the shapes to show the fractions and answer the equations.

5 a

b $\frac{3}{6} + \frac{2}{6} = \frac{\square}{6}$

6 a

b $\frac{5}{8} + \frac{2}{8} = \frac{\square}{8}$

7 a

b $\frac{4}{10} + \frac{3}{10} = \frac{\square}{10}$

8 a

b $\frac{1}{5} + \frac{3}{5} = \frac{\square}{5}$

9 Answer these equations.

a $\frac{2}{5} + \frac{1}{5} = \frac{\square}{5}$

b $\frac{2}{6} + \frac{2}{6} = \frac{\square}{6}$

c $\frac{4}{8} + \frac{2}{8} = \frac{\square}{8}$

d $\frac{5}{10} + \frac{3}{10} = \frac{\square}{10}$

e $\frac{2}{5} + \frac{3}{5} = \frac{\square}{5}$

f $\frac{1}{4} + \frac{2}{4} = \frac{\square}{4}$

g $\frac{5}{8} + \frac{2}{8} = \frac{\square}{8}$

h $\frac{4}{10} + \frac{4}{10} = \frac{\square}{10}$

i $\frac{1}{6} + \frac{2}{6} = \frac{\square}{6}$

  ISBN 978-1-923253-14-8

10 Label the fraction strips.

a
b
c

11 Fill in these equivalent fractions.

a 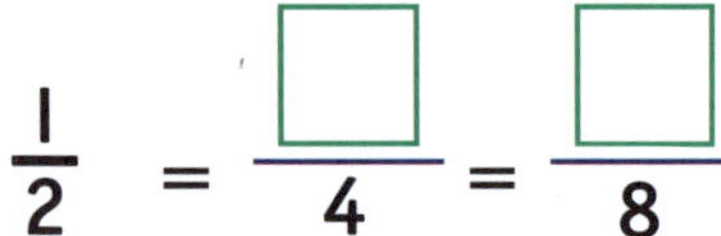

$\frac{1}{2} = \frac{\square}{4} = \frac{\square}{8}$

b $\frac{1}{4} = \frac{\square}{8}$

c $\frac{3}{4} = \frac{\square}{8}$

d $1 = \frac{\square}{2} = \frac{\square}{4} = \frac{\square}{8}$

12 Answer these equations. Find an equivalent fraction.

a $\frac{5}{8} + \frac{1}{8} = \frac{\square}{8} = \frac{\square}{\square}$

b $\frac{1}{8} + \frac{1}{8} = \frac{\square}{8} = \frac{\square}{\square}$

c $\frac{3}{8} + \frac{1}{8} = \frac{\square}{8} = \frac{\square}{\square}$

d $\frac{2}{8} + \frac{4}{8} = \frac{\square}{8} = \frac{\square}{\square}$

e $\frac{3}{8} + \frac{3}{8} = \frac{\square}{8} = \frac{\square}{\square}$

f $\frac{2}{8} + \frac{2}{8} = \frac{\square}{8} = \frac{\square}{\square}$

g $\frac{1}{4} + \frac{1}{4} = \frac{\square}{4} = \frac{\square}{\square}$

h $\frac{5}{8} + \frac{3}{8} = \frac{\square}{8} = \frac{\square}{\square}$

Mathseeds Year 3 Workbook © 3P Learning ISBN 978-1-923253-14-8

13 Complete the number line.

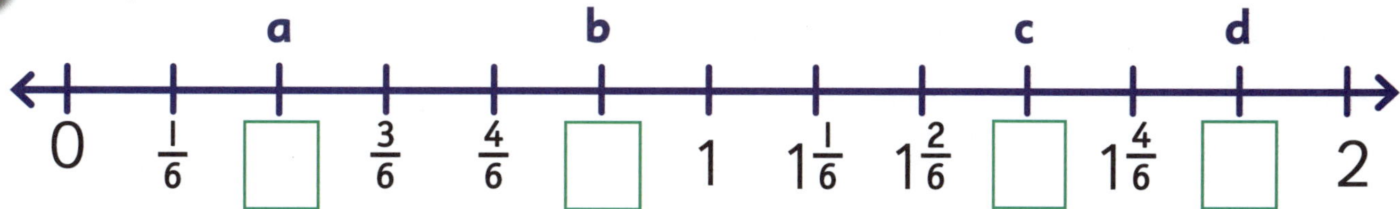

14 Order these mixed fractions from smallest to largest:

$1\frac{1}{2}$ $\frac{3}{4}$ $2\frac{1}{2}$ $1\frac{1}{4}$ $2\frac{3}{4}$ $\frac{1}{2}$ 2

a  **b** ☐ **c** ☐ **d** ☐ **e** ☐ **f** ☐ **g** ☐

15 Compare these pairs of mixed fractions using: **> < =**

a $1\frac{3}{4}$ ☐ $2\frac{3}{4}$ **b** $2\frac{1}{2}$ ☐ $3\frac{3}{4}$ **c** $4\frac{1}{4}$ ☐ $3\frac{3}{4}$

d $1\frac{3}{4}$ ☐ $1\frac{1}{4}$ **e** $2\frac{1}{2}$ ☐ $2\frac{3}{4}$ **f** $3\frac{1}{4}$ ☐ $3\frac{4}{8}$

g $1\frac{2}{8}$ ☐ $1\frac{1}{2}$ **h** $2\frac{6}{8}$ ☐ $2\frac{1}{2}$ **i** $4\frac{4}{8}$ ☐ $4\frac{1}{2}$

16 Write a fraction to complete the sum.

a $\frac{3}{4} > \frac{\square}{\square}$ **b** $1 = \frac{\square}{\square}$ **c** $\frac{1}{2} < \frac{\square}{\square}$

d $1\frac{1}{2} = \frac{\square}{\square}$ **e** $1 < \frac{\square}{\square}$ **f** $1\frac{6}{8} > \frac{\square}{\square}$

I finished this lesson online.

I can

- Find fractions of groups. ☐
- Add fractions with the same denominator, some with shape models. ☐
- Add quarters and 8ths with a fraction wall and find equivalent fractions. ☐
- Order and compare fractions and mixed numbers. ☐

We went to

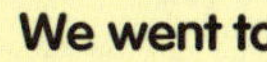

  ISBN 978-1-923253-14-8

LESSON 192 PERIMETER

1. Measure the sides with a ruler to find the perimeter of these shapes.

a

P = ______________

b

P = ______________

c

P = ______________

2. Write an addition number sentence to find the perimeter of each.

a soccer field

100 m

70 m

P = ______________________________

b swimming pool

25 m

20 m

P = ______________________________

c tennis court

37 m

18 m

P = ______________________________

Mathseeds Year 3 Workbook © 3P Learning ISBN 978-1-923253-14-8

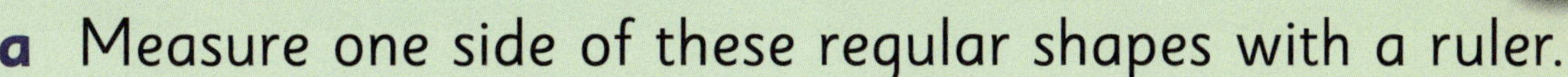

a Measure one side of these regular shapes with a ruler.

b Multiply by the number of sides to find the perimeter.

3 a ______

b ______________________

4 a ______

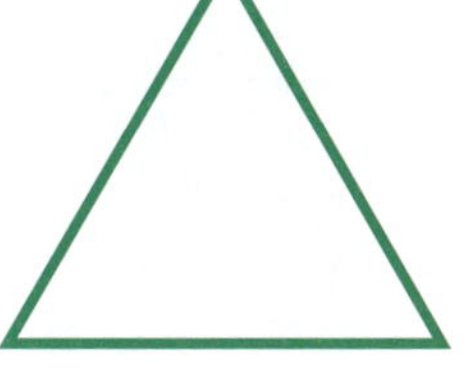

b ______________________

5 a ______

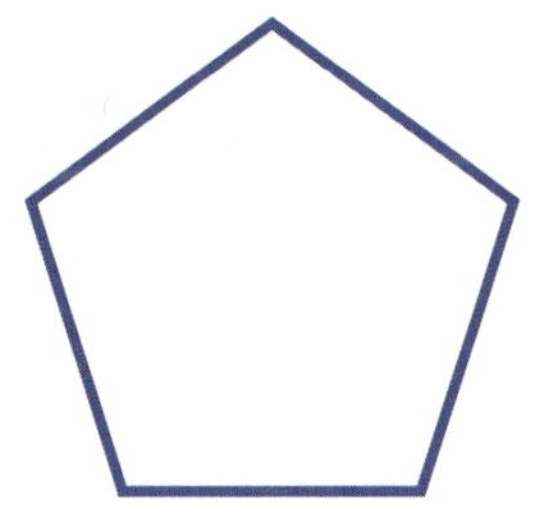

b ______________________

6 a ______

b ______________________

7 a ______

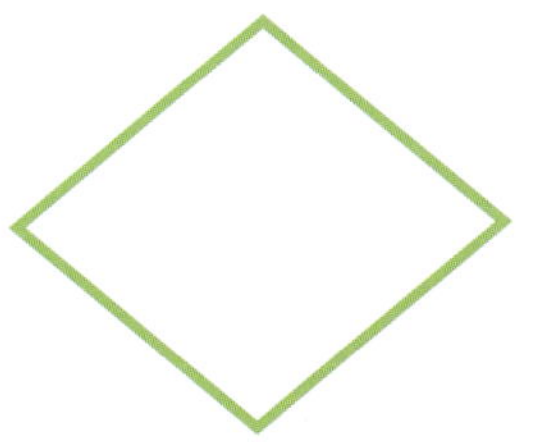

b ______________________

8 a ______

b ______________________

9 a ______

b ______________________

10 a ______

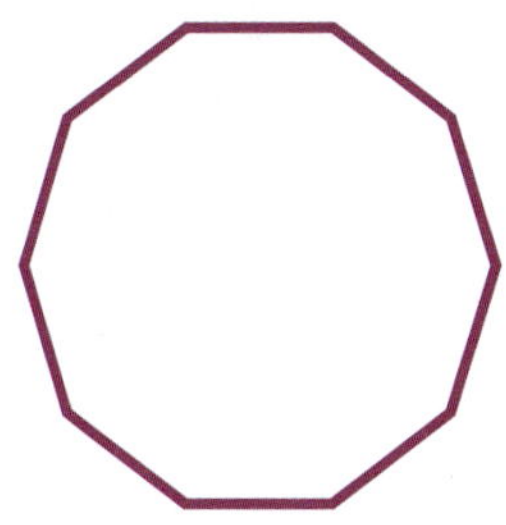

b ______________________

  ISBN 978-1-923253-14-8

Write an addition number sentence to find the perimeter of each letter.

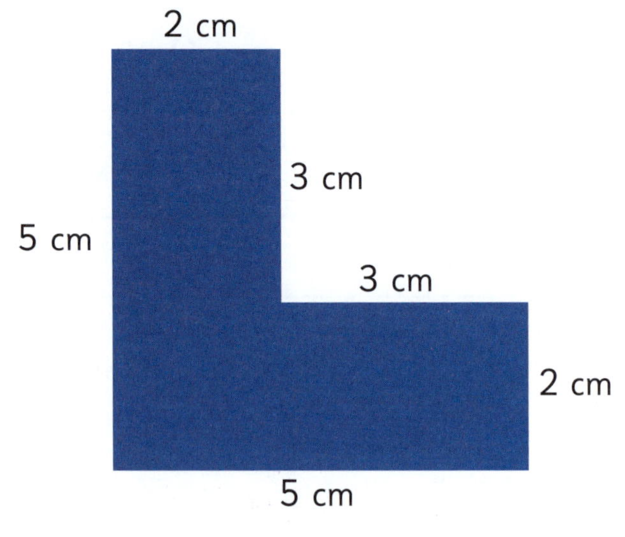

11 ______________________________

____

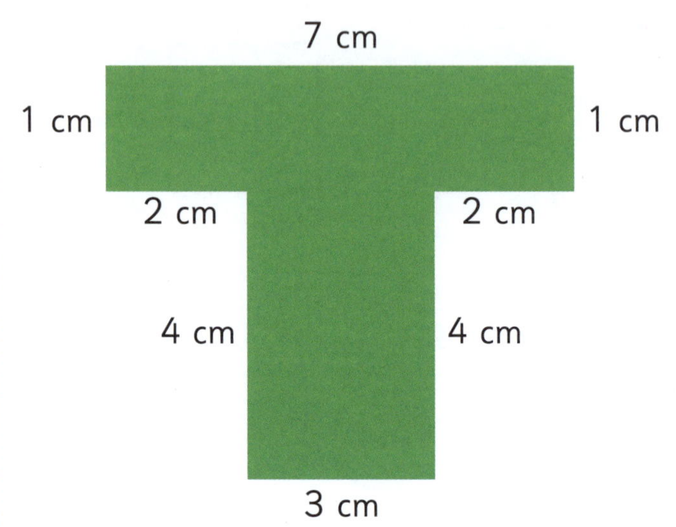

12 ______________________________

____

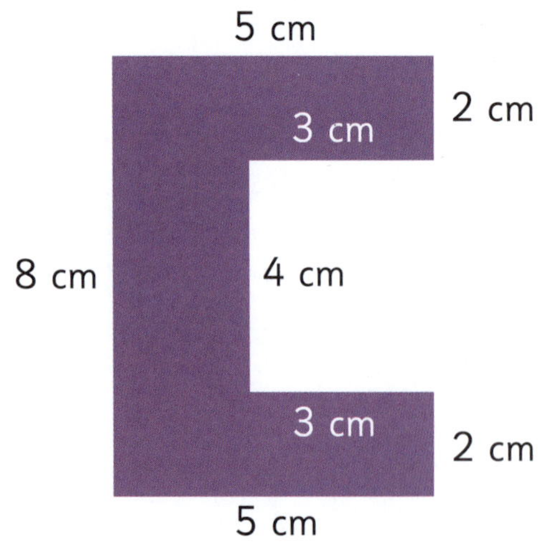

13 ______________________________

____

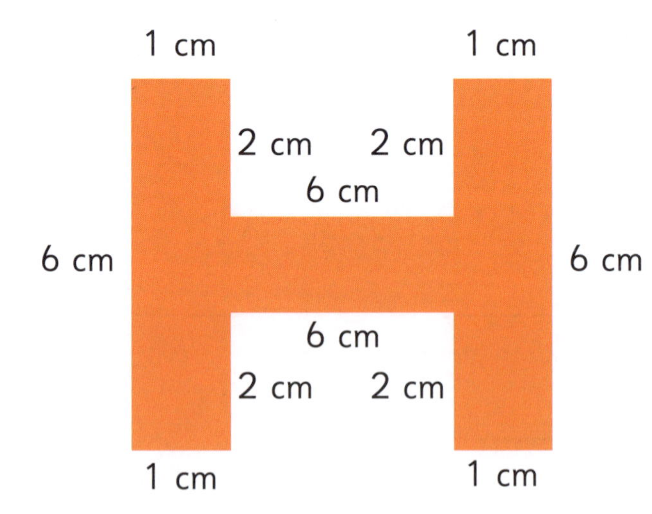

14 ______________________________

____

Mathseeds Year 3 Workbook © 3P Learning ISBN 978-1-923253-14-8

15 Waldo measured the insect enclosures. Find the perimeter of each. The cockroach tank is 120 cm long and 55 cm wide. The butterfly cage is 60 cm on all four sides. The spider chamber has five sides that are all 50 cm long. The stick insect enclosure has sides of 45 cm, 30 cm, 50 cm and 25 cm.

a Underline the question.

b Circle the facts.

c Draw a rough diagram and label the sides of each enclosure.

i The Cockroach Tank	**ii** The Butterfly Cage
iii The Spider Chamber	**iv** The Stick Insect Enclosure

d Write an addition equation to find the perimeter of each enclosure.

i ______________________

ii ______________________

iii ______________________

iv ______________________

I finished this lesson online.

I can

- Measure and add to find the perimeters of rectangles. ☐
- Measure and multiply to find the perimeters of regular polygons. ☐
- Add to find the perimeter of irregular shapes. ☐

We went to

1 Answer the algorithms.

a

Tens	Ones
	3
× 1	0

b

Tens	Ones
	8
× 1	0

c

Tens	Ones
	6
× 1	0

d

H	T	O
	4	2
×	1	0

e

H	T	O
	5	7
×	1	0

f

H	T	O
	1	9
×	1	0

2 Answer the equations.

a 23 × 10 = ______ **b** 76 × 10 = ______ **c** 38 × 10 = ______

d 69 × 10 = ______ **e** 81 × 10 = ______ **f** 94 × 10 = ______

3 Complete.

a

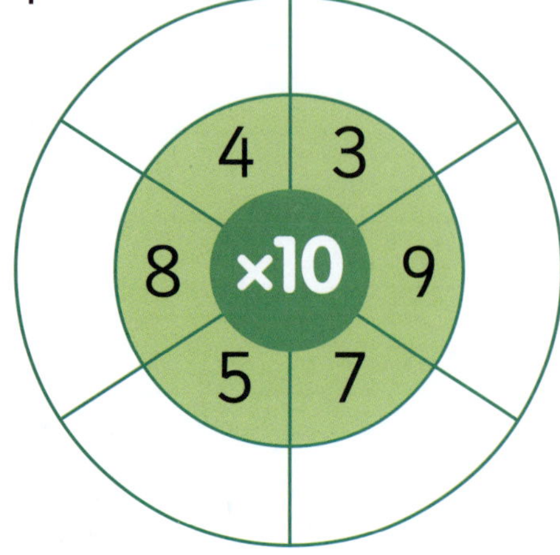

b

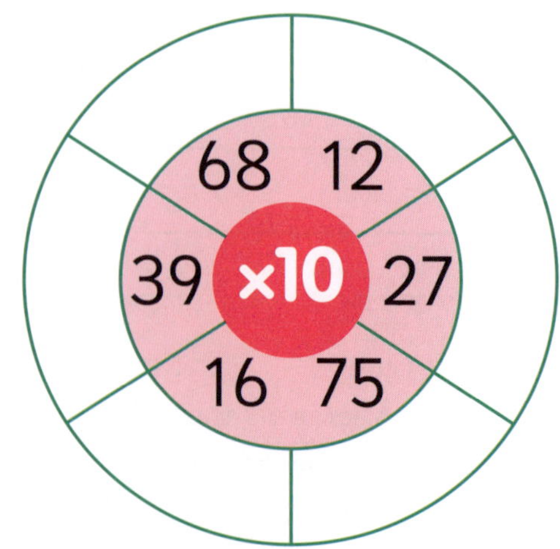

Mathseeds Year 3 Workbook © 3P Learning ISBN 978-1-923253-14-8

4 Split the multiple of ten to find the answer.

a $2 \times 30 =$ $2 \times 3 =$ ______ $\times 10 =$ ______

b $5 \times 20 =$ $5 \times 2 =$ ______ $\times 10 =$ ______

c $4 \times 40 =$ $4 \times$ ______ $=$ ______ $\times 10 =$ ______

d $7 \times 50 =$ $7 \times$ ______ $=$ ______ $\times 10 =$ ______

e $3 \times 80 =$ ____________________

f $6 \times 60 =$ ____________________

5 Answer the equations.

a $9 \times 20 =$ ______ b $7 \times 40 =$ ______ c $8 \times 50 =$ ______

d $3 \times 70 =$ ______ e $5 \times 90 =$ ______ f $6 \times 30 =$ ______

g $4 \times 60 =$ ______ h $5 \times 80 =$ ______ i $3 \times 30 =$ ______

j $7 \times 80 =$ ______ k $2 \times 50 =$ ______ l $9 \times 40 =$ ______

6 Complete.

a

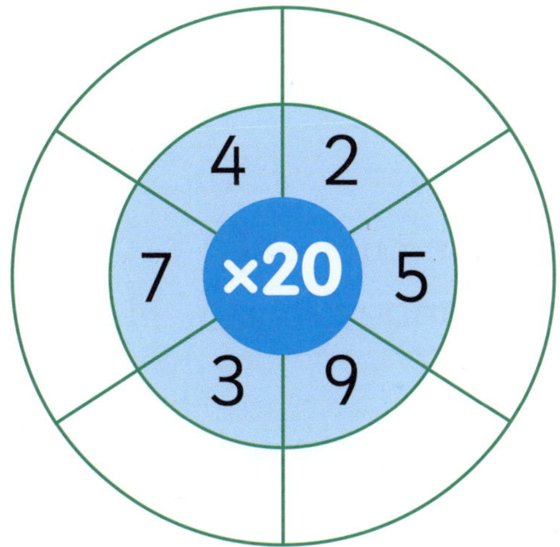

b

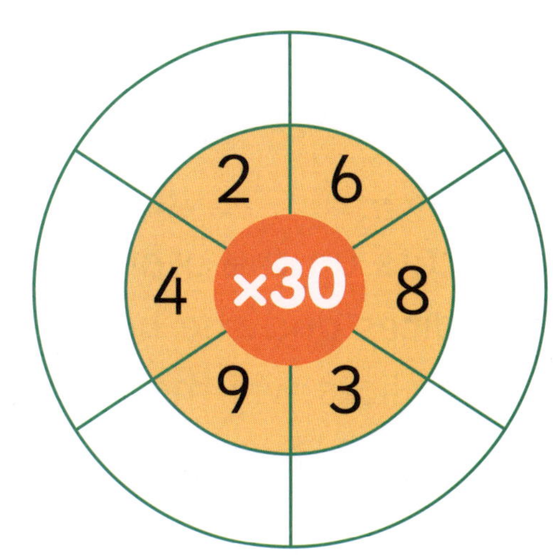

  ISBN 978-1-923253-14-8

Calculate the answers. Show your working.

7 Doc sees that there are twenty socks in each sock box. There are eight boxes of socks. How many socks altogether?

8 Dizzy has thirty bags of shirts in the storeroom. There are nine shirts in each bag. How many shirts in total?

9 Mango kicked four goals in every game this year. She played twenty games. How many goals did she kick over the year?

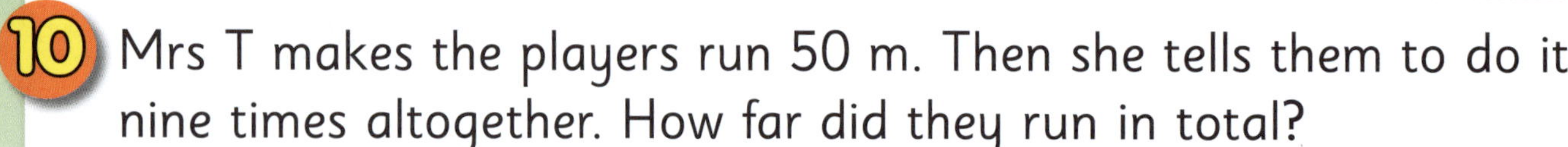

10 Mrs T makes the players run 50 m. Then she tells them to do it nine times altogether. How far did they run in total?

11 Ruby cuts up the oranges for half time. She cuts each orange into eight slices and she has a bag of thirty oranges to cut. How many orange slices will there be?

Mathseeds Year 3 Workbook © 3P Learning ISBN 978-1-923253-14-8

Calculate the answers. Show your working.

12 Mr Towers has thirty students in his science class. He gives each student four test tubes and five beakers. How many items has he handed out in total?

13 Mrs Fox has to mark four essays from every student she teaches. Her two English classes both have twenty students in them. How many essays is that altogether?

14 Ms Deacon takes two classes for circus arts on Friday afternoon. One class is twenty-five students and the other is thirty-five. If she plans to give each student three juggling pins, how many pins will she need?

15 Dr Evans needs to buy new laptops for his school. They want thirty laptops for each class. There are three classes in the lower grades and four classes in the upper grades. How many new laptops is that?

I finished this lesson online.

I can

- Use vertical algorithms and equations to multiply by 10. ☐
- Use the associative property to multiply multiples of ten. ☐
- Solve 1 and 2-step problems involving multiplying multiples of ten. ☐

We went to

LESSON 194 ROUNDING TO THE NEAREST 100

1 Round the number to the nearest ten. Circle your answer.

a

10 11 12 13 14 15 16 17 18 19 20

b

20 21 22 23 24 25 26 27 28 29 30

c

30 31 32 33 34 35 36 37 38 39 40

d

40 41 42 43 44 45 46 47 48 49 50

2 Round the number to the nearest hundred. Circle your answer.

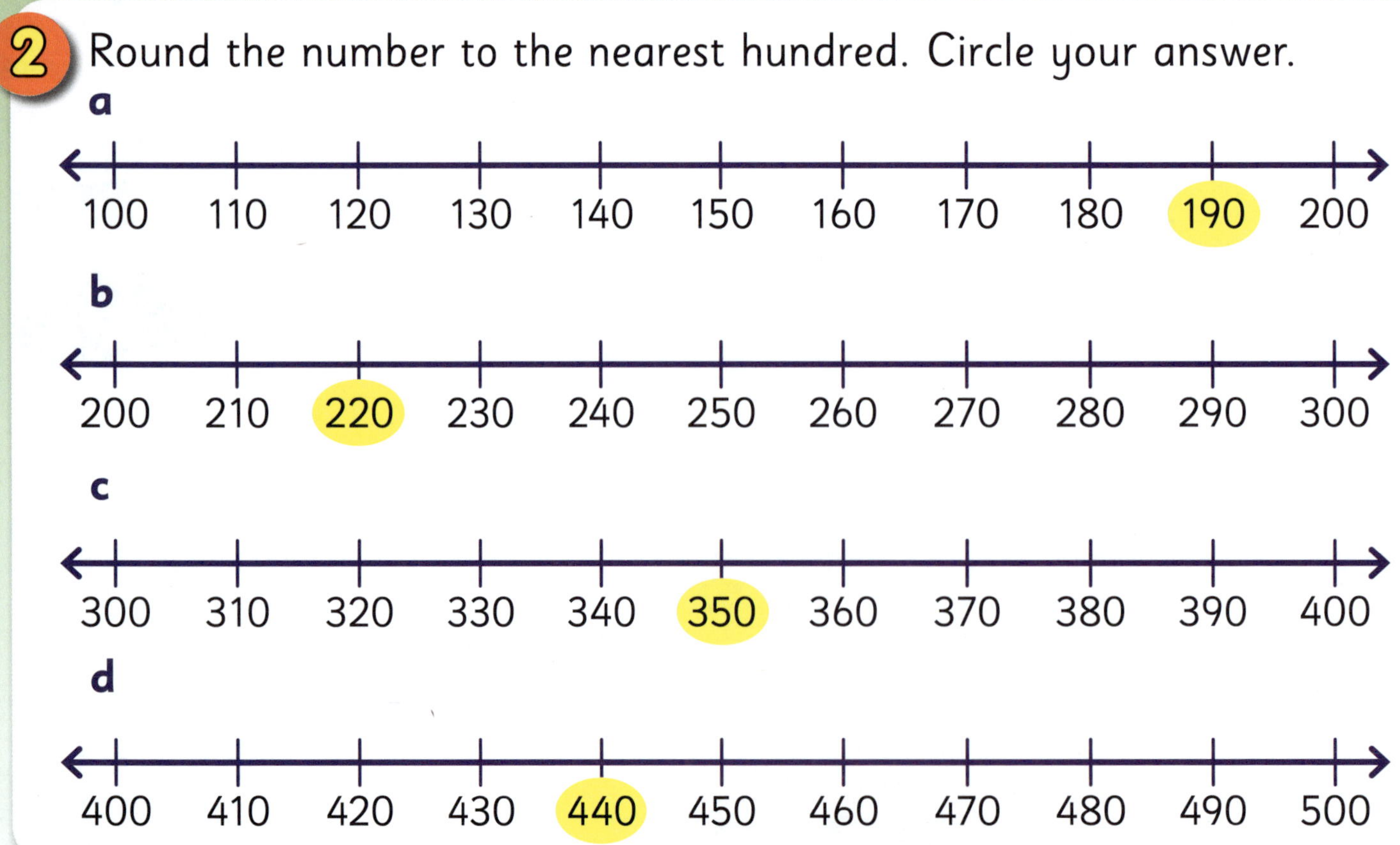

a

100 110 120 130 140 150 160 170 180 190 200

b

200 210 220 230 240 250 260 270 280 290 300

c

300 310 320 330 340 350 360 370 380 390 400

d

400 410 420 430 440 450 460 470 480 490 500

Mathseeds Year 3 Workbook © 3P Learning ISBN 978-1-923253-14-8

Rounding to the nearest 10

3 Draw a line for the midpoint.

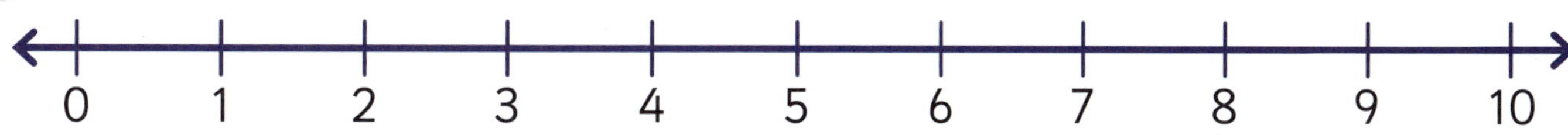

4 **a** Numbers from ________ to ________ will round up.

b Numbers from ________ to ________ will round down.

5 Round the number to the nearest 10.

a	52	☐	**b**	79	☐	**c**	84	☐
d	67	☐	**e**	31	☐	**f**	96	☐
g	23	☐	**h**	15	☐	**i**	48	☐

Rounding to the nearest 100

6 Draw a line for the midpoint.

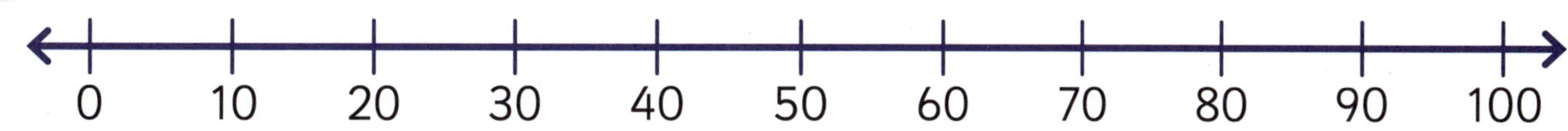

7 **a** Numbers from ________ to ________ will round up.

b Numbers from ________ to ________ will round down.

8 Round the number to the nearest 100.

a	710	☐	**b**	680	☐	**c**	550	☐
d	432	☐	**e**	999	☐	**f**	865	☐
g	101	☐	**h**	349	☐	**i**	251	☐

9 Round the number to the nearest 10.

a 143 ☐ **b** 578 ☐ **c** 851 ☐

d 602 ☐ **e** 985 ☐ **f** 329 ☐

10 Round the number to the nearest 100.

a 213 ☐ **b** 798 ☐ **c** 444 ☐

d 909 ☐ **e** 550 ☐ **f** 172 ☐

Use rounding to estimate an answer to these problems. Show your working.

11 Jon is buying timber for his building project. He needs seven lengths of 195 cm, but he has to order the timber in metres. About how much timber does he need?

Estimate: ☐ metres of timber

12 Anesh has 189 chickens. He lets about half of them brood and they hatch about two chicks each. About how many chicks are there?

Estimate: ☐ chicks

Mathseeds Year 3 Workbook © 3P Learning ISBN 978-1-923253-14-8

13 Doc wrote some clues for a number.
The nearest hundred is 300. The nearest ten is 30.
The number is even. What could the number be?

a Underline the question. **b** Circle the facts.

c Solve the problem using a number line.

The nearest hundred is 300.

Which numbers round up to 300?

Which numbers round down to 300?

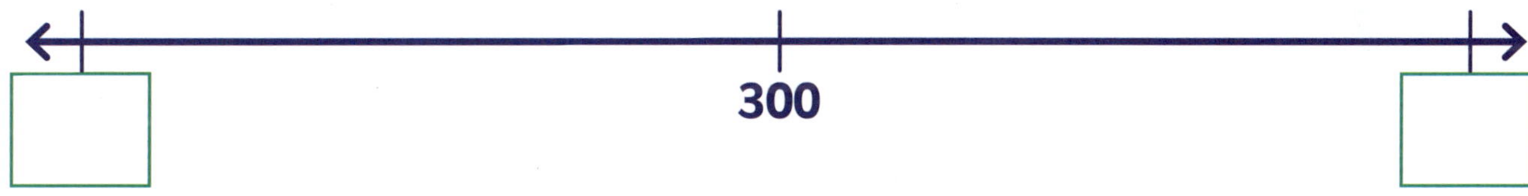

d *The nearest ten is 30.* Mark 30 on the number line.

e Let's zoom in on that section of the number line.

Which numbers round up to 330?

Which numbers round down to 330?

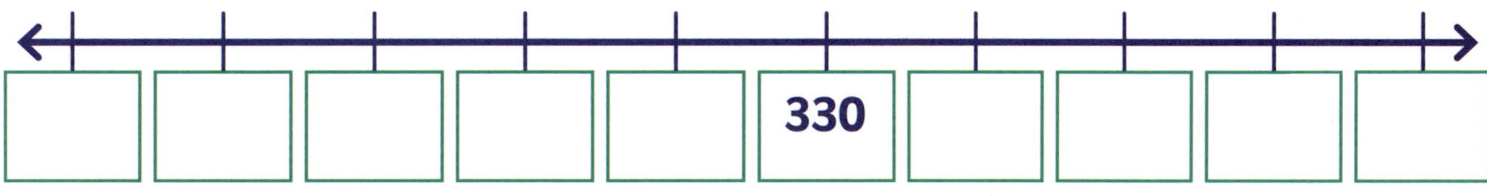

f *The number is even.* Highlight the even numbers above.

g What could the number be? ______________________

I finished this lesson online.

I can

- Use a number line to identify the 'midpoint' and round up or down. ☐
- Round 3-digit numbers to the nearest ten or hundred. ☐
- Use rounding and other clues to identify a number. ☐

We went to

  ISBN 978-1-923253-14-8

LESSON 195 ADDITION AND SUBTRACTION PATTERNS

1 Find the answers.

a

2 + 3 = ______

20 + 30 = ______

200 + 300 = ______

b

4 + 5 = ______

40 + 50 = ______

400 + 500 = ______

c

6 + 7 = ______

60 + 70 = ______

600 + 700 = ______

d

8 – 2 = ______

80 – 20 = ______

800 – 200 = ______

2 Complete the patterns.

a

8 + ______ = 16

80 + ______ = 160

800 + ______ = 1600

b

______ + 4 = 13

______ + 40 = 130

______ + 400 = 1300

c

14 – ______ = 7

140 – ______ = 70

1400 – ______ = 700

d

______ – 9 = 5

______ – 90 = 50

______ – 900 = 500

3 Fill in the patterns.

a

7 + 9 = ______

70 + ______ = ______

______ + ______ = ______

b

15 – 7 = ______

150 – ______ = ______

______ – ______ = ______

c

9 + 3 = ______

90 + ______ = ______

______ + ______ = ______

d

11 – 5 = ______

110 – ______ = ______

______ – ______ = ______

Mathseeds Year 3 Workbook © 3P Learning ISBN 978-1-923253-14-8

4 Find the answers.

a	b	c	d
5 + 4 = ____	6 + 6 = ____	3 + 17 = ____	28 + 9 = ____
15 + 4 = ____	6 + 16 = ____	13 + 17 = ____	28 + 19 = ____
25 + 4 = ____	6 + 26 = ____	23 + 17 = ____	28 + 29 = ____
35 + 4 = ____	6 + 36 = ____	33 + 17 = ____	28 + 39 = ____
45 + 4 = ____	6 + 46 = ____	43 + 17 = ____	28 + 49 = ____
55 + 4 = ____	6 + 56 = ____	53 + 17 = ____	28 + 59 = ____

5 Complete the patterns.

a	b	c
2 + 31 = ____	105 + 9 = ____	201 + 46 = ____
12 + 31 = ____	105 + 19 = ____	211 + 46 = ____
22 + 31 = ____	105 + 29 = ____	221 + 46 = ____
____ + 31 = ____	105 + ____ = ____	____ + 46 = ____
____ + 31 = ____	105 + ____ = ____	____ + 46 = ____
____ + 31 = ____	105 + ____ = ____	____ + 46 = ____

6 Add 10 to the first number.

12 + 325 = ____

____ + ____ = ____

____ + ____ = ____

____ + ____ = ____

____ + ____ = ____

____ + ____ = ____

7 Add 10 to the second number.

26 + 313 = ____

____ + ____ = ____

____ + ____ = ____

____ + ____ = ____

____ + ____ = ____

____ + ____ = ____

LESSON 195 ADDITION AND SUBTRACTION PATTERNS

8 Find the answers.

a	**b**	**c**	**d**
9 – 3 = ____	13 – 6 = ____	78 – 1 = ____	109 – 7 = ____
19 – 3 = ____	23 – 6 = ____	78 – 11 = ____	109 – 17 = ____
29 – 3 = ____	33 – 6 = ____	78 – 21 = ____	109 – 27 = ____
39 – 3 = ____	43 – 6 = ____	78 – 31 = ____	109 – 37 = ____
49 – 3 = ____	53 – 6 = ____	78 – 41 = ____	109 – 47 = ____
59 – 3 = ____	63 – 6 = ____	78 – 51 = ____	109 – 57 = ____

9 Complete the patterns.

a	**b**	**c**
217 – 12 = ____	804 – 101 = ____	325 – 23 = ____
227 – 12 = ____	814 – 101 = ____	325 – 33 = ____
237 – 12 = ____	824 – 101 = ____	325 – 43 = ____
____ – 12 = ____	____ – 101 = ____	325 – ____ = ____
____ – 12 = ____	____ – 101 = ____	325 – ____ = ____
____ – 12 = ____	____ – 101 = ____	325 – ____ = ____

10 Add 10 to the first number.

791 – 3 = ____

____ – ____ = ____

____ – ____ = ____

____ – ____ = ____

____ – ____ = ____

____ – ____ = ____

11 Add 10 to the second number.

575 – 18 = ____

____ – ____ = ____

____ – ____ = ____

____ – ____ = ____

____ – ____ = ____

____ – ____ = ____

Mathseeds Year 3 Workbook © 3P Learning ISBN 978-1-923253-14-8

Use two different strategies to solve each problem:
a a place value pattern **b** an algorithm.

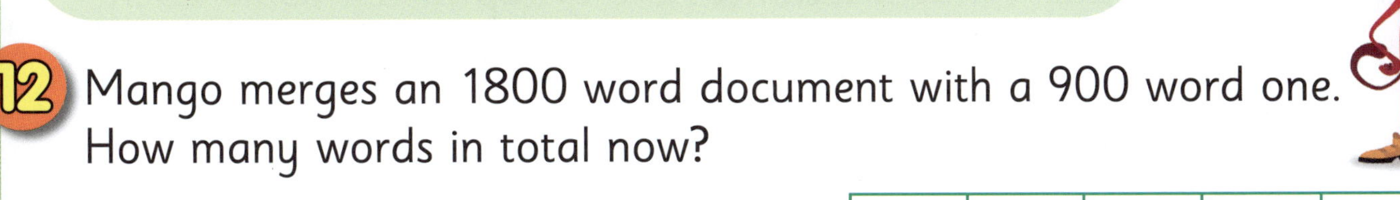

12 Mango merges an 1800 word document with a 900 word one. How many words in total now?

a 18 + 9 = _____

_____ + _____ = _____

_____ + _____ = _____

b

+				

13 Waldo has to choose 37 photos out of 654 to go in an album. How many photos will be left out?

a 654 – 7 = _____

_____ – _____ = _____

_____ – _____ = _____

_____ – _____ = _____

b

–			

14 Mrs T wants to own 1000 cacti but she only has 974. How many more cactus plants does she need?

a 1000 – 6 = _____

1000 – _____ = _____

1000 – _____ = 974

b

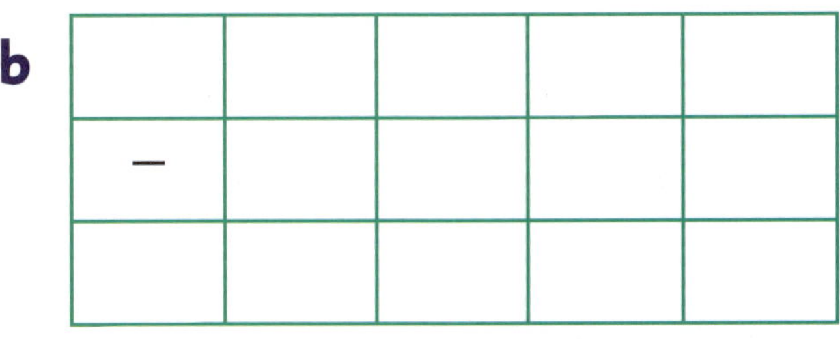

I finished this lesson online.

195

I can

- Complete place value patterns of addition and subtraction equations. ☐
- Use place value patterns and vertical algorithms to solve problems. ☐

We went to

1 Dizzy and Ruby bought ten pieces of fruit. They bought bananas, apples and pears. What fraction of the group of ten could each fruit be?

a Draw the 10 pieces of fruit.

b Write the fractions.

Bananas		Apples		Pears		Total
$\frac{\square}{\square}$	+	$\frac{\square}{\square}$	+	$\frac{\square}{\square}$	=	$\frac{\square}{\square}$

2 Calculate the perimeter of each shape. Write equations to show your working.

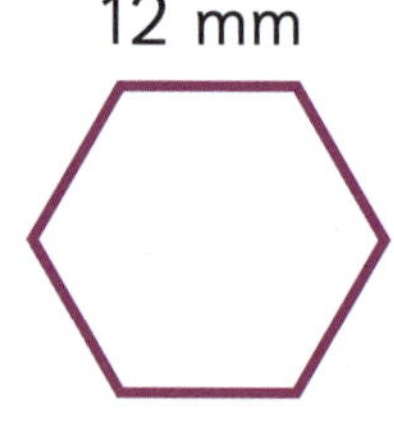

a ______________________

____

b ______________________

____

c ______________________

____

____

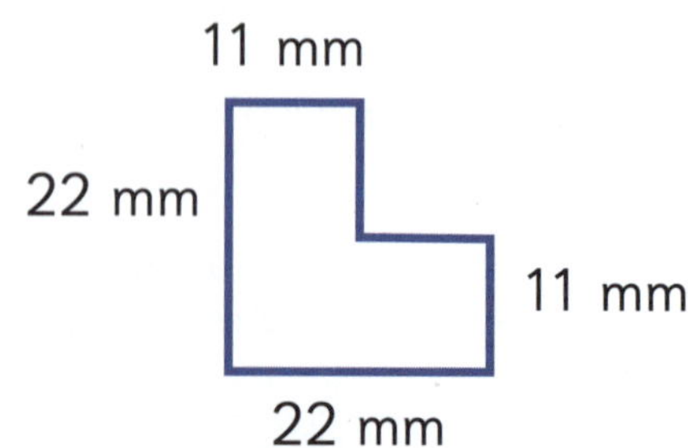

Mathseeds Year 3 Workbook © 3P Learning ISBN 978-1-923253-14-8

3 Split the multiple of ten to calculate the answer. Write equations to show your working.

Doc counted the seats in the stadium. There are 40 seats in a row and 9 rows in a stand. How many seats in a stand?

☐ × ☐ = ☐ × ☐ × ☐

☐ × ☐ = ☐ × ☐ = ☐

	Number	**4** Round to the nearest 10.	**5** Round to the nearest 100.
a	312		
b	667		
c	891		
d	205		
e	188		

6 Cross out the mistakes in these patterns. Write the correct number.

a

4 + 17 = 21

14 + 17 = 31

24 + 18 = 41

33 + 17 = 51

44 + 17 = 60

b

9 – 2 = 7

19 – 12 = 17

29 – 2 = 27

39 – 2 = 38

40 – 2 = 47

Awesome!

YOU COMPLETED

MAP 39

YOU CAN:

- [ ] Find **fractions** of a **group**.
- [ ] Calculate the **perimeter** of a rectangle, a regular hexagon and an irregular shape.
- [ ] Use the **associative property** to solve a multiplication problem.
- [ ] **Round** 3-digit numbers to the nearest **ten** or **hundred**.
- [ ] Correct mistakes in addition and subtraction **place value patterns**.

Signed:

Dated:

Mathseeds Year 3 Workbook © 3P Learning ISBN 978-1-923253-14-8

READ THE CODE

1 Match each answer to a letter. What is the message?

72	8	98	5	40	81	6	10	63	21	56
A	E	G	H	M	O	R	S	T	U	Y

7 × 8 = _____		9 × 9 = _____		74 – 53 = _____	
8 × 9 = _____		48 ÷ 8 = _____		64 ÷ 8 = _____	
42 + 56 = _____		54 ÷ 9 = _____		72 ÷ 9 = _____	
99 – 27 = _____		87 – 24 = _____		9 × 8 = _____	
7 × 9 = _____		5 × 8 = _____		55 + 17 = _____	
31 + 32 = _____		45 ÷ 9 = _____		80 ÷ 8 = _____	

2 What is the message?

____

____

LESSON 196 DIVISION WORD PROBLEMS

In each problem:
a circle the numbers and clues to numbers.
b fill in the equation and calculate the answer.

1 **a** Dizzy has 24 fishhooks. He shares them equally between himself, Ruby and Mrs T. How many fishhooks does each person get?

b _____ ÷ _____ = _____

2 **a** Mrs T makes 24 sandwiches. She puts an equal number into each of four boxes. How many sandwiches in each box?

b _____ ÷ _____ = _____

3 **a** Ruby has 24 m of fishing line. She cuts it into twelve equal lengths. How long is each short line?

b _____ ÷ _____ = _____

4 **a** Ruby, Mrs T and Dizzy each bring the same number of apples. Altogether they have 36 apples. How many did each person bring?

b _____ ÷ _____ = _____

5 Write a problem to go with this division equation.

36 ÷ 6 = 6

____

____

____

Mathseeds Year 3 Workbook © 3P Learning ISBN 978-1-923253-14-8

In each problem:

a circle numbers, clues for numbers and clues to the operation.

b write an equation and calculate the answer.

6 **a** Meg bought a hat for \$55 and a belt for \$37. How much did she spend altogether?

b ______________________________

7 **a** Ben has \$100 to spend. He got two books for \$38. How much money is left?

b ______________________________

8 **a** Peggy had \$80. She shared it equally between herself, her brother and her two sisters. How much did they each get?

b ______________________________

9 **a** Lenny bought six packets of rubber balls for \$9 each. How much did he spend in total?

b ______________________________

10 **a** Deb has fifty \$1 coins. She made ten equal groups of coins. How much is each group worth?

b ______________________________

11 **a** Ted was given \$50 for his birthday. He already had \$30. Then he spent \$60. How much is left?

b ______________________________

LESSON 196 DIVISION WORD PROBLEMS

Write 2 equations to solve these problems.

12 Dizzy made five pepperoni pizzas. He cut them into eight slices each and then shared them equally between himself, Ruby, Mango and Waldo. How many slices did each person get?

a ______________ b ______________

13 Mrs T made 18 cactus burritos. Yum! She put an equal number on plates for herself, cousin Carlotta and Doc. Doc and Mrs T ate all of theirs, but Carlotta only ate four. How many are left?

a ______________ b ______________

14 Mango picked 30 apples and shared them equally into five buckets. Next she gave two buckets to Carlotta. She kept the other buckets. How many apples did Mango keep?

a ______________ b ______________

15 Waldo caught 17 fish on Saturday and 19 on Sunday. On Monday night he put them in equal groups on six skewers and cooked them all up. How many fish were on each skewer?

a ______________ b ______________

16 Ruby shared 44 crackers equally between herself and Dizzy. Then Mrs T gave her 7 more. How many crackers does Ruby have now?

a ______________ b ______________

Mathseeds Year 3 Workbook © 3P Learning ISBN 978-1-923253-14-8

Solve the problems. Show your working.

17 Quinn has to put together a playlist for the party. He merges two lists – there are 37 songs in the rock list and 53 songs in the pop list. The playlist is three hours long. How many minutes long is each song?

18 Ling wants fairy lights all the way along the 90 m fence. She borrows two 12 m strings of lights from Rin. How many 11 m lengths of lights does Ling need to buy to finish the job?

19 Minh needs to make 45 invitations. She has made 21 already. It takes her ten minutes to make two invitations. How long will it take Minh to make the rest?

20 Pina is baking cupcakes. She does 12 in each batch and each batch takes 30 minutes. Plus, she needs an extra 10 minutes per batch to decorate them. If she aims to make 72 cupcakes, how long will it take altogether?

I finished this lesson online. 196

I can
- Solve division word problems by using equations and division facts. ☐
- Write equations to solve problems using all operations. ☐
- Solve multi-step word problems involving division. ☐

We went to

LESSON 197 WHOLE NUMBER FRACTIONS

1 Complete these sentences using the words **numerator** and **denominator**.

a In the whole number fraction $\frac{6}{3}$, 6 is the ________________.

b In the whole number fraction $\frac{6}{3}$, 3 is the ________________.

c In a whole number fraction, the ________________ is the number of parts in all the shapes, the total number of parts.

d In a whole number fraction, the ________________ is the number of parts one shape is divided into, the type of fraction.

2 Fill in the fractions to match.

a

b

c

d

e

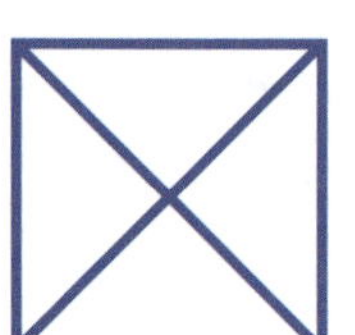

f

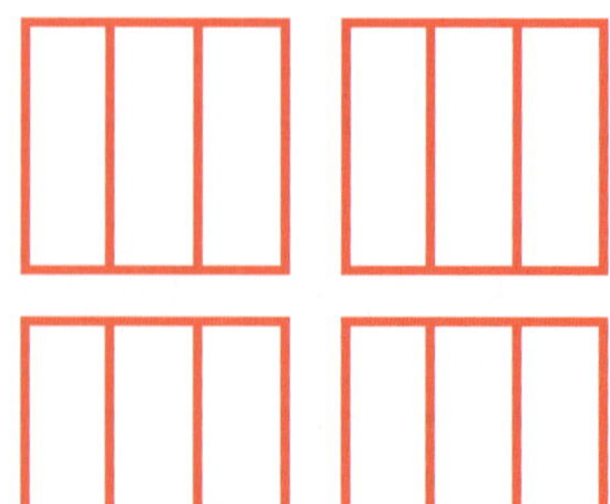

Mathseeds Year 3 Workbook © 3P Learning ISBN 978-1-923253-14-8

3 Match the fractions.

a

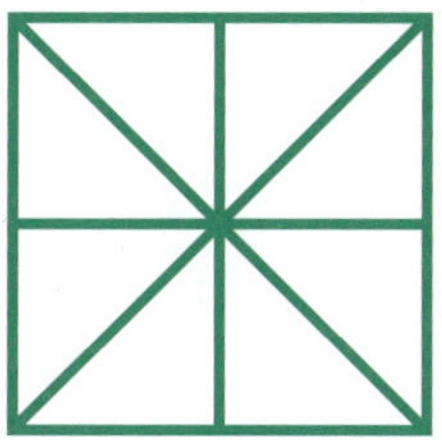

$\frac{18}{6}$

$\frac{20}{5}$

b

c

$\frac{18}{3}$

$\frac{12}{4}$

d

$\frac{8}{8}$

e

$\frac{10}{2}$

f

4 Draw shapes to show these fractions.

a $\frac{10}{5}$

b $\frac{6}{2}$

c $\frac{16}{4}$

d $\frac{9}{3}$

  ISBN 978-1-923253-14-8

5 Complete this sentence using the words **numerator** and **denominator**.

To find the whole number equivalent for a whole number fraction,

divide the ____________________ by the ____________________ .

6 Find the whole number equivalent.

a $\frac{12}{2}$ = 12 ÷ 2 = ____

b $\frac{20}{4}$ = 20 ÷ 4 = ____

c $\frac{16}{8}$ = ____ ÷ ____ = ____

d $\frac{21}{3}$ = ____ ÷ ____ = ____

e $\frac{30}{5}$ = ____ ÷ ____ = ____

f $\frac{12}{6}$ = ____ ÷ ____ = ____

7 Find the whole number equivalent.

a $\frac{2}{2}$ = ____ wholes

b $\frac{10}{1}$ = ____ wholes

c $\frac{15}{3}$ = ____ wholes

d $\frac{40}{4}$ = ____ wholes

e $\frac{30}{6}$ = ____ wholes

f $\frac{24}{8}$ = ____ wholes

8 Complete.

a $\frac{\square}{2}$ = 7 wholes

b $\frac{\square}{1}$ = 9 wholes

c $\frac{25}{\square}$ = 5 wholes

d $\frac{40}{\square}$ = 5 wholes

Mathseeds Year 3 Workbook © 3P Learning ISBN 978-1-923253-14-8

Write an equivalent whole number fraction and divide the shapes to match.

9 3 wholes

10 6 wholes

11 4 wholes

12 10 wholes

I finished this lesson online.

197

I can

- Understand the terms numerator and denominator.
- Write, draw and match whole number fractions and shape models.
- Use division to find a whole number equivalent for a whole number fraction.

We went to

LESSON 198 MEASUREMENT DATA

1 How far did each snail go?

a Anna ________ cm　　**b** Bob ________ cm

c Cleo ________ cm　　**d** Dan ________ cm

e Erin ________ cm　　**f** Finn ________ cm

g Gru ________ cm　　**h** Hera ________ cm

i Ian ________ cm　　**j** Jing ________ cm

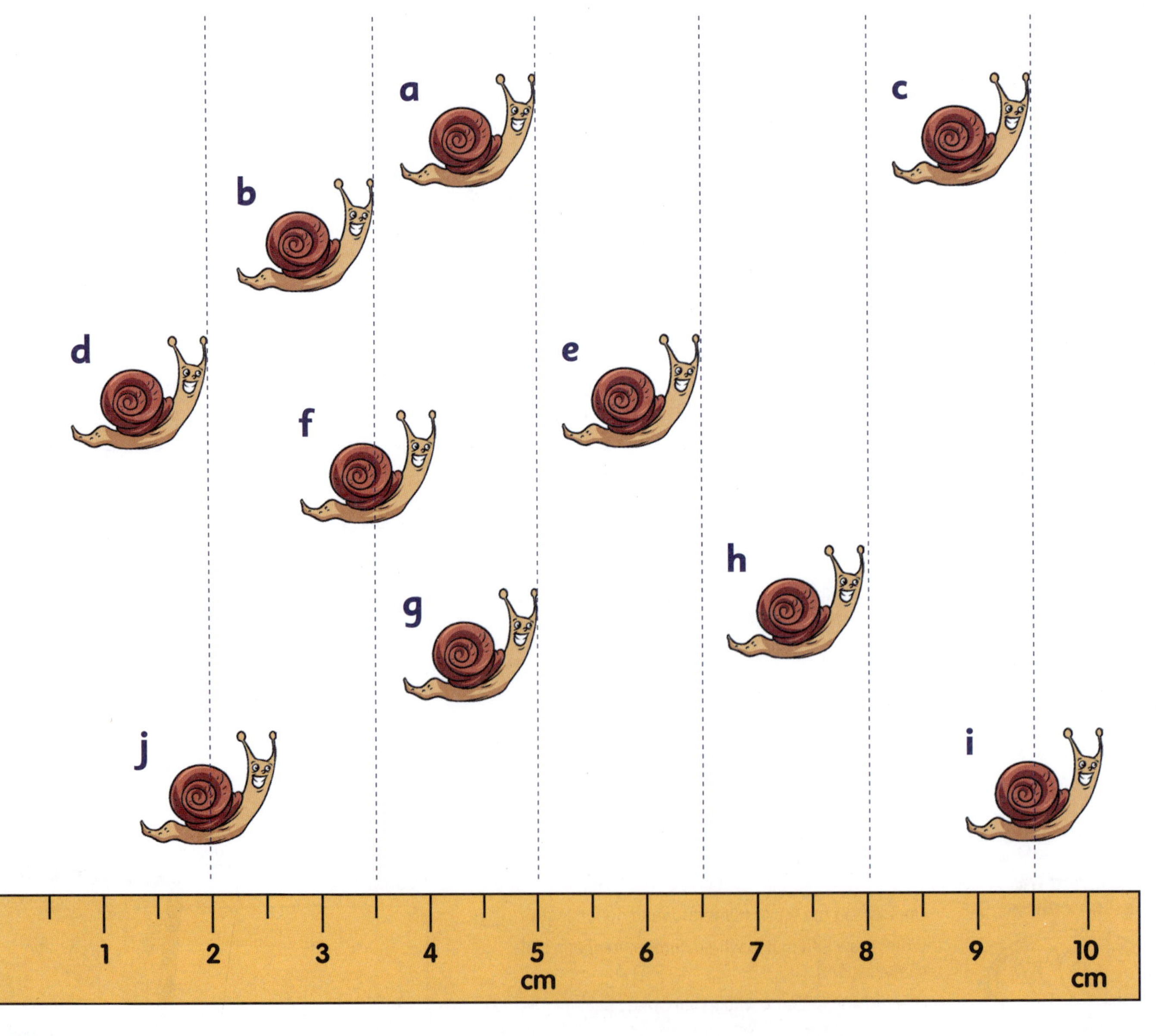

Mathseeds Year 3 Workbook © 3P Learning ISBN 978-1-923253-14-8

2 Use the distance measurements from page 230 to fill this data table.

Snail	Distance	Snail	Distance
a Anna		**f** Finn	
b Bob		**g** Gru	
c Cleo		**h** Hera	
d Dan		**i** Ian	
e Erin		**j** Jing	

3 Use the data in the table to fill in the column graph.

Snail Trail Distances

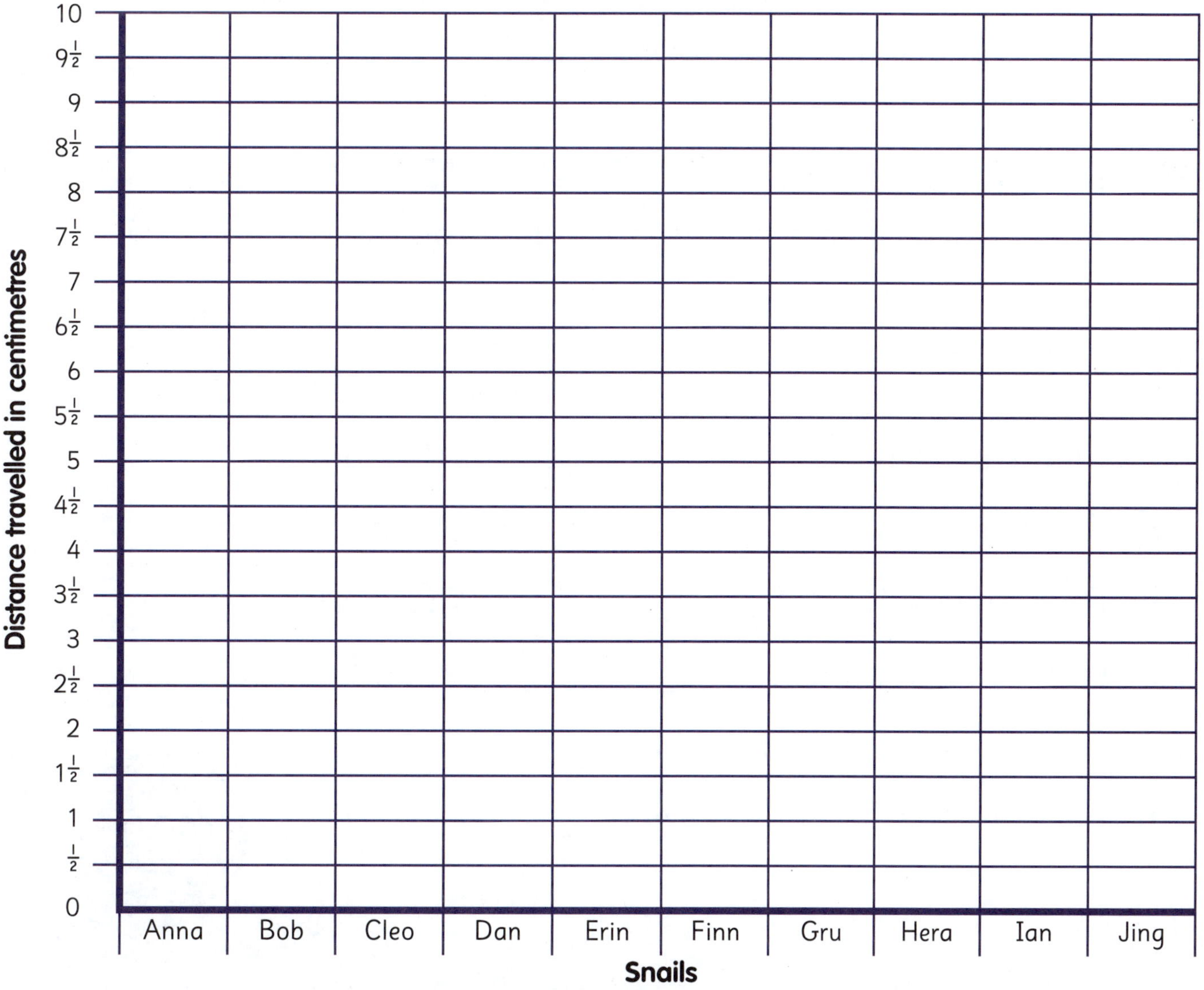

Distance travelled in centimetres: 10, $9\frac{1}{2}$, 9, $8\frac{1}{2}$, 8, $7\frac{1}{2}$, 7, $6\frac{1}{2}$, 6, $5\frac{1}{2}$, 5, $4\frac{1}{2}$, 4, $3\frac{1}{2}$, 3, $2\frac{1}{2}$, 2, $1\frac{1}{2}$, 1, $\frac{1}{2}$, 0

Snails: Anna, Bob, Cleo, Dan, Erin, Finn, Gru, Hera, Ian, Jing

  ISBN 978-1-923253-14-8

LESSON 198 MEASUREMENT DATA

4 Answer the questions based on the graph from page 231.

a Which snail travelled the shortest distance? ________________

b How far did it travel? ________________

c Which snail travelled the greatest distance? ________________

d How far did it travel? ________________

e Which two snails moved the same distance? ________________

f How far did they travel? ________________

g How many snails went over 5 cm? ________________

h How many snails went 5 cm or less? ________________

5 Complete the statements based on the graph from page 231.

a Bob and Hera travelled ________________ cm altogether.

b Jing and ________________ travelled $6\frac{1}{2}$ cm altogether.

c Cleo travelled ________________ cm further than Erin.

d Anna travelled ________________ cm less than Ian.

e Dan travelled 3 cm ________________ than Gru.

f Hera travelled 4 cm ________________ than Finn.

g Jing travelled 4 cm less than ________________.

h Ian travelled 5 cm more than ________________.

Mathseeds Year 3 Workbook © 3P Learning ISBN 978-1-923253-14-8

6 Measure the length of each of your ten fingers. Record the measurements.

Left	Thumb	Pointer Finger	Middle Finger	Ring Finger	Little Finger
Length					
Right	**Thumb**	**Pointer Finger**	**Middle Finger**	**Ring Finger**	**Little Finger**
Length					

7 Make a column graph of your data.

Title:

Fingers	Thumb	Pointer	Middle	Ring	Little	Thumb	Pointer	Middle	Ring	Little
Hands	Left hand					Right hand				

I finished this lesson online.

I can

- Measure distance in centimetres and half centimetres.
- Record distance data in a table and make it into a column graph.
- Interpret the data in the column graph.
- Collect data and make a column graph.

We went to

  ISBN 978-1-923253-14-8

1 Fold this sheet in half. Complete the top half. Time yourself.

a 8 × 2 = ______	**b** 7 × 7 = ______	**c** 3 × 9 = ______
d 6 × 5 = ______	**e** 4 × 9 = ______	**f** 5 × 5 = ______
g 10 × 3 = ______	**h** 9 × 8 = ______	**i** 7 × 4 = ______
j 8 × 8 = ______	**k** 9 × 2 = ______	**l** 4 × 6 = ______
m 3 × 8 = ______	**n** 9 × 9 = ______	**o** 6 × 10 = ______
p 7 × 9 = ______	**q** 8 × 4 = ______	**r** 6 × 6 = ______
s 5 × 4 = ______	**t** 6 × 8 = ______	**u** 6 × 3 = ______
v 10 × 10 = ______	**w** 7 × 5 = ______	**x** 9 × 6 = ______
y 5 × 9 = ______	**z** 6 × 7 = ______	**Time:** ______

2 Complete the bottom half. Time yourself. Were you faster?

a 4 × 4 = ______	**b** 7 × 8 = ______	**c** 8 × 6 = ______
d 8 × 5 = ______	**e** 3 × 7 = ______	**f** 9 × 4 = ______
g 8 × 3 = ______	**h** 9 × 5 = ______	**i** 4 × 5 = ______
j 8 × 9 = ______	**k** 7 × 6 = ______	**l** 5 × 7 = ______
m 9 × 3 = ______	**n** 4 × 8 = ______	**o** 9 × 7 = ______
p 5 × 6 = ______	**q** 2 × 9 = ______	**r** 4 × 7 = ______
s 6 × 9 = ______	**t** 10 × 4 = ______	**u** 7 × 10 = ______
v 6 × 4 = ______	**w** 8 × 7 = ______	**x** 3 × 5 = ______
y 4 × 3 = ______	**z** 5 × 8 = ______	**Time:** ______

Mathseeds Year 3 Workbook © 3P Learning ISBN 978-1-923253-14-8

3 What number completes the pairs of inverse operations?

a 3 × 4 = ______ ______ ÷ 4 = 3

b 6 × ______ = 30 30 ÷ ______ = 6

c 9 × 8 = ______ ______ ÷ 8 = 9

d 4 × ______ = 36 36 ÷ ______ = 4

e ______ × 10 = 70 70 ÷ 10 = ______

f ______ × 7 = 56 56 ÷ 7 = ______

4 Write the inverse operation.

a 6 × 10 = 60 ______________________

b 48 ÷ 8 = 6 ______________________

c 3 × 5 = 15 ______________________

d 20 ÷ 4 = 5 ______________________

e 7 × 9 = 63 ______________________

f 100 ÷ 10 = 10 ______________________

5 Complete the number fact families.

a 5 × 7 = ______

7 × 5 = ______

______ ÷ 5 = 7

______ ÷ 7 = 5

b 4 × 8 = ______

______ × ______ = ______

______ ÷ ______ = ______

______ ÷ 4 = 8

c 6 × 9 = ______

______ × ______ = ______

______ ÷ ______ = ______

______ ÷ ______ = ______

d ______ × ______ = ______

______ × ______ = ______

42 ÷ 6 = ______

______ ÷ ______ = ______

  ISBN 978-1-923253-14-8

6 Fold this sheet in half. Complete the top half. Time yourself.

a 16 ÷ 4 = ______	**b** 56 ÷ 7 = ______	**c** 48 ÷ 8 = ______
d 21 ÷ 3 = ______	**e** 36 ÷ 6 = ______	**f** 90 ÷ 9 = ______
g 40 ÷ 5 = ______	**h** 32 ÷ 4 = ______	**i** 54 ÷ 9 = ______
j 35 ÷ 5 = ______	**k** 60 ÷ 10 = ______	**l** 28 ÷ 7 = ______
m 63 ÷ 7 = ______	**n** 36 ÷ 4 = ______	**o** 45 ÷ 5 = ______
p 72 ÷ 9 = ______	**q** 64 ÷ 8 = ______	**r** 42 ÷ 6 = ______
s 24 ÷ 8 = ______	**t** 25 ÷ 5 = ______	**u** 81 ÷ 9 = ______
v 24 ÷ 4 = ______	**w** 30 ÷ 6 = ______	**x** 27 ÷ 9 = ______
y 18 ÷ 3 = ______	**z** 20 ÷ 5 = ______	**Time:** ______

7 Complete the bottom half. Time yourself. Were you faster?

a 80 ÷ 10 = ______	**b** 49 ÷ 7 = ______	**c** 54 ÷ 6 = ______
d 28 ÷ 4 = ______	**e** 63 ÷ 9 = ______	**f** 30 ÷ 5 = ______
g 100 ÷ 10 = ______	**h** 42 ÷ 7 = ______	**i** 35 ÷ 7 = ______
j 72 ÷ 8 = ______	**k** 20 ÷ 4 = ______	**l** 81 ÷ 9 = ______
m 27 ÷ 3 = ______	**n** 18 ÷ 6 = ______	**o** 45 ÷ 9 = ______
p 24 ÷ 6 = ______	**q** 48 ÷ 6 = ______	**r** 32 ÷ 8 = ______
s 70 ÷ 7 = ______	**t** 40 ÷ 8 = ______	**u** 21 ÷ 7 = ______
v 24 ÷ 3 = ______	**w** 64 ÷ 8 = ______	**x** 36 ÷ 9 = ______
y 36 ÷ 6 = ______	**z** 56 ÷ 8 = ______	**Time:** ______

Mathseeds Year 3 Workbook © 3P Learning ISBN 978-1-923253-14-8

Fluent ×÷ within 100

8 Use multiplication facts to solve each problem.

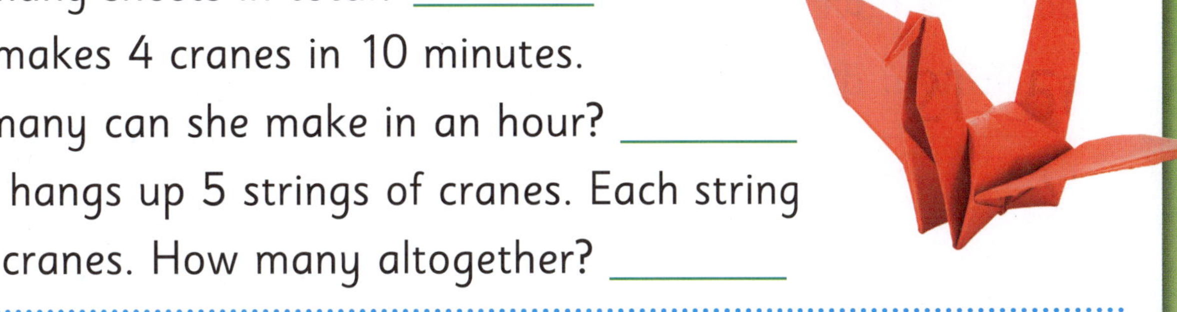

a Doc has 7 packs of paper. Each pack holds 7 sheets. How many sheets in total? ________

b Ruby makes 4 cranes in 10 minutes. How many can she make in an hour? ________

c Mrs T hangs up 5 strings of cranes. Each string has 8 cranes. How many altogether? ________

9 Use division facts to solve each problem.

a Dizzy has 90 cranes. He shares them between 10 strings. How many on each string? ________

b Mango made 81 cranes. She had 9 packs of paper. How many sheets in each pack? ________

c Waldo buys 6 packs of paper for $36 altogether. How much was each pack? ________

10 Write equations to show your solutions to these problems.

a Ruby has 3 packs of paper. Each pack holds 8 sheets. She makes all the sheets of paper into cranes and then shares them between 4 strings. How many cranes on each string?

____

b Doc buys 5 packs of paper for $30 altogether. Each pack has 3 sheets of super-special, fancy paper in it. How much is each sheet of paper?

____

I finished this lesson online.	I can	We went to
199	• Complete timed quizzes on multiplication and division facts. ☐ • Write inverse operations and number fact families. ☐ • Solve multiplication and division word problems. ☐	

LESSON 200 AREA PROBLEM-SOLVING

1 Mrs T's new kitchen is 5 m wide by 7 m long. She has a bench in the middle that is 2 m wide by 3 m long. How much floor space does she have?

a Draw a diagram of the kitchen.

b Calculate the area of the whole kitchen.

____

c Calculate the area of the bench.

____

d Calculate the floor space in the kitchen.

____

2 Calculate the green floor space.

a

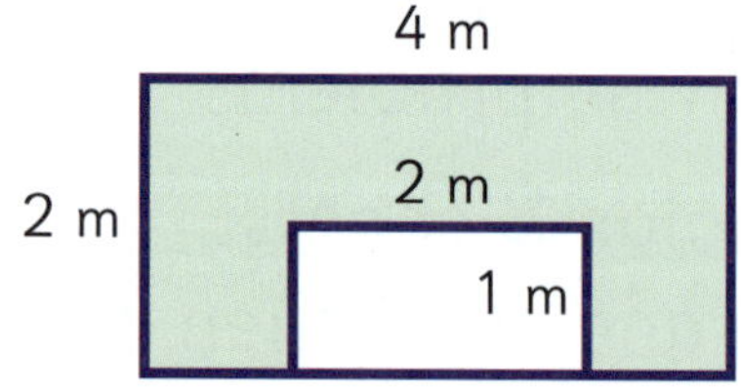

____ × ____ = ____

____ × ____ = ____

____ − ____ = ____

b

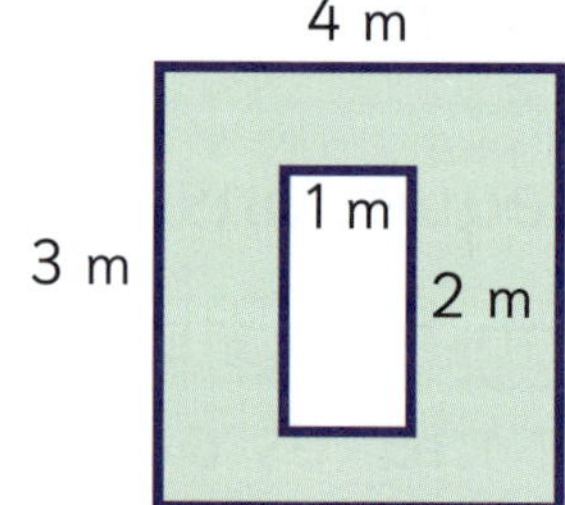

____ × ____ = ____

____ × ____ = ____

____ − ____ = ____

c

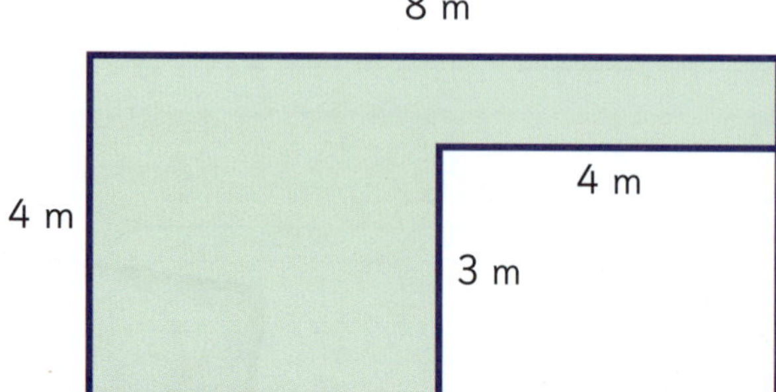

____

____

____

Mathseeds Year 3 Workbook © 3P Learning ISBN 978-1-923253-14-8

3 Mango made an enclosure for her bugs. How much space do the bugs have?

a Divide the shape into two rectangles.

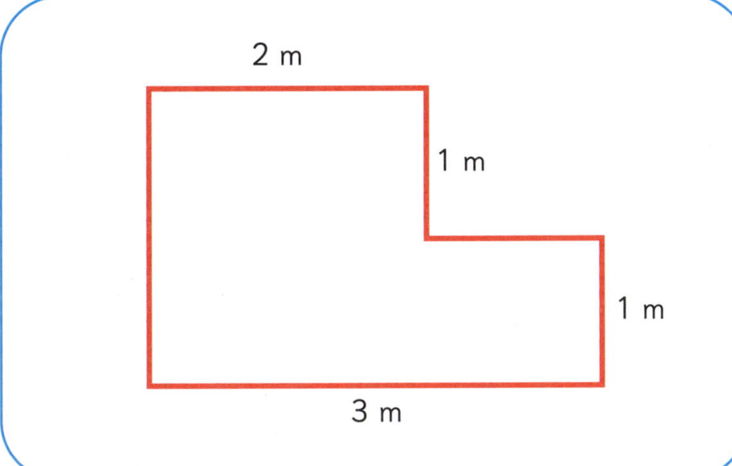

b Calculate the area of one rectangle.

____

c Calculate the area of the other rectangle.

____

d Calculate the area of the whole enclosure.

____

4 Calculate the area of each irregular shape.

a

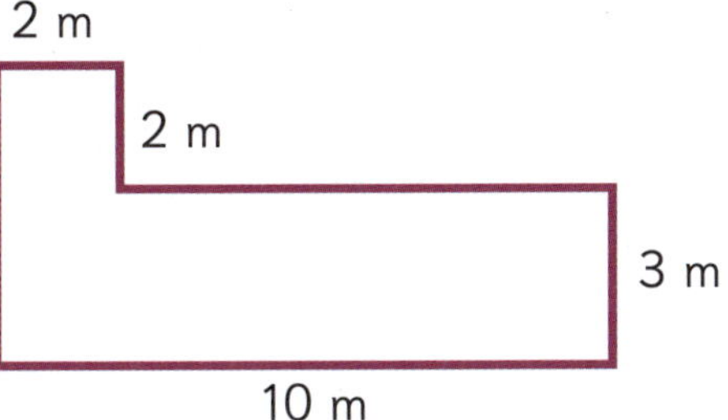

____ × ____ = ____

____ × ____ = ____

____ − ____ = ____

b

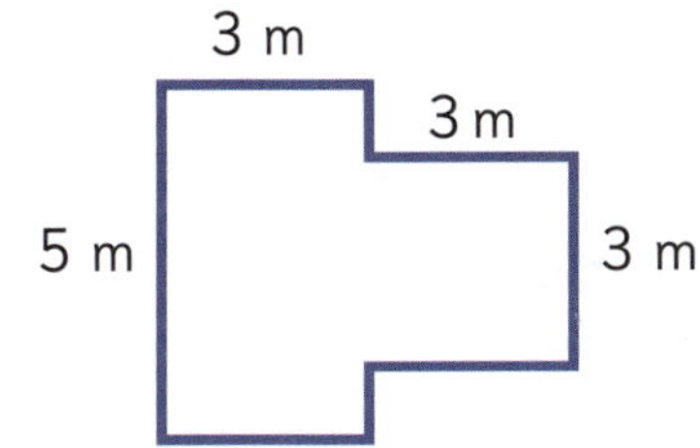

____ × ____ = ____

____ × ____ = ____

____ − ____ = ____

c

2 m   2 m

3 m

8 m

10 m

____

____

____

____

5 Calculate the area of each wall.

a
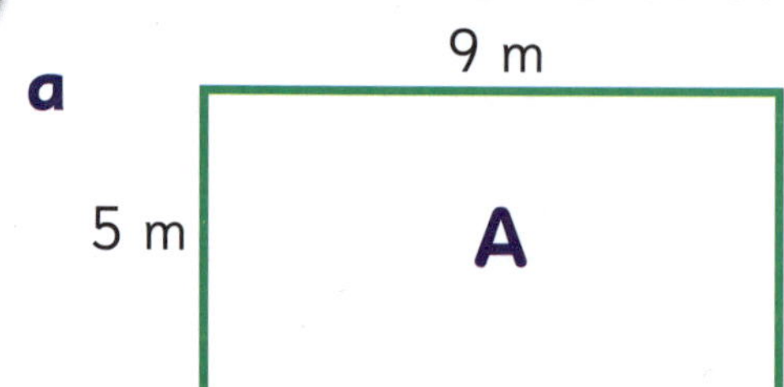

b
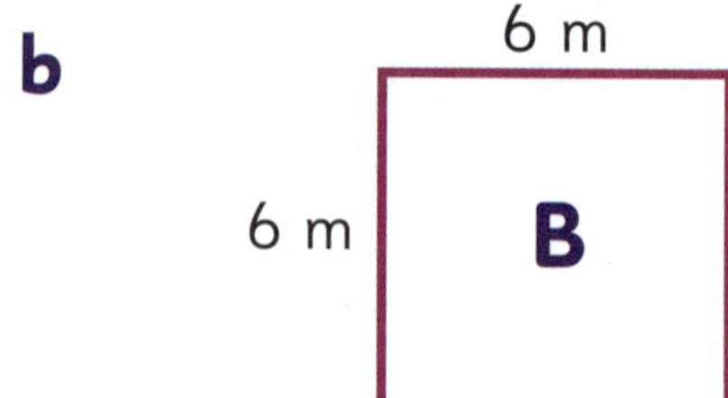

c
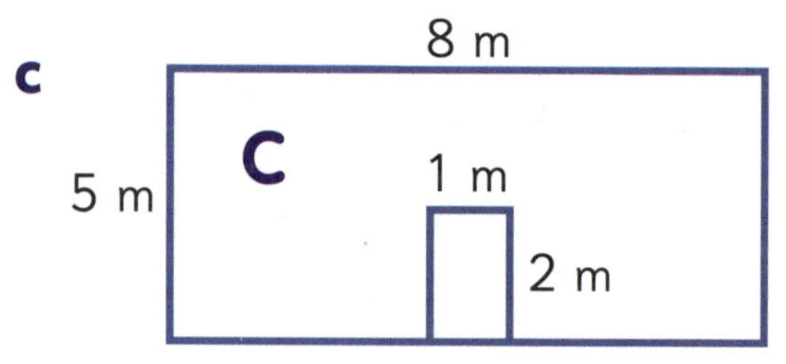

d
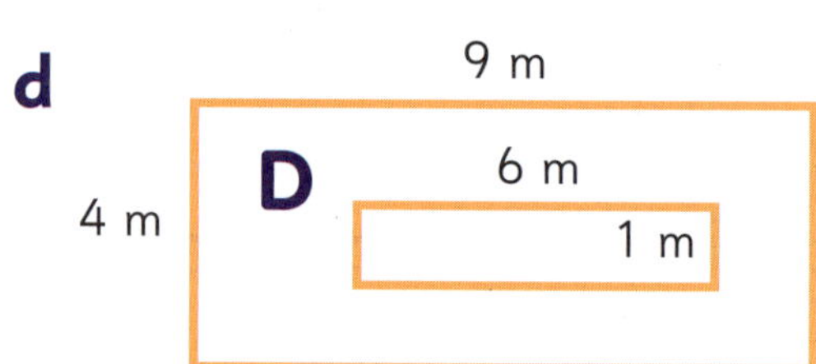

e
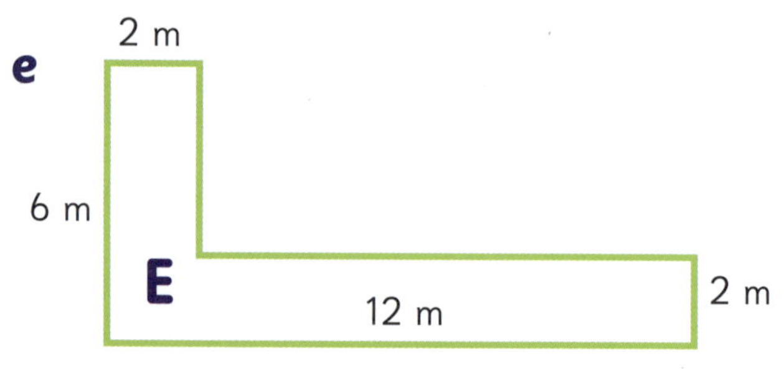

f
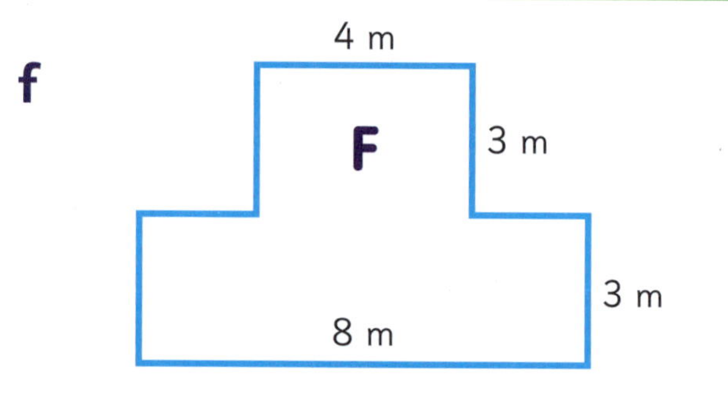

6 Colour:

a the wall with the largest area red.
b the wall with the smallest area blue.
c the walls with equal areas green.

7 A 5 L can of paint will cover 35 m^2. Circle which walls could be painted with a 5 L can of paint. **A B C D E F**

Mathseeds Year 3 Workbook © 3P Learning ISBN 978-1-923253-14-8

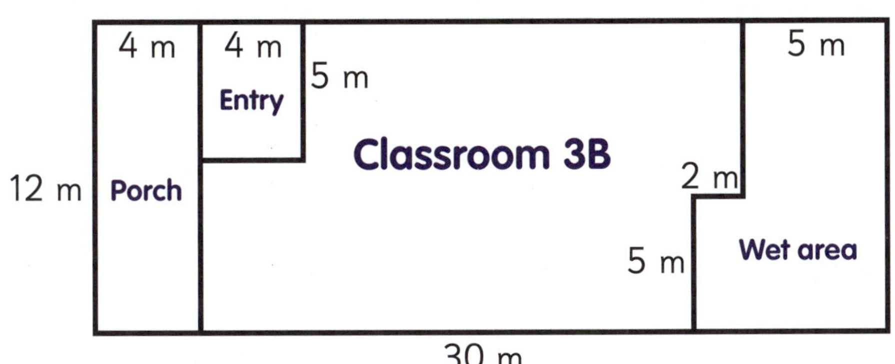

The classroom is getting new flooring. Help work out the cost.

8 Linoleum for the entry costs \$20 for 1 m^2.

a Calculate the area of the entry: ______________________

b Calculate the cost of linoleum for this area: ______________________

9 Paint for the porch costs \$25 a litre. 1 litre covers 30 m^2.

a Calculate the area of the porch: ______________________

b How many litres of paint will cover this area? ______________________

c Calculate the cost of the paint: ______________________

10 Tiles for the wet area cost \$30 per 1 m^2.

a Calculate the wet area: ______________________

____

b Calculate the cost of tiles for this area: ______________________

11 Carpet for the classroom costs \$10 for 1 m^2.

a Calculate the classroom area: ______________________

____

b Calculate the cost of the carpet: ______________________

____

I finished this lesson online.

I can
- Solve irregular area problems involving adding subtracting. ☐
- Compare areas. ☐
- Solve multi-step problems with area and money. ☐

We went to

QUIZ

END OF MAP 40 QUIZ

1 Write equations to solve the problem.

Ruby, Mrs T and Dizzy have six buckets, each with four fish. They share the fish equally between them. How many fish does each person get?

____

2 Complete these sentences using the words numerator and denominator.

In a whole number fraction, the ______________ is the number of parts one shape is divided into, the type of fraction.

In a whole number fraction, the ______________ is the number of parts in all the shapes, the total number of parts.

3 Find the whole number equivalent.

a $\frac{20}{4}$ = _____ ÷ _____ = _____ **b** $\frac{24}{6}$ = _____ ÷ _____ = _____

c $\frac{15}{5}$ = _____ **d** $\frac{27}{3}$ = _____ **e** $\frac{32}{8}$ = _____

4 Complete the number fact families.

a

7 × 5 = _____

_____ × _____ = _____

_____ ÷ _____ = _____

_____ ÷ _____ = _____

b

_____ × _____ = _____

_____ × _____ = _____

45 ÷ 9 = _____

_____ ÷ _____ = _____

Mathseeds Year 3 Workbook © 3P Learning ISBN 978-1-923253-14-8

5 Make a graph using the data from the results table.

a Write the title.

b Label the scale.

c Fill in the scale.

d Write the names.

e Fill in the columns.

Under 9 Long Jump Results	
Name	**Distance**
Kim	5 m
Lek	$4\frac{1}{2}$ m
Maria	2 m
Nin	3 m
Odin	$2\frac{1}{2}$ m
Pablo	1 m
Rob	$3\frac{1}{2}$ m
Sera	$4\frac{1}{2}$ m

c

a

b

d

6 Draw a diagram of the yard. Calculate the answer.

Dizzy's yard is 12 m wide. It is twice as long. It has a paved section measuring 6 × 4 m in the middle. A bag of grass seed covers 10 m^2. How many bags of grass seed does he need?

______ bags of grass seed

Excellent!

YOU COMPLETED

MAP 40

YOU CAN:

- [ ] Solve a 2-step **word problem** involving **division**.
- [ ] Complete sentences using the terms **numerator** and **denominator**.
- [ ] Find whole number equivalents for **whole number fractions**.
- [ ] Complete **number fact families** for multiplication and division.
- [ ] Make a **column graph**.
- [ ] Solve a **multi-step problem** with **area**.

Signed:

Dated:

Mathseeds Year 3 Workbook © 3P Learning ISBN 978-1-923253-14-8

FUN SPOT 10

MULTIPLICATION PUZZLES

1 Ruby has some multiplication puzzles for Mango. In each grid the numbers multiply across like an equation, and also down like vertical sums. Using your times tables knowledge, can you solve the puzzles?

a Underline the question. **b** Circle the facts.

c Mango started the first one. Can you solve the puzzles?

5	4	20
2	9	
10		

6	3	
5	9	

2 Mango says these are too easy. She makes the same type of multiplication puzzle, but with only the answers filled in. Can you solve these puzzles?

		14
		20
8	35	

		12
		32
24	16	

3 Then Ruby comes up with an even trickier version of this puzzle. Can you solve it?

2	4		72
3	3		72
			72
72	72	72	

	Number	1 Round to the nearest 10.	2 Round to the nearest 100.
a	742		
b	439		

3 Split one factor to make easier sums and find the answer.

Waldo has 25 tanks with six crabs in each. How many crabs in total?

_____ × _____ = _____ × _____ + _____ × _____ = _____

4 Split the multiple of ten to calculate the answer.

Doc counted the seats in the stadium. There are 40 seats in a row and 9 rows in a stand. How many seats in a stand?

☐ × ☐ = ☐ × ☐ × 10

☐ × ☐ = ☐ × 10 = ☐

5 Complete each number fact family.

a
3 × 6 = ☐
☐ × ☐ = ☐
☐ ÷ ☐ = ☐
☐ ÷ ☐ = ☐

b
☐ × ☐ = ☐
☐ × ☐ = ☐
45 ÷ 9 = ☐
☐ ÷ ☐ = ☐

6 Write equations to solve the problem.

Ruby, Mrs T and Dizzy have eight buckets, each with six fish. They share the fish equally between themselves and Waldo. How many fish does each person get?

____

Mathseeds Year 3 Workbook © 3P Learning ISBN 978-1-923253-14-8

7 Calculate the answer. Don't forget to regroup.

a
$$\begin{array}{r} 837 \\ -\ 756 \\ \hline \end{array}$$

b
$$\begin{array}{r} 629 \\ -\ 318 \\ \hline \end{array}$$

c
$$\begin{array}{r} 740 \\ -\ 536 \\ \hline \end{array}$$

d
$$\begin{array}{r} 518 \\ -\ 182 \\ \hline \end{array}$$

8 Lou buys a TV for $1600 and a new cabinet for $700.
How much did he spend in total?

a Use a place value pattern.

_____ + _____ = _____

_____ + _____ = _____

_____ + _____ = _____

b Use an algorithm.

+				

9 Draw a bar diagram or a number line to solve this problem.

There are 145 girls in the school and 289 boys. How many students in the school?

10 Write equations to solve the problem.

Every morning Amy walks 500 m to the supermarket.
Then she walks 200 m to the café and 300 m to the post office.
After that she walks home the same way. How far in metres does she walk? How far that is in kilometres?

11 Colour right angles red. Colour smaller angles blue.
Colour larger angles green.

a 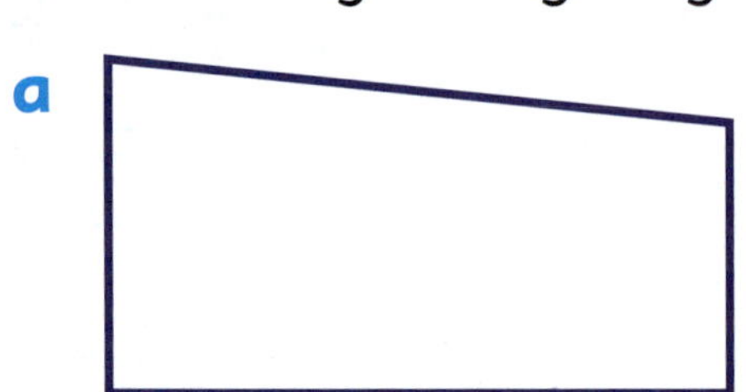

b 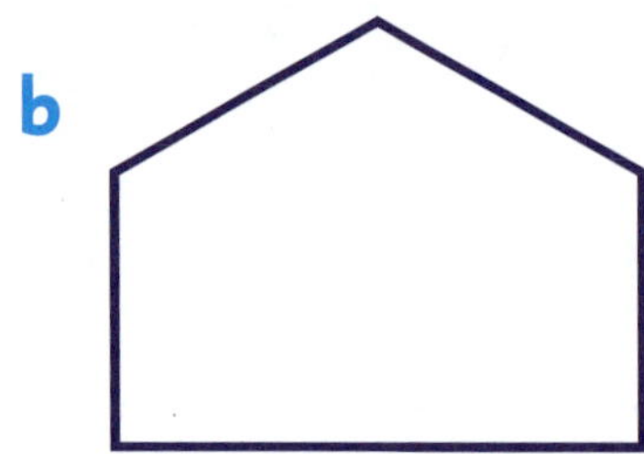

c 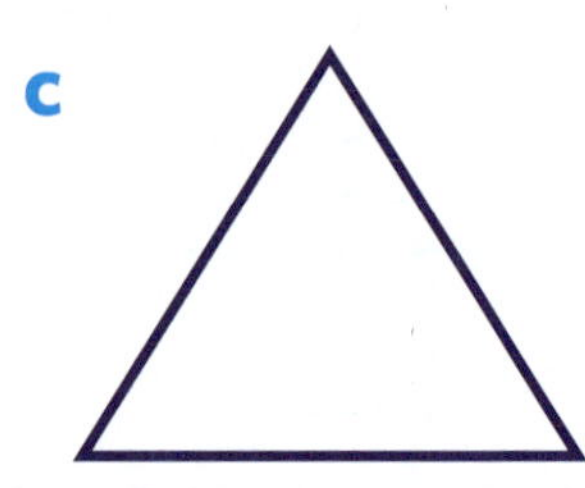

12 Write these times in words.

a 1:26 ______________________

b 2:02 ______________________

13 a Fill in the missing numbers.

Class	Start	End	Duration
Tennis	9:15 am	10:43 am	
Golf	10:35 am		1 hour 18 mins
Polo	9: am	11:22 am	hours 32 mins

b Which class is shortest? __________

14 a Circle the numerator.

$$\frac{5}{10}$$

b What is the other number called?

____

15 Find the whole number equivalents.

a $\frac{10}{5}$ = ____ ÷ ____ = ____ b $\frac{30}{3}$ = ____ c $\frac{28}{4}$ = ____

16 Add the fractions.

a $\frac{3}{8} + \frac{4}{8} = \frac{\square}{\square}$ b $\frac{2}{10} + \frac{5}{10} = \frac{\square}{\square}$ c $\frac{3}{6} + \frac{\square}{\square} = \frac{6}{6}$

Mathseeds Year 3 Workbook © 3P Learning ISBN 978-1-923253-14-8

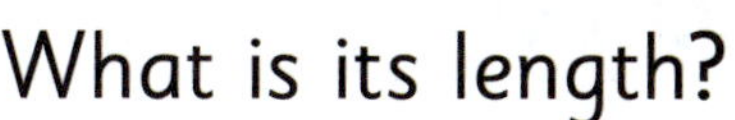

17 This is the end of the string being measured.
What is its length?

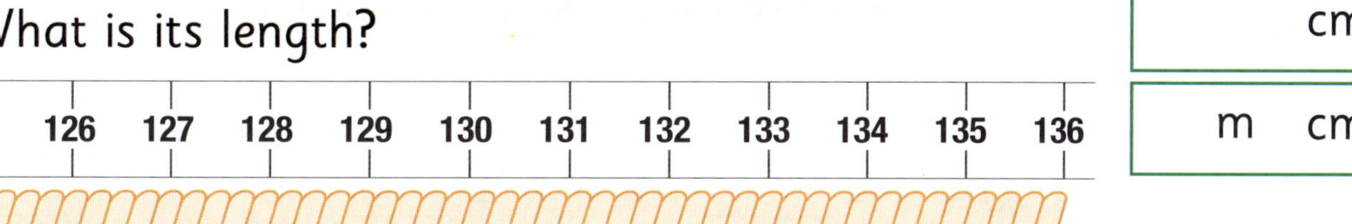

[ ] cm

[ ] m [ ] cm

18 Convert between units of measurement.

a 1 cm = _____ mm **b** 40 mm = _____ **c** 3 cm 5 mm = _____ mm

19 Find the perimeter of each insect enclosure. Write the equations.

a The cockroach tank is 120 cm long and 55 cm wide.

____

b The spider chamber has five sides that are all 50 cm long.

____

c The stick insect enclosure has sides of 45 cm, 30 cm, 50 cm and 25 cm. _______________________________

20 Calculate the total floor area of the house. _______ m^2

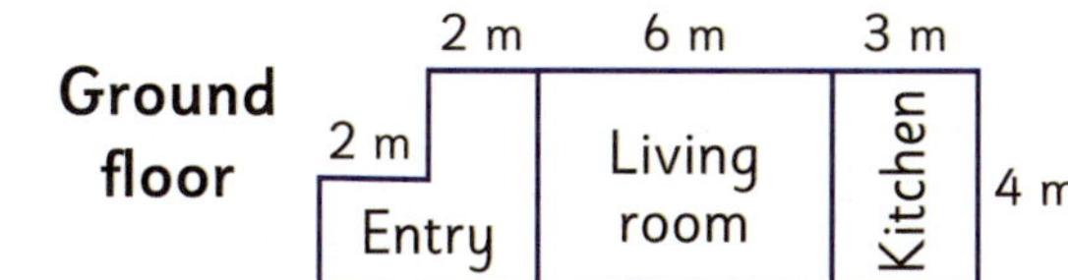

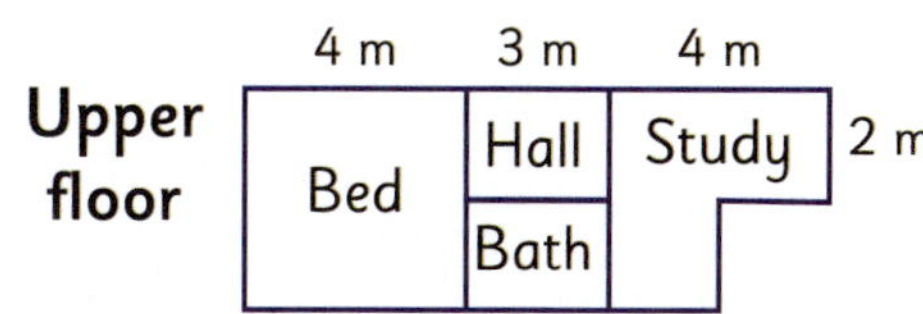

21 Number the survey steps in order 1 to 4.

[ ] **a** Record the data.

[ ] **b** Collect the data.

[ ] **c** Represent the data.

[ ] **d** Come up with a survey question.

22 Match each step to an action.

Ask people the question.

Write a table of possible answers.

Tally each answer to the question.

Make a graph.

  ISBN 978-1-923253-14-8

Add and Subtract to 10 and 20

10 + 0 = _____	10 – 5 = _____	4 + 4 = _____	9 – 6 = _____
3 + 7 = _____	7 – 2 = _____	9 + 1 = _____	10 – 7 = _____
5 + 5 = _____	8 – 5 = _____	2 + 6 = _____	9 – 4 = _____
8 + 2 = _____	10 – 2 = _____	6 + 3 = _____	8 – 4 = _____
1 + 6 = _____	7 – 3 = _____	7 + 2 = _____	10 – 6 = _____
8 + 9 = _____	20 – 7 = _____	15 + 4 = _____	17 – 6 = _____
13 + 6 = _____	18 – 5 = _____	9 + 9 = _____	16 – 6 = _____
12 + 5 = _____	19 – 7 = _____	14 + 6 = _____	17 – 4 = _____
7 + 9 = _____	18 – 12 = _____	8 + 8 = _____	19 – 11 = _____
10 + 10 = _____	20 – 5 = _____	11 + 9 = _____	16 – 8 = _____

Mathseeds Year 3 Workbook © 3P Learning ISBN 978-1-923253-14-8

Multiply and Divide by 0, 1, 2

7 ÷ 1 = _____	6 × 0 = _____	5 ÷ 1 = _____	4 × 0 = _____
3 × 1 = _____	9 ÷ 1 = _____	2 × 1 = _____	0 ÷ 1 = _____
2 ÷ 2 = _____	1 × 2 = _____	8 ÷ 2 = _____	5 × 2 = _____
2 × 3 = _____	4 ÷ 2 = _____	2 × 2 = _____	6 ÷ 2 = _____
10 ÷ 2 = _____	4 × 2 = _____	18 ÷ 2 = _____	2 × 7 = _____
2 × 9 = _____	12 ÷ 2 = _____	2 × 6 = _____	20 ÷ 2 = _____
14 ÷ 2 = _____	10 × 2 = _____	16 ÷ 2 = _____	2 × 8 = _____

Double and Half

Double 3 = _____	Half of 2 = _____	Double 5 = _____
Half of 8 = _____	Double 8 = _____	Half of 12 = _____
Double 7 = _____	Half of 4 = _____	Double 9 = _____

Multiply and Divide by 3, 4, 5, 10

21 ÷ 3 = _____	5 × 4 = _____	5 ÷ 5 = _____	4 × 10 = _____
3 × 1 = _____	40 ÷ 4 = _____	2 × 5 = _____	100 ÷ 10 = _____
12 ÷ 3 = _____	4 × 2 = _____	35 ÷ 5 = _____	5 × 10 = _____
2 × 3 = _____	4 ÷ 4 = _____	5 × 4 = _____	60 ÷ 10 = _____
18 ÷ 3 = _____	4 × 0 = _____	50 ÷ 5 = _____	10 × 7 = _____
3 × 9 = _____	24 ÷ 4 = _____	3 × 5 = _____	20 ÷ 10 = _____
9 ÷ 3 = _____	7 × 4 = _____	25 ÷ 5 = _____	10 × 8 = _____
5 × 3 = _____	36 ÷ 4 = _____	5 × 6 = _____	30 ÷ 10 = _____
30 ÷ 3 = _____	4 × 8 = _____	45 ÷ 5 = _____	9 × 10 = _____
3 × 8 = _____	16 ÷ 4 = _____	5 × 8 = _____	10 ÷ 10 = _____

  ISBN 978-1-923253-14-8

Multiply and Divide by 6, 7, 8, 9

24 ÷ 6 = ____	5 × 7 = ____	40 ÷ 8 = ____	4 × 9 = ____
6 × 1 = ____	42 ÷ 7 = ____	2 × 8 = ____	81 ÷ 9 = ____
12 ÷ 6 = ____	7 × 2 = ____	56 ÷ 8 = ____	9 × 10 = ____
5 × 6 = ____	49 ÷ 7 = ____	8 × 4 = ____	18 ÷ 9 = ____
18 ÷ 6 = ____	7 × 0 = ____	64 ÷ 8 = ____	3 × 9 = ____
6 × 9 = ____	21 ÷ 7 = ____	3 × 8 = ____	45 ÷ 9 = ____
60 ÷ 6 = ____	7 × 4 = ____	80 ÷ 8 = ____	9 × 8 = ____
6 × 6 = ____	63 ÷ 7 = ____	8 × 6 = ____	54 ÷ 9 = ____
42 ÷ 6 = ____	7 × 8 = ____	8 ÷ 8 = ____	9 × 0= ____
6 × 8 = ____	70 ÷ 7 = ____	9 × 8 = ____	63 ÷ 9 = ____

This is to certify that

____

has completed the

ABC Mathseeds

Essential Skills

YEAR 3

program.

____

Signature

____

Date

Mathseeds Year 3 Workbook © 3P Learning ISBN 978-1-923253-14-8

Lesson 151
1 1000, 2000, 3000, 4000, 5000
2 a two thousand b five thousand c one thousand
d four thousand e three thousand
3 a 4, 50, 200, 3000 b 1, 20, 500, 4000
c 3, 10, 1000, 4000
4 Teacher check
5 a 2510, 2520, 2530, 2540, 2550, 2560
b 4950, 4960, 4970, 4980, 4990, 5000
6 a $<$ b $>$ c $<$ d $>$ e $<$ f $<$ g $<$ h $>$
i $>$ j $<$ k $<$ l $>$
7 a 1563, 2945, 3890, 4798
b 1890, 2490, 3764, 4902
c 4165, 4398, 4629, 4890
8 2316, 3429, 3781, 4213, 4930
9 a 2539 b 4890
10 a-c Teacher check d 24
11 a 5421 b 1542 c 2541 d 4521
12 Teacher check

Lesson 152 1-9 Teacher check

Lesson 153
1 2, 3, 5, 8
2 13, 21, 34, 55
3 5 + 8 = 13, 8 + 13 = 21, 13 + 21 = 34, 21 + 34 = 55
4 34 + 55 = 89, 55 + 89 = 144, 89 + 144 = 233,
144 + 233 = 377
5 Add the last two numbers to get the next number
6 a 10, 13, 16, 19, 22, 25 b 46, 41, 36, 31, 26, 21
c 3, 5, 4, 6, 5 d 11, 8, 13, 10, 15
e 31, 34, 40, 43, 49 f 43, 41, 37, 35, 31
g 14, 24, 19, 29, 24 h 20, 11, 21, 12, 22
i 55, 65, 80, 90, 105 j 81, 76, 72, 67, 63
7 a 30, 40, 35; +10, –5 b 29, 21, 31; –8, +10
c 50, 52, 55; +2, +3 d 80, 71, 77; –9, +6
e 191, 190, 194; +4, –1 f 470, 477, 475; –2, +7
g 871, 875, 878; +3, +4 h 256, 246, 146; –100, –10
8 a 22, 29, 37; add ascending numbers
b 224, 234, 334; +1, +10, +100
c 64, 128, 256; double the last number to find the next
9 Teacher check
10 a 30; +5 b 33; –3 c 124; +10 –2
11-12 Teacher check

Lesson 154
1 a 1 L b more than 1 L c less than 1 L
2 a 2 L b 5 L c 4 L 3 Teacher check
4 a 500 mL b 100 mL c 400 mL d 200 mL
e 250 mL f 300 mL
5 a 100 mL b 400 mL c 350 mL
6 Teacher check
7 a 2 L b 5 L c 1 L
8 a 2000 mL b 5000 mL c 1000 mL
9 a mL b L c mL d L
10 a $\frac{1}{2}$ L b $1\frac{1}{2}$ L c $3\frac{1}{2}$ L d $4\frac{1}{2}$ L e $2\frac{1}{2}$ L
11 2 × 2 L = 4 L
12 3 × 300 mL = 900 mL
13 8 weeks
14 650 mL
15 500 mL + 500 mL = 1000 mL = 1 L

Lesson 155
1 a 2 + 2 + 2 + 2 + 2 + 2 = 12 b 3 + 3 + 3 = 9
c 5 + 5 = 10
2 a 2, 4, 6, 8, 10, 12, 14 b 3, 6, 9, 12, 15
c 5, 10, 15, 20
3 16 4 25 5 21 6 35 7 90 8 10
9 a 10 × 4 = 40 b 2 × 4 = 8 c 5 × 3 = 15
d 3 × 4 = 12 e 10 × 3 = 30 f 6 × 5 = 30
10 a 20 b 10 c 9 d 27 e 2 f 2
g 40 h 10 i 10
11 a-b Teacher check c 2 × 12 d Teacher check e 24
12 a-b Teacher check c 3 × 6 d Teacher check e 18

Quiz Map 31
1 2438, 2834, 3743, 4378, 4387
2 a five thousand, seven hundred and eighty-six
b one thousand, two hundred and three
3 Teacher check
4 a 20, 24, 27, 31; +3, +4
b 233, 333, 343, 443; +10, +100
c 280, 270, 265; –10, –5
d 24, 31, 39, 48; add by 1 then increase by 1.
5 a 400 mL b 3L c 250 mL d 1L
6 250 mL + 250 mL + 250 mL + 250 mL = 1000 mL = 1 L
7 a 40 b 35 c 30 d 18 e 12 f 35

Fun Spot 1
1 19 + 7 + 8 + 9 + 8 = 51

Lesson 156
1 Teacher check
2 a seven thousand, eight hundred and fifty-seven
b nine thousand, eight hundred and three
c five thousand, four hundred and ninety-one
d three thousand, eight hundred and ninety
3 a 5329, 6349, 7980, 8324
b 3892, 5928, 7829, 9342
c 2839, 4932, 5321, 7439
d 2562, 4031, 6611, 8172
4 1347, 3946, 6394, 8230, 9928
5 8294, 7305, 5720, 4897, 2934
6 a 3985 b 7827 c 2410 d 8275 e 5130 f 6711
7 a 9283 b 4830 c 6404 d 1010 e 5799 f 3220
8 a 5495 b 6574 c 8928 d 5027 e 9151 f 1110
9 a 2749 b 8352 c 4957 d 10 372
e 1622 f 6891

10 a 2000 + 800 + 50 + 6 b 5000 + 900 + 30 + 7
c 8000 + 300 + 60 d 4000 + 20 + 3
e 7000 + 800 + 4 f 900 + 10 + 4
g 1000 + 700 + 40 + 3 **11-13** Teacher check

Lesson 157

1 a 9 b 8 c 10 d 12
2 a $4 \times 4 = 16$ b $3 \times 5 = 15$ c $4 \times 5 = 20$
d $3 \times 6 = 18$
3 a $2 \times 6 = 12\ m^2$ b $5 \times 5 = 25\ m^2$ c $2 \times 3 = 6\ m^2$
d $4 \times 6 = 24\ m^2$
4 a $15\ m^2$ b $9\ m^2$ c $6\ m^2$ d $80\ m^2$
5 a $5\ m^2$ b $10\ m^2$ c $25\ m^2$
6 a $8\ m^2$ b $12\ m^2$ c $18\ m^2$
7 a $15\ m^2$ b $30\ m^2$ c $35\ m^2$
8 a $36\ m^2$ b $49\ m^2$ c $64\ m^2$ d $64\ m^2$
9 $10\ cm \times 10\ cm = 100\ cm^2$ **10-11** Teacher check

Lesson 158

1 a $2 \times 2 = 4$ b $5 \times 2 = 10$ c $3 \times 2 = 6$
d $4 \times 2 = 8$ e $1 \times 2 = 2$ f $6 \times 2 = 12$
2 0, 2, 4, 6, 8, 10, 12, 14, 16, 18, 20
3 a $4 \times 2 = 8$ b $7 \times 2 = 14$ c $3 \times 2 = 6$
d $9 \times 2 = 18$ e $5 \times 2 = 10$ f $8 \times 2 = 16$
4 **A** 3×4, 4×3, 12 **B** 7×4, 4×7, 28
C 2×4, 4×2, 8 **D** 5×4, 4×5, 20
E 9×4, 4×9, 36 **F** 4×4, 4×4, 16
G 8×4, 4×8, 32 **H** 6×4, 4×6, 24
I 10×4, 4×10, 40
5 0, 4, 8, 12, 16, 20, 24, 28, 32, 36, 40
6 0, 2, 4, 6, 8, 10, 12, 14, 16, 18, 20 **7** 2× table
8 0, 4, 8, 12, 16, 20, 24, 28, 32, 36, 40 **9** 4× table
10 a 10, 18, 6, 0, 12, 4 b 28, 12, 32, 8, 36, 16
11 a 4 b 2 c 4 d 4 e 2 f 2 g 4 h 4 i 2
12 Teacher check **13** Ostriches 8, Zebras 10
14 Teacher check

Lesson 159

1 a \$5.25 b \$12.50 c \$44.00 d \$15.80
e \$11.50 **2** Teacher check
3 a 20c, 10c, 5c b \$2, \$1, 10c, 5c
c \$1, 50c d 50c, 20c, 10c, 5c
e \$2, 50c, 5c f \$2, \$1, 50c, 20c
4 a \$4.40 b \$7.65 c \$0.05 d \$9.50
e \$11.95 f \$16.15
5 \$89.50 + \$5.70 = \$95.20
6 \$24.85 + \$52.20 = \$77.05
7 \$66.05 + \$19.95 = \$86.00
8 \$5.70 + \$24.85 = \$30.55
9 \$52.20 + \$19.95 = \$72.15
10 \$19.95 + \$5.70 = \$25.65
11 \$66.05 + \$24.85 = \$90.90
12 \$5.70 + \$52.20 = \$57.90
13 \$19.95 + \$24.85 = \$44.80 **14-17** Teacher Check

Lesson 160

1 a $\frac{3}{4}$ b $\frac{2}{3}$ c $\frac{6}{8}$ d $\frac{5}{8}$ e $\frac{4}{6}$ f $\frac{3}{5}$
2 a > b > c > d < e > f < g > h < I <
3 a $\frac{1}{5}, \frac{2}{5}, \frac{3}{5}, \frac{4}{5}, \frac{5}{5}$ b $\frac{1}{6}, \frac{2}{6}, \frac{3}{6}, \frac{4}{6}, \frac{5}{6}, \frac{6}{6}$
c $\frac{1}{8}, \frac{1}{4}, \frac{3}{8}, \frac{1}{2}, \frac{5}{8}, \frac{3}{4}, \frac{7}{8}, 1$
4 a $\frac{2}{3}$ b $\frac{1}{4}, \frac{3}{4}$ c 5, $\frac{3}{5}, \frac{4}{5}$
d $\frac{1}{6}, \frac{4}{6}, \frac{6}{6}$ e $\frac{1}{8}, \frac{2}{8}, \frac{3}{8}, \frac{5}{8}, \frac{7}{8}, 1$
5 a-d Teacher check
6 $\frac{1}{4}, \frac{3}{4}, 1\frac{2}{4}, 1\frac{3}{4}$ **7** $\frac{2}{3}, 1\frac{1}{3}, 1\frac{2}{3}$ **8** $\frac{2}{5}, \frac{3}{5}, 1\frac{2}{5}, 1\frac{3}{5}, 2$
9 a-c Teacher check d $\frac{4}{6} > \frac{1}{2}$ e Yes
10 a-c Teacher check d $1\frac{1}{2} > 1\frac{3}{8}$ e No

Quiz Map 32

1 a 6790, 6799, 6889 b 5933, 5942, 6032
2 a 7000 + 300 + 20 b 9000 + 800 + 40 + 3
3 a $10\ m^2$ b $16\ m^2$
4 a 16 b 14 c 24 d 16 e 20 f 28
5 Teacher check
6 a \$8.95 + \$3.50 = \$12.45 b \$7.55
7 $\frac{1}{3}, \frac{2}{3}, 1, 1\frac{1}{3}, 1\frac{2}{3}, 2$ **8** a < b > c <

Fun Spot 2

1 4021 **2** 1000 **3** 2864

Lesson 161

1 a 4 b 50 c 300 d 5000 e 70
f 3000 g 8 h 700 i 0
2 a 9000, 400, 70, 2 b 3000, 300, 20, 9
c 8000, 400, 10, 5 d 9000, 700, 30, 7
e 1000, 600, 3 f 2000, 800, 80
3 a 5000 + 600 + 40 b 2000 + 800 + 6
c 7000 + 30 + 3
4 a 3442 b 8966 c 6400
5 a 4737 b 9264 c 2582
6 a 1902 b 5548 c 9220
7 a 9353 b 4695 c 8066
8 Esperance **9** Wee Waa
10 Esperance, Roma, Tanunda, Wee Waa
11 2653 **12** 7006 **13** 4163 **14** 9920
15 a Harden b Roma c Kadina d Esperance
16 a-c Teacher check d 24 e 0
f 0 will make a 3 digit number
17 a 8630 b 3068
c 3068 3086 3608 3680 3806 3860
d 3680 3860 6380 6830 8360 8630

Lesson 162

1 a one minute past five b thirty-eight past eleven
c thirteen past eight d twenty-seven past nine
e forty-two past three f fifty-nine past seven
2 a two past ten b fifty-six past one
c forty-four past four d thirty-one past twelve
e twenty-eight past six f nineteen past two
3 a-i Teacher check

Mathseeds Year 3 Workbook © 3P Learning ISBN 978-1-923253-14-8

4 a 2 hours, 28 minutes b 9 hours, 7 minutes
c 2 hours, 38 minutes d 3 hours, 24 minutes
5 a 1 hour, 26 minutes b 6 hours, 25 minutes
c 49 minutes d 3 hours, 43 minutes
6 a 21 minutes b 38 minutes
c 1 hour, 15 minutes d 24 minutes
e 1 hour, 11 minutes
7 3 hours, 49 minutes

Lesson 163

1 a 68 b 13 + 72 = 85 c 25 + 69 = 94
d 17 e 59 – 23 = 36 f 91 – 48 = 43
2 a 84, 84 – 29 = 55 b 41, 41 + 41 = 82
c 89, 89 – 58 = 31 d 37, 37 + 38 = 75
e 79, 79 – 15 = 64 f 44, 44 + 53 = 97
3 a 32 + 46 = 78, 46 + 32 = 78, 78 – 46 = 32, 78 – 32 = 46
b 11 + 62 = 73, 62 + 11 = 73, 73 – 62 = 11, 73 – 11 = 62
c 75 + 23 = 98, 23 + 75 = 98, 98 – 23 = 75, 98 – 75 = 23
d 54 + 34 = 88, 34 + 54 = 88, 88 – 54 = 34, 88 – 34 = 54
4 a ✓ b ✗ c ✗ d ✓ e ✓ f ✗
5 a 5 b 1 c 30 d 20 e 93 f 30
6 a-h Teacher to check 7 a-f Teacher to check
8 a 10 b Max 16, Bella 9 c Lim 15, Yee 7
9 a 9 – 4 = 3 + 2 b 12 minutes, 17 + 8 = 13 + 12
10-11 Teacher check

Lesson 164

1 Teacher check
2 a Africa b North America c Asia
d Africa e South America f South America
g Europe h Asia i Atlantic Ocean
j Indian Ocean k Pacific Ocean
3 a A5 b D3 c C1 d F2 e A3 f C4
4 a flamingo b ticket entry c squirrel d gift shop
e parrot f elephant
5 F1 & F6 6 D1 & A6 7 E1 & E6 8 A1 & A2
9 (b) a path 10 Teacher check
11 A4 ➔ D4 ➔ D2 ➔ F2 ➔ F1 ➔ C1 ➔ C3 ➔ A3
12 a North b 16 c 1600 m d B2 e Teacher check
13 a-b Teacher check c E5 d C1 e Teacher check
14 Teacher check

Lesson 165

1 a 3 b 2 c 9 d 4
2 a 7 b 3 c 6 d 6
3 a 6 b 4 c 8 d 10 e 8 f 7
4 a 18 ÷ 6 = 3 b 12 ÷ 4 = 3 c 16 ÷ 8 = 2
d 20 ÷ 10 = 2 e 24 ÷ 8 = 3 f 28 ÷ 7 = 4
5 a 2 b 7 c 6 d 6 e 3 f 3 g 4 h 7
6 a ✓ b ✗ c ✗ d ✓ e ✗ f ✓ g ✓ h ✗
7 a 5, 20 ÷ 5 = 4 b 4, 36 ÷ 4 = 9 c 9, 63 ÷ 9 = 7
d 8, 48 ÷ 8 = 6 e 9, 27 ÷ 3 = 9 f 6, 54 ÷ 9 = 6
g 10, 40 ÷ 4 = 10 h 9, 72 ÷ 8 = 9
8-10 Teacher check

Quiz Map 33

1 a 200 + 10 + 3 b 4000 + 500 + 8
2 a 7603 b 3076
3 a 3:24 b two past ten c two to twelve, 11:58
4 Teacher check
5 760, 131 + 629 = 760, 760 – 629 = 131,
760 – 131 = 629
6 B2 ➔ C1 ➔ D3 ➔ F1 ➔ E4
7 a 8 b 6 c 8 d 9 e 3 f 7

Fun Spot 3

1 5, s, 9, I, 14, x, 4, f, 10, a, 2, t, 40, c, 10, a, 2, t, 5,
s, 30, e, 10, a, 2, t, 10, a, 40, c, 10, a, 6, k, 30, e
2 Six fat cats eat a cake.

Lesson 166

1 a ✗ b ✗ c ✗ d ✓ e ✓ f ✓ g ✗ h ✓
i ✓ j ✗ k ✗ l ✓
2 a-f any digits from 0, 2, 4, 6, 8
3 a-f any digits from 1, 3, 5, 7, 9
4 red bottom row, blue top row
5 a 10, even b 18, even c 38, even d 56, even
e 54, even f 80, even
6 a 8, even b 18, even c 42, even d 52, even
e 68, even f 78, even
7 a 13, odd b 23, odd c 35, odd d 47, odd
e 63, odd f 85, odd
8 a 5, odd b 15, odd c 47, odd d 51, odd
e 69, odd f 73, odd
9 a even b even c odd d odd
10 a odd b even c even d odd
e odd f odd
11 a even 408 b even 492 c odd 711 d even 1270
e odd 1241 f odd 919
12 a 1410 even b 1221 odd c 11 044 even
d 181 971 odd e 71 284 even
13 a-d Teacher check e 18
14 a 6 b No c Teacher check

Lesson 167

1 a certain b equal chance c impossible
2 a all yellow marbles b no blue flowers
c 2 red & 2 black cards d no green pencils
e 3 pink & 3 purple bows f all orange lollies
3 a 1 b 2 c 3 d 4 e 5 f 6
4 a equal chance b impossible c certain
5 a 1 b 1 c 1 d 1 e 1 f 1
6 4 for each outcome
7 5 for each outcome 8-9 Teacher check

  ISBN 978-1-923253-14-8

10 red 6, blue 12, green 3, yellow 3
11-12 Teacher check
13 a-b Teacher check c likely, unlikely, equal chance
14 Teacher check

Lesson 168

All **part a** to be checked by teacher. **Part b**:
1 8 × 2 = 16 2 5 × 4 = 20 3 3 × 5 = 15
4 4 × 6 = 24 5 7 × 3 = 21 6 2 × 9 = 18
7 5 × 5 = 25 8 2 × 3 = 6 9 10 × 4 = 40
10 10 × 5 = 50 11 8 × 3 = 24 12 5 × 6 = 30
13 7 × 7 = 49
14 a 2 × 3 = 6 b 6 × 4 c 24
15 a 2 × 5 = 10 b 10 × 10 c 100
16 a 2 × 2 = 4 b 4 × 8 c 32
17 Teacher check 18 a-c Teacher check d 120
19 Teacher check

Lesson 169

1 a-d Teacher check
2 a triangular b rectangular c hexagonal
d pentagonal
3 a 2 triangles, 3 rectangles b 6 rectangles
c 2 hexagons, 6 rectangles
d 2 pentagons, 5 rectangles 4 a-d Teacher check
5 a triangular b rectangular c pentagonal
d square
6 an apex
7 a 4 triangles b 1 rectangle, 4 triangles
c 1 pentagon, 5 triangles d 1 square, 4 triangles
8 a triangular prism b pentagonal pyramid
c rectangular prism d triangular pyramid
e square pyramid
9 a E b D c A d C e B 10-11 Teacher check

Lesson 170

1 a-b Teacher check c 392
2 a-b Teacher check c 836
3 a-b Teacher check c 622
4 a 64 b 42 c 87 d 80 e 96 f 42 g 91 h 74
5 a 90 b 81 c 90 d 82 e 80 f 91 g 65 h 83
6 a 796 b 446 c 791 d 829 e 683 f 839
g 864 h 715
7 a 845 b 700 c 845 d 874 e 934 f 987
g 432 h 650 i 631
8 61 9 82 10 528 11 402 12 747 13 $840

Quiz Map 34

1 a even b odd c even d odd
2 a 5 in 10 b 2 in 10 c 3 in 10
3 a 5 × 4 = 20 b 20 × 2 c 40
4 a face b vertices c apex d face
e base f edge
5 triangular prism, square pyramid, Teacher check nets
6 a 957 b 932 c 775 d 1220

Fun Spot 4

1 a cone b cube c cylinder d triangular pyramid

Lesson 171

1 a 3 × 4 = 12 b 6 × 4 = 24 c 8 × 4 = 32
d 4 × 4 = 16 e 5 × 4 = 20 f 7 × 4 = 28
2 0, 4, 8, 12, 16, 20, 24, 28, 32, 36, 40
3 a 2 × 4 = 8 b 5 × 4 = 20 c 7 × 4 = 28
d 8 × 4 = 32 e 3 × 4 = 12 f 6 × 4 = 24
4 0, 8, 16, 24, 32, 40, 48, 56, 64, 72, 80
5 a 8 × 1 = 8 b 8 × 10 = 80 c 8 × 4 = 32
d 8 × 6 = 48 e 3 × 8 = 8 × 3 = 24
f 8 × 8 = 8 × 8 = 64 g 2 × 8 = 8 × 2 = 16
h 5 × 8 = 8 × 5 = 40 i 9 × 8 = 8 × 9 = 72
j 7 × 8 = 8 × 7 = 56
6 a 2 b 5 c 4 d 7 e 3 f 6
7 a 3 × 4 = 12 b 4 × 4 = 16
c 5 × 4 × 10 = 200 d 4 × 2 × 7 = 56
e 2 × 3 × 8 = 48 f 20 × 4 × 2 = 160
8 a 6 b 10 c 8 d 2 e 4 f 10
9 a-b Teacher check c 5 × 8 × 2
d Teacher check e 80
10 a-b Teacher check c 2 × 5 × 8
d Teacher check e 80

Lesson 172

1 a 1 kg b 5 kg c 2 kg d 80 kg e 11 kg f 15 kg
2 a 4 b 2 c 3 d 5 e 1
3 a 250 g b 500 g c 750 g d 700 g e 50 g
f 900 g
4 a 4 b 1 c 3 d 5 e 2
5 a 150 g b 3 kg c 750 g d 1 kg e 300 g
f 4.5 kg
6 a 7.5 kg b 3.15 kg c 8.25 kg d 4.15 kg
e 4.45 kg f 9.7 kg
7 a-b Teacher check c 1000
8 a 600 g 400 g 250 g 250 g b 1500 g
9 a Yes b 500 g 10 Teacher check

Lesson 173

1 a 85 – 3 = 82 b 87 + 4 = 91
c 56 + 30 = 86 – 1 = 85
d 78 + 10 = 88 + 3 = 91 e 46 + 50 = 96 – 3 = 93
f 59 + 30 = 89 + 2 = 91
2 a 55 + 4 = 59 b 28 – 2 = 26
c 98 – 80 = 18 + 1 = 19 d 84 – 60 = 24 – 3 = 21
e 52 – 30 = 22 + 3 = 25 f 66 – 40 = 26 – 4 = 22
3 a 99 b 55 c 89 d 18 e 81 f 34
g 52 h 38 i 100
4 a 65 + 3 = 68 b 87 + 8 = 95
c 62 + 30 = 92 + 4 = 96 d 59 + 20 = 79 + 9 = 88
e 17 + 10 = 27 + 8 = 35 f 48 + 30 = 78 + 5 = 83
5 a 78 – 6 = 72 b 34 – 8 = 26
c 52 – 20 = 32 – 8 = 24 d 78 – 40 = 38 – 2 = 36
e 63 – 10 = 53 – 6 = 47 f 49 – 20 = 29 – 4 = 25

Mathseeds Year 3 Workbook © 3P Learning ISBN 978-1-923253-14-8

6 a 65 b 26 c 85 d 39 e 82 f 36 g 95 h 58 i 88

7 a 75 b 58 c 9 d $93 e 27 g

8 a 26 b $71 c 85 minutes d 101 L e 13

9 a-b Teacher check c-d 101

10 a-b 35 11 Teacher check

Lesson 174

1 a Total b 卌 卌 卌 c 卌 d 20 e 卌 卌 卌

2 Teacher check

3 a 25 b caramel c 10 d chocolate e 151

4 a 2, 1 b Stayrite, Colour Brite, Hi Lite, Paint Delite
c Teacher check
d 5 paint cans, 7 cans, 6 cans, $6\frac{1}{2}$ cans

5 a 58 b paper c rock d two of the same thing
e paper f no g Teacher check 6-7 Teacher check

Lesson 175

1 a-e Teacher check

2 a $\frac{4}{8}$ b $\frac{3}{9}$ c $\frac{3}{12}$ d $\frac{2}{10}$ 3 a $\frac{3}{15}$ b $\frac{1}{5}$

4 a $\frac{4}{12}$ b $\frac{1}{3}$ 5 a $\frac{2}{12}$ b $\frac{1}{6}$ 6 a $\frac{2}{8}$ b $\frac{1}{4}$

7 a $\frac{10}{20}$ b $\frac{1}{2}$ 8 Teacher check

9 a < b > c > d < e > f < g < h >

10 a-b Teacher check c 8 d Teacher check e $\frac{4}{8} = \frac{1}{2}$

11 Teacher check

Quiz Map 35

1 a 12 b 40 c 36 d 64 e 16 f 72

2 a 40 b 48 3 20 kg 4 3900 grams

5 50 g, 750 g, $\frac{1}{2}$ kg

6 a 102 b 89 c 67 d 94

7 a 50 b 35 c 30 d 35

8 a Comedy b Fantasy & Adventure c 20
d 150 e Teacher check

9 a 4 b $\frac{4}{20}$ c $\frac{1}{5}$

Fun Spot 5

1 1234, 4321, 3142, 2413

2 1342, 3421, 2134, 4213

3 4321, 1432, 2143, 3214

4 2431, 3142, 4213, 1324

Lessons 151 to 175 Review

1 a 9283, 9823 b 3928, 3982, 8392, 9283, 9823
c 9000 + 800 + 20 + 3
d three thousand, nine hundred and twenty-eight
e odd f 8393, 8402, 8492

2 a 678, 789, 900 b 400, 425, 375 c 13, 21, 34

3 a +111 b –50, +25 c Add the last two numbers

4 a 16 b 14 c-d Teacher check

5 629 + 131 = 760 275 + 432 = 707
131 + 629 = 760 432 + 275 = 707
760 – 629 = 131 707 – 275 = 432
760 – 131 = 629 707 – 432 = 275

6 a 905 b 1000 c 815

7 a $12.35 b $7.65 c-d Teacher check

8 a 18 b 21 c 32 d 25 e 56 f 90
g 70 h 36 i 9 j 6 k 10 l 9
m 5 n 6

9 a 2 × 3 = 6 b 6 × 4 = 36 apples

10 $\frac{1}{5}$, $\frac{3}{5}$, $1\frac{2}{5}$, $1\frac{4}{5}$ 11 a > b < c >

12 a 4 b $\frac{4}{16}$ c $\frac{1}{4}$ 13-14 Teacher check

15 a 1000 b 4 c 3500 d 1 e 2500 f 3.5

16 15 m^2 17 8 hours & 27 minutes 18 3 in 12

Lesson 176

1 a 6 × 3 = 18 b 9 × 3 = 27 c 8 × 3 = 24
d 5 × 3 = 15 e 7 × 3 = 21 f 10 × 3 = 30

2 0, 3, 6, 9, 12, 15, 18, 21, 24, 27, 30

3 a 6 b 5 × 3 = 15 c 7 × 3 = 21
d 8 × 3 = 24 e 3 × 3 = 9 f 6 × 3 = 18

4 0, 6, 12, 18, 24, 30, 36, 42, 48, 54, 60

5 a 6 × 6 = 36 b 9 × 6 = 54 c 8 × 6 = 48
d 5 × 6 = 30 e 7 × 6 = 42 f 10 × 6 = 60
g 4 × 6 = 24 h 3 × 6 = 18

6 a 15 + 6 = 21, 7 × 3 = 21
b 15 + 12 = 27, 9 × 3 = 27
c 24 + 24 = 48, 8 × 6 = 48
d 30 + 12 = 42, 7 × 6 = 42 7 a-d Teacher check

8 a 81 b 48 c 56 d 42 9 a 63 b 36

Lesson 177

1 a arm b angle c vertex d arm

2 a g, b h, c e, d f 3 b

4 a bottom left angle b all 4 angles
c all 4 angles d bottom 2 angles
e bottom 2 angles f none

5 Teacher check 6 a B b C c A

7 a arm at 3 or 9 b arm at 3 or 9
c arm at 6 or 12 d arm at 5 or 11

8-12 Teacher check

Lesson 178

1 a 9 b 18 c 29 d 37 e 8 f 29 g 17 h 34

2 a 12 b 6 c 16 d 47 e 18 f 29 g 41 h 18

3 a 192 b 270 c 271 d 122 e 163 f 377
g 177 h 185

4 a 371 b 782 c 190 d 271 e 282 f 288

5 a 186 b 279 c 169 d 277 e 186 f 289
g 78 h 178

6 a 169 b 166 c 57 d 146 e 269 f 117

7 18 8 7 9 26 10 111 11 146 12 264

Lesson 179

1 a 37 mins b 1 hr 53 mins c 3 hrs 15 mins
d 41 mins e 1 hr 9 mins f 2 hrs 20 mins

2 a 1:45 b 2:19 c 0:31 d 4:52 e 0:08 f 3:27

3 a Doc b Waldo c Mango d Ruby

4 Doc, Ruby, Mango, Dizzy, Waldo

5 a Doc b Waldo c 0:59 & 1:03
d 1 hr 6 mins 6 4 hrs 45 mins

7 a 3:50 b 12:14 c 9:22
8 a 2:28 b 9:08 c 12:55
9 a 2:20 b 11:33 c 3:43 d 8:19
10 a-b Teacher check c 12:30pm
11 a 12:45pm b 12:36pm c 12:42pm d 12:39pm
e 12:48pm
12 Teacher check

Lesson 180
1 a $\frac{1}{2}$ b $\frac{2}{4}$ c $\frac{3}{6}$ d $\frac{4}{8}$ 2-3 Teacher check
4 a 1 whole b $\frac{1}{2}$ c $\frac{1}{4}$ d $\frac{1}{8}$
5 a $\frac{2}{4}$ b $\frac{4}{8}$ c $\frac{2}{8}$ d $\frac{6}{8}$ 6 a 1 whole b $\frac{1}{3}$ c $\frac{1}{6}$
7 a $\frac{2}{6}$ b $\frac{4}{6}$ 8 $1 = \frac{2}{2} = \frac{4}{4} = \frac{8}{8} = \frac{3}{3} = \frac{6}{6}$
9 a $\frac{2}{5}, \frac{3}{5}, \frac{4}{5}$ b $\frac{3}{10}, \frac{4}{10}, \frac{5}{10}, \frac{6}{10}, \frac{7}{10}, \frac{8}{10}, \frac{9}{10}$
10 a $\frac{2}{3}, \frac{3}{3}$ b $\frac{2}{9}, \frac{3}{9}, \frac{4}{9}, \frac{5}{9}, \frac{6}{9}, \frac{7}{9}, \frac{8}{9}, \frac{9}{9}$
11 a $\frac{1}{5}$ b $\frac{4}{10}$ c $\frac{5}{5} = \frac{10}{10}$ d $\frac{1}{3} = \frac{3}{9}$ e $\frac{2}{3} = \frac{6}{9}$ f $\frac{3}{3} = \frac{9}{9}$
12 a-c Teacher check d $\frac{2}{6} = \frac{3}{9}$
13 a-c Teacher check d $\frac{1}{5} = \frac{2}{10}$

Quiz Map 36
1 a 15 b 21 c 24 d 30 e 42 f 48
2 39 3 Teacher check
4 a 427 b 240 c 159 d 649
5 a 1:19 b 11:53 am c 12:11 pm d 3:24 pm
e 1:54
6 a Waldo b Mrs
7 a i $\frac{1}{8}$ ii $\frac{2}{8}$ iii $\frac{1}{4}$ b i 3 ii $\frac{3}{9}$ iii $\frac{1}{3}$

Fun Spot 6
1 a 2 b 6 c 5 d 3 e 4 f 10

Lesson 181
1 a 4 × 2 = 8 b 5 × 3 = 15 c 6 × 4 = 24
d 6 × 5 = 30 e 10 × 6 = 60 f 4 × 7 = 28
2 a 50 ÷ 10 = 5 b 36 ÷ 4 = 9 c 72 ÷ 9 = 8
d 42 ÷ 6 = 7 e 32 ÷ 8 = 4 f 21 ÷ 3 = 7
3 a 2 × 7 = 14, 14 ÷ 2 = 7
b 5 × 4 = 20, 20 ÷ 5 = 4
c 6 × 8 = 48, 48 ÷ 6 = 8
4 a 12, 12, 12, 12 b 9, 9, 9, 9 c 5, 5, 5, 5
5 a 12, 3, 3, 12 b 18, 9, 9, 18 c 40, 5, 5, 40
d 70, 10, 70, 10 e 54, 9, 54, 9 f 35, 7, 35, 7
6 a 21, 21, 21, 21, 21 b 9, 9, 9, 9, 9
c 10, 10, 10, 10, 10
7 a 30, 5 × 6 = 30, 6 × 5 = 30, 30 ÷ 5 = 6, 30 ÷ 6 = 5
b 72, 8 × 9 = 72, 9 × 8 = 72, 72 ÷ 8 = 9, 72 ÷ 9 = 8
c 42, 7 × 6 = 42, 6 × 7 = 42, 42 ÷ 7 = 6, 42 ÷ 6 = 7
8 Teacher check
9 a It's the same number.
b Yes because the number being divided has to go first.
10 Teacher check

Lesson 182
1 a 90 mm b 9 cm 2 a 60 mm b 6 cm
3 a 110 mm b 11 cm 4 a 38 mm b 3 cm 8 mm
5 a 57 mm b 5 cm 7 mm
6 a 23 mm b 2 cm 3 mm
7 a 75 mm b 7 cm 5 mm
8 a 3 m 56 cm b 215 cm c 4 m 60 cm
d 184 cm
9 a 587 cm b 8 m 31 cm c 2 m 48 cm
d 1 m 50 cm e 10 m 10 cm f 495 cm
10 a 32 mm b 6 cm 7 mm c 122 mm
d 9 cm 9 mm
11 a 37 mm b 97 mm c 7 cm 1 mm
d 5 cm 5 mm e 112 mm f 6 cm 6 mm
12 a 1 cm 2 mm b 5 cm 6 mm c 6 cm 9 mm
d 4 cm 7 mm e 7 cm 4 mm f 9 cm 5 mm
13 a 6 mm b 8 mm c 27 mm d 7 mm
14 a 2 cm 6 mm b 2 cm 7 mm c 0 cm 6 mm
d 5 cm 0 mm
15 a-b Teacher check c the length is the same
16 Teacher check

Lesson 183
1 a 503; 247, 256 b 247 + 256 = 503
2 a 440; 172, 156, 112 b 172 + 156 + 112 = 440
3 a 147; 35, 112 b 147 – 35 = 112
4 a 120 + 62 = 182 + 1 = 183
b 90 + 42 = 132 – 1 = 131
5 a 10 + 50 = 60, 6 + 3 = 9, 60 + 9 = 69
b 30 + 40 = 70, 1 + 5 = 6, 70 + 6 = 76
6 a 147 b 326
7 a 72 – 30 = 42 + 1 = 43
b 238 – 90 = 148 + 1 = 149
8 a 90 – 70 = 20, 5 – 3 = 2, 20 + 2 = 22
b 60 – 20 = 40, 7 – 4 = 3, 40 + 3 = 43
9 a 59 b 188
10 a Barbara 39, 59, 98 Robin 31, 66, 97 b Barbara
11 a Diana 15, 22, 37 Etta 16, 16, 32 b Diana

Lesson 184
1 flat, straight, closed
2 Colour b, d, e, h, j, l, m, o, r, s
3 a curved side f open shape
g open shape with a curved side k curved side
p curved sides q open shape with a curved side
4 a flat, closed shape with four sides and four vertices.
5 a parallelogram & rectangle
b rhombus & square c two trapeziums
6 kite
7 a top green, bottom blue b all green
c left red, top right green, bottom right blue
d all green e all red f all green g all blue
h top & bottom blue, left & right green
i top left & bottom right green, top right & bottom left blue

Mathseeds Year 3 Workbook © 3P Learning ISBN 978-1-923253-14-8

8-9 Teacher check

10 **a** 4 equal sides, 2 pairs of parallel sides
b square has 4 right angles, rhombus has opposite angles equal

11 **a** 4 sides, 2 pairs of parallel sides, 4 right angles
b square has all sides equal, rectangle has opposite sides equal

12 **a** 4 sides, 2 pairs of parallel sides
b square has 4 right angles & 4 equal sides, parallelogram has opposite angles & sides equal

13 **a** 4 sides, 2 pairs of parallel sides, opposite sides equal
b parallelogram has opposite angles equal, rectangle has 4 right angles

14 **a** 4 sides, 2 pairs of parallel sides, opposite angles equal
b parallelogram has opposite sides equal, rhombus has all sides equal

Lesson 185

1 **a-f** Teacher to check
2 **a** 4 minutes past 8 **b** 7 minutes to 3
c 22 minutes to 11 **d** 14 minutes to 6
e 29 minutes past 12 **f** 17 minutes past 9
3 **a** f **b** h **c** e **d** g
4 **a** 27 minutes past 1 **b** 12 minutes past 7
c 28 minutes to 11 **d** 1 minute to 5
e 19 minutes past 8 **f** 13 minutes to 12
5 **a** 1:23 **b** 10:56 **c** 4:07 **d-f** Teacher check
g 11:02 **h** 4:54 **i** 6:41
6 **a** Start 8:45 am, Finish 5:25 pm
b Go to sleep 11:41 pm, Wake up 8:01 am
c Set out 8:25 am, Arrive 1:47 pm

Quiz Map 37

1 4 × 10 = 40 8 × 2 = 16 9 × 10 = 90
10 × 4 = 40 2 × 8 = 16 10 × 9 = 90
40 ÷ 4 = 10 16 ÷ 8 = 2 90 ÷ 9 = 10
40 ÷ 10 = 4 16 ÷ 2 = 8 90 ÷ 10 = 9
2 **a** 218 **b** 132 **c** 267
3 **a** 30 **b** 5 **c** 27
4 177 boys **5** 156 books **6** Teacher check
7 Start 4:40 pm, Finish 5:55 pm

Fun Spot 7

1 **a**
b
c
d

Lesson 186

1 **a** 3 × 8 = 24 **b** 4 × 9 = 36
c 6 × 7 = 42 **d** 5 × 6 = 30
2 **a** 56 **b** 54
3 **a** $\begin{array}{r}5\\ \times\ 8\\ \hline 40\end{array}$ **b** $\begin{array}{r}5\\ \times\ 7\\ \hline 35\end{array}$ **c** $\begin{array}{r}3\\ \times\ 9\\ \hline 27\end{array}$ **d** $\begin{array}{r}4\\ \times\ 8\\ \hline 32\end{array}$
4 **a** 21 **b** 24 **c** 45 **d** 28
e 25 **f** 48 **g** 63 **h** 64
5 **a** $\begin{array}{r}3\\ \times\ 9\\ \hline 27\end{array}$ **b** $\begin{array}{r}4\\ \times\ 7\\ \hline 28\end{array}$ **c** $\begin{array}{r}5\\ \times\ 6\\ \hline 30\end{array}$
6 **a** 21 **b** 32 **c** 45
7 **a** $\begin{array}{r}6\\ \times\ 4\\ \hline 24\end{array}$ **b** $\begin{array}{r}5\\ \times\ 7\\ \hline 35\end{array}$ **c** $\begin{array}{r}9\\ \times\ 8\\ \hline 72\end{array}$ **d** $\begin{array}{r}6\\ \times\ 9\\ \hline 54\end{array}$
8 **a** $\begin{array}{r}3\\ \times\ 3\\ \hline 9\end{array}$ **b** $\begin{array}{r}9\\ \times\ 9\\ \hline 81\end{array}$

Lesson 187

1 **a** 26 **b** 23 **c** 12 **d** 18 **e** 9
2 **a** how many items of clothing were sold on Saturday
b 12 **c** t-shirts **d** hats **e** 88
f 14 **g** clothing shop
3 Clothing Sales (or similar) **4** Teacher check
5 t-shirts, jeans, jackets, shorts, hats **6** Teacher check
7 **a** 20 **b** 40 **c** 50 **d** 30 **e** 25
8 pegasus **9** unicorn **10** griffin **11** dragon
12 165 **13** 5 **14-15** Teacher check

Lesson 188

1 **a** × **b** 5 × 4 = 20
2 **a** + **b** 10 + 12 = 22
3 **a** ÷ **b** 24 ÷ 8 = 3
4 **a** – **b** 40 – 18 = 22
5 **a** × **b** 10 × 5 = 50
6 **a** – **b** 50 – 33 = 17
7 **a** + × **b** 14 + 1 = 15, 15 × 2 = 30
8 **a** × – **b** 3 × 5 = 15, 20 – 15 = 5
9 **a** × + **b** 6 × 4 = 24, 24 + 5 = 29
10 **a** + ÷ **b** 3 + 3 = 6, 60 ÷ 6 = 10
11 **a** ÷ – **b** 300 ÷ 10 = 30, 30 – 19 = 11
12 **a** one of three shares **b** total number of pieces
c multiply & add **d** divide **e** 3 × 4 = 12
f 12 + 21 + 27 = 60 **g** 60 ÷ 3 = 20
13 **a** 21 ÷ 3 = 7 **b** 27 ÷ 3 = 9 **c** 4 **d** 20
14 **a-b** Teacher check
c Green 24 ÷ 4 = 6 Purple 24 ÷ 6 = 4
d Green \$60 Purple \$44 **e** Purple
15 **a-b** Teacher check **c** 3 Green & 3 Purple
d 3 × \$10 + 3 × \$11 = \$63

Lesson 189

1 11:10 am 2 3:55 pm 3 10:55 am 4 7:32 pm
5 2:01 pm 6 1 hr 40 mins 7 2 hrs 55 mins
8 3 hrs 31 mins 9 44 mins 10 2 hrs 8 mins
11 a 7:31 am, 48 mins b Ruby
12 a 10:03 pm, 10:24 pm b Block Build
13 a 1:27 pm, 3 hrs 33 mins b Coding
14 a 2 hrs 29 mins, 2 hrs 19 mins b Bus 4321
15 2 hrs 23 mins 16 1:21 pm 17 Doc 18 12:01 pm

Lesson 190

1 a $6 \times 5 = 30$, $30 \div 5 = 6$, $30 \div 6 = 5$
b $7 \times 4 = 28$, $28 \div 4 = 7$, $28 \div 7 = 4$
c $9 \times 8 = 72$, $72 \div 8 = 9$, $72 \div 9 = 8$
2 a $3 \times 9 = 27$, $9 \times 3 = 27$, $27 \div 3 = 9$, $27 \div 9 = 3$
b $4 \times 8 = 32$, $8 \times 4 = 32$, $32 \div 4 = 8$, $32 \div 8 = 4$
c $6 \times 7 = 42$, $7 \times 6 = 42$, $42 \div 6 = 7$, $42 \div 7 = 6$
3 a $5 \times 9 = 45$, $9 \times 5 = 45$, $45 \div 5 = 9$, $45 \div 9 = 5$
b $6 \times 8 = 48$, $8 \times 6 = 48$, $48 \div 6 = 8$, $48 \div 8 = 6$
c $7 \times 10 = 70$, $10 \times 7 = 70$, $70 \div 7 = 10$, $70 \div 10 = 7$
4 a 32 b 10 c 6
5 a $4 \times 8 = 32$, $8 \times 4 = 32$, $32 \div 4 = 8$, $32 \div 8 = 4$
b $4 \times 10 = 40$, $10 \times 4 = 40$, $40 \div 4 = 10$, $40 \div 10 = 4$
c $6 \times 9 = 54$, $9 \times 6 = 54$, $54 \div 6 = 9$, $54 \div 9 = 6$
6 a 6 b 5 c 6 d 5 e 4 f 5
7 a 18, 3, 3, 18 b 35, 7, 7, 35 c 36, 9, 9, 36
d 56, 8, 8, 56 e 50, 5, 5, 50 f 24, 3, 3, 24
8 a 7 b 24 c 8 d 54 e 7 f 90 g 5 h 15
i 10 j 72 k 8 l 49 m 8 n 28 o 10
9-10 Teacher check

Quiz Map 38

1 a $5 \times 9 = 45$ b $4 \times 6 = 24$
2 a Gym/Hall b 18 c Office d 4 e 14 f 24
3 a 1 hr × 5 = 5 hr, 30 – 5 = 25 hr
b $32 + 19 + 15 = 66$, $66 \div 6 = 11$
4 a 7 hr 13 min b 6:46 pm c 8:11 pm
5 a 35 b 9 c 12

Fun Spot 8

1 a 12 b 27 c 100, 10, 10 d 4, 4, 1
e 10, 5, 2 f 8, 2, 2 g 10, 2, 5 h 6, 2, 3
I 6, 3, 4 j 4, 6, 2 k 9, 9, 3 l 5, 8, 1

Lesson 191

1 a 10 b 2 c 4 d 3 e 1 2 a $\frac{2}{10}$ b $\frac{4}{10}$ c $\frac{3}{10}$ d $\frac{1}{10}$
3 a $\frac{2}{8}$ b $\frac{3}{8}$ c $\frac{3}{8}$ 4 a $\frac{1}{6}$ b $\frac{2}{6}$ c $\frac{3}{6}$
5 a 5 parts coloured b $\frac{5}{6}$ 6 a 7 parts coloured b $\frac{7}{8}$
7 a 7 parts coloured b $\frac{7}{10}$ 8 a 4 parts coloured b $\frac{4}{5}$
9 a $\frac{3}{5}$ b $\frac{4}{6}$ c $\frac{6}{8}$ d $\frac{8}{10}$ e $\frac{5}{5}$ f $\frac{3}{4}$ g $\frac{7}{8}$ h $\frac{8}{10}$ i $\frac{3}{6}$
10 a $\frac{1}{2}$ S b $\frac{1}{4}$ S c $\frac{1}{8}$ S
11 a $\frac{1}{2} = \frac{2}{4} = \frac{4}{8}$ b $\frac{1}{4} = \frac{2}{8}$ c $\frac{3}{4} = \frac{6}{8}$ d $1 = \frac{2}{2} = \frac{4}{4} = \frac{8}{8}$
12 a $\frac{6}{8} = \frac{3}{4}$ b $\frac{2}{8} = \frac{1}{4}$ c $\frac{4}{8} = \frac{1}{2}$ or $\frac{2}{4}$ d $\frac{6}{8} = \frac{3}{4}$
e $\frac{6}{8} = \frac{3}{4}$ f $\frac{4}{8} = \frac{1}{2}$ or $\frac{2}{4}$ g $\frac{2}{4} = \frac{1}{2}$ h $\frac{8}{8} = \frac{4}{4}$ or $\frac{2}{2}$
13 a $\frac{2}{6}$ b $\frac{5}{6}$ c $\frac{3}{6}$ d $\frac{5}{6}$
14 a $\frac{1}{2}$ b $\frac{3}{4}$ c $\frac{1}{4}$ d $1\frac{1}{2}$ e 2 f $2\frac{1}{2}$ g $2\frac{3}{4}$
15 a < b < c > d > e < f < g < h > i =
16 Teacher check

Lesson 192

1 a 12 cm b 12 cm c 12 cm
2 a 100 + 100 + 70 + 70 = 340 m
b 20 + 20 + 25 + 25 = 90 m
c 37 + 37 + 18 + 18 = 110 m
3 a 2 cm b $2 \times 4 = 8$ cm
4 a 3 cm b $3 \times 3 = 9$ cm
5 a 2 cm b $2 \times 5 = 10$ cm
6 a 2 cm b $2 \times 6 = 12$ cm
7 a 2 cm b $2 \times 4 = 8$ cm
8 a 1 cm b $1 \times 12 = 12$ cm
9 a 2 cm b $2 \times 6 = 12$ cm
10 a 1 cm b $1 \times 10 = 10$ cm
11 2 + 3 + 3 + 2 + 5 + 5 = 20 cm
12 7 + 1 + 2 + 4 + 3 + 4 + 2 + 1 = 24 cm
13 5 + 2 + 3 + 4 + 3 + 2 + 5 + 8 = 32 cm
14 6 + 1 + 1 + 2 + 2 + 6 + 6 + 2 + 2 + 1 + 1 + 6 = 36 cm
15 a-c Teacher check
d i 120 + 120 + 55 + 55 = 350 cm
ii $60 \times 4 = 240$ cm iii $50 \times 5 = 250$ cm
iv 45 + 30 + 50 + 25 = 150 cm

Lesson 193

1 a 30 b 80 c 60 d 420 e 570 f 190
2 a 230 b 760 c 380 d 690 e 810 f 940
3 a 30, 90, 70, 50, 80, 40
b 120, 270, 750, 160, 390, 680
4 a $6 \times 10 = 60$ b $10 \times 10 = 100$
c $4 \times 4 = 16 \times 10 = 160$ d $7 \times 5 = 35 \times 10 = 350$
e $3 \times 8 = 24 \times 10 = 240$ f $6 \times 6 = 36 \times 10 = 360$
5 a 180 b 280 c 400 d 210 e 450 f 180
g 240 h 400 i 90 j 560 k 100 l 360
6 a 40, 100, 180, 60, 140, 80
b 180, 240, 90, 270, 120, 60
7 160 8 270 9 80 10 450 m 11 240
12 270 13 160 14 180 15 210

Lesson 194

1 a 10 b 30 c 30 d 50
2 a 200 b 200 c 400 d 400
3 Line between 4 and 5.
4 a 5 to 9 will round up. b 1 to 4 will round down.
5 a 50 b 80 c 80 d 70 e 30 f 100
g 20 h 20 i 50
6 Line between 40 and 50.
7 a 50 to 99 will round up. b 1 to 49 will round down.
8 a 700 b 700 c 600 d 400 e 1000 f 900
g 100 h 300 i 300
9 a 140 b 580 c 850 d 600 e 990 f 330
10 a 200 b 800 c 400 d 900 e 600 f 200

Mathseeds Year 3 Workbook © 3P Learning ISBN 978-1-923253-14-8

11 195 cm ≈ 2 m, × 7 ≈ 14 m of timber
12 189 ≈ 200 chickens, ≈ 100, × 2 ≈ 200 chicks
13 **a-b** Teacher check **c** 252, 348 **d** Teacher check
e 325, 326, 327, 328, 329, 331, 332, 333, 334
f Teacher check **g** 326, 328, 332, 334

Lesson 195

1 **a** 5, 50, 500 **b** 9, 90, 900
c 13, 130, 1300 **d** 6, 60, 600
2 **a** 8, 80, 800 **b** 9, 90, 900
c 7, 70, 700 **d** 14, 140, 1400
3 **a** 16, 90 = 160, 700 + 900 = 1600
b 8, 70 = 80, 1500 – 700 = 800
c 12, 30 = 120, 900 + 300 = 1200
d 6, 50 = 60, 1100 – 500 = 600
4 **a** 9, 19, 29, 39, 49, 59 **b** 12, 22, 32, 42, 52, 62
c 20, 30, 40, 50, 60, 70 **d** 37, 47, 57, 67, 77, 87
5 **a** 33, 43, 53, 32, 63, 42, 73, 52, 83
b 114, 124, 134, 39, 144, 49, 154, 59, 164
c 247, 257, 267, 231, 277, 241, 287, 251, 297
6 337, 22 + 325 = 347, 32 + 325 = 357, 42 + 325 = 367, 52 + 325 = 377, 62 + 325 = 387
7 339, 26 + 323 = 349, 26 + 333 = 359, 26 + 343 = 369, 26 + 353 = 379, 26 + 363 = 389
8 **a** 6, 16, 26, 36, 46, 56 **b** 7, 17, 27, 37, 47, 57
c 77, 67, 57, 47, 37, 27 **d** 102, 92, 82, 72, 62, 52
9 **a** 205, 215, 225, 247, 235, 257, 245, 267, 255
b 703, 713, 723, 834, 733, 844, 743, 854, 753
c 302, 292, 282, 53, 272, 63, 262, 73, 252
10 788, 801 – 3 = 798, 811 – 3 = 808, 821 – 3 = 818, 831 – 3 = 828, 841 – 3 = 838
11 557, 575 – 28 = 547, 575 – 38 = 537, 575 – 48 = 527, 575 – 58 = 517, 575 – 68 = 507
12 **a** 27, 180 + 90 = 270, 1800 + 900 = 2700
b 1800, 900, 2700
13 **a** 647, 654 – 17 = 637, 654 – 27 = 627, 654 – 37 = 617
b 654, 37, 617
14 **a** 994, – 16 = 984, 26 **b** 1000, 26, 974

Quiz Map 39

1 Teacher check **2** **a** 130 mm **b** 72 mm **c** 88 mm
3 9 × 40 = 9 × 4 × 10, 9 × 4 = 36 × 10 = 360
4 **a** 310 **b** 670 **c** 890 **d** 210 **e** 190
5 **a** 300 **b** 700 **c** 900 **d** 200 **e** 200
6 **a** 3rd line, 17 **b** 2nd line, 2

Fun Spot 9

1 56, y, 81, 0, 21, u, 72, a, 6, r, 8, e, 98, g, 6, r, 8, e, 72, a, 63, t, 72, a, 63, t, 40, m, 72, a, 63, t, 5, h, 10, s
2 You are great at maths.

Lesson 196

1 **a** circle: 24; himself, Ruby and Mrs T **b** 24 ÷ 3 = 8
2 **a** circle: 24; four **b** 24 ÷ 4 = 6
3 **a** circle: 24; twelve **b** 24 ÷ 12 = 2
4 **a** circle: Ruby, Mrs T and Dizzy; 36 **b** 36 ÷ 3 = 12
5 Teacher check
6 **a** circle: $55; $37; altogether **b** $55 + $37 = $92
7 **a** circle: $100; $38; left **b** $100 – $38 = $62
8 **a** circle: $80; shared; herself, her brother & two sisters
b $80 ÷ 4 = $20
9 **a** circle: six packets; $9 each; total **b** 6 × $9 = $54
10 **a** circle: fifty; ten; equal groups **b** $50 ÷ 10 = $5
11 **a** circle: $50; $30; spent $60; left
b $50 + $30 – $60 = $20
12 **a** 5 × 8 = 40 **b** 40 ÷ 4 = 10
13 **a** 18 ÷ 3 = 6 **b** 6 – 4 = 2
14 **a** 30 ÷ 5 = 6 **b** 3 × 6 = 18
15 **a** 17 + 19 = 36 **b** 36 ÷ 6 = 6
16 **a** 44 ÷ 2 = 22 **b** 22 + 7 = 29
17 37 + 53 = 90 songs, 3 × 60 = 180 mins, 180 ÷ 90 = 2 mins per song
18 2 × 12 = 24 m, 90 – 24 = 66 m, 66 m ÷ 11 m = 6 strings
19 45 – 21 = 24 left, 24 ÷ 2 = 12, 12 × 10 = 120 mins = 2 hours
20 72 ÷ 12 = 6 batches, 30 + 10 = 40 mins, 40 × 6 = 240 mins = 4 hours

Lesson 197

1 **a** numerator **b** denominator **c** numerator
d denominator
2 **a** $\frac{1}{1}$ **b** $\frac{6}{6}$ **c** $\frac{8}{2}$ **d** $\frac{15}{5}$ **e** $\frac{8}{4}$ **f** $\frac{12}{3}$
3 **a** $\frac{8}{8}$ **b** $\frac{12}{4}$ **c** $\frac{18}{6}$ **d** $\frac{10}{2}$ **e** $\frac{18}{3}$ **f** No match
4 **a** 2 shapes cut into 5ths **b** 3 shapes cut in half
c 4 shapes cut into 4ths **d** 3 shapes cut into 3rds
5 divide the numerator by the denominator.
6 **a** 6 **b** 5 **c** 16 ÷ 8 = 2 **d** 21 ÷ 3 = 7
e 30 ÷ 5 = 6 **f** 12 ÷ 6 = 2
7 **a** 1 **b** 10 **c** 5 **d** 10 **e** 5 **f** 3
8 **a** 14 **b** 9 **c** 5 **d** 8
9-12 Teacher check

Lesson 198

1 **a** 5 **b** $3\frac{1}{2}$ **c** $9\frac{1}{2}$ **d** 2 **e** $6\frac{1}{2}$ **f** 4 **g** 5 **h** 8 **i** 10 **j** $2\frac{1}{2}$
2 **a** 5 cm **b** $3\frac{1}{2}$ cm **c** $9\frac{1}{2}$ cm **d** 2 cm **e** $6\frac{1}{2}$ cm
f 4 cm **g** 5 cm **h** 8 cm **i** 10 cm **j** $2\frac{1}{2}$ cm
3 Teacher check
4 **a** Dan **b** 2 cm **c** Ian **d** 10 cm
e Anna & Gru **f** 5 cm **g** 4 **h** 6
5 **a** $11\frac{1}{2}$ cm **b** Finn **c** 3 cm **d** 5 cm
e less **f** more **g** Erin **h** Anna & Gru
6-7 Teacher check

Lesson 199

1 **a** 16 **b** 49 **c** 27 **d** 30 **e** 36 **f** 25 **g** 30
h 72 **i** 28 **j** 64 **k** 18 **l** 24 **m** 24 **n** 81
o 60 **p** 63 **q** 32 **r** 36 **s** 20 **t** 48 **u** 18
v 100 **w** 35 **x** 54 **y** 45 **z** 42

2 **a** 16 **b** 42 **c** 48 **d** 40 **e** 21 **f** 36 **g** 24
h 45 **i** 20 **j** 72 **k** 42 **l** 35 **m** 27 **n** 32
o 63 **p** 30 **q** 18 **r** 28 **s** 54 **t** 40 **u** 70
v 24 **w** 56 **x** 15 **y** 12 **z** 40
3 **a** 12 **b** 5 **c** 72 **d** 9 **e** 7 **f** 8
4 **a** 60 ÷ 10 = 6 **b** 6 × 8 = 48 **c** 15 ÷ 5 = 3
d 5 × 4 = 20 **e** 63 ÷ 9 = 7 **f** 10 × 10 = 100
5 **a** 35, 35, 35, 35 **b** 32, 8 × 4 = 32, 32, 32 ÷ 8 = 4
c 54, 9 × 6 = 54, 54 ÷ 6 = 9, 54 ÷ 9 = 6
d 6 × 7 = 42, 7 × 6 = 42, 7, 42 ÷ 7 = 6
6 **a** 4 **b** 8 **c** 6 **d** 7 **e** 6 **f** 10 **g** 8
h 8 **i** 6 **j** 7 **k** 6 **l** 4 **m** 9 **n** 9
o 9 **p** 8 **q** 8 **r** 7 **s** 3 **t** 5 **u** 9
v 6 **w** 5 **x** 3 **y** 6 **z** 4
7 **a** 8 **b** 7 **c** 9 **d** 7 **e** 7 **f** 6 **g** 10
h 6 **i** 5 **j** 9 **k** 5 **l** 9 **m** 9 **n** 3
o 5 **p** 4 **q** 8 **r** 4 **s** 10 **t** 5 **u** 3
v 8 **w** 8 **x** 4 **y** 6 **z** 7
8 **a** 49 **b** 24 **c** 40 **9** **a** 9 **b** 9 **c** $6
10 **a** 3 × 8 = 24, 24 ÷ 4 = 6
b $30 ÷ 5 = $6, $6 ÷ 3 = $2

Lesson 200

1 **a** Teacher check **b** 5 × 7 = 35 m^2
c 2 × 3 = 6 m^2 **d** 35 – 6 = 29 m^2
2 **a** 2 × 4 = 8, 2 × 1 = 2, 8 – 2 = 6 m^2
b 3 × 4 = 12, 1 × 2 = 2, 12 – 2 = 10 m^2
c 4 × 8 = 32, 4 × 3 = 12, 32 – 12 = 20 m^2
3 **a** Teacher check **b** 2 × 1 = 2 m^2
c 3 × 1 = 3 m^2 **d** 2 + 3 = 5 m^2
4 **a** 2 × 2 = 4, 3 × 10 = 30, 30 + 4 = 34 m^2
b 3 × 5 = 15, 3 × 3 = 9, 15 + 9 = 24 m^2
c 2 × 3 = 6, 2 × 3 = 6, 5 × 10 = 50, 50 + 6 + 6 = 62 m^2
5 **a** 45 m^2 **b** 36 m^2
c 5 × 8 = 40, 1 × 2 = 2, 40 – 2 = 38 m^2
d 4 × 9 = 36, 1 × 6 = 6, 36 – 6 = 30 m^2
e 2 × 6 = 12, 10 × 2 = 20, 12 + 20 = 32 m^2
f 4 × 3 = 12, 8 × 3 = 24, 12 + 24 = 36 m^2
6 Colour **a** A red **b** D blue **c** B & F green
7 Circle D, E
8 **a** 20 m^2 **b** $400
9 **a** 48 m^2 **b** 2 **c** $50
10 **a** 5 × 12 = 60, 2 × 5 = 10, 60 + 10 = 70 m^2
b $2100
11 **a** 12 × 30 = 360 – (20 + 48 + 70) = 360 – 138 = 222 m^2
b $2220

Quiz Map 40

1 6 × 4 = 24, 24 ÷ 3 = 8
2 numerator, denominator
3 **a** 20 ÷ 4 = 5 **b** 24 ÷ 6 = 4 **c** 15 ÷ 5 = 3
d 27 ÷ 3 = 9 **e** 32 ÷ 8 = 4
4 **a** 35, 5 × 7 = 35, 35 ÷ 7 = 5, 35 ÷ 5 = 7
b 8 × 4 = 32, 4 × 8 = 32, 4, 32 ÷ 4 = 8

5 **a** Under 9 Long Jump Results **b** Distance
c-e Teacher check
6 Teacher check, 27 bags

Fun Spot 10

1 **c** 18, 36 18, 45, 30, 27 2 2, 7, 4, 5 6, 2, 4, 8 3
9, 8, 12, 6, 1

Review Lesson 176 to 200

1 **a** 740 **b** 440
2 **a** 700 **b** 400
3 25 × 6 = 20 × 6 + 5 × 6 = 150
4 9 × 40 = 9 × 4 × 10, 9 × 4 = 36 × 10 = 360
5 **a** 3 × 6 = 18 **b** 9 × 5 = 45
6 × 3 = 18 5 × 9 = 45
18 ÷ 3 = 6 45 ÷ 9 = 5
18 ÷ 6 = 3 45 ÷ 5 = 9
6 16
7 **a** 81 **b** 311 **c** 204 **d** 336
a $16 + $7 = $23 **b** 1600
$160 + $70 = $230 + 700
$1600 + $700 = $2300 2300
9 434
10 2000 m = 2 km
11 **a** Colour red: bottom left & right,
Colour blue: top left & right
b Colour red: bottom left & right,
Colour green: top left, middle & right
c Colour blue: all angles
12 **a** 26 minutes past 1 **b** 2 minutes past 2
13 **a** 1 hr 28 min, 11:53 am, 9:50 am & 1 hr 32 min
b Golf
14 **a** Circle 5 **b** denominator
15 **a** 10 ÷ 5 = 2 **b** 10 **c** 7 **16** **a** $\frac{7}{8}$ **b** $\frac{7}{10}$ **c** $\frac{3}{6}$
17 136 cm & 1 m 36 cm **18** **a** 10 **b** 4 cm **c** 35
19 **a** 120 + 120 + 55 + 55 = 350 cm
b 50 × 5 = 250 cm **c** 45 + 30 + 50 + 25 = 150 cm
20 88 **21** **a** 3 **b** 2 **c** 4 **d** 1 **22** d, b, a, c

Number Facts

+– to 10 & 20	**×÷ 0, 1, 2**	**×÷ 3, 4, 5, 10**	**×÷ 6, 7, 8, 9**
10, 5, 8, 3	7, 0, 5, 0	7, 20, 1, 40	4, 35, 5, 36
10, 5, 10, 3	3, 9, 2, 0	3, 10, 10, 10	6, 6, 16, 9
10, 3, 8, 5	1, 2, 4, 10	4, 8, 7, 50	2, 14, 7, 90
10, 8, 9, 4	6, 2, 4, 3	6, 1, 20, 6	30, 7, 32, 2
7, 4, 9, 4	5, 8, 9, 14	6, 0, 10, 7	3, 0, 8, 27
17, 13, 19, 11	18, 6, 12, 10	27, 6, 15, 2	54, 3, 24, 5
19, 13, 18, 10	7, 20, 8, 16	3, 28, 5, 80	10, 28, 10, 72
7, 12, 20, 13	**Double &**	15, 9, 30, 3	36, 9, 48, 6
16, 6, 16, 8	**Half**	10, 32, 9, 90	7, 56, 1, 0
20, 15, 20, 8	6, 1, 10	24, 4, 40, 1	48, 10, 72, 7
	4, 16, 6		
	14, 2, 18		

Mathseeds Year 3 Workbook © 3P Learning ISBN 978-1-923253-14-8